The German Family

This book surveys the history of the German family in the nineteenth and twentieth centuries. The contributions deal with the influence of industrialisation on family life in town and country, with rural families and communities under the impact of social and economic change, and with the role and influence of the family in the lives of men and women in the newly-emerged working class.

Research on the history of the family had so far, at the point of this book's publication in 1981, concentrated on England and France; this book adds an important comparative dimension by extending the discussion into Central Europe and bringing fresh evidence and interpretation to bear on the wider debate about the effects of industrialisation on family structure and family life as a whole. The authors approach the subject from a variety of perspectives, including social anthropology, oral history, economic history and feminist studies.

This book is ideal for students of history, particularly the history of Germany.

The German Family

Essays on the Social History of the Family in
Nineteenth- and Twentieth-Century Germany

Edited by
Richard J. Evans and W. R. Lee

Routledge
Taylor & Francis Group

First published in 1981
by Croom Helm Ltd

This edition first published in 2015 by Routledge
2 Park Square, Milton Park, Abingdon, Oxon, OX14 4RN
and by Routledge
711 Third Avenue, New York, NY 10017

Routledge is an imprint of the Taylor & Francis Group, an informa business

ISBN 13: 978-1-138-84378-3 (hbk)
ISBN 13: 978-1-315-73085-1 (ebk)

The German Family

ESSAYS ON THE SOCIAL HISTORY OF THE FAMILY
IN NINETEENTH- AND TWENTIETH-CENTURY
GERMANY

EDITED BY RICHARD J. EVANS AND W.R. LEE

CROOM HELM LONDON

BARNES & NOBLE BOOKS
TOTOWA, NEW JERSEY

© 1981 Richard J. Evans and W.R. Lee
Croom Helm Ltd, 2-10 St John's Road, London SW11

British Library Cataloguing in Publication Data

The German family.
1. Family – Germany – History – 19th century
2. Germany – Social life and customs – 19th century
3. Family – Germany – History – 20th century
4. Germany – Social life and customs – 20th century
I. Evans, Richard John
II. Lee, William Robert
943.07   HQ626   80-41571

ISBN 0-7099-0067-8

First published in the USA 1981 by
Barnes & Noble Books,
81 Adams Drive,
Totowa, New Jersey, 07512

ISBN: 0-389-20101-4

Typesetting by Elephant Productions, London SE15
Printed and bound in Great Britain
by Billing and Sons Limited
Guildford, London, Oxford, Worcester

To Jody, Kitty Stoat, Silver Sands, Tibs and Tigger, who, alas, are no longer able to have families of their own.

CONTENTS

TABLES

FIGURES

PREFACE

This book is a collection of essays, all of which appear in English for the first time, and only one of which has been published anywhere before, on the history of the German family in the nineteenth and twentieth centuries. The authors and their contributions are drawn from a number of disciplines, and they approach the subject from a variety of perspectives, including social anthropology, oral history, quantitative demography, economic history, feminist studies, political history, collective biography and the history of ideas. The research techniques represented range from participant observation to computer-assisted statistical analysis. The study of family history, a relatively recent development in historical scholarship, must necessarily be interdisciplinary in orientation if it is to realise its full potential, and while quantitative studies have a vital role to play, it is important to realise that they have their limitations as well. These limitations can only be overcome by recourse to other disciplines, methods and sources, though this does not mean, of course, that the historian should be indiscriminate or uncritical in doing so. By presenting a wide range of different theoretical and methodological perspectives on the subject, this volume hopes to make a general contribution to family history as an area of historical investigation as well as a particular contribution for the country with which it is concerned.

A second purpose of this collection is to extend the discussion of central problems of family history to a new geographical area. The pioneers of new methods and approaches to the history of the family, above all, historical demographers and the social historians of the *Annales* school, concentrated their attention on pre-industrial France. More recently, studies have begun to appear on rural England and America. Historians of these countries have also started to turn their attention to family life in industrial towns. It is only within the last few years, however, that the history of the family has become an acceptable subject for scholars in Germany, for its perversion for 'racial' and 'eugenic' purposes during the Third Reich rendered it taboo for a whole generation of German historians during the 1950s and 1960s. Despite this, however, Germany has a long tradition of the sociology of the family, submerged or driven into exile by the Nazi regime. There are numerous empirical sociological studies of family life dating from the period before the First World War, and the sources available for original research are at least as rich as those for France, and in some respects better. Moreover, unlike France or England, Germany underwent an industrialisation and urbanisation process of extreme rapidity and intensity, making it an exceptionally valuable field for the investigation of the relationship of industrialisation and social change, not only in the area of family history, but in other spheres as well. It is largely for this reason – but also as a reflection of the existing focus of historical scholarship – that we have chosen to concentrate in this collection of essays on the period of industrialisation and the spread of the capitalist mode of production.

The contributions deal with rural society under the impact of social and economic change and the growth of State power, with the adjustments that workers made in their family life as they settled down to factory labour, and with the role of the family in the newly-emerging working-class environment. They illustrate the stresses and strains that industrialisation brought to bear on family life in the countryside as well as in the towns. By focusing our attention on a specific period and a particular set of problems, therefore, we hope not only to add a further comparative dimension to the history of the family but also to intervene directly in the more general debate about the effects of industrialisation on family life as a whole. The book opens with a survey of the state of research into the history of the German family by Robert Lee. The full bibliographical notes which are appended to this essay will, it is hoped, provide interested readers with a starting-point for further study. The second essay, by Karin Hausen, discusses the general framework of the development of the bourgeois ideology of family roles during the nineteenth century. It is particularly relevant to the social roles of middle-class women, but it also has a more general application, which is why we have placed it at the beginning of the collection. The next three contributions deal with the peasant family in the era of industrialisation. Finally, there are four essays on the working-class family, of which the first, by Heilwig Schomerus, occupies a central place in the book through its analysis of changing family structures and family life-cycles in first-generation industrial workers who still retained ties with their rural origins. Running through all the essays are a number of common themes – the impact of social change, the nature of women's work, the variety of structures and functions concealed beneath the global term 'family', the relationship of the family to wider social and economic structures such as the household, the community or the labour market – which link the essays together and, it is hoped, make the book into more than the sum of its parts.

The family was (and is) no universal, biologically-determined institution; on the contrary, its nature varies from one social milieu to another. A reading of the contributions to this book will, we hope, confirm this argument and illustrate something of the variety of forms which 'the family' can take, the range of social and economic influences by which it is affected, and the multiplicity of effects which it can have on societies and individual lives alike. Beyond this, the present collection of essays also seeks to demonstrate that the history of the family is not merely another aspect of social history, but that an understanding of it is necessary for a whole range of wider questions, from obvious problems such as the growth of population in early nineteenth-century Germany or the nature, conditions and remuneration of women's work in the early industrial period, to less obvious topics such as the adjustment of workers to the industrial environment, the complex and contradictory relationship between theory and practice in the politics of the German labour movement, and the impact of the Third Reich on life in the German countryside. Of course, it is not the only way of looking at such subjects; the role of women in society, for example, which figures prominently in several of the studies in this volume, can only be partially and imperfectly understood if it is approached solely through the history of the family. But this does not invalidate approaching this subject, and many others, in this way; the history of the family remains a necessary element in the history of women, of peasant society and of the industrial proletariat, and as long as the limits of its explanatory power are clearly understood, it will continue to be a vitally important one. We hope, therefore, that this book will not be used simply for the study or teaching of family history: its contributions have a relevance to many other areas of modern social, economic and political history as well.

A book of this length cannot hope to be comprehensive, even within the strict chronological limits which we have set to it. We hope, however, that we have indicated at least something of the range of research currently in progress in Germany and elsewhere on the subject. A more wide-ranging survey of recent work and of possibilities for future research is provided in the introductory essay. All the essays appear in English for the first time, and only one has been published before – Karin Hausen's contribution (Chapter 2), which first appeared in German as 'Die Polarisierung der Geschlechtscharaktere – Eine Spiegelung der Dissoziation von Erwerbs- und Familienleben', in Werner Conze (ed.), *Sozialgeschichte der Familie in der Neuzeit Europas* (Industrielle Welt, Band 21, Klett-Cotta Verlag, Stuttgart, 1977), pp. 363-93. We are grateful to the Ernst Klett Verlag, Stuttgart, to Werner Conze and to Karin Hausen for permission to print a translation of this essay. We would also like to express our thanks to the translators, Cathleen Catt (Chapter 2) and Carla Wartenberg (Chapter 4), to Marjan Bhavsar, who undertook a great deal of the typing, to Richard Johnson, of the Audio-Visual Centre at the University of East Anglia, who prepared the artwork, and to David Croom for being a patient and understanding publisher.

Norwich, New York   Richard J. Evans
Liverpool, Münster   W.R. Lee

Note

The present volume has its origin in the first meeting of the Social Science Research Council Research Seminar Group on Modern German Social History, held at the University of East Anglia in July 1978, when the topic discussed was the history of the family. A report of this meeting can be found in *Social History*, Vol.4, No.1 (January 1979), pp. 103-10.

Five of the contributors to this book took part in the conference, and a number of the essays collected here are revised versions of papers delivered to the meeting. The aim of the group is to provide a forum in which British, American and German scholars can meet to discuss major problems in the social history of Germany in the nineteenth and twentieth centuries. I am grateful to the SSRC for providing the initial and continuing support for the meetings, under Grant No. HG 113/6/7, and to the participants in the July 1978 conference for their contribution to the discussion and to the improvement of the papers presented. It should be emphasised, of course, that the opinions presented in this book are those of the authors alone, and are in no way attributable to the SSRC.

Richard J. Evans

1 THE GERMAN FAMILY: A CRITICAL SURVEY OF THE CURRENT STATE OF HISTORICAL RESEARCH

Robert Lee

I

The crisis of history as an academic discipline has been voiced on innumerable occasions. History, it has been claimed, 'fails to fulfil its social function – in government, in administration, in all the manifold affairs of men'.[1] In a society increasingly orientated according to the criterion of social utility, the absence of a recognisable and accepted social function could indeed be viewed as a severe, if not insuperable, hindrance for any academic discipline. The position of what is known as *Fach-historie* (academic history) in Germany would, however, seem to be even more precarious than in the United Kingdom. Indeed its latent dilemma was already pinpointed after the First World War, when Theodor Heuss, the first President of the German Federal Republic, referred to the need to reappraise Nietzsche's original questioning of the usefulness of history as a whole as far as the practical problems of life were concerned.[2] The American historian Fritz Stern, while stressing that the tensions between history and the social sciences were a common phenomenon in the Western world, nevertheless viewed this essentially as a 'German problem'.[3] Without at this juncture initiating a debate as to why this has become a specifically German concern, it is nevertheless clear that throughout the late 1950s and early 1960s, the so-called 'New Social History', with its distinctive and substantive links with many areas of the social sciences, found little response within the weighty and traditional world of German historical writing. Jürgen Kocka, for example, has already stressed the extent to which research on social structures and processes, including migration, social mobility, family history and stratification patterns, was simply not undertaken during this critical period.[4] With perhaps a few notable exceptions, such as Blaschke and Köllman, the important sphere of historical demography was hardly explored.[5] And yet research into the history of the family could be said to exercise a central function, simply because as a subject of historical analysis it incorporates a wide variety of different subject areas including, of course, economics, anthropology, demography and sociology. The growth of historical research into this essentially diffuse and diverse subject area over the last few years can therefore be taken perhaps as a touchstone for the general progress of the 'New Social History' in Germany as a whole. German involvement in the initial development of studies in the history of the family in the previous decade was very limited indeed. The publication of the proceedings of the Cambridge conference of 1969[6] marked a turning-point in the development of historical interest in the composition and structure of the European family. Significantly at this juncture German research was only in its developmental stage and no German contribution was included in this important volume. However in the opening years of the 1970s the situation in Germany was to change fairly radically, with the appearance of a number of contributions relating either directly or indirectly to the role and function of the family in historical perspective. Sabean's work on household formation and migration patterns in Württemberg,[7] the research of Engelsing and Schneider on living costs and working-class budgets,[8] and the publications of Shorter and Phayer on illegitimacy and the problem of 'modernisation' in German society,[9] are good examples of the increasing involvement of historians in family history and its allied subject areas. The appearance of the double issue of the periodical *Geschichte und Gesellschaft* in 1975[10] devoted to the history of the family could be said to indicate an important breakthrough in this discipline. Not only did the contributions of Rosenbaum[11] and Mitterauer[12] pinpoint crucial weaknesses in the restrictive nature of Laslett's emphasis on 'Mean Household Size' (the infamous 'mean of means') and the inherent danger of excluding non-numerative evidence in family analysis, but Karin Hausen was able expertly to identify key areas of weakness in current research.[13] At the same time a possible framework was suggested for future work in this field. In contrast to the established direction of the 'Cambridge School', future research was to emphasise the role of the family within the existing productive system and as a function of its specific location within the established hierarchy of social class. The family was to be viewed as a process rather than as a static unit. It was therefore quite reasonable for a recent commentator to claim that a 'take-off' as far as research in this general area was concerned was indeed 'imminent'.[14] German historians appeared increasingly in a position not only to develop this subject as a dynamic new element within the traditional school of history, but also to provide a significantly original contribution to the further development of the discipline as a whole.[15] The following discussion will attempt to provide an analysis of existing trends, particularly within the context of a generally accepted need to relate research into the family to underlying socio-economic parameters. It will examine existing literature from a number of specific general approaches – studies concerned with family and household analysis, with historical demography, with the function of the family within the economy, and finally research connected with folklore, legal history and other ancillary fields.

II

A turning-point in the overall development of historical studies of the family was the publication of an important collection of essays in historical social structure edited by Laslett and Wall.[16] Laslett was determined to provide an effective scheme of classification which would facilitate a comparative analysis of family structure both spatially and across time. It was believed that such a scheme would allow historians to determine the evolution of family and household structure from the late Middle Ages onward. As a result of the empirical research associated with Laslett's approach the traditional hypothesis which envisaged a distinct evolution from the large, extended, multi-generational household of the pre-industrial age to the nuclear family of the industrial age has been completely refuted. In its place has emerged a nuclear family structure which essentially has remained constant over time, and which remained relatively unaffected by the onset and progress of the industrial revolution. Nevertheless despite the value of Laslett's empirical approach, which has dominated studies into the history of the family throughout the 1970s, there has been increasing criticism of the scheme of classification and of the methodological framework of analysis as a whole. Furthermore, the mounting criticism levied at the Laslett approach would seem to be largely justified. Although it would be inappropriate at this juncture to present a further critique, two particular points will suffice for the moment to highlight the inherent weakness of his general approach to family history. First, Laslett's methodology cannot control for the age of the household head, although this clearly represents a critical variable in determining household structure. Secondly, the process of classification and quantification (family, household and houseful) only serves to introduce an artificial distinctness and rigidity into any discussion of household organisation. It is therefore encouraging to note that German research on family structure *per se*, as a comparative late-starter in the field, has been able to avoid at least some of the pitfalls inherent in the original methodology. Brunner's early emphasis on the concept of *das ganze Haus* (the 'whole house' or household)[17] may well have benefited later research workers in more than one respect. His emphasis on the inherent unity between production and consumption, on the one hand, and physical reproduction, on the other hand, focused attention on the inherent limitations implicit in an undue concentration on a simple numerative analysis of household and family structure. As a result the more detailed work on census material and the clearly more profitable *Seelenbeschreibungen* (an early form of census) has not suffered from a too rigid approach.[18] Certainly Mitterauer's work on Austria deserves note in this respect, particularly as he has confirmed the earlier impression that 'blood and marriage' were relatively unimportant in determining household composition.[19] Equally important is his emphasis on household role and the structure of the co-resident domestic group, including non-relatives. However even within this sphere insufficient attention is often devoted to the effect of the life-cycle. In Hartinger's recent analysis of family and social structure in Bavaria, for example, which utilises identical material reaching back into the mid-seventeenth century, the tendency to revert to an unduly narrow static approach, as embodied in Laslett's methodological framework, is only too evident.[20] It can only be hoped that future exploitation of this comparatively rich source of information, particularly the *Seelenbeschreibungen* in the Catholic areas of Germany, will realise the optimal potential that can be obtained from the available material.

A similar criticism can be levied at more general attempts to chart the history of the German family as a whole. Although it is clearly useful to have general histories even if specific research results are still meagre, such publications are still rather premature and frequently unsatisfactory. Weber-Kellermann does emphasise the role of the family as a centre of production and does devote an important section to the 'emancipation of the child',[21] but the almost total dependence on contemporary literary evidence hints perhaps at some fundamental weaknesses. Helmut Möller's earlier work on the '*kleinbürgerliche Familie*' (lower middle-class family), however, is clearly in a different category.[22] It emphasises the need to chart the overall socialisation process of the lower middle class and to take into consideration such factors as living standards, income levels, accommodation, orientation systems and the significance of day-to-day events such as births, marriages and deaths, as well as local festivals. It would be highly desirable to have at one's disposal a greater range of similar studies of different social groups, whether urban or rural based, and in particular of the middle class which has not yet really received adequate treatment. And yet Möller's analysis of household size is very poor, dependent largely on the evidence provided by the pioneering work of O. K. Roller and other earlier writers.[23] The section on the socialisation process, for example, would have benefited from the inclusion of additional information on a number of other factors, including fluctuations in the average number of children per family.

A basic problem common to most existing publications in this sphere is the failure to adopt a sufficiently rigorous theoretical framework. Elder has recently outlined five developments in sociology since the early 1960s that bear closely on the framework for the general examination of family life: the evolution of family development as a theoretical framework; cohort analysis of life patterns; life-span developmental psychology; life history methods in data collection and retrieval; and time allocation research.[24] Clearly the applicability of these developments to the historical study of the family is dependent on the data and archival base, but few attempts have as yet been made to assess their possible contribution to German research in this field. Although sound work has already been achieved in charting such aspects of family life as the choice of marriage partner with its resultant influence on the pattern of social homogeny,[25] no attempt has been made to establish a general typology of different life course types. Many areas of family life and interaction have still to be explored. The physical constraints on family life in relation to housing and accommodation have not been examined, apart from Niethammer's treatment of working-class housing in the latter decades of the nineteenth century.[26] The socialisation of children within the family and the emergence of conforming or deviant behaviour patterns are also areas in need of examination, particularly as the socialisation process impinged directly on the formation of personality roles and general attitudes to authority. Inter-generational conflict, as well as the family role of the elderly in historical perspective, have also been largely ignored, apart from studies, such as that by Baumert, dealing principally with the more recent past.[27] Indeed this is once again doubly unfortunate — not simply because a theoretical framework to a large extent already exists, but also because adequate data are already available. What one is left with at the moment is simply a number of studies, such as Stahleder's discourse on the *Landjugend* of Bavaria,[28] which skips over important ground such as social behaviour forms, work and employment, socialisation and education, without ever penetrating to the crucial and significant issues. Only in the context of the family and its role in the rise of fascism in Germany have inter-family relationships been rigorously studied.[29] But if it is well worth exploring the link between political and family authoritarianism in the twentieth century as highlighted by Adorno and Theweleit, a plea could also be made for similar research during the earlier stages of German economic development.[30]

It is also perhaps significant that the very first issue of *Geschichte und Gesellschaft* was concerned entirely with problems of social mobility,[31] even if it is true that the contributions represent simply 'workmanlike pieces of empirical scholarship based on highly controversial but unreflected notions of social stratification'.[32] Nevertheless it is still very important that interest in this sphere is currently being extended, given its role in family history as a whole. Sabean's study of geographical mobility in the village of Weilimdorf in Württemberg is a good example of what a fairly simple analysis can produce at the micro-level.[33] The results emanating from the so-called 'Württemberg project'[34] are also important, both in terms of the analysis of inter-generational mobility in an industrialising context broken down according to occupational structure, and in relation to the general pattern of geographic migration. It is interesting to note, for example, that income levels affected the direction of migration. On the basis of an analysis of the disparate industrialising centres of Esslingen and Kuchen,[35] evidence shows that children from poorer families tended to migrate into rural areas, and those from comparatively richer artisan families were more inclined to seek employment in the expanding urban centres. However it is often more difficult to evaluate these findings, given the overt concentration on individual localities and the failure to relate specific research to general national trends. The textile factory at Esslingen was one of the most extensive and dynamic firms in Germany in the mid-nineteenth century and this factor, in turn, gives rise to problems of representativeness and implicit bias. Analyses of migration at the macro-level, on the other hand, and there have been very few of these relating to intra-urban or inner German patterns since the pioneering work of Fritz Meyer in 1937,[36] are more concerned with relating migration trends to secular swings in the economy, as in the case of Langewiesche's recent contribution.[37] They therefore tend to neglect those areas primarily related to family or community pressures. And yet migration and mobility studies are clearly an integral part, not only of social history as a whole, but also of the history of the family in particular. Migration, both in the pre-industrial and industrialising period, affected not only the transmission of attitudes and ideologies particularly along generational lines and therefore the general process of social change, but also impinged directly on the structure and nature of family life by influencing the sex and age ratios of specific communities. Although David Crew's work on Bochum perhaps comes closest to a full appraisal of the significance of mobility and migration,[38] touching upon such problems as the ability of individuals to define themselves socially within the context of a changing social structure and the relative propensity towards upward social and occupational mobility, there is still a wide range of issues to be dealt with in this sphere. If the cultural formation of the new working class in the nineteenth century is to be understood more perceptively, then future studies of the mobility and migration will have to pay more attention to a wide range of ancillary issues closely related to the function and role of the family.

III

A development that has strongly influenced the direction of historical research on the family is the recent explosion of interest in demographic history, which only really began in the early 1960s.[39] Despite the significant contribution of German academics such as Süssmilch, Jastrow, Neumann and Roller[40] to the early growth of this discipline, however, the rehabilitation of historical demography after the Nazi era is only now beginning to get under way. Indeed this is long overdue, given the comprehensive nature of extant archival material, much of which still awaits analysis.[41] Interpretative demography, to use a phrase coined by Hollingsworth,[42] clearly plays a crucial role in any analysis of the history of the family, particularly as changes in vital rates such as births, marriages and deaths have an immediate bearing on family composition and structure. Low life expectancy and high mortality in an eighteenth-century context, for example, would have had important consequences for the pattern of the family life-cycle. Age at marriage was also a factor of crucial strategic significance in pre-industrial Western Europe and would have been influenced, if not determined, by shifts in age-specific mortality. The mechanism of the demographic transition and the responsiveness of European populations to the economic constraints on fertility would also invariably affect the composition and role of the family.

To this extent the development of historical demography in Germany over the recent years should have produced substantial spin-offs for family analysis. The number of publications on German historical demography has increased remarkably, with research centred around a number of separate Universities, including Berlin, Bochum and Mainz.[43] Given the widespread availability not only of parish registers and earlier pioneering publications, but also of a unique and compact archival source in the form of *Ortssippenbücher*,[44] the potential contribution of work in this field to family history could be very impressive indeed. To a certain extent this potential is already being realised. Imhof, for example, in the context of a very extensive research project on Giessen and its surrounding settlements, has been able to highlight the structural composition of rural families.[45] His increasing involvement in mortality phenomena and the problem of individual passivity or self-expression in the face of death, does not deprive this work of its inherent significance for family history. The theoretical framework employed is still concerned to 'establish correlations between a specific group of the population, the average marriage age, migration, the proportion of married and single, the frequency of legitimate and illegitimate births; and to relate the results to the situation in the whole population'.[46] Indeed the development of new analytical techniques of 'synchronous representation' to assess the historical diagnosis of disease and epidemics should facilitate a more effective treatment of crisis mortality and the impact of changing mortality and morbidity rates on the structure of the family, family roles and inheritance patterns.[47]

Equally important has been the confirmation provided by recent research of the earlier practice of family limitation. Evidence of such a practice has been forthcoming from Giessen as well as from a number of individual Bavarian settlements,[48] and corresponds well with the findings described in Wrigley's classical study of Colyton.[49] Connected with the general problem of fertility and its impact on the family there has been an increasing interest in the problem of infant feeding and infant mortality. Knodel, for example, has utilised German data from the Imperial Statistical Office to test the biometric analysis of infant mortality as developed by Bourgeois-Pichat,[50] and an attempt has also been made to relate regional shifts in infant mortality in the early nineteenth century, not only to the general rate of population growth, but also to the predominant form of sectoral economic development.[51] Areas of extensive agricultural growth, such as the eastern provinces of Prussia, were marked by an increase in labour-intensive production and an increasing incorporation of women into the active labour force. As a result the practice of breast-feeding declined, infant mortality rose, and the long-term reproductive cycle of the family was severely affected. Further examination of the frequency and socio-economic distribution of breast-feeding over time may well produce interesting results, not only in terms of the history of the family, but also in relation to wider issues germane to 'psycho-history', given the possiblity that there may be some connection between the length of breast-feeding and later psychological security.[52]

Furthermore as a result of Knodel's seminal analysis of the decline of fertility in Germany,[53] increasing interest is now being shown in the mechanism of the demographic transition, specifically as this related to individual socio-economic and family groups. Demographic transition theory in any case is primarily concerned with the impact of urbanisation, industrialisation and mortality decline on fertility and hence on the family, with important control variables including marriage patterns, migration and religious composition. It is hoped that the use of multivariate models[54] and the increasing concern with the position of specific class groupings[55] will cast more light on the factors influencing relative fertility levels, in both urban and rural communities, and in families of different religious persuasion, before, during and after the critical transition period. Finally, as far as the genealogical side of demographic history is concerned, German research is arguably very well placed indeed. Schaub has recently utilised genealogical material to analyse family structure in Oldenburg.[56] Significantly this initiative has coincided with a general call to utilise more effectively genealogical data on an international scale.[57]

However as far as the direction of present research is concerned, a great deal is still left to be desired. Castell has recently complained of the continuing lack of substantive coordination between family history and historical demography.[58] Unfortunately this is all too clearly the case. The number of full family reconstitution studies is still pitifully small[59] and Köllmann's treatment of demographic history in the *Handbuch der Deutschen Wirtschafts- und Sozialgeschichte* contains little, if anything, on the implicit interrelationship between population change and family structure.[60] Indeed a fundamental weakness of a great deal of research in this area remains the obtuse avoidance of a full treatment of economic determinants of family behaviour in the demographic sphere. The family as the centre of 'production and re-production' is only too frequently absent from the analysis. Indeed it is to some extent ironic that an overriding concern with Mackenroth's concept of 'generative behaviour'[61] has frequently led to the perpetuation of economic myths and hence a misunderstanding of the relationship between the role and function of the family, demographic trends and economic parameters. Castell's own contribution to a recent volume on the German family edited by Conze is highly instructive in this particular case.[62] It assumes without any qualification an inevitable Malthusian interdependence of population size on relative levels of food supply and availability. The improvement in life expectancy and the general increase in German population growth rates from the late eighteenth century onwards are explained on the basis of this assumption. The process of agrarian reform and *Landesausbau*, as originally postulated by Ipsen, are viewed as having played a critical role in this context.[63] The Prussian legislation of 1807 and 1811, which reflected similar structural changes in the primary sector of a number of German states, is accordingly regarded as the causative mechanism behind the growth in population.[64] However none of these traditional arguments is fully convincing.[65] The evidence at present available on key components of overall fertility rates in Germany do not support Castell's case. Even in the eastern provinces of Prussia, where an endogenous mechanism of population growth was arguably present, the recent work of Harnisch has successfully refuted Ipsen's emphasis on the contribution of Prussian legislative reforms.[66] Family history invariably needs to be located within a realistic socio-economic framework. Where such a framework is not adopted the conclusions can be both unhelpful and misleading.

Indeed the gaps in present research in demographic history, as far as these relate to the history of the family, are still frighteningly large. Mortality is generally accepted as a major determinant of family size, but as yet cross-sectional analysis of age-specific and class-specific death-rates specifically for the pre-census period is still lacking.[67] This is all the more important, given the mutual interdependence of disease patterns, environmental change and social structure, as originally pointed out by Ackerknecht and Rosenberg.[68] Even if it can be shown that the upper classes benefited historically from lower mortality and morbidity rates in urban Giessen, and that age-specific death-rates in rural Bavaria varied considerably according to socio-economic criteria,[69] too little is at present known to chart the differentiated effect of these vital rates, and their relative shifts in the modern period, on the life-cycle of the German family. Equally the inherent psychological impact of family loss, as a consequence of short-term movements in mortality, on the pattern of family reproduction and inter-family relationships, has hardly been examined at all.

A further problem is the continuing absence of regional analysis. Given the wide regional variety in Germany in relation to social structure, inheritance customs and the sectoral distribution of employment, a more rigorous approach to the problem of regional dissimilarity or convergence would be highly desirable. Even at an aggregate level few attempts have been made to analyse shifts and fluctuations in vital rates and in the selection of settlements for family reconstitution there is still perhaps a natural, but unfortunate, emphasis on rural, as opposed to industrialising, communities. The major plea as far as future research in historical demography in Germany is concerned, however, would simply be for more and extended analyses, bearing in mind the continuing need to take into consideration the overall socio-economic context of population development. Too often, as perhaps in Schmidt's contribution to the Giessen project,[70] the full potential of historical analysis is overlooked. At the other extreme there always exists a danger that historical demography will limit itself to an elucidation of trends in vital rates.[71] In such a context it is clearly preferable to err in the direction of a wider, more comprehensive brand of 'total history' than to become embroiled in mere technical issues, irrespective of their intrinsic importance to demographic history as a whole.

IV

It has of course been argued that the focus of the 'New Social History' is not coterminous with parallel trends in economics and economic history. Thus in the case of long-term changes in economic structure, the basic preoccupation of social historians is assumed to be not with the source of these changes, but more with their human consequences.[72] Such a division of interests, however, would seem to be far too arbitrary, particularly as the growth process itself on a macro-economic level was clearly susceptible to influences directly generated by the structure of family life and family labour. Any effective analysis of the family in historical perspective must in essence pay close attention to economic parameters. Indeed the interdependence of family structure, inheritance patterns and economic growth was pointed out by

Habakkuk as early as 1955.[73] The family, both as a source of labour supply and as a unit of consumption, was a critical element in the functioning of the pre-industrial and industrialising Germany economy. In a rural context, therefore, a history of the family must by definition include as an integral part of the analysis, as Sabean has correctly stressed,[74] such facets as the division of land, the size of peasant holdings, the nature of the peasant land market, as well as the interrelationship of the family life-cycle with the labour requirements of an agrarian economy. A similarly extended focus for research would be necessary for any study dealing with an urban community.

Indeed in this particular sphere the impact of German research in recent years has been most significant. Starting from the theoretical and empirical findings of Kisch and Mendels in relation to the proto-industrial family,[75] the Göttingen research group has clearly extended our appreciation of the structural role of the family in the specific transition from feudalism to nascent capitalism.[76] The development of proto-industrial activity in Germany effectively disrupted the traditional homeostatic balance which had characterised early modern society and replaced a pattern of late marriage, conditioned by the inelastic demand for labour, by a declining marriage age, which heightened the destabilising role which proto-industrial producing units came to play within the existing agrarian community. There are naturally a number of criticisms which arise from such a potentially stimulating synthesis,[77] but it is sufficient at this juncture to stress the degree to which this general approach to the role of the family in past time, with its emphasis on 'reproduction, production and consumption' effectively replaces the rigid emphasis on the categorisation and enumeration of household or family structure. It can only be hoped that further research will either confirm or qualify some of the assumptions of the original model. Significantly, Hohorst's pioneering work on the Kreis Hagen has failed to corroborate the active role of the so-called 'Mendels-Medick model' in an early nineteenth-century context, and evidence from Bavaria does not seem to confirm the posited cycle of reproduction ascribed to families connected with domestic craft production.[78] But this in itself does not in any way devalue the major contribution to family history which this approach has constituted. What would be desirable in this context, however, would be an extension in the remit of future studies on specific groups, such as the *Handwerker*, to include those aspects of family role and structure emphasised by the Göttingen group. Adolf Noll's recent study of structural change in craft production in the second phase of German industrialisation, for example, although concerned both with demographic forms and economic potential, unfortunately fails to trace the ramifications of these developments in the most immediate sphere of reference for small-scale producers – namely their own family and kinship groupings.[79] A change in the emphasis of current research along these lines would benefit both economic historians and historians of the family.

Indeed this emphasis in research on the position of the family within a given economic framework, although following to some extent the earlier investigations of Sax, Frankenstein and Schnapper-Arndt,[80] has also served as a means of testing a further hypothesis intimately connected with family history, where considerable German data have been used to support a general case. Shorter's rather tendentious explanation of the evolution of the 'modern' family, with its emphasis on the transformation of relationships within the community through a 'sentimentalising' of relationships within the family as an increasingly emotional unit rather than a productive and reproductive one, certainly marked a milestone in the general growth of studies in the history of the family.[81] Many aspects of his case, however, have been subjected to rigorous criticism, particularly those arguments relating to the concept of 'modernisation' and the impact of an increasing capitalist market mentality on family and sexual relationships. This is particularly evident in his treatment of the significance of rising illegitimacy rates towards the end of the eighteenth century, which provide an essential corroboration for the posited 'modernisation' process itself.[82] The danger of divorcing general theory from underlying empirical research quickly becomes evident if the German data employed by Shorter are re-examined. It is particularly difficult to argue for a 'sexual revolution' on the basis of contemporary medical topographies, administrative reports and 'statistical' descriptions of lower-level bureaucrats, simply because their inherent bias frequently fostered a tendency to misinterpretation. Bavaria, of course, which features extensively in Shorter's analysis, certainly had some of the highest illegitimacy rates in early nineteenth-century Germany, and yet it remained comparatively unaffected by the development of modern capitalism during this critical period. Shorter's hypothesis is essentially too simplistic and in terms of its diagnostic assessment of socio-economic phenomena clearly evinces fundamental weaknesses. The general argument would have benefited from a closer attention to underlying economic parameters. The effect of improved nutrition and better standards of female health on reproductive biology, as well as shifts in

the real wage rates of domestic and agricultural servants or *Gesinde*, as
a function of changing economic conditions at the macro-level, are only
two examples of crucial variables affecting illegitimacy rates which
were clearly related to long-term trends in the economic infrastructure
of contemporary German states, and yet ignored by Shorter.

It has also been increasingly recognised, however, that family
structure together with kinship relations were often closely interlinked
with the position of the family as a unit of labour supply.[83] The
presence of non-relatives within the household, whether boarders,
lodgers or servants – a group that has been largely ignored by historians –
was frequently a reflection in agrarian communities of a temporary
short-fall in the supply of indigenous family labour. Peasant farmers
in many parts of South Germany and Austria frequently hired
outsiders when their own children were too young for full-time farm
work, and then replaced them as their own children reached maturity.[84]
However, research into many of the aspects relating to labour supply
and family structure is only just beginning. Köllmann's concept of
Arbeitskräftepotential (potential labour force) is indeed a useful
analytical tool and can be used for such purposes as assessing the
increase in full-time female participation in the workforce,[85] but little
attempt has been made to relate shifts in this index over time to
changes in family structure and the division of work within the family
unit. This omission is all the more surprising, given the dramatic
changes in the age composition of the indigenous population and in
the workforce during the early stages of capitalist development. In
Prussia, for example, there was a 46.68 per cent increase in the
proportional representation of the age group 20–39 to total
population within the period 1816 to 1840, and evidence from other
individual states confirms the fact that the crucial expansion in this
age group was primarily a phenomenon of the first half of the
nineteenth century.[86]

Of equal interest is the division of labour within the family itself
and the significant effect this had on both production and reproduction.
The increasing penetration of the market in the eighteenth century, for
example, would have influenced the family role of women by
encouraging the substitution of domestically produced goods and
foodstuffs by manufactured items.[87] Equally improvements in nutrition
would have affected the female life-cycle and hence the operative
structure and function of the family. Earlier puberty and a later onset
of the menopause, for example, may well have added a further ten
years to the average fertility of women, with important repercussions on

family life. On the other hand in those areas of Germany where agricultural growth in the early nineteenth century was achieved by an increasing full-time exploitation of residual female labour, the reproductive ability of women may well have deteriorated, generating a significantly different response curve in the life-cycle of the family.[88] The pattern of economic development and the labour role of women within the family were closely related and may well have influenced the general process of population growth throughout the various German states. However very little research has been undertaken in this field, apart from the general analysis conducted by Tilly, Scott and Cohen,[89] and Robyn Dasey's contribution to the present volume is therefore doubly valuable (pp. 221–55 below).

The problem of child labour and its role within the family structure is also quite crucial in this particular context. Certainly there has already been some considerable work on the employment of child labour in a factory situation initiated to a large extent by Kuczynski.[90] However comparatively little effort has been made to provide a rigorous survey of the significance of child employment in the primary sector, particularly in relation to the labour requirements of specific types of holding and the process of the family life-cycle. Certainly in the case of Bavaria it can be argued, on the basis of contemporary secondary material, that peasant attitudes to children were largely predetermined by their awareness not only of inheritance problems connected with an extensive family, but also of the relative level of labour requirements on the family holding. Too many children were seldom regarded as a benefit to the family and after the birth of the fourth child it was claimed by contemporaries that parental attitudes noticeably deteriorated. Indeed later children were frequently regarded as 'undesirable creatures', with a value below that of a calf or other farm animal.[91]

Both areas of research — female and child employment — are also vital to an understanding of the impact of increasing industrialisation on the traditional role structure of the family. Current French evidence would seem to indicate that factory development did not inevitably lead to a total break with the past, or a radical dislocation of the social and familial ties upon which earlier society had been based.[92] It is equally possible that kinship ties were maintained in the German textile sector in the early nineteenth century, just as in England children frequently worked alongside adult spinners. An examination of such issues in the German context would be particularly valuable. Not only would research provide further evidence of the general nature of the modernisation process as it affected family relationships, but it would also facilitate a testing of Smelser's earlier ideas and a closer analysis of the precise impact of industrialisation on the nuclear family.[93] Indeed any model of the working of the social structure as a whole in the context of the nineteenth century, whether Marxist or bourgeois, in as far as it employs analytical categories which depart from those perceived by contemporaries directly involved in the events under examination, must inevitably be verifiable on the basis of such empirical research.

Finally it must not be forgotten that the family and household was the basic unit of consumption within the German economy. As Engelsing has pointed out 'the standard of life of a social stratum did not result from transparent income of a market and money economy, but from a household economy in which the producer and consumer belonged to the one social unit'.[94] Thus there is a clear connection, for example, between family structure, social class and expenditure schedules, which, in turn, have a significant impact on the general functioning of the economy and the relative balance over time between producer and consumer goods industries. Equally important was the impact of the middle-class doctrine of thrift in the nineteenth century on the development of the savings ratio, as well as the issue of general expenditure preferences and the propensity towards family limitation from the late nineteenth century onwards. Indeed the subject of family consumption has an even wider significance than its immediate effect on the economy, as consumption itself was symptomatic of the pattern of self and/or family evaluation in terms of social class, and a useful indicator of family involvement in a developing mass culture. However very little work has been undertaken in this important area of family history. Apart from Lothar Schneider's examination of working-class budgets in the eighteenth century, and Engelsing's important contributions,[95] only Sandra Coyner has attempted to deal with the wider significance of consumption patterns in terms of family role and class consciousness.[96]

V

Studies in local folklore frequently tend to be rather anecdotal, focusing attention on curiosities and relics rather than central issues in social history. However folklore studies can provide important information on the nature and quality of family life in past time.

Germany, in this respect, is favourably placed. Historical folklore has tended to be a highly developed scholarly field and one which has benefited from a recent revival.[97] Increasingly the discipline is viewed as a history of culture 'from below'.[98] Both in West Germany and in the GDR there has been an increasing concern with the history of workers' culture.[99] Particularly in the former case folklore studies have been seen by younger practitioners as an historical science, combining local investigations and research into social associations within the framework of a wider discussion of the precise meaning and significance of 'tradition' and 'change'. As a result such studies have helped to elucidate issues of vital interest to historians of the family, particularly where there are aspects of family life and behaviour which are not easily subject to quantification.[100] The work of Kramer provides a good example of the value of such work.[101] There are also usable social histories of the Silesian weavers and of certain aspects of German peasant life and work, compiled by folklorists.[102] Wiegelmann's recent publication, moreover, provides clear testimony of the potential value of such material for the family historian, and indeed for those historians primarily concerned with such social phenomena as *Heimgarten* and 'charivari'.[103] It is also encouraging to note that this element of family history is also receiving some attention in the GDR.[104] A more rigorous analysis of folklore publications, utilising modern sociological theory, will undoubtedly shed important light on a wide spectrum of issues connected with the role and function of the family, as Rudolf Braun's seminal work on the Swiss textile workers in the eighteenth century has shown[105] in relation to such topics as teenage sexual customs and parental control over children's earnings.

Another area which has provided important spin-offs for family history has been the field of legal studies, where legal historians generally have created a significant body of literature relating to local and regional family law, particularly legal enactments dealing with marriage and succession. Certainly almost every region in Germany has generated specific studies on its own legal system. In Bavaria, just to take one example, the earlier publications of Bader, Fick and Wilhelm have established a useful typology of legal customs relating to property inheritance and the role of the local *Gemeinde*.[106] However only Berkner and Mendels, and to a lesser extent Schröder, have so far utilised this rich material in an effective way by attempting to relate the various legal systems of inheritance with the shaping of particular social structures.[107] Legal history can be of even more use in other areas relevant to family roles and individual behaviour patterns. A link might

well have existed between changes in the legal code and shifts in social
and family behaviour. In Bavaria, for example, changes in the law had
a direct effect on the level of infanticide and illegitimate conceptions.[108]
If the 'stone of infamy' and public degradation had been prominent as
punishments for illegitimate conceptions under the 'Law of Levity' in
the early eighteenth century, by the following century legal constraints
on extra-marital relationships had almost completely disappeared. By
1827 the degradation pole had vanished from all cities and markets and
the edict of 1808 had prohibited monetary fines for pregnancies arising
from illicit relationships.[109] Changes in the legal system, therefore,
could well have facilitated the dramatic rise in illegitimacy, unrelated
to any vague process of social modernisation. It would clearly be
desirable if legal history could be brought more closely into the
mainstream of social history, particularly as far as research into the
history of the family was concerned.

There are, however, a number of other subject areas where the
overlap with family history is very considerable indeed and where a
study of the family in historical perspective would gain substantially
from close collaboration. Education, for example, is not simply to be
viewed as a process of human capital formation, but as something with
wider social significance, affecting not only the functioning of the
family and its openness to alternative forms of social behaviour, but
also the impact of state socialisation processes on its continuous role in
society. Late eighteenth-century educational reformers, such as
Steinbart and Zerrenner, viewed the role of education in terms of
explicit social control, designed to inculcate higher levels of loyalty and
productivity, and to make the indigenous peasantry 'sensible'.[110] It is
clear, for example, that the significant improvements in female literacy
in the early nineteenth century and the increasing synchronisation of
literacy skills between the sexes, at least in rural Bavaria, could have
had an important influence on family and sexual roles.[111] A further
insight into social and familial attitudes can be derived from an
examination of the development of the book market in Germany and
the growing popularity in the second half of the nineteenth century
of popular forms of literature, such as the 'colporteur' novel, with its
deliberate emphasis as far as working-class women were concerned on
'honeyed idyllic phrases' and images of romantic attachment.[112]
Moreover just as a great deal of popular, as opposed to middle-class,
culture, tended to mirror basic and recurrent themes, such as poverty,
misfortune, violent crime, sadism and sex, as illustrated in Rudolf
Schenda's work *Volk ohne Buch*,[113] so an examination of both literate

and popular culture could well illuminate many aspects of family life, class consciousness and sexual roles.[114]

A similar plea could also be made for more research into such subjects as the role of the public holiday and the development over time of attitudes to work and leisure. Apart from Reulecke's recent contribution, almost nothing has so far appeared in this context.[115] And yet the transition from a society geared to frequent feast days and a philosophy that there were in any case enough days for work and that man did not live by work alone,[116] to one dependent on organised and structured factory holidays, provides an important insight into changing attitudes to work, together with the social consequences of this transition in terms of the family division of labour. Finally family and generational roles were frequently expressed in clothing styles, which often served as symbols not only of community attachment, but also of psychological needs and individualistic expressionism. The early nineteenth-century complaints against illegitimacy significantly also included criticism of changing clothing styles, which offended not only the traditional social order, but the implicit respect which dress conformity was designed to secure for older generational groups in German society. Once again, however, these are further areas where the need for new and original research is desperately apparent.

VI

I hope that it is clear from this brief survey of contemporary trends in the history of the family in Germany, that a considerable amount of work is already in the process of being undertaken, and that the 'late starter' is at least showing signs of considerable growth potential. It is equally clear, however, that progress in certain areas has been very limited and still stands in an initial phase. Complaints are still voiced concerning the continuing 'theory deficit', not only in connection with the history of the family, but in relation to social history as a whole.[117] There is, of course, a great deal of ongoing research, which deals directly with family history and related subject areas,[118] but the preponderance of foreign initiative is still uncomfortably too extensive as far as the long-term viability of studies in German family history is concerned. Furthermore the impact of recent research on the traditional school of German historicism remains surprisingly limited and perhaps the attempt to evolve a 'special variant' of social history designed to mirror the reputed uniqueness of German experience may well constitute an additional barrier to future research. In conclusion, therefore, I would like to pinpoint a number of areas which should perhaps be taken into consideration and act as an outline for future research in this critical subject discipline.

(a) First, there is a need to explore the potentialities of a more rigorous theoretical approach. Too often empiricism has superseded the need for a secure theoretical framework. Indeed even the *Annales* school, perhaps because of its limitations, has found few enthusiastic followers in Germany.[119] In particular future research on the history of the family in Germany would benefit from an exploration of the applicability of Marxist theory, not on the basis of what has been described as 'institutionalised historical materialism',[120] but along the lines established in the sphere of social history in the United Kingdom by Hobsbawm and E. P. Thompson. Whatever its inherent shortcomings, and this would equally apply to any other general theoretical model, the Marxist school cannot be faulted for ignoring the evolving structural aspects of economic and social systems. At its best, devoid of the constraints of narrow theoretical assumptions, it fully constitutes in its broadest sense *l'histoire engagée*. German historical research into the history of the family would undoubtedly benefit from the perspective that a wider theoretical approach might offer.

(b) Secondly, research into the history of the family must by definition transcend the barriers of a specific discipline. In order to examine the role and function of the family over time, research in this important area must continue to depend on many areas of the social sciences, and implicitly on the 'New Economic History'. Indeed the thrust of research in the latter case is increasingly concerned with the allocative implications of specified changes in property rights, transaction costs, the regulation of the household and non-market decision-making.[121] Medick has already shown the need to base any analysis of family role and structure within the framework of economic parameters, and there is clearly already a great deal of common ground and common interest between social and economic historians, as far as the role and function of the family in past time is concerned.

(c) Thirdly from a methodological point of view, there are two specific requirements which future research will probably have to fulfil. On the one hand there is a need for far more macro- and longitudinal studies, particularly since changes in the family itself tend to be slow.[122] Equally comparative perspectives, in relation to international research, must be retained, as it is clearly extremely difficult, if not totally impossible, to measure 'adjustment', 'adaptability' or 'stability' within the family or household unit, without utilising extensively comparative criteria. On the other hand, because of the early developmental stage of German research into the history of the family, there is abundant scope for micro-level analysis of specific socio-economic groups, which can take into consideration the full range of problems connected with the family as a unit of production and reproduction. Of course in recent years there has been a fairly significant number of group-specific studies,[123] but only rarely, as in the case of Linse's treatment of working-class structures and the birth-rate,[124] have they effectively encompassed the central problems of behaviour patterns specific to different social groups.

(d) Fourthly in terms of periodisation, both in relation to studies of the family *per se*, as well as in the field of demographic history, there is a clear need for more research on the twentieth century. The pre-industrial phase, the transition to capitalism, and the Wilhemine period have all to varying degrees received some treatment over the recent past. In total contrast the publications on family history for the modern period are relatively few and far between. As Tim Mason has recently observed, 'since Clifford Kirkpatrick published his thoughtful and detailed empirical study in 1938, *Nazi Germany: its Women and Family Life*, very little new research has been done into this aspect of modern German social history'.[125] Although this situation is gradually being rectified, a great deal of important work still remains to be done.[126]

Family history may indeed still be in its early stages, not only in Germany, but in the international scene as a whole. Equally Goubert may be correct in claiming that the 'family phase' in historical fashion will hardly last longer than 'the fad for mini-skirts'.[127] But a sound argument can be made out that interest in this subject area will not be simply a transitory phase. Indeed with its inevitably close links with other social science disciplines, and with an increasing attention to methodology and theoretical frameworks, as well as to quantitative techniques, further research into German family history could play a critical role in the long-term development of both *Fach-historie* and the social sciences as a whole. Certainly there are many opportunities still to be grasped by future research workers, particularly as the groundwork for future development has already been largely laid. But the proof of the pudding in this particular case will be in the response of German historians to this exciting challenge. A late starter may indeed benefit from the earlier mistakes of its rivals and from the replication of advanced methodologies and analytical techniques. A note of caution, however, still needs to be sounded, as far as future research into the history of the family in Germany is concerned, as 'underdevelopment' can easily become a self-perpetuating or at least a self-perpetuated state. However it would be wrong to conclude this cursory survey on a pessimistic note. Germany, as far as studies in family history are concerned, will undoubtedly benefit from the presence of extensive archival source material, including unusually detailed parish registers, *Ortsippenbücher,* medical topographies and all the administrative reports even in the early decades of the nineteenth century that reflected the implementation of J.P. Frank's concept of 'medical police'[128] and the further development of established centralised state bureaucracies. As a result historians of the family in Germany are in a promising position to contribute a great deal to the further discussion of central issues in this field which are part and parcel of a wider international debate.

Notes

This essay is a revised and extended version of a paper delivered to the first meeting of the SSRC Research Seminar Group on Modern German Social History at the University of East Anglia in July 1978.

1.   J.H. Plumb (ed.), *Crisis in the Humanities* (London, 1964), p. 44.
2.   R. Koselleck, 'Wozu noch Historie?', *Historische Zeitschrift,* Bd. 212 (1971), p.1.
3.   F. Stern, 'Rationalismus und Irrationalismus in Deutschland' (Arbeitsgruppenbericht), in *Aufklärung heute – Probleme der deutschen Gesellschaft* (Freiburg, 1967), p.57.
4.   J. Kocka, 'Recent Historiography of Germany and Austria', *Journal of Modern History,* Vol. 47 (1975), p. 112.
5.   K. Blaschke, 'Soziale Gliederung und Entwicklung der sächsischen Landbevölkerung im 16. bis 18. Jahrhundert', *Zeitschrift für Agrargeschichte und Agrarsoziologie,* Bd. 4 (1956); idem., 'Zur Bevölkerungsgeschichte Sachsens vor der industriellen Revolution', in E. Giersiepen and D. Lösche (eds.), *Beiträge zur deutschen Wirtschafts- und Sozialgeschichte des 18. und 19. Jahrhunderts* (Berlin, 1962), pp.133-70; idem., *Bevölkerungsgeschichte von Sachsen bis zur industriellen Revolution* (Göttingen, 1974); idem., 'Bevölkerungsgeschichte, 1800-1970' in H. Aubin and W. Zorn (eds.), *Handbuch der deutschen Wirtschafts- und Sozialgeschichte* (Stuttgart, 1976), Vol. II, pp. 9-50.
6.   P. Laslett and R. Wall (eds.), *Household and Family in Past Time* (Cambridge, 1972).

7.   D. Sabean, 'Household Formation and Geographical Mobility: a Family Register Study for A Württemberg Village, 1760-1900', *Annales de démographie historique* (1970), pp. 275-94.

8.   R. Engelsing, 'Probleme der Lebenshaltung in Deutschland im 18. und 19. Jahrhundert', *Zeitschrift für die gesamte Staatswissenschaft*, Bd. 128 (1970), pp. 290-308; L. Schneider, *Der Arbeiterhaushalt im 18. und 19. Jahrhundert. Dargestellt am Beispiel des Heim- und Fabrikarbeiters* (Berlin, 1967).

9.   E. Shorter, 'Illegitimacy, Sexual Revolution and Social Change in Modern Europe', *The Journal of Interdisciplinary History*, Vol. 2 (1971/2), pp. 237-72; idem., 'Bastardy in South Germany: A Comment', *The Journal of Interdisciplinary History*, Vol. 8 (1978), pp. 459 *et seq.*; idem., *The Making of the Modern Family* (New York, 1975); J.M. Phayer, *Religion und das gewöhnliche Volk in Bayern in der Zeit von 1750 bis 1850* (Miscellanea Bavarica Monacensia, Munich, 1970); idem., 'Lower Class Morality: the Case of Bavaria', *Journal of Social History*, Vol. 7 (1974), pp. 79-95; idem., *Sexual Liberation and Religion in 19th-century Europe* (London, 1977).

10.   H.-U. Wehler (ed.), 'Historische Familienforschung und Demographie' (= *Geschichte und Gesellschaft*, Vol. I, 1975).

11.   H. Rosenbaum, 'Zur neueren Entwicklung der Historischen Familienforschung', *Geschichte und Gesellschaft*, Vol. I, Bd. 2/3 (1975), pp. 210-25.

12.   M. Mitterauer, 'Familiengrösse – Familientypen – Familienzyklus. Probleme quantitativer Auswertung von österreichischem Quellenmaterial', *Geschichte und Gesellschaft*, Vol. I, Bd. 2/3 (1975), pp. 226-55.

13.   K. Hausen, 'Familie als Gegenstand Historischer Sozialwissenschaft. Bemerkungen zu einer Forschungsstrategie', *Geschichte und Gesellschaft*, Vol. I, Bd. 2/3 (1975), pp. 171-209.

14.   H. Medick in a personal communication.

15.   K. Hausen, 'Historische Familienforschung', in R. Rürup (ed.), *Historische Sozialwissenschaft. Beiträge zur Einführung in die Forschungspraxis* (Göttingen, 1977), pp. 59 *et seq.*

16.   P. Laslett and R. Wall (eds.), *Household and Family in Past Time* (Cambridge, 1972).

17.   O. Brunner, 'Das Ganze Haus und die alteuropäische Oekonimik' (1950), in idem, *Neue Wege der Verfassungs- und Sozialgeschichte* (Göttingen, 1968), pp. 103-27). See also the contribution by Wilke and Wagner in the present volume (pp. 120-47, below).

18.   P. Schmidtbaur, 'The History of Family Structure in Austria: Sources and Research Problems', *Local Population Studies*, No. 23 (1979), pp. 36-8; idem., *Bevölkerung und Haushaltsstruktur in Oesterreich vom 17. bis zum 20. Jahrhundert* (Vienna, 1980); M. Mitterauer, 'Zur Familienstruktur in ländlichen Gebieten Oesterreichs im 17. Jahrhundert', in H. Helczmanovski (ed.), *Beiträge zur Bevölkerungs- und Sozialgeschichte Oesterreichs* (Vienna, 1973), pp. 167-222.

19.   M. Mitterauer and R. Sieder, *Vom Patriarchat zur Partnerschaft. Zum Strukturwandel der Familie* (Munich, 1977); M. Mitterauer, 'Vorindustrielle Familienformen. Zur Funktionsentlastung des "ganzen Hauses" im 17. und 18. Jahrhundert', *Wiener Beiträge zur Geschichte der Neuzeit*, Vol. 2 (1975), pp. 123 *et seq.*; M. Mitterauer and R. Sieder, 'The Developmental Process of Domestic Groups: Problems of Reconstruction and Possibilities of Interpretation', *Journal of Family History*, Vol. 4 (1979), pp. 257-84.

20.   W. Hartinger, 'Zur Bevölkerungs- und Sozialstruktur von Oberpfalz und Niederbayern in vorindustrieller Zeit', *Zeitschrift für bayerische Landesgeschichte*, Bd. 39 (1976), pp. 785-822.

21.   I. Weber-Kellermann, *Die Familie* (Frankfurt a.M, 1976); idem., *Die deutsche Familie* (Frankfurt a.M., 1977).

22.   H. Möller, *Die kleinbürgerliche Familie im 18. Jahrhundert* (Berlin, 1969).

23.   O.K. Roller, *Die Einwohnerschaft der Stadt Durlach im 18. Jahrhundert* (Karlsruhe, 1907).

24.   G.H. Elder, 'Family History and the Life Course', *Journal of Family History*, Vol. 2 (1977), pp. 279-304.

25.   A. Simonis, 'Sippen- und bevölkerungskundliche Untersuchungen eines Eifeldorfes', *Archiv für Bevölkerungswissenschaft (Volkskunde) und Bevölkerungspolitik* (1936), Vol. I, p. 42; H. Zwerenz, *Westheim (bei Kitzingen am Main). Ein sterbendes Bauerndorf in Mainfranken* (Würzburg, 1937), pp. 15 *et seq.*; W. Klenck, *Das Dorfbuch von Mulsum (Land Wursten)* (1959) pp. 273-4.

26.   L. Niethammer, 'Wie wohnten Arbeiter im Kaiserreich?', *Archiv für Sozialgeschichte*, Bd. XVI (1976), pp. 61-134. See the contribution by James H. Jackson in the present volume (pp. 194-220).

27.   G. Baumert, 'Changes in the Family and the Position of Older Persons in Germany', *International Journal of Comparative Sociology*, Vol. I (1960), pp. 202-10.

28.   E. Stahleder, 'Altbayerische Landjugend im Griff der "Aufklärung"', *Zeitschrift für Agrargeschichte und Agrarsoziologie*, Vol. 25 (1977), pp. 170-95.

29.   W. Koomen, 'A Note on the Authoritarian German Family', *Journal of Marriage and the Family* (1974), pp. 634-6; R. König, 'Family and Authority: the German Father in 1955', *The British Sociological Review*, Vol. 5 (1957), pp. 107-27; B. Schaffner, *Father Land: A Study of Authoritarianism in the German Family* (New York, 1948).

30.   T.W. Adorno, *The Authoritarian Personality* (New York, 1968); K. Theweleit, *Männerphantasien*, 2 vols. (Frankfurt, 1977/8).

31.   J. Kocka (ed.), 'Soziale Schichtung und Mobilität in Deutschland im 19. und 20. Jahrhundert' (= *Geschichte und Gesellschaft*, Vol. I/I, 1975).

32.   G. Eley, 'Memories of Under-development: Social History in Germany', *Social History*, No. 6 (1977), p. 788.

32.   D. Sabean, 'Household Formation'.

34.   See the contribution by Schomerus to the present volume (pp. 175-93); and P. Borscheid and H. Schomerus, 'Mobilität und soziale Lage der württembergischen Fabrikarbeiterschaft im 19. Jahrhundert', in P.J. Müller (ed.), *Die Analyse prozess-produzierter Daten* (Historisch-Sozialwissenschaftliche Forschungen, Bd. 2, Stuttgart 1977), pp. 119-224; P. Borscheid, *Textilarbeiterschaft in der Industrialisierung. Soziale Lage und Mobilität in Württemberg (19. Jahrhundert)* (Stuttgart, 1978); H. Schomerus, 'Soziale Differenzierung und Nivellierung der Fabrikarbeiterschaft Esslingens 1846-1914', in H. Pohl (ed.), *Forschungen zur Lage der Arbeiter im Industrialisierungsprozess* (Stuttgart, 1978), pp. 20-64; idem., 'Ausbildung und Aufstiegmöglichkeiten württembergischer Metallarbeiter 1846-1914 am Beispiel der Maschinenfabrik Esslingen', in U. Engelhardt, V. Sellin and H. Stuke (eds.), *Soziale Bewegung und politische Verfassung* (Stuttgart, 1976), pp. 372 *et seq.*; idem., *Die Arbeiter der Maschinenfabrik Esslingens. Untersuchungen zum innerbetrieblichen und innerstädtischen Status 1848-1914* (Stuttgart, 1977).

35.   P. Borscheid, 'Arbeitskräftepotential, Wanderung und Wohlstandsgefälle', in R. Fremdling and R.H. Tilly (eds.), *Industrialisierung und Raum. Studien zur regionalen Differenzierung in Deutschland des 19. Jahrhunderts* (Historisches-Sozialwissenschaftliche Ferschungen, Vol. 7, (Stuttgart, 1979), pp. 230-50.

36.   F. Meyer, *Die Grossstädte im Strome der Binnenwanderung. Wirtschafts- und bevölkerungswissenschaftliche Untersuchungen über Wanderung und Mobilität in deutschen Städten* (Leipzig, 1937).

37.   D. Langewiesche, 'Wanderungsbewegungen in der Hochindustrialisierungsperiode. Regionale, interstädtische und innerstädtische Mobilität in Deutschland 1880-1914', *Vierteljahrschrift für Sozial- und Wirtschaftsgeschichte* (1977/I), pp. 1-40.

38.   D. Crew, 'Definitions of Modernity: Social Mobility in a German Town: Bochum 1880-1901', *Journal of Social History*, Vol. 7 (1973) pp. 51-74; idem., 'Regionale Mobilität und Arbeitersklasse. Das Beispiel Bochum 1880-1901', *Geschichte und Gesellschaft*, Vol. I/I (1975), pp. 99-120; idem., *Town in the Ruhr* (New York, 1979).

39.   See the works cited by L.K. Berkner, 'Recent Research on the History of the Family in Western Europe', *Journal of Marriage and the Family* (1973), pp. 395-405.

40.   J.P. Süssmilch, *Die göttliche Ordnung in der Veränderungen des menschlichen Geschlechts, aus der Geburt, dem Tode und der Fortpflanzung desselben erwiesen* (3rd edn., Berlin, 1765); J. Jastrow, *Die Volkszahl deutscher Städte zu Ende des Mittelalters. Ein Ueberblick über den Stand und Mittel der Forschung* (Berlin, 1886); F.J. Neumann, *Beiträge zur Geschichte der Bevölkerung in Deutschland* (Tübingen, 1885-1903); O.K. Roller, *Die Einwohnerschaft der Stadt Durlach im 18. Jahrhundert* (Karlsruhe, 1907).

41.   W.R. Lee, 'Zur Bevölkerungsgeschichte Bayerns 1750-1850: Britische Forschungsergebnisse', *Vierteljahrschrift für Sozial- und Wirtschaftsgeschichte*, Vol. 63/3 (1975), pp. 310-11.

42.   T. Hollingsworth, 'Relationships between Historical Sciences and Historical Demography', in *Proceedings of the International Population Conference* (Liège, 1973), Vol. 3, p. 89.

43.   A.E. Imhof (Berlin), 'Historical Demography as Social History: Possibilities in Germany', *Journal of Family History* (1977), pp. 305-32; idem., 'Bevölkerungsgeschichte und Historische Demographie', in R. Rürup (ed.), *Historische Sozialwissenschaft. Beiträge zur Einführung in die Forschungspraxis* (Göttingen, 1977), pp. 16-58; idem, *Einführung in die Historische Demographie* (Munich, 1977); W. Köllman (Bochum), *Bevölkerung in der industriellen Revolution* (Göttingen, 1974); W. Köllmann and P. Marschalck (eds.), *Bevölkerungsgeschichte* (Cologne, 1972); W.G. Rödel (Mainz), 'Untersuchungen zur Bevölkerungsgeschichte der Pfarrei (Mainz-) Gonsenheim (1686-1797)', *Geschichtliche Landeskunde* Vol. XIV (1976), pp. 152-69; idem (ed.), 'Bevölkerungsbewegung und soziale Strukturen in Mainz zur Zeit des Pfälzischen Krieges (1680-1700). Eine historisch-demographische Fallstudie', *Geschichtliche Landeskunde*, Vol. XIX (1978).

44.   J. Knodel and E. Shorter, 'The Reliability of Family Reconstitution Data in German Village Genealogies (*"Ortssippenbücher"*)', *Annales de Démographie Historique* (1976), pp. 115-54. Stemming from the foundation in 1937 of the *Arbeitsgemeinschaft für Sippenforschung und Sippenpflege* there has been a useful stream of published material, one of the most recent being the volume edited by A. Köbele and H. Scheer, *Ortssippenbuch Altdorf. Stadt Ettenheim, Ortenau-Kreis in Baden* (Frankfurt a.M., 1976). For further information concerning Ortssippenbücher see A.E. Imhof, *Einführung in die Historische Demographie* (Munich, 1977), pp. 26, 101, 120, 135 and below, pp. 157-8.

45.   A.E. Imhof, 'Ländliche Familienstrukturen an einem hessischen Beispiel: Heuchelheim 1690-1900', in W. Conze (ed.), *Sozialgeschichte der Familie in der Neuzeit Europas* (Stuttgart, 1977), pp. 197-230; G. Schmidt, 'Hofgrösse – Familiengrösse – Familiengewohnheiten. Eine Fallstudie über fünf Familien auf Grund des Heuchelheimer Geschossbuches aus dem 18. Jahrhundert', in A. E. Imhof, *Historische Demographie als Sozialgeschichte. Giessen und Umgebung vom 17. zum 19. Jahrhundert* (Darmstadt and Marburg,

1975), Vol. II, pp. 687-708.
46.　A.E. Imhof, 'Historical Demography'.
47.　A.E. Imhof, 'The Hospital in the 18th century: for whom?', *Journal of Social History*, Vol. 10 (1977), pp. 448-70. See also Imhof's contribution to the present volume (pp. 148-74).
48.　A.E. Imhof, 'Historical Demography'; W.R. Lee, *Population Growth, Economic Development and Social Change in Bavaria, 1750-1850* (New York, 1977), pp. 41-51.
49.　E.A. Wrigley, 'Family Limitation in Pre-industrial England', *Economic History Review*, Vol. XIX (1966), pp. 86 *et seq*.
50.　J. Knodel and H. Kintner, 'The Impact of Breast-feeding Patterns on the Biometric Analysis of Infant Mortality', *Demography*, Vol. 14, No. 4 (1977), pp. 391-409.
51.　W.R. Lee, 'Regionale Differenzierung im Bevölkerungswachstum Deutschlands im frühen neunzehnten Jahrhundert', in R. Fremdling and R.H. Tilly (eds.), *Industrialisierung und Raum. Studien zur regionalen Differenzierung im Deutschland des 19. Jahrhunderts* (Historisch-Sozialwissenschaftliche Forschung, Vol. 7, Stuttgart, 1979), pp. 212 *et seq*.
52.　A.H. Maslow and I. Syilagi-Kessler, 'Security and Breast Feeding', *Journal of Abnormal Social Psychology*, Vol. 41 (1946), pp. 83-5.
53.　J. Knodel, *The Decline of Fertility in Germany, 1871-1939* (Princeton, 1974).
54.　T. Richards, 'Fertility Decline in Germany: An Econometric Appraisal', *Population Studies*, Vol. 31, No. 3 (1977), pp. 537-53.
55.　R. Spree, 'Strukturierte soziale Ungleichheit im Reproduktionsbereich. Zur historischen Analyse ihrer Erscheinungsformen in Deutschland 1870 bis 1913,' in J. Bergmann *et al.*, (eds.), *Geschichte als politische Wissenschaft* (Stuttgart, 1979), pp. 68-96.
56.　W. Schaub, 'Städtische Familienformen in sozialgenealogischer Sicht (Oldenburg 1743/1870)', in W. Conze (ed.), *Sozialgeschichte der Familie in der Neuzeit Europas* (Stuttgart, 1977), pp. 292-323.
57.　S.P. Hays, 'History and Genealogy: Patterns of Change and Prospects for Cooperation', *Prologue* (Spring, Summer, Fall 1975); A.v. Nell, 'Die Entwicklung der Generativen Strukturen bürgerlicher und bäuerlicher Familien von 1750 bis zur Gegenwart' (Diss., Bochum, 1973), pp. 19-21.
58.　A Gräfin zu Castell, 'Forschungsergebnisse zum gruppenspezifischen Wandel generativer Strukturen', in W. Conze (ed.), *Sozialgeschichte der Familie in der Neuzeit Europas* (Stuttgart, 1977), pp. 161-72.
59.　A.E. Imhof, 'Demographische Stadtsstrukturen der frühen Neizeit. Giessen in seiner Umbegung im 17. und 18. Jahrhundert als Fallstudie', *Zeitschrift für Stadtgeschichte, Stadtsoziologie und Denkmalpflege*, Vol. 2 (1975), pp. 190-227; F.M. Phayer, *Religion und das gewöhnliche Volk in Bayern in der Zeit von 1750 bis 1850* (Miscellanea Bavarica Monacensia, Munich, 1970); J. Knodel, 'From Natural Fertility to Family Limitation: The Onset of Fertility Transition in a Sample of German Villages' (Manuscript submitted for publication, 1979); J. Knodel and S. de Vos, 'Preferences for the Sex of Offspring and Demographic Behaviour: An examination of Evidence from German Village Genealogies for the Eighteenth and Nineteenth Centuries' (Paper presented to the 1979 Annual Meeting of the Population Association of America); also notes 42 and 48 above.
60.　W. Köllmann, 'Bevölkerungsgeschichte, 1800-1970', in H. Aubin and W. Zorn (eds.), *Handbuch der deutschen Wirtschafts- und Sozialgeschichte* (Stuttgart, 1976), Vol. II, pp. 9-50.
61.　G. Mackenroth, *Bevölkerungslehre. Theorie, Soziologie und Statistik der Bevölkerung* (Berlin – Göttingen – Heidelberg, 1953).

62. A. Gräfin zu Castell, 'Forschungsergebnisse'.

63. G. Ipsen, 'Die preussische Bauernbefreiung als Landesausbau', *Zeitschrift für Agrargeschichte und Agrarsoziologie*, Vol. 2 (1954), pp. 29 *et seq*; W. Köllmann, 'Grundzüge der Bevölkerungsgeschichte Deutschlands im 19. und 20. Jahrhundert', *Studium Generale*, Vol. 12 (1956), p. 384. The cultivable area in the North-east provinces of Prussia, including East Prussia, Brandenburg, Pommerania and Posen was increased from 3.2 million to 7.4 million hectares within the period 1815-49.

64. W. Köllmann, 'Die deutsche Bevölkerung im Industriezeitalter', *Mitteilungen der Deutschen Gesellschaft für Bevölkerungswissenschaft*, Vol. 27 (1962), p. 57. Similarly in Baden and Württemberg the precise chronology of agricultural reform in the early nineteenth century apparently determined the precise onset of population growth, according to the analysis of J. Griesmeyer, 'Die Entwicklung der Wirtschaft und der Bevölkerung von Baden und Württemberg im 19. und 20. Jahrhundert', *Jahrbücher für Baden-Württemberg*, Vol. I, No. 2 (1954), p. 125.

65. W.R. Lee, 'Germany' in idem (ed.), *European Demography and Economic Growth* (London, 1979), pp. 146-7.

66. H. Harnisch, 'Die Bedeutung der kapitalistischen Agrarreform für die Herausbildung des Inneren Marktes und die Industrielle Revolution in den östlichen Provinzen Preussens in der ersten Hälfte des 19. Jahrhunderts', *Jahrbuch für Wirtschaftsgeschichte* (1977), Pt. IV, pp. 83 *et seq*; idem, 'Bevölkerungsgeschichtliche Probleme der Industriellen Revolution in Deutschland', in K. Lärmer (ed.), *Studien zur Geschichte der Produktivkräfte. Deutschland zur Zeit der Industriellen Revolution* (Berlin, 1979), pp. 267-339.

67. This is equally true of other states, including America: G.N. Grob, 'The Social History of Medicine and Disease in America: Problems and Possibilities', *Journal of Social History*, Vol. 10, No. 4 (1977), pp. 391-409.

68. E.H. Ackerknecht, *Malaria in the Upper Mississippi Valley 1760-1900* (Baltimore, 1945); C.E. Rosenberg, *The Cholera Years: the United States in 1832, 1849, and 1868* (Chicago, 1962).

69. A.E. Imhof, 'Demographische Stadtstrukturen'; W.R. Lee, *Population Growth*, pp. 60-3.

70. G. Schmidt, 'Hofgrösse'.

71. As in the contribution by E. Simon, H. Immel and E. Rettinger, 'Untersuchungen zur Bevölkerungsgeschichte der Pfarrei St. Ignaz in Mainz (1603-1650)', *Geschichtliche Landeskunde*, Vol. XIV (1976), pp. 138-52.

72. R.E. Gallmann, 'Some Notes on the New Social History', *Journal of Economic History*, Vol. 37 (1977), p. 11.

73. H.J. Habakkuk, 'Family Structure and Economic Change in 19th Century Europe', *Journal of Economic History*, Vol. 15, No. 1 (1955), pp. 1-12.

74. D. Sabean, 'Verwandtschaft und Familie in einem württembergischen Dorf 1500 bis 1870: einige methodische Ueberlegungen', in W. Conze (ed.), *Sozialgeschichte der Familie in der Neuzeit Europas* (Stuttgart, 1977), pp. 231-46.

75. H. Kisch, 'The Textile Industries in Silesia and the Rhineland: a Comparative Study in Industrialization', *Journal of Economic History*, Vol. XIX (1959), pp. 541-64; idem, 'The Impact of the French Revolution on the Lower Rhine Textile Districts: Some Comments on Economic Development and Social Change', *Economic History Review*, 2nd series, Vol. XV (1962), pp. 304-27; F.F. Mendels, 'Proto-industrialization: the First Phase of the Industrialization Process', *Journal of Economic History*, Vol. XXXII (1972), pp. 241-61; idem, 'Industrialization and Population Pressure in Eighteenth-century Flanders', *Journal of Economic History*, Vol. XXXI (1971), pp. 269-71; idem, 'Agriculture and Peasant Industry in Eighteenth-century Flanders', in W.N. Parker and E.L. Jones (eds.), *Economic Issues in European Agrarian History* (Princeton, 1975).

76.   P. Kriedte, H. Medick and J. Schlumbohm, *Industrialisierung vor der Industrialisierung: Gewerbliche Warenproduktion auf dem Lande in der Formationsperiode des Kapitalismus* (Göttingen, 1977); H. Medick, 'The Proto-industrial Family Economy: the Structural Function of Household and Family during the Transition from Peasant Society to Industrial Capitalism', *Social History*, No. 3 (1976), pp. 291-315; idem, 'Zur strukturellen Funktion von Haushalt und Familie im Uebergang von der traditionellen Agrargesellschaft zum industriellen Kapitalismus: die proto-industrielle Familienwirtschaft', in W. Conze (ed.), *Sozialgeschichte der Familie in der Neuzeit Europas* (Stuttgart, 1979), pp. 254-82; J. Schlumbohm, 'Der saisonale Rhythmus der Leinenproduktion im Osnabrücker Lande während des späten 18. und der ersten Hälfte des 19. Jahrhunderts: Erscheinungsbild, Zusammenhänge und interregionaler Vergleich', *Archiv für Sozialgeschichte*, Vol. XIX (1979), pp. 263-98.

77.   A number of points were made in my review of the book jointly written by the Göttingen research group in *Social History*, Vol. IV, No. 2 (1979), pp. 375-9. The interpretation advanced in this book to explain population growth is essentially Malthusian in nature and ignores what might have been an exogenous decline in mortality. Equally it could be argued that there is an insufficient differentiation between the different substrata in rural society and a failure to determine the precise geographical extent of genuine proto-industrial production. One must also query the overall applicability of Chayanov's model of self-exploitation to German experience, as well as the function of the 'demo-economic paradox' in relation to the specific role of children in domestic craft production. The empirical work at present being undertaken by the Göttingen group will be an important test of the viability of many of these concepts.

78.   G. Hohorst, *Wirtschaftswachstum und Bevölkerungsentwicklung in Preussen 1816 bis 1914* (New York, 1977); W.R. Lee, as yet unpublished findings from Upper Bavarian data.

79.   A. Noll, *Sozio-ökonomischer Strukturwandel des Handwerks in der zweiten Phase der Industrialisierung* (Studien zum Wandel von Gesellschaft und Bildung im 19. Jahrhundert, Bd. 10, Göttingen, 1978). The more traditional school of studies into craft production in Germany, however, seldom poses such central questions, and is more concerned with charting the approximate extent of craft production in the late eighteenth and early nineteenth century and the relative level of income operative in each specific trade. K.H. Kaufhold, 'Umfang und Gliederung des deutschen Handwerks um 1800', in W. Abel *et al.* (eds.), *Handwerkgeschichte in neuer Sicht* (Göttinger handwerkswirtschaftliche Studien, Vol. 16, Göttingen, 1970); E. Wiest, *Die Entwicklung des Nürnberger Gewerbes zwischen 1648 und 1806* (Stuttgart, 1968); K. Assman, *Zustand und Entwicklung des städtischen Handwerks in der ersten Hälfte des 19. Jahrhunderts* (Göttinger handwerkswirtschaftliche Studien, Vol. 18, Göttingen, 1971).

80.   E. Sax, *Die Hausindustrie in Thüringen* (Halle, 1882); K. Frankenstein, *Bevölkerung und Hausindustrie im Kreise Schmalkaden seit Anfang dieses Jahrhunderts* (Tübingen, 1883); G. Schnapper-Arndt, *Fünf Dorfgemeinden auf dem Hohen Taunus. Eine sozialstatistische Untersuchung über Kleinbauerntum, Hausindustrie und Volksleben* (Leipzig, 1883).

81.   E. Shorter, *The Making of the Modern Family* (New York, 1975).

82.   For example the review by R.T. Vann, *Journal of Family History*, Vol. I, No. 1 (1976), pp. 106-17; W.R. Lee, 'Bastardy and the Socio-economic Structure of South Germany', *Journal of Interdisciplinary History*, Vol. 7 (1977), pp. 403-25; idem, 'Bastardy in South Germany: A Reply', *Journal of Interdisciplinary History*, Vol. 8 (1978), pp. 471-6; M. Mitterauer, 'Familienformen und Illegitimität in ländlichen Gebieten Oesterreichs', *Archiv für Sozialgeschichte*, Bd. XIX (1979), pp. 123-88.

83.   M. Mitterauer, 'Familiengrösse' (note 12, above).
84.   L.K. Berkner, 'Recent Research' (note 39 above).
85.   W. Köllmann, 'Bevölkerung und Arbeitskräftepotential in Deutschland 1815-1865. Ein Beitrag zur Analyse der Problematik des Pauperismus', *Jahrbuch des Landes Nordrhein-Westfalen*, 1968 (published by the Minister-präsident des Landes Nordrhein – Westfalen, Landesamt für Forschung), pp. 209-54; J. Reulecke, 'Veränderungen des Arbeitskräftepotentials im Deutschen Reich 1900-1933' in H. Mommsen, D. Petzina and B. Weisbrod (eds.), *Industrielles System und politische Entwicklung in der Weimarer Republik* (Verhandlungen des Internationalen Symposiums in Bochum vom 12–17 Juni 1973, Düsseldorf, 1974), pp. 84-95. However a word of caution needs to be expressed concerning certain aspects of Reulecke's analysis for the period 1900-33, as he ignores the fact that a large number of women were added to the workforce during this period simply by a reclassification of categories. This was particularly the case between the census of 1895 and 1907. It is also important to note that the process of reclassification of the *mithelfende Familienange-hörigen* occurred among rural female labourers. I am grateful to Richard Evans for bringing my attention to these points.
86.   G. Meyer, 'Die Mittlere Lebensdauer', *Jahrbücher für National-ökonomie und Statistik*, Vol. 5, Jena (1867), p. 31; W.R. Lee, 'Germany', in idem (ed.), *European Demography and Economic Growth* (London, 1979), p. 156.
87.   P. Branca, *Women in Europe since 1750* (London, 1978), p. 87.
88.   W.R. Lee, 'Germany', pp. 192-227.
89.   J. Scott and L. Tilly, 'Women's Work and the Family in Nineteenth-century Europe', *Comparative Studies in Society and History*, Vol. XVII (1975), pp. 36-64; L.A. Tilly, J.W. Scott and M. Cohen, 'Women's Work and European Fertility Patterns', *Journal of Interdisciplinary History*, Vol. 3 (1976), pp. 447-76.
90.   J. Kuczinski, *Geschichte der Kinderarbeit in Deutschland 1750 bis 1939* (2 vols., Berlin, 1958); K.-H. Ludwig, 'Die Fabrikarbeit von Kindern im 19. Jahrhundert', *Vieteljahrschrift für Sozial- und Wirtschaftsgeschichte*, Vol. 52 (1965), pp. 63-85; L. Adolph, *Industrielle Kinderarbeit im 19. Jahrhundert* (Duisburger Forschungen, Beiheft 15, Duisburg, 1972).
91.   J.v. Hazzi, *Statistische Aufschlüsse über das Herzogtum Baiern*, Bd. II (Munich, 1802), p. 181; W.R. Lee, *Population Growth*, pp. 282-3.
92.   J.M. Reddy, 'Family and Factory: French Linen Weavers in the Belle Epoque', *Journal of Social History*, Vol. 8 (1975), pp. 110 *et seq.*
93.   N.J. Smelser, *Social Change in the Industrial Revolution* (London, 1959); idem, 'Sociological History: the Industrial Revolution and the British Working-class Family', *Journal of Social History*, Vol. I (1967), pp. 18-35. Smelser takes as his theoretical starting-point a system-based model society where the different elements are essentially interdependent and integrated in functional, normative and structural terms. The primary concern of his research, which is illustrated by the historical development of the Lancashire textile industry, is to examine how economic change affected society through an increasing and destabilising division of labour. He is also concerned to examine the subsequent process of reintegration. One of his major findings is that the initial impact of industrialisa-tion on the family was not necessarily disruptive and that the family continued to perform important economic functions within a new industrial context. For a rigorous critique of these views, see M. Anderson, 'Sociological History and the Working-class Family: Smelser Revisited', *Social History*, No. 3 (1976), pp. 317-34.
94.   R. Engelsing, 'Probleme' (note 8, above).
95.   L. Schneider, *Der Arbeiterhaushalt* (note 8, above); R. Engelsing, 'Lebenshaltungen und Lebenshaltungskosten im 18. und 19. Jahrhundert in den

48   The German Family

Hansastädten Bremen und Hamburg', *International Review of Social History*, Vol. II (1966), pp. 90 *et seq.*
    96.   S.J. Coyner, 'Class Patterns of Family Income and Expenditure during the Weimar Republic: German White-collar Employees as Harbingers of Modern Society' (Ph.D. Rutgers University, 1975); idem, 'Class Consciousness and Consumption: The New Middle Class during the Weimar Republic', *Journal of Social History*, Vol. 10 (1977), pp. 310-31.
    97.   Particularly from the mid nineteenth century onwards there was a steady stream of useful studies into German folklore and practice. For South Germany, the following publications may be taken as typical of the genre –
A. Birlinger and M.R. Buck, *Sagen, Märchen, Volksaberglauben* (Volksthümliches aus Schwaben, Bd. I, Freiburg im Breisgau, 1861); J.W. Lipwosky, *Die sozialen und volkswirtschaftlichen Zustände des Landgerichtes Eggenfelden* (Landshut, 1862); Bavaria, *Landes- und Volkskunde des Königreichs Bayern* (5 vols., Munich, 1862-7). As far as the history of the family was concerned, an important general publication was that by W.H. Riehl, *Die Familie* (Stuttgart, 1889).
    98.   M. Scharfe, 'Towards a Cultural History: Notes on Contemporary Volkskunde (folklore) in German-speaking Countries', *Social History*, Vol. 4, No. 2 (1979), p. 336.
    99.   W. Jacobeit and U. Mohrmann (eds.), *Kultur und Lebensweise des Proletariats. Kultur-historisch-volkskundliche Studien und Materialen* (Berlin (East), 1973); D. Kramer, 'Kreativität in der "Volkskultur" ', *Zeitschrift für Volkskunde*, Vol. LXVIII (1972), pp. 26-41; idem, 'Literatur zur Kultursoziologie der Arbeit', *Zeitschrift für Volkskunde*, Vol. LXXXI (1975), pp. 88-103.
    100.   U. Jeggle, *Kiebingen – eine Heimatgeschichte* (Tübingen, 1977); J. Brückl, *Zolling. Aus Vergangenheit und Gegenwart* (Munich, 1968).
    101.   K.-S. Kramer, *Grundriss einer rechtlichen Volkskunde* (Göttingen, 1974); idem, 'Die Nachbarschaft als bäuerliche Gemeinschaft', *Bayerische Heimatforschung*, Vol. 9 (Munich, 1954); idem, *Bauern und Bürger im nachmittelalterlichen Unterfranken* (Würzburg, 1957); idem, 'Nachrichten zum Komplex "Haus und Hof im Volksleben" vorwiegend aus Holstein', *Kieler Blätter zur Volkskunde*, Bd. 2 (1970), pp. 63 *et seq.*
    102.   W.E. Peuckert, *Volkskunde des Proletariats* (Frankfurt, 1931); K.S. Kramer, 'Arbeitsanfang und -anschluss als Kernelement des Brauchtums', in *Arbeit und Volksleben. Deutsche Volkskunde-Kongress 1965* (Göttingen, 1967), pp. 354 *et seq.*; I. Weber-Kellermann, *Erntebrauch in der ländlichen Arbeitswelt des 19. Jahrhunderts* (Marburg, 1965); idem, 'Arbeitsbräuche und Arbeitsfeste der Drescher' in *Arbeit und Volkskunde. Deutsche Volkskunde-Kongress 1965* (Göttingen, 1967), pp. 363-72).
    103.   G. Wiegelmann (ed.), *Kultureller Wandel im 19. Jahrhundert. Verhandlungen des 18. Deutschen Volkskunde-Kongresses in Trier 1971* (Göttingen, 1973); F.W. Zipperer, *Das Haberfeldtreiben. Seine Geschichte und seine Deutung* (Weimar, 1938); J.M. Phayer, *Sexual Liberation and Religion in 19th century Europe* (London, 1977), pp. 14-16, 40-1, 52-3. The ongoing work of Ian Farr (University of East Anglia) on charivari in South Germany is also highly important in this particular context.
    104.   See also E. Hofmann, 'Volkskundliche Betrachtungen zur proletarischen Familie in Chemnitz um 1900', *Wissenschaftliche Zeitschrift der Humboldt Universität zu Berlin* (1971).
    105.   R. Braun, *Industrialisierung und Volksleben: Die Veränderungen der Lebensformen in einem ländlichen Industriegebiet vor 1800 (Züricher Oberland)* (Zürich, 1960); idem, 'The Impact of Cottage Industry on an Agricultural Population', in D.S. Landes (ed.), *The Rise of Capitalism* (New York, 1966),

pp. 53-64.

106. K.-S. Bader, *Das Mittelalterliches Dorf als Friedens- und Rechtsbereich* (Munich, 1957); idem, *Dorf und Dorfgemeinde im Zeitalter von Naturrecht und Aufklärung. Festschrift für K.G. Hugelmann* (Aalen 1959); L. Fick, *Die bäuerliche Erbfolge im Gebiet des bayerischen Landrechtes* (Munich, 1895); R. Wilhelm, *Rechtspflege und Dorfverfassung nach nieder-bayerischen Ehehaftordnungen vom 15. bis 18. Jahrhundert* (Verhandlungen des historischen Vereins für Niederbayern, Bd. 80, 1954), pp. 163 *et seq.*

107. L.K. Berkner and F.F. Mendels, 'Inheritance Systems, Family Structures and Demographic Patterns in Western Europe, 1700-1900', in C. Tilly (ed.), *Historical Studies of Changing Fertility* (Princeton, 1978), pp. 209-24; L.K. Berkner, 'Peasant Household Organization and Demographic Change in Lower Saxony (1689-1766)', in R. Lee (ed.), *Population Patterns in the Past* (New York, 1976), pp. 53-70; U. Planck, 'Hofstellenchronik von Bölgental 1650-1961: Strukturwandlungen in einem Fränkischen Weiler', in H. Haushofer and W. Boelcke (eds.), *Wege und Forschungen der Agrargeschichte. Festschrift zum 65. Geburtstag von Günther Franz* (Frankfurt a.M., 1967), pp. 242-67; R.H. Schröder, 'Realteilung und Industrialisierung als Ursachen agrargeographischer Wandlungen in Württemberg', *Zeitschrift für Erdkunde*, Vol. 10 (1942), pp. 542-8. Social anthropology in general can contribute a great deal to historical studies on the family. Indeed there is already a fair number of publications drawing on social anthropological theory and dealing with the historical development of the family unit. See D. Sabean, 'Intensivierung der Arbeit und Alltagserfahrung auf dem Lande', *Sozialwissenschaftliche Information für Unterricht und Studium*, Vol. 6, No. 4 (1977), pp. 148-52; F. Brüggemeier, 'Bedürfnisse, gesellschaftliche Erfahrung und politisches Verhalten – Das Beispiel der Ruhr-Bergarbeiter', *Sozialwissenschaftliche Information für Unterricht und Studium*, Vol. 6, No. 4 (1977), pp. 152-9; J. Goody, 'Strategies of Heirship', *Comparative Studies in Society and History*, Vol. 15 (1973), pp. 3-20; idem, (ed.), *The Character of Kinship* (Cambridge, 1973); J. Goody, J. Thirsk, E.P. Thompson (eds.), *Family and Inheritance: Rural Society in Western Europe 1200-1800* (Cambridge, 1976).

108. W. Peitzsch, *Kriminalpolitik in Bayern unter der Geltung des Codex Juris Criminalis Bavarici von 1751* (Münchener Universitätsschriften, Vol. 8, Munich, 1968).

109. W.R. Lee, *Population Growth*, p. 311.

110. G.S. Steinbart, *Vorschläge zu einer allgemeinen Schulverbesserung, insofern sie nicht Sache der Kirche, sondern des Staats ist* (Züllichau, 1789), p. 10; H.G. Zerrenner, *Volksaufklärung. Uebersicht und freimütige Darstellung ihrer Hindernisse nebst einigen Vorschlägen denselben wirksam abzuhelfen* (Magdeburg, 1786), p. 7.

111. W.R. Lee, *Population Growth*, pp. 337-55.

112. R.A. Fullerton, 'The Development of the German Book Markets 1815-1888' (Ph.D., University of Wisconsin-Madison, 1975); idem, 'Creating a Mass Book Market in Germany: the Story of the Colporteur Novel 1870-1880'. *Journal of Social History* (1977), pp. 265-83.

113. R. Schenda, *Volk ohne Buch. Studien zur Sozialgeschichte der populären Lesestoffe 1770-1910* (Frankfurt, 1970); idem, *Die Lesestoffe der kleinen Leute. Studien zur populären Literatur im 19. und 20. Jahrhundert* (Munich, 1976).

114. In this context, see the contribution by Karin Hausen to the present volume (pp. 51-83).

115. J. Reulecke, 'Vom blauen Montag zum Arbeiterurlarb. Vorgeschichte und Entstehung des Erholungsurlaubs für Arbeiter vor dem Ersten Weltkrieg',

Archiv für Sozialgeschichte, Vol. XVI (1976), pp. 205-48; W. Nahrstedt, *Die Entstehung der Freizeit, dargestellt am Beispiel Hamburgs* (Göttingen, 1972); idem, 'Freizeit und Aufklärung. Zum Funktionswandel der Feiertage seit dem 18. Jahrhundert in Hamburg (1743-1860)', *Vierteljahrschrift für Sozial- und Wirtschaftsgeschichte*, Vol. 57 (1970), pp. 46-92; idem, 'Die Entstehung des Freiheitsbegriffs der Freizeit. Zur Genese einer grundlegenden Kategorie der modernen Industriegesellschaften (1755-1860)', *Vierteljahrschrift für Sozial- und Wirtschaftegeschichte*, Vol. 60 (1973), pp. 311-42; A. Timm, *Verlust der Musse. Zur Geschichte der Freiheitgesellschaft* (Buchholz-Hamburg, 1968).

116.   Sentiments voiced in a contemporary publication – E. Schneider, 'Die Geringhaltung der Sonn- und Feiertage und die Heiligung der abgewürdigten Feiertage auf dem Lande', *Wochenblatt des landwirtschaftlichen Vereins*, (Munich, 1821), No. II.

117.   H. Berding, 'Begriffsgeschichte und Sozialgeschichte', *Historische Zeitschift*, Vol. 223 (1976), pp. 98-110.

118.   As an illustration of the breadth of contemporary research some mention must be made of the work being undertaken by John Breuilly (University of Manchester) on family life and urbanisation in nineteenth-century Hamburg. Further examples can be found in the recently completed research of J.H. Jackson, 'Family Life and Urbanization in the Ruhr Valley 1840-1890 (Ph.D. diss. University of Minnesota, 1980) (see also pp. 194-220 in the present volume).

119.   G.G. Iggers, 'Die "Annales" und ihre Kritiker. Probleme moderner französischer Sozialgeschichte', *Historische Zeitschrift*, Vol. 219 (1974), pp. 578-608.

120.   J. Kocka, 'Recent Historiography of Germany and Austria. Theoretical Approaches to Social and Economic History of Modern Germany: Some Recent Trends, Concepts and Problems in Western and Eastern Germany', *Journal of Modern History*, Vol. 47, No. 1 (1975), pp. 101-19.

121.   R.E. Gallman, 'Some Notes on the New Social History', *Journal of Economic History*, Vol. 37 (1977), p. 11.

122.   T.K. Hareven, 'The Family as Process: The Historical Study of the Family Cycle', *Journal of Social History*, Vol. 7, No. 3 (1974), p. 328.

123.   P.N. Stearns, 'The Unskilled and Industrialization. A Transformation of Consciousness', *Archiv für Sozialgeschichte*, Vol. XVI (1976), pp. 249-82; H. Grees, 'Ländliche Unterschichten und ländliche Siedlung in Ostschwaben', *Tübingen Geographische Studien*, Heft 58 (Sonderband 8), Tübingen, 1975; R. Engelsing, 'Das häusliche Personal in der Epoche der Industrialisierung', in idem, *Zur Sozialgeschichte deutscher Mittel- und Unterschichten* (Göttingen, 1973), pp. 225-61.

124.   U. Linse, 'Arbeiterschaft und Geburtenentwicklung in Deutschen Kaiserreich von 1871', *Archiv für Sozialgeschichte*, Vol. XII (1972), pp. 205-72. This study, however, contains very little empirical data.

125.   C. Kirkpatrick, *Nazi Germany: Its Women and Family Life* (Indianapolis/New York, 1938); T.W. Mason, 'Women in Nazi Germany, Pt. I', *History Workshop*, No. 1 (1976), p. 75.

126.   J. Stephenson, *Women in Nazi Society* (London, 1975); D. Winkler, *Frauenarbeit im Dritten Reich* (Hamburg, 1977); idem, 'Frauenarbeit versus Frauenideologie. Probleme der weiblichen Erwerbstätigkeit in Deutschland 1930-1945', *Archiv für Sozialgeschichte*, Vol. XVII (1977), pp. 99-126; L.J. Rupp, *Mobilizing Women for War. German and American Propaganda 1939-45* (Princeton, 1978).

127.   P. Goubert, 'Family and Province: A Contribution to the Knowledge of Family Structures in Early Modern France', *Journal of Family History*, Vol. 2 (1977), p. 192.

128.   W.R. Lee, 'Medicalisation and Mortality Trends in South Germany in the Early 19th Century', in A.E. Imhof (ed.), *Mensch und Gesundheit in der Geschichte* (Berlin, 1980), pp. 79-113.

2 FAMILY AND ROLE-DIVISION: THE POLARISATION OF SEXUAL STEREOTYPES IN THE NINETEENTH CENTURY — AN ASPECT OF THE DISSOCIATION OF WORK AND FAMILY LIFE

Karin Hausen

I

The German notion of *Geschlechtscharakter* (the character of the sexes), which has nowadays fallen into disuse, emerged in the eighteenth century. In the nineteenth century it was generally used to describe the mental characteristics which were held to coincide with the physiological distinctions between the sexes. In their own terms, statements about the 'character of the sexes' are intended to convey the quintessential nature of man and woman. The following is an attempt to outline and interpret the value-system behind the term 'character of the sexes'. At the basis of this analysis lies the assumption that the investigation of norms pertaining to family life will indicate a line of approach to the qualitative aspects of family life which are neglected in the contemporary preference for quantitative research. Statements about the sex-specific character traits of man and woman are in the first instance normative statements, and as such their relationship to reality is problematic. But at the same time they are almost certainly based on common experience of the real socio-economic sexual division of labour. Because of this, they can lay claim to a certain degree of relevance. It can be assumed, therefore, that at the very least they do not contradict the accepted model for the sexual division of labour. The fact that the sexual division of labour traditionally plays a central functional role in the organisation of family and household must also be taken into account, as must its decisive influence on the socialisation of children, the theory and practice of which it thoroughly permeates. However, socialisation, in so far as it forms the later behaviour and actions of the adult, is a complex amalgam of material and normative, direct and indirect forces and experiences. This dialectical interaction between reality and norms, hinted at here, is obviously particularly relevant for the family as the 'natural' location of the sexual division of labour. The study of norms pertaining to family life thus belongs necessarily to the historical study of the family in general.

　Another opportunity to explain the analysis which follows in the present essay is offered by the theoretical and empirical work of the social sciences, based on the concept of roles.[1] This concept, rich in colloquial associations, and its derivatives (role behaviour, role expectations, role prescription, role configuration, etc.) means basically that particular behaviour patterns are socially prescribed in accordance with various structurally determined social positions. The actual holder of the position is not at liberty to contravene these patterns. The interaction of individuals is totally determined neither by subjective behavioural decisions made anew as the situation demands, nor by material circumstances. Rather, social behaviour is based on culturally prescribed behaviour patterns. Keeping to these patterns is controlled either by force or consensus. Some of the questions that concern researchers working with role theory are the uniformity of role behaviour, role behaviour in certain groups or by particular individuals that deviates from 'normal' behaviour, the extent of congruity or incongruity between the role ideal and normal role behaviour (i.e. the distance between the ideal and the actual norm), the learning of and acting out of roles by the actors, and finally the social position and normative powers of those who define the roles. For our purposes, the indisputable advantage of the concept of role consists in the fact that the diverse points of view of sociology, social psychology, psychiatry and psychology can be integrated into a general interpretation.[2] The danger that, by using the concept of role, human behaviour threatens to become divided up into endless series of more or less discrete roles, should not be underestimated. But in particular in the analysis of the social positions of the sexes, this danger will be limited. This is because with sex-specific behaviour patterns for man and woman, husband and wife, father and mother we are dealing with very general behaviour patterns which are part of the generalised pattern of the division of labour; and because, secondly, we are also dealing with patterns of high intensity which are rooted in the primary phases of socialisation.

　Formulated in the language of role theory, the present investigation will first raise the question of how the new definition of one aspect of sex roles, which originated with treatises on the 'character of the sexes', arose. We shall ask who formulated this new definition, and with what authority? We shall also ask, how and for whom this value system was able to influence sex roles. And there is a related, more general question: why did the system of values embodied in the 'character of the sexes' work, and what was its function? This question, indeed, extends beyond the framework of role theory, and is directed at the relationship between socio-economic development and its ideological interpretation. It thus addresses itself to the ideological content of the successful prescription of complementary sex roles in the specific format of the 'character of the sexes'. This programme is an ambitious one, and in several respects it cuts across the prevailing trend in the fast-growing body of research on the family.[3] In addition, the actual execution is further hampered by the fact that I am not presenting the results of completed research, merely making observations which seem interesting in this context. The following preliminary remarks outline an important problem area in the history of the family, and should revitalise the discussion of how normative statements and beliefs which were current at a particular time, but not institutionalised, can be socially located with respect to their origin and effect, and how social history can and must incorporate intellectual history without becoming engulfed by it.[4]

II

A major German encyclopaedia, Meyer's *Grosses Konversationslexikon* (1904), under the heading *Geschlechtseigentümlichkeiten* (the disposition of the sexes), after an exposition on the anatomical and physiological distinctions, briefly summed up in the following terms:[5]

Mental distinctions are also to be found; in the female, emotion and sensibility, in the male, intelligence and thought predominate; the imagination of the female is livelier than that of the male, but seldom achieves the heights and boldness of the latter.

The stereotyping of the 'character of the sexes', here reduced to a brief formula, suggests that the working-out and definition of sexual character traits continued unabated from the last third of the eighteenth century on into the twentieth. This lively interest in definition, and likewise the matter-of-factness with which this was carried out, is impressively documented in the numerous encyclopaedias of the nineteenth century under headings such as *Frau* (woman), *Weib* (female), *Geschlecht* (sex), *Geschlechtscharakter* (character of the sexes), *Geschlechtseigentümlichkeiten* (disposition of the sexes), etc.

A quote from Brockhaus, another important encyclopaedia, in 1815, serves to illustrate the value system we are dealing with: here the character of the sexes in man and beast was defined as 'the natural opposition of forces which belong and work together in a common enterprise'. For humans this opposition was supposed to operate in both mind and body:[6]

> Thus in the male form the idea of power prevails, in the female more the idea of beauty . . . the male spirit is more creative, having greater effect on the outside world, more inclined to strive, to process abstract subjects, to form wide-ranging plans; of the passions the swift, volatile ones belong to the man, the slow, secretive, inward ones to the woman. The man is eager, loud in his desires, the woman knows quiet longing. The female is confined to a small intimate circle; she has more patience and perseverance in small tasks. The man must acquire, the woman seeks to preserve, the male with force, the female with her virtue or her wiles. The former belongs to bustling public life, the latter to the quiet domestic circle. The man works by the sweat of his brow, and, exhausted, requires repose; the woman is always busy, always active. The man will oppose his very fate and even when laid low remains defiant; the woman willingly bows her head and finds comfort and help in her tears.

Similarly in Meyer, 1848, in a ten-page article on the 'disposition of the sexes' the sexes were characterised thus: 'the male is in preference individual, the female, universal', in which individuality had the character of 'self-confidence, independence, power and energy, completeness, antagonism'. Universality, however, entailed 'dependence, uncertainty, sacrifice, sympathy'.[7] This list of characteristics was supposed not only to describe the physiological differences between the sexes generally observable in the animal kingdom, but also the corresponding mental traits in human beings:[8]

> In accordance with the more universal character of women, sensibility predominates – the female is a more feeling creature; in the man, because of his greater individuality, reaction predominates – he is a more thinking creature . . . In relation to the universality of the woman, sympathy, love prevail; in the man, due to his predominant individuality, antagonism, hate – and thus the former is more sympathetic, kinder, more moral, more religious than the rougher, often hard-hearted man who inclines to measure everything

in terms of self. He is firm and steady, bold and certain of purpose; he is above pettiness and has less vanity than pride; in regard to the latter, he can sacrifice all for a friend. The character of the woman is more fickle. Decisions, however, are often taken more hastily; in suffering she is generally more composed and endures the worst trials and tribulations with greater forebearance than the man. Everything that mainly lays a claim on the emotions affects the woman more, and it is woman's nature to love, not her own sex, but rather the other and the tender, helpless little ones. Her virtue is innocence of spirit and purity of heart; her honour inward participation and sympathy.

Next the different destinies of the sexes in the external world must be looked at . . . Reproduction is only possible through the cooperation of both; however, the female has unmistakably the largest part to play in this operation — while the woman in the main lays the foundation for the ties which bind the family, the man is the link with the external world; he is the bond between family and family, it is he who is the basis of the State.

These richly varied statements about the 'character of the sexes' mixed biology, social destiny and inner nature in their definitions and were intended to form a typology of the characteristics of man and woman. According to the 'disposition of the sexes', conceived of as a series of opposites, the man was by nature predestined for public life, the female for a domestic role. The destiny and talents of the man were concerned with social production, those of the woman with private reproduction. Constantly recurring characteristics were, for the man, activity and rationality, for the woman, passivity and emotionality, in which the dual concept activity-passivity was derived from the sexual act and rationality-emotionality from the social arena. These main categories could be found in combination with a multitude of additional characteristics, so that the essence of masculinity and femininity was described in a mixture of traditional and modern, physiological, mental and social qualities. If the sex-specific character traits commonly met with in these dictionaries and encyclopaedias are arranged in order,[9] the following groups are found:

Man	*Woman*
Social destiny	
External life	Inner life

Far	Near
Public life	Domestic life
Activity	*Passivity*
Energy, power, willpower	Weakness, yielding, devotion
Steadfastness	Fickleness
Bravery, boldness	Modesty
Doing	*Being*
Independent	Dependent
Striving, ambition, effective	Industrious, busy
Acquisitive	Protective
Giving	Receiving
Ability to get his own way	Self-denial, adaption
Force	Love, goodness
Antagonism	Sympathy
Rationality	*Emotionality*
Mind	Feeling, emotion
Reason	Intuition
Intellect	Perception
Thought	Receptiveness
Knowledge	Religion
Abstraction, judgement	Understanding
Virtue	*Virtues*
	Retiring, modest
	Resigned
	Loveable
	Tactful
	Gift of beautifying
Worthy	Grace, beauty

The body and mind of the woman were primarily intended for the
reproductive or generative purpose and the patriarchal monogamous
marriage, socially regarded as optimal. Those of the man on the other
hand were destined for a cultural purpose. In Marianne Weber's words:
'The woman is defined as the sexual creature, the man as the cultural'.[10]
These character schemata, which did not begin to lose their persuasive-
ness until the second half of the twentieth century, were 'discovered' in
the last third of the eighteenth. During the nineteenth century the

underlying principles remained the same and were 'scientifically' supported by medical science, anthropology, psychology and psychiatry.[11] At the same time, preconceptions about the essential nature of the sexes were so successfully popularised that ever greater sectors of the population came to accept them as the proper standards of masculinity and femininity well into the twentieth century.[12]

The bald fact of the comparison of men and women is historically not very informative, for statements about the 'other sex' have long formed a model for male self-definition in patriarchal societies.[13] However it is probably historically significant that with the appearance of the 'character of the sexes' in the last third of the eighteenth century the nature of this comparison changed. 'The character of the sexes' was derived from nature as a combination of biology and destiny, and at the same time was transferred (as the essence of masculinity and femininity) to human mentality. In contrast to this, older statements about man and woman preserved in sermons and almanacs (*Hausväterliteratur*) were all about status, social position and the corresponding virtues and duties.[14] In the first third of the eighteenth century Wolff divided men and women according to their social position (in a conjugal, parental or master's household) and laid down the corresponding virtues of authority or obedience, and of abilities of housekeeping or the direction of labour.[15] Similarly in 1735 in Zedler (another early encyclopaedia) the following is found:[16] 'The female or woman is a married person, who, subject to her husband's will and rule, runs the household, and in the latter is the servants' superior.' On the female sex in general: 'Their humour, spirit, character, inclination and nature seem to be different in every land and condition.' Krünitz as well, in 1778, listed under the heading 'woman' (*Frau*) not character traits, but the rights and duties of the housewife and specified that his remarks were meant for artisans' and merchants' wives.[17] The first instance in which the household did not constitute the sole frame of reference occurred in Adelung (a linguistic dictionary), 1796/1801. In comparison however to the elaborate definition of 'the character of the sexes' in the 1815 Brockhaus the entry here ('the female sex, which in humans is also called the fair sex, the weaker sex and the other sex') was remarkably reticent.[18]

Evidently what was new in the definition of the 'character of the sexes' was the choice of reference system. From the end of the eighteenth century, character definitions took the place of status definitions. Thus a particularistic classificatory principle was replaced by a universal one; instead of the head of the household and his wife the entire male and female sexes were included, and instead of duties deriving from the household, it was the general nature of each that was described. This change in reference systems seems to constitute a significant historical phenomenon, not least as it coincided with a series of other developments. In particular it coincided with the transition – long recognised in intellectual history – from the household or 'whole house' (*ganzes Haus*) to the bourgeois family,[19] which occurred when both the aspect of domestic economy and the notion of house servants subject to the master's rule disappeared from the concept of family.[20] There are many indications that in Germany at the end of the eighteenth century this transition was experienced as a profound change in the social institution of the family. According to Schwab, the theoretical questioning of the old family concept evidently reached such a pitch between 1780 and 1810 that the 'social role of the family' threatened to become completely overwhelmed.[21] As the following period saw the emergence of a new family concept it seems likely that the vehicle of the 'character of the sexes' was instrumental in bringing about this change. Thus the keen interest in the definition of the 'character of the sexes' can be interpreted as an attempt to replace the obsolete code of values with a new, more secure one. This seems all the more plausible if we take a look at the 'critical' situation between 1780 and 1810.

It is necessary to start with the growing interest in the individual and his inner and external autonomy, which took its impulse from humanism and, ultimately, the Reformation. At first this interest was directed solely at the man, the paterfamilias: human and man in the discussion of fundamental natural rights were self-evidently synonymous[22] and the demand for human rights for the man did not at first affect the woman or wife, traditionally subject to male authority, a state of affairs sanctioned by the Bible. This only changed when the model of the social contract, introduced to counter the theological legitimation of State power, was applied to the domestic structure as well, which, as a result of the traditional 'structural analogy of state and family',[23] was a logical next step. The application of contractual principles to the family however was no longer meant, as in Catholic and Protestant tradition, to refer solely to the marriage ceremony. It implied that marriage itself should be conceived of as a contract. This interpretation meant that the prevailing institutional framework of the family, the rule of the paterfamilias (i.e. the authority of the husband and father), and even the sexual monopoly and the indissolubility in principle of marriage, came under fire and demanded justification. This theoretical discussion, with its interpretation of the family based on the rights of the individual, 'absolved it from political duty'.[24] So marriage, formerly the joining of man and woman for the purpose of sexual intercourse, the rearing of children, running a household and carrying out common religious and economic duties, was transformed during the age of sensibility into the mainly spiritual union of the marriage partners through love alone. Finally, when for the Romantics marriage came to be seen as primarily and even solely founded on love and thus relating only to the individual man and woman, marriage and family tended to disappear as an institution.[25]

These ideas, clearly no longer dictated by the system of values pertaining to the *ganzes Haus* ('household') had far-reaching consequences, particularly with respect to the reinterpretation of the social and domestic role of women. One result was the demand for female emancipation from conjugal or paternal authority and integration on equal terms with men into bourgeois society. This demand was raised in the wake of the French Revolution and was immediately regarded as a threat both to the established order and to the family in particular.[26] The other result, which was a component of the new view of love and at the same time a reaction against socially unacceptable demands for emancipation, was the search for a new form of legitimation for the traditional subjection of the woman to her husband and her limitation to the domestic sphere. It attempted to reconcile for women the postulated development of a rational personality with marriage and family affairs. The interest in the 'character of the sexes' developed in connection with these efforts.[27] One of the achievements of German Classicism is that it succeeded in creating the legitimation and code of values that were sought: it managed to integrate heterogeneous points of view, at the same time intellectualising the potentially revolutionary elements. It is not necessary to describe in detail this process of ideological renovation, which was successfully completed by the turn of the century. It is sufficient to point out that in this period everything pertaining to the sexes, marriage and the family was subjected to careful scrutiny and all the attempted interpretations sprang from the general desire to decode the rational plan and purpose of Nature. The aim was to work out the different natural destinies and the corresponding different natural gifts and talents of man and woman according to the God-given order of the world.

In this sense Fichte[28] in 1796 continued the discussion about marital law (*Eherecht*), in which he deduced that the aim of marriage was the 'total union of two people' and that marriage was a relationship demanded by nature and reason. For the man the satisfaction of his sexual drive in the act of procreation was as rational as it was active; for the woman, regarded as passive in the act of procreation, the active and thus rational motive force was love, i.e. the need to 'satisfy a man'. According to Fichte, love was the total surrender of the personality and thus also the surrender of all property and rights to the man, who on his side was duty-bound, by the total surrender of the woman, to generosity and marital tenderness. In its practical handling, and because it was aimed at education, the argument was reduced to the constantly recurring formula of educational tracts: 'woman's destiny is to be a wife, housekeeper and mother'.[29] This 'polarised philosophy of the sexes',[30] which was developed over a relatively short time-span, finally provided the theoretical basis so long sought by dividing the rational personality regarded since the Enlightenment as the ideal, into two separate halves – the male and female personalities – and at the same time reconciling them. The differing qualities of the sexes were defined expressly emphasising the equal status and value of man and woman. Only through the combination of femininity, which came to fruition in the woman, with masculinity, could the ideal of humanity be approached.

The notion that these currents of thought, originating from different sources and coming together here, really created a new code of values is supported by contemporaneous developments in philosophical anthropology and psychology.[31] In 1798 Kant held his lecture on 'pragmatic anthropology' in which the 'character of the sexes' figured as part of his exposition. It interested him pragmatically in terms of 'what human beings as free creatures do, can and should make of themselves'.[32] Even more directly, Humboldt's 'Plan for a Comparative Anthropology' (1795) included the specification of the 'character of the sexes', which he regarded as necessary to a knowledge of humanity: 'what it is' and 'how it can develop'.[33] Taken together, the development of 'characterology' and the philosophy of the sexes did seem to be directly related to the acute need for orientation. Finally the growing interest in the moral history of the female sex can also be related to these intellectual currents.[34] This preoccupation is clearly evident in nineteenth-century encyclopaedias. Statements about the character of women were generally combined with a summary of the moral history of women in order to add an historical proof that the original, true character of woman could only be realised when the family was correctly regarded as a 'worthy' and 'high' institution – which in

Germany was only the case from the end of the eighteenth century.[35]
In all these arguments it was clear that woman was defined by
marriage and the family and vice versa. In contrast to previous
generations however it was *only* the woman, and no longer the man,
who was defined by the family; and also in contrast to earlier times it
was the laws of nature, history and morality that set the boundaries
within which the female sex had to develop, under the penalty of
'going against nature' if they were transgressed.[36]

III

If the observations made up to this point do not deceive, then these
statements about the 'character of the sexes' comprised a surprisingly
unified, astonishingly lasting and evidently widespread system of values
in the modern period. Looked at in this way the next, more fruitful
question becomes: what could the social function of this value-system
have been, and whose interests, and whose self-understanding was
being expressed here?

Without doubt the social destiny of the sexes served to reinforce
patriarchal authority.[37] It is not only the coincidence in the emergence
of this system of values and the crisis in patriarchal authority that
speaks in favour of this thesis. It is clear that, later on, for example, the
emergence of the 'character of the sexes' served the purpose of
reinforcing male legal privileges. An example of this can be seen in Carl
Theodor Welcker's line of argument in the *Staatslexicon*, under the
heading *Geschlechtsverhältnisse* ('relations between the sexes').[38]
Welcker regarded the aim of equality under the law, based on the rights
of man, as problematic with respect to women; there was so great an
inequality between the man and the woman, such great differences in
their life's tasks and powers and in their legal relationship,[39] 'laid down
by Nature herself'. Well aware that the 'voice of Nature is not readily
decipherable' and that 'custom, prejudice and the interests of the
stronger party here, as always where despotic and aristocratic
relationships are involved, have corrupted the judgement even of the
best enquirers' it is only after careful scrutiny that he came to regard it
as correct to withold from women the legal equality demanded by a
theory of the State based on natural rights. So he called on 'history
and the common judgement of all voices worthy of regard' in order to
establish the connection between the progress of civilisation on the one
hand and the 'juster, worthier treatment of women' and the 'high regard

for family' on the other. He went on to demonstrate that the realisation of this connection occurred in Christian culture and to 'investigate the nature of the two sexes and their relations', concluding that the position of women and family realised in Christian culture must be preserved,[40] 'even in the highest stages of rational civilisation':[41]

> It hardly now needs further proof, that in the face of such differences between the sexes in the nature and purpose of their relations, that to grant the woman equality with the man in domestic and public laws and duties and in the execution of these, would contradict human destiny and happiness and destroy family life; would deny women their lofty destiny in the domestic circle, degrade true femininity and endanger their greatest joy. It would also be detrimental to the formation of the following generation . . . Those theories that are indifferent to the rights of women, regarding them as tools to be used for men's purposes, must renounce the highest good of man and State — the domestic or family life and the moral upbringing of children. Those that, blindly following an abstract ideal of equality, disregard the laws of Nature and her limits, demanding more rights for women than they, in accordance with these laws and limits, can possibly desire, destroy the most sacred, secure foundation of human and civil virtue and happiness.

Welcker expressly includes the supporters of women's emancipation and Socialists and Communists in the latter.

The aspects of power became even more pronounced in the last third of the nineteenth century as woman's natural character was argued with greater vehemence in response to concrete demands for emancipation raised by the now organised women's movement. So, for example, the demand that women should be allowed to attend grammar schools and universities was countered on the lines that it would endanger motherhood or that it was nonsense in the light of the 'physiological feeble-mindedness of women'.[42] The equal value of men and women, emphasised at the end of the eighteenth century, was completely overshadowed in this type of argument. The high ideal of femininity was clearly damaged by the ferocity of these battles and the notion of 'motherliness' formulated by the Romantics often came to mean no more than sexuality defined by the tasks of child-rearing.[43] Examples in support of the idea that the 'character of the sexes' was developed and used as an ideology to support the ruling group can easily be multiplied. But it would be a mistake to limit the analysis to this one aspect and thus overlook the fact that the justification of power was only one element in a much more complex system of values, which contained hints at other, qualitatively different aspects of social and family relations. An historical interpretation can establish, over and above the fundamental fact of patriarchal authority, significant changes in the nature of this authority in society and family. In this respect the fact that the main criteria for ascribing positions to the sexes were no longer the ability to rule on the one hand and the predisposition to subordination on the other, in particular requires interpretation. The man was now clearly predestined for the outside world and the woman for domestic life; the man by his activity/rationality constellation of character traits, which expressly rejected qualities pertaining to familial authority; the woman by her character based on passivity/emotionality. Thus the polarisation of 'home' and 'world' was reflected in the contrasted 'character of the sexes'. At the same time the essence of male and female nature was so conceived that only together were they able to realise the sum of all human virtues and needs. Man and woman were destined by nature for union and accordingly it was impossible for a single person to develop into a balanced personality. This idea of complement, formulated by Romanticism and Classicism, generalised and transformed the purpose of marriage based on sexuality into a communion of souls. The idea of complement seems to be the root definition in the polarisation of the 'character of the sexes'. To quote Welcker once again:[44]

> For the nature and destiny of both sexes — the perfection of higher humanity — do not represent higher or lower levels of development, but different, complementary directions. They can only fully be realised in the presence of both, by the preservation of their differences and mutual ties.

From the idea of complement it follows that, independently of whether or not mental differences between the sexes were regarded as determined by natural or social causes,[45] overstepping the boundaries between the two to create 'mannish' or 'womanish' characters was regarded as the degradation of humanity:[46] 'Humanity is complete in both sexes when both virtues, masculinity and femininity, are united, without either having to disregard or deny its own sex.'[47] Regulated by this notion of complement, the opposition of the sexes was not antagonistic in effect but, on the contrary, of advantage to both.

Opposites united to form a harmonious whole. The idea of complement reconciled not only the sexes, but also the social spheres of action, public and family life, which were regarded as appropriate to either man or woman. Thus on the basis of the definition of the 'character of the sexes' derived from the 'natural' world order, it was possible to declare that the dissociation of productive and family life was natural and at the same time to regard their opposition not simply as necessary, but as ideal, and to reconcile them. The reconciliation of the separate spheres of action was at first (*c.* 1800) only implicitly contained in the definition of the 'character of the sexes'. In the course of the following decades however it was increasingly clearly specified that the complement to the public productive and political life dominated by the man was that of marriage and family life based on the woman, and that this area was essential to the satisfaction of basic human needs: 'Without woman present day life would be unbearable for every sensitive soul', wrote Gervinus in 1853; for it was the woman

> who is the basis of the poetic side of society in modern times . . .
> because the woman of today, like the Greek citizen of ancient times,
> is removed from the common bustle of life, because she is not
> concerned with a sense of status, does not suffer the degradation of
> lowly occupations, the turmoil and heartlessness of work, and
> because the woman is by nature more fitted than the man to unite
> with a highly developed social sense a feeling for naturalness and the
> original simplicity of humanity.[48]

The image of the man, returning exhausted from his labours, greeted by his wife in a home filled with love and peace, as depicted by L. von Stein *inter alia*, demonstrated forcefully how closely interconnected the ideology of home was with the division of life into hostile world and friendly home. Despite this increasingly negative evaluation of the external world it was still firmly maintained that the character of the man was defined by his destiny in precisely this hostile outer world.[49]

At any rate the harmony so emphatically insisted on at the beginning of the nineteenth century became increasingly precarious in the second half. The ideal of the motherly, loving woman in the peace of the home, protected from society at large, became less persuasive. At the same time, the refuge cultivated by the woman appeared more desirable than ever before in the light of the growing criticism of the world of men. One of the first examples of an awareness of this problem was provided by Ferdinand Tönnies in *Gemeinschaft und*

Gesellschaft ('community and society'), which first appeared in 1887.
Indicatively his remarks were also based on the contrasted 'character of
the sexes': he saw in the organic group relations of his category
Gemeinschaft a feminine approach which contrasted with the abstract
and mechanical group relations of *Gesellschaft*, a male-dominated
system. For Tönnies, woman, with her direct relationships to things and
people, embodied the natural spirit, while man was calculating, artificial,
even capable in his manifestation as merchant of using his fellow beings
as means and tools for gain. Tönnies diagnosed an accelerated decline in
Gemeinschaft as *Gesellschaft* became ever more powerful, and saw in
this a long-term threat to the family and female virtues. A factory girl,
for example, who was directly exposed to the influences of *Gesellschaft*,
'becomes enlightened, cold, knowing. Nothing is more alien to her
original character, nothing more harmful'.[50] Clearly the kind of model
of society based on the polarity of the sexes, as formulated by Tönnies,
was widespread. Informative and at the same time an indication of the
possible social relevance of such preconceptions was the fact that the
bourgeois women's movement at the end of the nineteenth century
shared them. These women based their demands for educational and
legal equality from the end of the 1860s on the assertion that it was
'the cultural task of women' to bring humanity, through their
femininity, 'into the inhuman world of men'. In their eyes the woman,
up till now only active in the domestic sphere of family life, had a
mission to fulfil in the hostile outside world.[51]

Today this belief in the harmonisation of human affairs, the
complementary nature of society and home, man and woman, has
disappeared just as surely as the belief that it is possible decisively to
improve social affairs through femininity *per se*. What has remained is
the preconception that only the family can provide the individual with
a refuge from the effects of a society regarded as hostile. In this
assumption such politically diverse scholars as Horkheimer and Parsons
are agreed. In the middle of the 1930s Horkheimer not only
characterised the family as the originator of socially desirable
authoritarian character types. At the same time he emphasised that
family and society stood in an antagonistic relation to each other and
that in the family the economic and competitive relationships prevailing
in society made way for relationships in which the individual was in a
position to 'act humanly'. He thus saw in the family 'on the basis of the
human relationships determined by the woman, a reservoir of resistance
to the complete dehumanisation of the world'.[52] The same observation
led Parsons to emphasise, not the antagonism, but the complementary

functions of family and society. In the process of increasing social differentiation, the functions of the family became concentrated on the 'purely personal relations between the members', namely 'on the socialization of children and tension management of the adult members on a psychological or personal level'. Accordingly the differentiation of the specifically female role meant that the woman was 'defined as a specialist in "human relations" and in mastering subtle psychological problems'.[53] Thus in the mid-twentieth century what is referred to as a social function and the aim of education is the same as that which formerly was designated the character of the female sex. Even in formulations like this it is the family alone that is the location for the realisation of humanity, and within the family it is the woman who is supposed to cultivate the desired and necessary human environment for the man, returning home from the inhuman working world, and for the defenceless children. However, the resources of this humanity remain unquestioned.

It is only an interpretation like this, starting from the idea of complement, that makes clear why the value-system behind the polarised 'character of the sexes' gained rather than lost attraction during the course of a century characterised by considerable structural change. Marriage, family and the woman as the personification of special familial qualities were defined on the basis of a series of desirable characteristics at a time when these characteristics lost their value in the extra-familial social structures and were discarded as encumbrances by the man, who was under pressure to succeed in this restructured larger society. The exclusive assignation of the characteristics rationality-activity to the man and emotionality-passivity to the woman should therefore be understood as a reaction against and at the same time an adaption to the development of a society which increasingly denied the ideal stemming from the Enlightenment of the autonomous, harmonious, developed personality.[54]

IV

The previous section concluded on the connection between social preconceptions and social reality. This interpretation, in the manner of traditional intellectual history, will rightly be greeted with scepticism. On the one hand the value-system has been generalised to cover what possibly only had partial social validity, and on the other hand awareness or interpretation of reality has been taken as a direct expression of reality or the experience of it. In order to counter these objections, it is necessary to pose the question of the reality content and relevance of the normative and ideological statements about 'the character of the sexes' more explicitly. The clear distinction between the public, professional and private/family areas of life and the prevailing notion of the characteristics of man and woman indicate a starting-point. First, it can hardly be maintained that statements about man and woman in the eighteenth century referred to peasants, for their living and working conditions were quite adequately covered by traditional role assignments and continued to be so for a long time afterward. Interestingly, Riehl, in the second half of the nineteenth century, explicitly stated that he had found that in country people 'occupation is in many respects the same . . . the voice, facial features and behaviour of both sexes in this lower class are very similar, thus the characteristic difference clearly only unfolds in the atmosphere of more educated circles'.[55]

It is less easy to decide how far the definition of the 'character of the sexes' was relevant to the living conditions of wage-workers. It can probably be safely assumed that while domestic production prevailed, and later, in the transition to centralised industrial production, when the income of the man alone was not sufficient to support his family and thus neither domestic nor productive work could be carried out exclusively by one sex, that not only was the contrasting of the 'character of the sexes' irrelevant, but also that even the sexual division of labour diverged from the accepted norm.[56] For a sharper division of sex roles and thus receptivity to the idea of a different destiny for man and woman it seems likely that the necessary socio-economic preconditions were only created as the development of industrial capitalism made the distinction between industrial and domestic work more pronounced in terms of location and quality and the man could be regarded, at least ideally, as the family's sole bread-winner. The fact that the women and daughters of workers continued in paid employment, although their work became increasingly distinct from that of the men and that *de facto* women were never regarded as solely responsible for their families, could have proved a serious obstacle to the adoption of these values. At any rate during the nineteenth century there were several concerted attempts to persuade workers to cultivate the 'correct' sense of family and in particular to educate the women of the lower strata of society for their 'destiny as wife, housekeeper and mother' with the corresponding mental and practical skills. As the restabilisation of family life was regarded as the best solution to the 'social question' it seems permissable to assume that in attempts to 'educate' the workers, special efforts were made to popularise the doctrine of the 'character of the sexes' which formed a central concept in the preconceptions about family life.[57]

Quite clearly the polarisation of the sexes only coincided with real social phenomena in the educated bourgeoisie[58] – the group responsible for the appearance of this code of values at the turn of the nineteenth century. If it is assumed that the main occupations of the educated bourgeoisie were to be found in the administrative, educational and clerical services, this provides a series of arguments in support of our general hypothesis. In the first place the qualities assigned to women refer to a great extent to the care of children. Motherliness in this sense can only develop where the offspring have already been accorded the special status of childhood. In the educated bourgeoisie child-rearing is assigned great importance in accordance with the child's future career prospects, which are laid down by the father.[59] Another indication in support of this idea is the fact that in the value-system behind the 'character of the sexes', public life and family, productive and domestic work are contrasted. Almost certainly, the separation of these areas of life happened first and foremost in the group of civil servants (*Beamtentum*). True, this group not only included representatives of the bourgeoisie but also, in the higher positions in particular, members of the aristocracy. A detailed analysis would have to go into both the differences and similarities in the living and working conditions of noble and bourgeois civil servants and likewise the particularities pertaining to the different ranks within the bureaucratic hierarchy.[60]

But for the present, the gradual separation of private and working life is of greater interest.[61] This separation was considerably accelerated at the beginning of the nineteenth century by the general triumph of bureaucratic principles in the reorganisation of government and the emergence of a class of career civil servants. Apart from the phenomenon of bureaucratic centralisation, it is also important to note the development of set educational entry requirements, the payment of regular salaries, paid increasingly solely in money, and the growing demand for pensions.[62] For the civil service household this development of the bureaucratic system meant that, amongst other things, in contrast to peasant and artisan households, production and consumption were divorced and there was no longer any provision for the joint enterprise of the marriage partners, as the husband was now paid a set salary. Certainly throughout the whole of the nineteenth century the wife's property and/or thrift was of great importance in maintaining the family in a manner 'fitting to their station in life'. However with his secure, and in the course of his career increasing, salary the man was identified as the family bread-winner; service to the State as a source of income was reserved exclusively for men.[63] A further observation is interesting in this context. In the developing contrast between working and family life things to do with child-rearing and working life were transformed into qualities of character, but the management of the home, which became increasingly the woman's exclusive responsibility, was ignored. A possible explanation for this could be that work concerned with running the home no longer appeared relevant when it lost its direct connection to income. It could be argued, following on from this, that productive work, with the activity it demanded, was being contrasted with an area of life which appeared to be free from these demands and thus developed passively. This interpretation takes greater account of the refuge function of the family, emphasised in the nineteenth century, and can also be linked to explicit preconceptions found in German Classicism.

The contrasting of rationality and emotionality in the 'character of the sexes' provides the final and at the same time most decisive indication that the educated bourgeoisie is the social class with whom we are concerned. Rationality as a specifically human achievement must be highly regarded and explicitly cultivated before it makes sense to contrast it with and separate it from emotionality as mode of behaviour. The people who, up to the nineteenth century, had been in a position to enjoy and had learned to value the luxury and toil of an external formal education were, apart from a few exceptions, men from the aristocracy and the bourgeoisie. Grammar schools, colleges and universities remained closed to women.[64] Girls continued to be educated even in the eighteenth century at home, in better-off families by tutors and governesses, but mainly through the successive adoption of domestic duties, following the example set by the mother. The aim and result of such an education could not be 'rationality' if by this is meant the facility for abstract formulation of thought, fostered by schooling with the aim of creating calculated, self-controlled behaviour. Education, which in general since the sixteenth century had been aimed at men, and in the bourgeoisie in particular was a necessary precondition for their future employment, almost certainly brought about considerable real though socially engendered character differences between the men and women of the eighteenth-century bourgeoisie with respect to rationality.[65] The women, socialised in the traditional manner at home, had evidently preserved modes of behaviour which diverged from those of the formally educated men as irrational, emotional, spontaneous, uncontrolled, etc. . . . . When rationalism began to prevail as a general principle, these modes of behaviour were no longer regarded as a matter of course, but came to be seen as a noteworthy phenomenon. Indicatively, from the late eighteenth century it was general to take the behaviour of men as the standard for adult behaviour and, thus measured, the behaviour of women was equated with that of children or savages.[66]

It was not only on the basis of education, however, but also because of their actual fields of activity that the modes of behaviour of bourgeois man and woman in the eighteenth century clearly developed in opposite directions. Characteristic of reproduction and consumption, centred on the family, was the continued variety of the work and its concentration on the satisfaction of the needs of all the household members. In contrast, in the increasingly specialised fields of productive, distributive and administrative activity, an increasingly disciplined, rational and impersonal behaviour was demanded of the man. The difference in the fields of activity for man and woman must have been particularly clearly visible in families where the man was employed by the State. This was above all the case in the administration, where the rationality of the bureaucratic principle became more pronounced from the end of the eighteenth century, and where the fulfilment of duties in the service of a larger and therefore more abstract whole became the drive for achievement. Whether a similar contrast in areas of work can also be found in the financial and commercial *grande bourgeoisie* in this period remains to be seen. It is possible that since the late Middle Ages, with the separation of business and family accounts, the wives of the financial and commercial bourgeoisie had lost their business capacity and their share of responsibility.[67] But in principle they did retain the option of working together in contrast to the civil servants and this remained an economic necessity for small-scale businesses well into the twentieth century. When and how the 'luxury' of restricting the woman's contribution to domestic work, or, as in the aristocracy, absolving her of all responsibility and obliging her to lead a life of leisure and luxury, prevailed in the *grande bourgeoisie*, has until now attracted as little research as the question of the penetration of this prestige behaviour into the middle bourgeoisie.[68]

If, however, during the course of the nineteenth century, the polarisation of the 'character of the sexes' became increasingly widespread in the bourgeoisie, then the cause of this should not be sought solely in the ever-increasing differences between domestic and non-domestic work. At least equally important, if not more so, is the fact that at the same time educational policies had the effect of widening the gap between the sexes.[69] All the things which evidently originally came into existence unconsciously in the different modes of behaviour of man and woman, were from the late eighteenth century even more consciously proclaimed as the aim of education. The definition of the 'character of the sexes' was also a programme for education. When it was decided that girls too should have a planned education, the judgement on the 'nature' of woman had already been fixed. Education was intended solely to foster this nature and thus fit the woman for her destiny. These premises had wide-ranging consequences for the development of a school system for girls, in so far as we are concerned with the formal education of the daughters of the higher classes and not with the State-run lower school system, which was coeducational through necessity. The education of young ladies was intended on the one hand to equip the young woman with the requisite accomplishments and social graces, and on the other, partly in opposition to the former, to develop in her the qualities necessary to fit her for her 'natural profession'; 'domesticity' and 'motherliness'. This education, intended solely to fit the recipient for marriage and family life, was regarded as a purely family concern not worthy of public support. Accordingly, the State institutionalisation of higher education for women was delayed until the late nineteenth century. The schools available for the daughters of the bourgeoisie either arose through private initiative as commercial enterprises or were charitable institutions founded by interested citizens and occasionally communities. In educational debate even these institutions were at times regarded with suspicion, as the family, with the mother as example, was often seen as the only suitable place for female education.[70]

As regards the educational content of what was to be taught to girls, it is clear that any subject which could possibly inhibit emotionality was to be kept from them. Mathematics in particular fell into this category, as it fostered the calculating, rather than the feeling side of the personality.[71] In addition, every incitement to ambition was to be avoided,which was probably a fairly effective way of preserving 'feminine passivity'.[72] The actual success of this planned education of the female character cannot be ascertained — such research as was carried out by contemporaries is not of a standard to allow this. However, in the nineteenth century, parallel to the education of 'young ladies', State-sponsored education for the sons of the bourgeoisie was intensified and rapidly specialised in accordance with the demands of the working world. So it seems reasonable to suppose that in the course of the nineteenth century, character differences between the sexes, at least in terms of demands on behaviour, increased rather than decreased. The disposition of women for the functions of spouse, housekeeper and mother, thus for their role in the 'perfecting of private life',[73] was elevated to part of a conscious educational programme, while in the education of men the later extra-mural occupational function increasingly took over more completely from the function of spouse, household head and father. During the nineteenth century increasingly fewer men were employed as domestic personnel,[74] and in the same period, when bourgeois women were, in exceptional cases, driven by economic necessity to seek paid employment outside the home, they were only able to find it in the areas of education and welfare, because these alone were regarded as suitable for women. These two developments acted as a further impulse to, and at the same time were also a result of, this increasing contrast in the 'character' of man and woman.

This classification of occupations into those of a 'masculine' and those of a 'feminine' type began to cause problems only at the end of the nineteenth century, when new white-collar jobs, crossing the boundaries between occupations regarded as feminine on the one hand and industrial work regarded as 'unfeminine' on the other, clearly proved attractive to single bourgeois women.[75] In accordance with what has already been said, the value-system which was implied in 'the character of the sexes' had a considerable and probably increasing relevance for certain groups of the bourgeoisie, groups which during the course of the nineteenth century probably increased in numbers. How and with what success these social groups, whose influence on the dissemination and generalisation of social norms is generally considered to have been very high, succeeded in bringing about a popularisation of this code of values, is an important social-historical question that needs a good deal of further research before it can be answered.

V

Up to this point in the discussion, the term 'character of the sexes' has been described formally as a 'value-system'. This has made it possible to demonstrate the relationship referred to in the introduction between statements about the 'character of the sexes', the definition of sex roles and ideological interpretations of reality. It has also, however, enabled us to avoid in the first instance a wider ranging interpretation. In this last section we shall attempt to broaden out the analysis and to discuss the *general* social significance of the argument which so emphatically insisted on the different 'nature' and 'destiny' of the sexes in order to separate out an area of 'inner' life presided over by the woman and family free from the taint of the principles of an efficiency-oriented rationalism which governed the external world represented by the man. It is first necessary to state that the 'character of the sexes' is intended to describe *both* differences arising from the sexual division of labour, on which the bourgeois family is in principle founded, *and* the dissociation and contrasting of work and family life, the public and private domains in general. This leads us to regard the bourgeois family as a kind of model. Its cultivation of intimacy is the criterion usually used to distinguish bourgeois from socially open peasant and noble families. The bourgeois family, emerging in the form of a patriarchal nuclear family, is interpreted as 'an area of mental liberation'[76] or as a reaction to the loss of '*densité sociale*'.[77]

Starting from the 'character of the sexes', the next step is to demonstrate the differing quality of work within and outside the home. From the eighteenth century, social production became increasingly distinct from work carried out within the family circle, as the satisfaction of the needs of specific people no longer determined the type, extent, purpose and value of the work done. While objectively structured social production was increasingly rationalised, and regulated according to criteria of economy and efficiency, work aimed directly at the fulfilment of the needs of family members was not 'modernised' in the way that work highly valued by society was. Housework, increasingly carried out solely by women, remained traditional. In comparison to work measured in terms of time and salary, it came to appear uneconomic. Thus it became an occupation which increasingly lost its character as work. The objective and subjective reasons why the difficult and demanding job of social consumption and reproduction, which is responsible for the next generation of social producers, retained the older approach to work cannot be fully investigated here. It is, however, important that, at least for the bourgeoisie, this traditional approach to work was maintained despite the increasing rationalisation of social production, by the housekeeper and mother acting within the private family unit and thus outside the sphere of influence of the prevailing rationalism. This form of the division of socially necessary labour was ideologically interpreted as a natural relationship. Responsibility for the one or the other area was prescribed for a person from birth on the basis of sex by the 'laws of nature' argument. This meant that the relationship of the sexes was immunised against the competitiveness of society in general. On the other hand, and probably more important, this division of responsibilities in principle removed from the individual the onus of choice, and so ensured the 'natural' smooth running of the system. This type of the sexual division of labour was lastingly guaranteed by socialisation within the family and was more or less brought to the pitch of perfection.

The significance of the actual and at the same time ideological polarisation of the sexes for the inner structure of the family cannot be overestimated. As far as the relationship between the marriage partners was concerned, the fact that they were not regarded as united through a common enterprise but through love, and that the idea of complement had less to do with the complementary nature of their work than with modes of communication and behaviour, is decisive. However, the demands of the dualism of society and family reflected in the 'character of the sexes' were hard to reconcile with the notion of an organic development of an ideal marital and family life, and made the latter hard to realise. In particular the position of the man returning from the world to the refuge of the family, but ill-equipped with his masculine character traits for family life, gave rise to both ideological and practical problems.

The polarisation of the 'character of the sexes' has had a lasting effect on the relationship of parents to children, and therefore also on primary socialisation even into our own time. The socialisation of small children became increasingly the exclusive responsibility of the mother. Only the mother, whose nature is defined as feeling, is supposed to be in the position – and *de facto* there is generally no alternative for her – to foster through her maternal love the necessary emotional ties and provide the child with the emotional security it needs. The exclusive responsibility of the mother for the child's welfare however ends as soon as training in the desire to succeed and deal with reality make their appearance on the educational agenda. Now the man, defined by nature as rationality, assumes an active paternal function. Instead of the principle of gratification connected with the mother the child is now taught by the father on the basis of the principles of realism. In this of course the father will, in accordance with the future functions and duties of the child, pay more attention to a son than to a daughter. The socially determined sexual division of labour between family and society finds its equivalent within the familial upbringing which efficiently ensures its continuity through the generations. Psychiatry, with Freudian theory as a prototype of the contemporary polarisation of the sexes, indicates where an historically relevant interpretation might lie.[78] The child is subject first to the mother's influence, followed by the father's: this is seen as a contrast and Parsons,[79] writing in the second half of the twentieth century with a new vocabulary, refers to it as the 'tearing apart of the expressive and instrumental' functions in the socialisation process, a necessary and in his eyes positive function of modern society. This has clearly had the effect of nurturing the ambition of men – deemed socially desirable – who have been brought up in this manner. Taking present-day empirical work as a basis, this is probably not least because emotionality, mediated originally by the mother, has been successfully repressed, following the father's example, in favour of socially accepted values.[80]

In general, the present essay has dealt exclusively with Germany. But the functional aspects of the phenomena which we have been discussing are surely typical of bourgeois society as a whole. If this is true, then value systems comparable to the German 'character of the sexes' (*Geschlechtscharaktere*) should be evident in the bourgeois societies of other nations. Viola Klein[81] has indicated the similarity and generality of the characterisation of man and woman at the end of the nineteenth century in other countries. In connection with the interpretation put forward here it would be interesting to work out the probable temporal and cultural differences in the emergent phase of the ideology of the sexes in different societies.[82] The fact that in Germany statements on the ideal of womanhood frequently contain comparative references to the position of women in France and England further recommends this course. In these comparative references the German woman, due to the high moral value placed on family life, always comes off best, while the sophisticated Frenchwoman is always referred to disparagingly well into the nineteenth century. To support the (by no means original) hypothesis that reality and ideology in the sense of this study of the bourgeois family comprise a central element of bourgeois society, the points raised in this analysis, which have in some cases only been partially or hypothetically worked out, not only need to be investigated in more detail but also on a comparative basis, alongside the study of similar developments in other nations.

Notes

This essay was first published in W. Conze (ed.), *Sozialgeschichte der Familie in der Neuzeit Europas* (Stuttgart, 1976) and is reprinted here by kind permission of the publishers (Klett-Cotta Verlag). It has been translated for this volume by Cathleen Catt.

1.   On the concept of role see the article 'Role' by Th.R. Sarbin and R.H. Tuner in *International Encyclopaedia of the Social Sciences* (New York, 1968), Vol. 13, pp. 546-7; A.M. Rocheblave-Spenlé, *La notion de la rôle en psychologie sociale. Etude historico-critique* (2nd edn., Paris, 1969); idem, *Les rôles masculins et féminins* (Paris, 1964); K.H. Bömmer (ed.), *Die Geschlechterrollen* (Munich, 1973).

2.   F. Haug, *Kritik der Rollentheorie* (Frankfurt am Main, 1972) advances a critique of various sociological role theories developed in West Germany since the fifties – she ascribes the deep involvement of sociology in role theories as an attempt to reduce the analysis of society to the analysis of interaction. This strong criticism of role theory, more evident in the formulation than in the argumentation, certainly draws attention to important deficits in individual theories and in the approach in general. But it does not succeed in convincing one that every approach based on role theory must be avoided.

3.   In comparison to the quantitative results of a family research based on the methods of historical demography the present work – as yet unquantified and possibly not amenable to quantification – runs the risk of being branded unscientific. In my opinion this methodological failing is at any rate less theoretically problematic than restricting research to such topics as can be easily quantified.

4.   See Laslett's critical remarks on 'The History of Family Attitudes' in P. Laslett, R. Wall (eds.), *Household and Family in Past Time* (Cambridge, 1972), pp. 10-13.

5.   *Meyer's grosses Konversationslexicon* (6th edn., Leipzig, Vienna, 1904), Vol. 7, p. 685.

6.   *Conversations-Lexicon oder Handwörterbuch für die gebildeten Stände* (3rd edn., Leipzig/Altenburg, 1815), Vol. 4, p. 211.

7.   J. Meyer, *Das grosse Conversations-Lexicon*, Part 1, Vol. 12 (Hildburghausen, 1848), p. 742.

8.   Ibid., pp. 748f.

9.   Apart from various encyclopaedias, medical, pedagogical, psychological and literary works were also investigated.

10.   Marianne Weber, *Ehefrau und Mutter in der Rechtsentwicklung* (Tübingen, 1907, reprinted Aalen 1971), pp. 300f. This was systematically carried to its logical conclusion by O. Weiniger, *Geschlecht und Charakter* (Vienna, 1903) (25th edn., 1925).

11.   E.g. the often quoted tracts of the doctor K.F.v. Burdach, *Der Mensch nach den verschiedenen Seiten seiner Natur. Anthropologie für das gebildete Publicum* (Stuttgart, 1837), pp. 470-7; also V. Klein, *The Feminine Character. History of an Ideology* (2nd edn., London, 1971); L.E. Tyler's article 'Sex Differences', *International Encyclopaedia of the Social Sciences* (New York, 1968), pp. 207-13.

12.   See R. Hofstätter, 'Männlich und weiblich', in *Wiener Archiv für Psychologie, Psychiatrie und Neurologie*, Vol. 6 (1956), pp. 154-67, who comes to grips empirically with this kind of stereotyped preconception. Even at the end of the fifties, of 138 German professors and lecturers questioned 40 per cent were decidedly negative towards and 39 per cent essentially opposed to the idea of

women college teachers: the most common reason was 'lack of intellectual or creative/productive capacity' and the idea that 'teaching in the higher education system contradicts women's biological purpose of their natural inclination'. See H. Anger, *Probleme der deutschen Universität* (Tübingen, 1960), pp. 23, 491.

13.   See S. de Beauvoir, *Das andere Geschlecht. Sitte und Sexus der Frau* (Reinbeck, 1968).

14.   See J. Hoffmann, *Die 'Hausväterliteratur' und die 'Predigten über den christlichen Hausstand'* (Weinheim/Berlin, 1959).

15.   Chr.Frh.v. Wolff, *Vernünftige Gedancken von dem gesellschaftlichen Leben der Menschen und insonderheit der gemeinen Wesen* (. . .) (2nd edn., Frankfurt/Leipzig, 1725), part 1, ch. 5 'Von dem Hause'.

16.   J.H. Zedler, *Grosses vollständiges Universal-Lexicon*, Vol. 9 (Halle/ Leipzig, 1735), cols. 1767, 1782.

17.   J.G. Krünitz, *Ökonomisch-technologische Encyclopädie oder allgemeines System der Staats, Haus-, und Landwirtschaft und der Kunst-Geschichte*, Vol. 14 (Berlin, 1779), pp. 789-95.

18.   J.C. Adelung, *Versuch eines vollständigen grammatischen-kritischen Wörterbuchs der hoch-deutschen Mundart*, Vol. 2, (2nd edn., Leipzig, 1796), col. 10; see also the article 'Weib', Vol. 4, 1801.

19.   See D. Schwab's article 'Familie' in O. Brunner *et al.* (eds.), *Geschichtl. Grundbegriffe. Historisches Lexikon zur politisch-sozialen Sprache in Deutschland*, Vol. 2 (Stuttgart, 1975), pp. 253-301. See also the essay by Gerhard Wilke and Kurt Wagner in the present volume (pp. 120-47).

20.   Schwab, 'Familie', p. 273.

21.   Ibid., p. 271.

22.   This equation taken as a matter of course can be found in e.g. A.L. Schlözer, *Allgemeine Staatsrecht und Statsverfassungslehre* (Göttingen, 1793), p. 31. 'The human existed before the subject . . . and before he entered a state-controlled society he had tasted as husband, father, master of the home and citizen the joys and sorrows of communal life.'

23.   Schwab, 'Familie', p. 280.

24.   Ibid., p. 284.

25.   P. Kluckhohn, *Der Auffassung der Liebe in der Literatur des 18. Jahrhunderts und in der deutschen Romantik* (2nd edn., Halle, 1931).

26.   In 1791-2 A. Condorcet, *Sur l'instruction publique*, demanded equal education for both sexes. In 1792 Th.G.v. Hippel, *Über die bürgerliche Verbesserung der Weiber*, and M. Wollstonecraft, *A Vindication of the Rights of Women* (German edn., 1793/4) were published. See K.M. Grass, R. Koselleck, 'Emanzipation' in *Geschichtliche Grundbegriffe*, Vol. 2, pp. 153-97, and the section 'Frauenemanzipation', pp. 185-91.

27.   In the terminology of D. Riesman *et al.*, *Die einsame Masse* (Reinbek, 1958), it was a case of strengthening the inner motivation over the traditional for the social character of the woman. cf. Riesman, p. 56.

28.   J.G. Fichte, *Grundlagen des Naturrechts nach den Prinzipien der Wissenschaftslehre*, Appendix 1: Familienrecht (1796), in: *Werke, Auswahl in 6 Bänden*, ed. F. Medicus, Vol. 2 (Leipzig, 1908), p. 319. Also Marianne Weber, *Ehefrau und Mutter*, pp. 306-12.

29.   On the preconceptions behind this formula used in 1789 by J.H. Campe see E. Blochmann, *Das 'Frauenzimmer' und die 'Gelehrsamkeit'. Eine Studie über die Anfänge des Mädchenschulwesens in Deutschland* (Heidelberg, 1966), pp. 29-41. These preconceptions are directly related to the principles for the education of Sophie developed by J.J. Rousseau, 1762, in the fifth book of *Emile*.

30.   Ibid., pp. 44 and 42-8.

31.   On this M. Dessoir, *Geschichte der neueren deutschen Psychologie*

(2nd edn., Berlin, 1902), in particular pp. 116-356. The nature of the accelerated development of psychological science in the late eighteenth century strengthens the assumption that Pietism was of great significance in the creation and dissemination of the new code of values. Unfortunately, as far as I know, there has been no research into this problem comparable to that on Puritanism.

32. Kant's *Gejammelte Schriften*, ed. Königlich Preussische Akademie der Wissenschaften, Vol. 7 (Berlin, 1907), p. 117.

33. W.v. Humboldt, *Werke*, ed. A. Leitzmann, Vol. 1 (Berlin, 1903), p. 378. Humboldt's essays 'Über den Geschlechtsunterschied und dessen Einfluss auf die organischen Natur' and 'Über die männliche und weibliche Form' appeared in Schiller's *Horen* at the same time.

34. The first approach of this kind is clearly Ch. Meiners, *Geschichte des weiblichen Geschlechts*, 4 vols. (Hannover, 1788-1800).

35. A particularly detailed example of this line of argument can be found in: J.S. Ersch and J.G. Gruber, *Allgemeine Encyclopaedie der Wissenschaften und Künste*, sect. 1, part 63 (Leipzig, 1856), pp. 30-44; also K. Biedermann, *Frauen-Brevier, Kulturgeschichtliche Vorlesungen* (Leipzig, 1856), or as a variant the foundation of a 'healthy social policy based on history' by K. Bücher, *Die Frauenfrage im Mittelalter* (Tübingen, 1882), pp. 55-7, according to whom one of the most powerful forces of history consisted in 'relieving the woman more and more of the toil of working life'.

36. E.g. Ersch and Gruber, *Allgemeine Encyclopaedie*, p. 40.

37. This interpretation brought forward recently by the women's movement was developed by S. de Beauvoir (see above, note 13); S. Firestone, *The Dialectic of Sex* (New York, 1970); K. Millett, *Sexual Politics* (New York, 1970), amongst others.

38. C. Welcker's article 'Geschlechtsverhältnisse' in K. Rotteck, C. Welcker (eds.), *Staatslexicon oder Encyclopädie der Staatswissenschaft*, Vol. 6 (Altona, 1938).

39. The following quotes from ibid., pp. 630-2.

40. Ibid., p. 644.

41. Ibid., p. 635.

42. E.g. P. Mobius, *Über den physiologischen Schwachsinn des Weibes* (Halle, 1900). The discussion of the 'true' vocation of women became more heated from the sixties, as the debate over the German edition of J.S. Mill's *On the Subjection of Women*, which appeared in 1869, clearly demonstrated. Cf. M. Twellmann, *Die deutsche Frauenbewegung. Ihre Anfänge und erste Entwicklung 1843-1849*, Vol. 1 (Meisenheim, 1972), pp. 55-62. The connection between the bourgeois women's movement's struggle for the right to attend Grammar schools and universities, which from c. 1890 increased in intensity, and the stepping up of anti-feminist polemic is documented in the bibliography H. Sveistrup, A.v. Zahn-Harnack, *Die Frauenfrage in Deutschland* (Burg b.M., 1934), pp. 202-18, 470-9.

43. Doctors were particularly quick to defend their domain. E.g. A. Ander (Dr.med.), *Mutterschaft oder Emanzipation. Eine Studie über die Stellung des Weibes in der Natur und im Menschenleben* (Berlin, 1913), in particular p. 28. In 1899 the *Bundesrat* decided to allow women to sit state medical and pharmaceutical examinations.

44. Welcker, 'Geschlechtsverhältnisse', p. 642.

45. Ersch and Gruber, *Allgemeine Encyclopaedie*, p. 39f.

46. Ibid., p. 40.

47. *Kleineres Brockhaus'sches Conversations-Lexicon f.d. Handgebrauch*, Vol. 2 (Leipzig, 1854), p. 557.

48. G.G. Gervinus, *Geschichte der deutschen Dichtkunst*, Vol. 1 (4th edn.,

Leipzig, 1853), p. 302, correctly quoted in Ersch and Gruber, *Allgemeine Encyclopaedie*, p. 36.

49.   Particularly explicit in L.v. Stein, *Die Frau, ihre Bildung und Lebensaufgabe* (1st edn., 1851, 3rd edn., Dresden, 1890), pp. 1-5, 33-5, 51-6; *Die Frau auf dem Gebiete der National-ökonomie* (6th edn., Stuttgart, 1886), p. 93f. Similarly, K. Biedermann (see note 35 above), p. 9: 'Only an intelligent woman can ensure that the man, when he returns from his difficult business tasks, exhausted, seeking repose, to his hearth, finds the rest he needs, that he is surrounded by domestic comfort, attention to his usual needs and that a harmonious and agreeable environment soothes his worried brow, like oil poured on troubled waters; that he is not denied the healing stimulus of a conversation at once sensible and trusting necessary for his weary spirit; nor the balm of friendly agreement, springing from deep understanding and sure estimation of his worth, needful for his perhaps injured sensibility; nor the comforting support of a woman who sees life simply and often more clearly in his manifold business cares and worries.'

50.   F. Tönnies, *Gemeinschaft und Gesellschaft, Grundbegriffe der reinen Soziologie* (2nd edn., Berlin, 1912), p. 197.

51.   E.g. H. Lange, *Die Frauenbewegung in ihren modernen Problemen* (Berlin, 1907), p. 118, or the programme of the *Bund deutscher Frauenvereine* 1919, printed in *Jahrbuch des Bundes deutscher Frauenvereine*, 12 (1928-31), (Leipzig, 1932); Twellmann, *Die deutsche Frauenbewegung*, Vol. 1, pp. 55-67. As late as 1928 G. Bäumer in her election speeches was putting forward goals 'derived from the cultural ideal of women', and thus for the representation of 'objective values in social life . . . life against property, against the consumer culture i.e. inner being against civilisation', *Die Frau*, Vol. 35 (1928), p. 193. On the line of argument in the twentieth century see J. Zinnecker, *Sozialgeschichte der Mädchenbildung* (Weinheim, 1973), pp. 123-7.

52.   M. Horkheimer, in E. Fromm *et al.*, *Autorität und Familie*, Vol. 1 (Paris, 1936), pp. 63-7, where Hegel is interpreted in this connection.

53.   T. Parsons's 'Über den Zusammenhang von Charakter und Gesellschaft' (1961), in Parsons, *Sozialstruktur und Persönlichkeit* (Frankfurt, 1968), p. 269f.

54.   The equation of family and woman and the fear that a change in the social position of women means the loss of the chance to form human relationships has been clearly expressed since the turn of the century. In 1902 the Prussian *Kultusminister* Studt in relation to the proceedings to allow more women to sit for the *Abitur* and study higher education observed that 'The German family should as far as possible be maintained as the uniquely ideal setting for the German woman', quoted in Zinnecker, *Sozialgeschichte*, p. 88. The German woman in the German family was still even in the twenties, even if less optimistically than prior to 1914, seen as a contrast to 'working humanity', drawn into 'the heartlessness and brutality of economic competition'. E.g. B.G. Steinhausen, *Geschichte der deutschen Kultur*, Vol. 2 (2nd edn. Leipzig/ Vienna, 1913), p. 495, and *Deutsche Geistes- und Kulturgeschichte von 1870 bis zur Gegenwart* (Halle, 1931), pp. 471-3.

55.   K.A. Schmidt *et al.* (eds.), *Enzyclopädie des gesamten Erziehungs- und Unterrichtswesens bearb. v. einer Anzahl Schulmänner und Gelehrten*, Vol. 2 (2nd edn., Gotha, 1878), p. 1918.

56.   Hans Medick, 'The Proto-Industrial Family Economy: The Structural Function of Household Production in the Transition from Feudalism to Capitalism,' *Social History*, Vol. 1, No. 3 (1976), pp. 291-315.

57.   E.g. L.v. Stein, *Die Frau auf dem sozialen Gebiet* (Stuttgart, 1880), pp. 125-8, recommended educating the lower classes in this manner. See also the

introduction to *Das häusliche Glück. Vollständiges Haushaltungsunterricht nebst Anleitung zum Kochen für Arbeiterfrauen* (11th edn., M. Gladbach/Leipzig, 1882, reprinted Munich, 1975). An analysis, based on this approach, of the lower school system would be very informative about the popularisation of bourgeois norms. See also the essays by Richard J. Evans and Robyn Dasey in the present volume (pp. 256-88 and 221-55).

58.　This rather crude category is still waiting for socio-historical refinement. On the problem see H. Henning, *Das westdeutsche Bürgertum in der Epoche der Hochindustrialisierung, 1860-1914* (Wiesbaden, 1972), pp. 5-38; H. Möller, *Die kleinbürgerliche Familie im 18. Jh.* (Göttingen, 1969), pp. 2-8. Still good, H. Gerth, 'Die sozialgeschichtliche Lage der bürgerlichen Intelligenz um die Wende des 18. Jahrhunderts' (Diss. phil., Frankfurt, 1935).

59.　P. Ariès, *L'enfant et la vie familiale* (Paris, 1960), has indicated the connection between the development of childhood as a special category and interest in formal education in France. On the passing on from father to son of an academic career and the bourgeoisification of academics see H. Mitgau, *Gemeinsames Leben, 1500-1770* (Göttingen, 1955), pp. 66-75.

60.　On the Prussian case, still the best studied, see H. Rosenberg, *Bureaucracy, Aristocracy and Autocracy. The Prussian Experience, 1660-1815* (Boston, 1966); R. Koselleck, *Preussen zwischen Reform und Revolution* (Stuttgart, 1967), pp. 78-115. On socio-cultural aspects see N. Elias, *Über den Prozess der Civilisation* (Berne, Munich, 1969), Vol. 1, pp. 10-42.

61.　In the words of Maxim von Montgelas: 'the strict division of the official and the private', quoted in E. Weis, *Montgelas, 1759-1799. Zwischen Revolution und Reform* (Munich, 1971), p. 180.

62.　On the category of bureaucratic administration see M. Weber, *Wirtschaft und Gesellschaft* (Tübingen, 1922), pp. 124-7, 650-78; on the development from a *Standesbeamtentum* to a class of career civil servants see O. Hintze 'Der Beamtenstand' (1911), in his *Soziologie und Geschichte* (2nd edn., Göttingen, 1964), pp. 66-125; rich in material is S. Isaacsohn, *Geschichte des preussischen Beamtentums*, 3 Vols. (Berlin, 1874-84); for the nineteenth century in particular, see W. Bleek, *Von der Kameralausbildung zum Juristenprivileg. Studium, Prüfung und Ausbildung der höheren Beamten des allgemeinen Verwaltungsdiensten im 18. und 19. Jahrhundert* (Berlin, 1972).

63.　On the possible situation of the household M. Freudenthal, 'Gestaltwandel der städtischen bürgerlichen und proletarischen Hauswirtschaft unter besonderer Berücksichtigung des Typenwandels von Frau und Familie, 1760-1910' (Phil.diss. Frankfurt, Würzburg, 1934). The fact that state civil servants from the eighteenth century needed permission to marry, and later junior civil servants were forbidden to marry until properly instated, refers to the function of the man as bread-winner. Cf. D. Schwab, *Grundlagen und Gestalt der staatlichen Ehegesetzgebung in der Neuzeit* (Bielefeld, 1967), pp. 198, 235. The postponement of marriage until obtaining a post which allowed the 'decent maintenance' of a family is a well-known phenonemon. The following comments of a Göttingen professor on the precariousness of supporting a family for academics from a lower-class background is interesting in this respect: 'few professors own, marry or inherit money. Most therefore must pass their lives in uninterrupted labour, otherwise they would not be in a position to cover the increasing requirements of their family. An unavoidable result then of the education and position of most professors is a certain one-sidedness, as they are only able to exercize and strengthen one side of their personality; the mind at the expense of the body, the heart and the capacity for social life.' In C. Meiners, *Über die Verfassung und Verwaltung deutscher Universitäten* (Göttingen 1801/2, rep. Aalen, 1970), Vol. 2, p. 12.

64.　F. Paulsen, *Geschichte des Unterrichts auf den deutschen Schulen und Universitäten vom Ausgang des Mittelalters bis zur Gegenwart*, 2 vols. (2nd edn., Leipzig, 1896/97); F. Eulenburg, 'Hochschule und höhere Schule in der deutschen Sozialgeschichte der Neuzeit' in K. Repgen, S. Skalweit (eds.), *Spiegel der Geschichte. Festgabe f. M. Braubach* (Münster, 1964), pp. 321-39; W. Roessler, *Die Entstehung des modernen Erziehungswesens in Deutschland* (Stuttgart, 1961). The way in which planned education was meant exclusively for boys can be seen in J.A. Comenius, *Pampaedia* (1676/77), ed. by D. Tschizewsky *et al.* (Heidelberg, 1960). Comenius, it is true, did refer to males and females in his introduction, but then he went on to deal exclusively with the male child. Also interesting in this context is Ariès's remark that the status of childhood was in the first instance only accorded to boys (Ariès, *L'enfant et la vie familiale*, pp. 46, 54).

65.　Marianne Weber, *Ehefrau und Mutter*, pp. 281f., and J.v. Ussel, *Sexualunterdrückung. Geschichte der Sexualfeindschaft* (Reinbek, 1970), p. 50 confirm that the difference between man and woman developed in those groups, where from the Renaissance rational behaviour became increasingly relevant. Also S. Firestone, *Dialectic of Sex*, pp. 200f., who bases her ideas on the notion of a complete division of the cultural sphere into an aesthetic (feminine) and technological (masculine), a process which started in the sixteenth century and is now becoming apparent.

66.　G.W.F. Hegel, *Grundlinien der Philosophie des Rechts*, para. 165, and A. Schopenhauer, *Über die Weiber*, ch. 27, paras. 364, 366; A. Comte, *Cours de Philosophie Positive*, Vol. 4 (5th edn., Paris, 1893), mentioned the 'child-nature' of the woman. Comte, p. 456 (in 1839) held 'une sorte d'état d'enfance' to be the decisive characteristic of women, because they were not in a position, like men, to develop their 'facultés intellectuelles' at the expense of their 'facultés affectives'. Likewise the radical J. Fröbel, *System der sozialen Politik* (2nd edn., Mannheim, 1847), p. 226, although his conclusion was emancipatory, remarked: 'To the man, who was the first to tread the way of reflection and put thought into practice, the woman, stubbornly maintaining the view-point of naturalness must appear simply as a means, one of the chattels of life, as property . . .'. S. Firestone, *Dialectic of Sex*, p. 99, hints at interesting parallels between the myths of childhood and femininity.

67.　Indications to this effect: E. Mannheim, 'Beiträge zu einer Geschichte der autoritären Familie', in E. Fromm *et al., Autorität und Familie*, Vol. 2, pp. 566f.

68.　Freudenthal, 'Gestaltwandel der städtischen bürgerlichen', p. 41, calculates that this could only have occurred after 1860 in rich or small bourgeois households. The memoir literature of the nineteenth-century feminist movement is very informative on the situation of women from the *grande bourgeoisie* in the second half of the nineteenth century. The best-selling novel by J. Stinde, *Die Familie Buchholz*, probably gave an apt characterisation of middle-class conspicuous consumption aimed at increasing marriage prospects. A more thorough analysis can be found in T. Veblen, *The Theory of the Leisure Class* (New York, 1899).

69.　Relevant for the following: Blochmann, *Das 'Frauenzimmer' und die 'Gelehrsamkeit'* and Zinnecker, *Sozialgeschichte*. Until about 1740 the moral weeklies regarded an aquaintance not only with the humanities but also the practical sciences as desirable even for women and thought that learning from experience should be supplemented by knowledge. Cf. W. Mertens, *Die Botschaft der Tugend. Die Aufklärung im Spiegel der deutschen Moralischen Wochenschriften* (Stuttgart, 1968), pp. 520-42.

70.　See for example the chapter on 'Die Erziehung der Mädchen', in

K.v. Raumer, *Geschichte der Pädagogik vom Wiederaufblühen klassischer Studien bis auf unsere Zeit*, Vol. 3 (3rd edn., Stuttgart, 1857), pp. 450, 537.

71.   The *Encyclopädie für das gesamte Erziehungs- und Unterrichtswesen* (see note 55 above) (1881, Vol. 4, p. 816), gives the following timetable for a higher girls school:

	Lessons	
	Middle School	*Sixth form*
Religion	2	2
German	6	4
Arithmetic	2	2
French	4	3
English	–	3
Geog., Hist., Biology	2 each	2 each
Needlework	4	2
Drawing, singing	2 each	2 each
	28	26

E. Schildkamp-Kündiger, 'Geschlechtervorstellungen und Mathematikleistung bei Mädchen' (Diss. phil., Saarbrücken, 1973), shows that it is still widely assumed that women and mathematics are incompatible.

72.   For 'young ladies' schooling ended after 8-10 years, at an age of 14-16; classes were not systematically graded according to age and until the end of the nineteenth century girls were excluded from the grading system used in boys' schools.

73.   Cf R.v. Mohl, *Die deutsche Polizei Wissenschaft nach den Grundsätzen des Rechtsstaats*, Vol. 1 (2nd edn., Tübingen, 1844), p. 484.

74.   Cf. R. Engelsing, 'Das häusliche Personal in der Epoche der Industrialisierung', in his: *Zur Sozialgeschichte deutscher Mittel- und Unterschichten* (Göttingen, 1973), p. 235.

75.   The difficulty of placing female white-collar workers in the schema of femininity is clearly evident in the studies on women's careers published by the women's movement; e.g. J. Levy-Rathenau, *Die deutsche Frau im Beruf* (5th edn., Berlin, 1917); *Handbuch der Frauenbewegung*, ed. H. Lange, C. Bäumer, part 5.

76.   J. Habermas, *Strukturwandel der Öffentlichkeit* (Neuwied, 1962), p. 60. On the separation of the private sphere pp. 58-65 and 169-77.

77.   Cf. Ariès, *L'enfant et la vie familiale*, p. 460.

78.   The modern study of socialisation, decisively influenced by psychiatry, should be a fruitful source for the socio-historical analysis of these connections, as should Freud's interpretation and theoretical generalisation of clinical data; very different attempts in this direction are: E. Fromm and M. Horkheimer, in: E. Fromm, *Autorität und Familie*, Vol. 1; F. Weinstein, G.M. Platt, *The Wish to be Free. Society, Psyche and Value Change* (Berkeley, 1969), in particular pp. 137-96; K. Millett, *Sexual Politics*, pp. 233-68, with her historical-social interpretation of Freud's sexual theories.

79.   T. Parsons, R.F. Bales, *Family, Socialization and Interaction Process* (London, 1956), in particular pp. 16f., 45-54, 81-3.

80.   Indications in this direction in F. Neidhardt, 'Schichtenspezifische Vater- und Mutterfunktionen im Sozialisationsprozess', in *Soziale Welt*, Vol. 16 (1965), pp. 338-48.

81.   Cf. note 11 above.

82.   Interesting in this connection is the investigation of the position in England by M. George: 'From "Goodwife" to "mistress". The Transformation of the Female in Bourgeois Culture', *Science and Society*, Vol. 37 (1973),

pp. 152-77. Also on American ideologies B. Welter, 'The Cult of True Womanhood, 1 820-1 860', *American Quarterly*, 78 (1966), pp. 151-74.

3 FAMILY AND 'MODERNISATION': THE PEASANT FAMILY AND SOCIAL CHANGE IN NINETEENTH-CENTURY BAVARIA

Robert Lee

I

The opening decades of the nineteenth century, according to many historians, constituted a critical transition period as far as the function and role of the Western European family was concerned. Edward Shorter, for example, in attempting to compress the transformation of the family and family relations within the framework of modernisation theory, has argued that the beginning of the nineteenth century witnessed the end of 'traditional society'.[1] This view has been accepted by other historians. This period coincided with the end of a formerly static village society and was characterised, even in rural Bavaria, by 'an immense dynamic of social, economic and cultural change'.[2] The first half of the nineteenth century was a time of 'partial' but nevertheless significant change in the daily life of rural society.[3] Indeed superficial evidence of radical social change prior to any industrial take-off in Germany is relatively easy to find. The dramatic rise in illegitimacy rates, particularly in many areas of South Germany, has been taken as signifying the onset of a sexual revolution which was ultimately to transform sexual attitudes and family roles in general.[4] The breakdown of traditional social standards and the trend to 'anomie'[5] was widespread and constituted a severe threat to the existing social order. In the torrent of sexual permissiveness in Central Europe after 1800, business and inheritance considerations which had previously been paramount in regulating family affairs, were 'soon dissolved'.[6] Even before the onset of industrialisation, secularisation and agrarian reform had fostered the 'breakdown of authority in traditional rural society'.[7] But if the extension of the capitalist mode of production to German agriculture had undermined traditional values in rural society, the process of social change was reinforced by the increasing manipulative power of the State over most aspects of peasant life. As a result of the interplay of these factors rural society was characterised by a 'changed self-awareness and heightened self-consciousness',[8] although the increasing apathy, fear and deviance evident in the early nineteenth century eventually culminated in a collective reorientation to the conditions of a modernising society.[9] The belief in the essential unity of the medieval world picture, which had still been evident in the late eighteenth century, was now finally shattered.[10]

Bavaria is a critical test case for this general hypothesis, and many protagonists of 'social modernisation' have explicitly utilised Bavarian data.[11] Not only did the country retain its agrarian base throughout the first half of the nineteenth century, but indigenous illegitimacy rates, as a rough index of the breakdown in the traditional value-system of rural society, were among the highest in Germany.[12] In fact, all the factors which are reputed to have contributed to the process of social change in the early nineteenth century were clearly at work in Bavaria.

First, the changes in the primary sector were significant. Peasant emancipation, the creation of a rural land market through the abolition of the traditional '*Hoffuss-*system', the redistribution of common land and legal changes affecting land ownership, amounted to an important transformation in the conditions of production in Bavarian agriculture. Output indices confirm the fact that agrarian reform contributed significantly to a marked increase in production.[13] The social ramifications of these institutional changes were supposedly immense, providing a dynamic impulse to the modernisation process.[14] The growth of agrarian individualism, signified by the termination of common pasturing and the division of common land, had an immediate impact on social relations. Conflicts between different social groups in rural society became more pronounced and the village community, it is argued, lost its traditional integrative function.[15]

Secondly, the pace of social change in rural areas was accelerated by the process of secularisation. Although the traditional role of the Roman Catholic Church had already been somewhat undermined by the Enlightenment before the end of the eighteenth century,[16] secularisation in 1803, the reduction in ecclesiastical personnel, the enforced sale of Church lands and the reorganisation of parish boundaries amounted to a complete cessation of the traditional influence on the Church on both the social and economic aspects of rural life. Traditional moral norms, which had always rested on a firm Christian basis, were finally displaced in the process of a 'secularisation of sexual life'.[17] Evidence for this radical change has been found not only in rising illegitimacy rates, but also in changes in clothing styles and popular dances. The functional norms of the eighteenth century, it is argued, were rapidly abandoned in favour of new and more modern ones.[18]

State integration and State control apparently replaced the vacuum created through secularisation. Although a trend towards 'reglementation' existed in the late eighteenth century,[19] secularisation and the dysfunctional impact of two decades of military conflict during the Napoleonic period necessitated an extension in State power, if the existing political order was to be securely legitimised. The means adopted to achieve this end were also to determine the value-system of Bavarian society throughout the nineteenth century. If the local community had been the key integrative force in 'traditional' society, this function was now taken over by the new State bureaucracy. Administrative weaknesses at the local level facilitated an extension in direct State involvement and enabled State officials to restructure rural society along lines laid down by the central authorities.[20] The Bavarian state increasingly determined the value-systems operative in contemporary peasant society in a variety of ways.

In terms of medical provision the late eighteenth century and particularly the early nineteenth century witnessed a dramatic expansion in direct State involvement. Fuelled by an ideological emphasis on the need to develop human potential and a general acceptance of cameralist ideas embodied in J.P. Frank's concept of medical police, there was an important extension in the State's role in the medical sphere. Even in rural areas the impact of increasing State initiative could well have been considerable.[21] The formation of local medical districts and the appointment of local authority doctors (*Gerichtsärzte*) was designed on the one hand to strengthen State control over medical practice. On the other hand the new centralised system of medical provision was to eliminate indigenous medical practices and finally to destroy peasant belief in the effectiveness of 'magical' medicine and the cures provided by itinerant charlatans and lay practitioners. The reforms undertaken in this field in the early nineteenth century were therefore directly linked with an extension in State power. At the same time they were also designed to produce a modernisation of peasant attitudes towards medical care and treatment.

Educational reform was designed in the same mould, namely to free the ordinary citizen from the influence of previous authorities and to bind him effectively to the newly constituted State.[22] The break-through in this field occurred in 1802 when school attendance was made compulsory for all children in Bavaria between six and twelve years of age.[23] The duration of the school year, the level of school fees and the daily hours of educational instruction were now to be subject to State regulation. Further attempts at centralised control and standardisation were embodied in the revised teaching plan of 1804 and in additional legislation of 1806 and 1811.[24] The role of the State was strengthened by the creation of an inspectorate system and by the establishment of compulsory teacher-training seminaries throughout the country. Educational reform was designed to serve a number of distinct purposes. It was to have a normative function in inculcating values such as obedience, patriotism and industriousness, of immediate value to the State.[25] It was also designed to influence the 'mental structure' of future generations.[26] By emphasising the power of the State, it was also to contribute to a reduction in the activities and significance of smaller social groups, such as the village and parish authorities. Changes in the sphere of education in the first half of the nineteenth century were therefore conceived as being in the wider interests of both the State and the indigenous population who stood to benefit from a general acceptance of the need for social change.

Finally increasing State control and social integration within the wider process of modernisation was also achieved through an expansion in the Bavarian armed forces. Bavaria's standing army, based entirely on compulsory conscription, grew considerably in the years after 1815. The number of non-commissioned officers and ordinary conscript soldiers rose from 42,352 (1819/20) to 96,150 (1862).[27] The trend towards an increasingly higher rate of conscription per generation had important implications. Not only did it serve to bring a larger proportion of Bavaria's youth under direct military control during a key developmental stage, but military service, it could be argued, served indirectly to undermine the cohesiveness of traditional rural attitudes. Garrisoned in major towns and subjected to the influence of urban life, military service heightened the growing contrast between urban and rural communities and facilitated the transmission of more 'modern' attitudes. Indeed the existence of a standing army, in itself, was regarded by one contemporary as a factor which would inevitably contribute to a loosening of family ties and the disappearance of traditional values.[28]

II

It is clear, therefore, that the protagonists of modernisation theory can find in Bavaria a number of key factors in the early decades of the nineteenth century, which apparently contributed to a transformation of traditional familial, sexual and social attitudes. Even before the onset of widespread industrialisation a significant transition process had occurred in rural society. The changes that took place, it is argued, not only served to stabilise the political hegemony of the Bavarian state, but also to reduce the barriers to 'modern' socialisation. At one level the passing of the old order was marked by 'the demise of the village'[29] and a weakening of the cooperative system of community and family control. On a more personal basis the institutional reforms of the early nineteenth century implied a freer and wider choice for the individual. The sexual revolution, which involved a fundamental reassessment of individual and associative values, was already under way.

However as far as the impact of exogenous structural reform in the early nineteenth century on the internal function and role of the family was concerned, the existing studies tell us very little. And yet an analysis of family role and structure is central to any understanding of the changes that took place in the first half of the nineteenth century. If external intrusions and the growth of agrarian individualism did become predominant, how did they affect the nature of family relationships? If public structures, embodied in administrative and educational reforms, were increasingly applied in rural society, how did the family function in response? Did it act as a mediator designed to reproduce the dominant values and ideas of the State, or as a bulwark in the defence of existing and traditional values? Despite the general acceptance of the need for a greater sensitivity to transactions between historical change and the family unit,[30] this has not been evident in the treatment of Bavarian data relevant to this central debate. Most historians have assumed that the family and household in early nineteenth century Bavaria were passive recipients of social change, rather than active agents, and that the 'traditional' values governing family life simply responded to economic and institutional pressures. Despite Hareven's plea that historians should be willing to accept that the family was not necessarily a dependent variable[31] and despite evidence that the working class in the nineteenth century was able to resist and transform attempts to intervene in the management of the family,[32] most existing studies have tacitly assumed a positive and functionalist correlation between socio-economic reform, imposed from above, and the modernisation of family relationships and household structure. Shorter has been justly criticised for his espousal of modernisation theory, with its assumption of unilinear progress and an ethnocentric model of modernity.[33] But the predominant analysis of social change in early nineteenth-century Bavaria, as far as this affected the position of the individual and the role of the family, is deficient in a number of other important aspects. Despite the assumed dysfunctional impact of military involvement before 1815 and the specific timing of reform legislation in the agrarian, ecclesiastical, educational and medical fields, no attempt has been made on the basis of cohort analysis to examine the impact of these changes on role accumulation in rural society, or the function of social network groups. Rapid social change clearly differentiates the specific historical context of successive birth cohorts,[34] yet confirmation of the modernising effect of socio-economic reform in early nineteenth-century Bavaria has not been sought along these lines. In a wider context the social and economic factors determining the structure and nature of family relationships during this period have been largely ignored and the possible resilience of rural society in the face of externally imposed 'modernisation' underestimated. It is to be hoped that the present contribution will to some extent provide a more objective analysis of the extent of social change in early nineteenth-century Bavaria. It will examine the specific changes in the role and function of the peasant family and the peasant household and will focus attention on the nature of social network contacts at the kinship and community levels. Such an analysis may also facilitate a reappraisal of the role of the family not only as an agent capable of responding to the exigencies of a specific mode of production, but as a critical factor affecting the overall process of social change.

At first sight it would appear that Bavaria, of all German states, should have witnessed the least degree of social change and transformation of familial and individual relationships during the first half of the nineteenth century. Rapid population growth is frequently viewed as one of the major exogenous factors contributing to rapid social change and the destabilisation of traditional values.[35] However, the overall rate of population growth between 1818 and 1852 stood at only 0.67 per cent per annum and compares unfavourably with corresponding annual rates for other German territories. Only Württemberg of the major states had a lower growth rate in the early nineteenth century and many regions of Prussia enjoyed a rate of population growth three or four times in excess of that of Bavaria.[36] If high rates of population growth and the resultant shift in supply and demand conditions were significant factors in changing traditional social attitudes, this was clearly unlikely to have been the case in Bavaria during the period under consideration.

A similar difficulty lies in the interpretation of the social impact of agrarian reform, and the further extension of the capitalist mode of production into rural areas. Two important facets of this development need to be emphasised at this juncture. First, the net effect of land redistribution was not to exacerbate existing social differences within rural communities, but to reduce socio-economic divisions within peasant society.[37] Although this was not uniformly the case, a variety of local studies confirms that this was a fairly general trend.[38] By the mid-nineteenth century, Bavaria was a country of medium-sized peasant holdings, with the average family land endowment varying from 9.3 hectares in Upper Bavaria to 7.9 hectares in the Palatinate.[39] By 1882, two-thirds of all agricultural holdings were less than 5 hectares.[40] Land redistribution, associated with agrarian reform legislation of the early nineteenth century, had therefore contributed to a reduction in social differentials. Small-holders, day-labourers and families involved in domestic craft production were now able to extend their land endowment, at the direct expense of integral holdings, whose owners were now finally able to resolve their economic difficulties by the sale of surplus land. Far from encouraging agrarian individualism on the part of the peasantry, the process of land redistribution in Bavaria would have reinforced the existing level of economic interdependence in peasant communities. Even until late in the nineteenth century cooperation between two or three families in rural areas appears to have been usual, particularly in fulfilling specific economic tasks, such as house construction and repair, wood transport, assistance at fires, and ploughing.[41] Land redistribution would also have had an integrative function in terms of community and kinship relationships.

Secondly, agrarian reform in Bavaria, as in most other cases, was inevitably labour-intensive. Increased levels of output were achieved not through significant technological advance, but by a more effective and labour-intensive exploitation of existing resources.[42] To the extent that class relationships depend specifically on the type of agricultural production,[43] few changes could be expected in this sphere, as the nature of production remained essentially the same. Furthermore, as far as the role of the family was concerned, the increased emphasis on labour as the key factor of production would have heightened the importance of family labour in the domestic economy. This in turn would have reinforced the traditional function of the peasant family as an institution of work[44] and would have weakened the family's receptiveness for new and more 'modern' social attitudes. If the division of labour can be regarded, as Sabean has argued,[45] as one of the crucial institutions that channels the force of change into new sets of social relationships, then the nature of agrarian reform in early nineteenth-century Bavaria would not in itself have created the conditions favourable to rapid social change, particularly in relation to the function and role of the family unit and the significance of kinship networks.

But any critical appraisal of the process and extent of social change in the early nineteenth century must be anchored in the reality of the function and structure of the Bavarian peasant family. The family in early nineteenth-century Bavaria, as in most pre-industrial economies, constituted the basic unit within society. Its importance was consistently reinforced by the attitude of the Roman Catholic Church, which viewed the family as constituting a solid rock and an indispensable base for the maintenance of a unified society.[46] If the protagonists of modernisation theory are correct in their assumptions, then the period of agrarian reform, secularisation and the extension in the manipulative powers of the State in the opening decades of the nineteenth century should have found an immediate impact in the sphere of the family. The dysfunctional effects of these structural and institutional changes should inevitably have disrupted the traditional pattern of family relationships and fostered increasing generational conflict, specifically as a response to the rapid growth in illegitimacy rates and sexual independence. They should also have weakened community and kinship bonds, as economic relations in the primary sector became increasingly governed by capitalist and individualistic principles, rather than traditional forms of social obligations and community interdependence. An analysis of the role of the peasant family in Bavaria is therefore central to a wider understanding of the social impact of institutional change during the period under consideration. The reaction of the rural community to new demands and pressures, expressed primarily in family and kinship relations, will provide an insight into the actual mechanism of 'modernisation'. Indeed such an analysis is essential if the role of the family in the general process of social change is to be understood.

III

Average family size in Bavaria in the eighteenth century conformed closely with the well-established Western European pattern.[47] In the villages of the *Landgericht* Dachau average family size (parents and children) fluctuated between 5.3 and 5.7.[48] The overall figure for Upper Bavaria in 1811/12 stood at 5.2.[49] (Table 3.1). Socio-economic

changes in the early nineteenth century did not affect this pattern
(Table 3.2), primarily because the apparent stability of the small
nuclear family was itself a function of other critical factors which
determined the life–cycle of peasant communities. By and large parents
tended to delay the devolution of the family holding until their own
working life was at an end (Table 3.3). This was a common
phenomenon in both North and South Germany[50] and reflected
economic and status considerations implicit in the traditional role of
the *Hausvater* or head of household.[51] As a result, average age at first
marriage for inheriting children remained high and actually tended to
rise in the course of the nineteenth century (Table 3.4). The
combination of a late average age at first marriage and excessively high
infant and child mortality rates naturally reduced the final average size
of peasant families. Furthermore the advanced age of parents at the
time of devolution only served to shorten the length of time during
which the elder generation remained physically present in the newly
constituted household. The demographic, legal and social factors which
traditionally determined average family size were not affected to any
extent by the reform legislation of the early nineteenth century.

The inheritance system in most areas of Bavaria was based on
traditional laws of 1346, which were essentially re-confirmed in 1818.
All children were accorded equal rights in the holding, although
management of the holding was to pass to only one specified heir.[52]
The choice of a direct heir, however, was determined by a number of
external factors, such as the comparative age of surviving children,
adult mortality rates and the frequency of re-marriage within the
peasant community, as well as personal preference. In this respect there
was no significant change in the first half of the nineteenth century,
and the traditional laws of inheritance in Bavaria remained intact until
1855.[53] Equally agrarian reform did not promote the emergence of
larger family units. Increased output from the primary sector was not
accompanied by a reduction in age-specific mortality. It has been
argued elsewhere that the pattern of agricultural reform in Bavaria,
with its emphasis on a more extensive utilisation of available labour,
specifically female labour, had an adverse effect on indigenous levels of
mortality.[54] The further deterioration in infant mortality rates in the
early nineteenth century also meant that the final completed family
size in rural areas remained relatively small. Finally the late age at
which parents handed on the family holding was a reflection of the
traditional *Hausvater* principle, which legitimised the dependence of
family members on the head of the household.[55] The devolution of a

Table 3.1: Average Size of the Family Group (Parents and Children) in Upper Bavaria: 1811/12

District	Average size	District	Average size
Stadt Munich	4.6	Ldg.Pfaffenhofen	4.7
Ldg.Dachau	4.8	Ldg.Tölz	4.8
Ldg.Ebersberg	4.9	Ldg.Trostberg	5.0
Ldg.Freising	4.2	Ldg.Wasserburg	4.2
Ldg.Friedberg	4.1	Ldg.Weilheim	5.3
Ldg.Munich	4.5	Ldg.Wolfratshausen	5.1
Ldg.Mühldorf	4.5	Ldg.Landshut	4.7

Table 3.2: Average Size of the Family Group (Parents and Children) in Selected *Landgerichte* of Upper Bavaria: 1818–37

District	Average size				
Landgericht	1818	1827	1830	1834	1837
Freising	5.4	4.7	4.7	4.9	5.1
Friedberg	4.7	5.1	4.9	5.0	4.9
Pfaffenhofen	5.0	5.0	4.8	4.7	4.8
Wasserburg	4.4	5.3	5.3	4.8	4.7
Weilheim	5.1	4.9	5.3	5.0	4.9

Table 3.3: Age of Parents at the Time of Devolution: Hofmark Massenhausen, 1750–1849 (in years)

Village	Average age of father	Average age of mother
Massenhausen	59.4	60.5
Fürholzen	61.6	52.5
Hetzenhausen	63.0	59.8
Gross Eisenbach	63.1	61.2
Klein Nöbach	63.1	59.6
Average	62.0	58.7

Table 3.4: Mean Age at First Marriage on the Estates of Massenhausen and Thalhausen *(Landgericht* Freising) (in years), 1740–1849

Decade	Hofmark Massenhausen		Hofmark Thalhausen	
	brides	grooms	brides	grooms
1740-9	25.3	—	30.6	32.0
1750-9	28.7	29.2	29.1	26.7
1760-9	25.5	27.4	33.2	31.0
1770-9	27.0	27.6	32.4	30.6
1780-9	25.9	29.1	31.2	31.0
1790-9	27.4	28.6	29.6	30.5
1800-9	27.3	28.4	29.0	31.1
1810-9	26.9	30.5	28.8	33.3
1820-9	26.6	28.8	27.8	28.3
1830-9	27.1	29.0	29.2	31.1
1840-9	27.8	29.5	32.0	33.3

holding implied an immediate loss of control and also of social status.[56] The continuing rights of surviving parents in the holding were rigidly defined by law and the detailed nature of parental settlements typified the need for these interests to be stipulated and defended. Once devolution had taken place the claims of surviving parents were of secondary importance as far as the management of the holding was concerned. Aged parents were frequently looked after badly by their children and even in the present century a premature loosening of the reins of control was viewed with little sympathy in rural communities.[57] All these factors, however, which directly influenced the average size of peasant families in Bavaria, remained constant throughout the period under consideration. Indeed agrarian reform, in the short term, only served to emphasise the predominance of the small nuclear family.

However the continued prominence of the nuclear family in nineteenth-century Bavaria also reflected the degree to which the peasant family had retained its primary economic function. The concept of the family was largely dependent on the economic significance of the holding. The unifying bond which provided an important element of stability in rural society was the family holding rather than a complex of personal relationships. Within this framework, work-orientation determined the relationship between parents and children and the role obligations of all household members. The social role of women, with its attendant ramifications for the socialisation of children, was also determined by this factor. The sexual division of labour played a central part in the organisation of both the family and the household, and the role of peasant women during this period continued to be determined by the nature of the rural economy. Financial considerations, particularly the dowry of a future bride, were very important in the choice of a marriage partner. It is not surprising, therefore, that as far as the social background of marriage partners was concerned, rural society evinced a high degree of class endogamy. However, this pattern was just as prominent in the first half of the nineteenth century as it had been in the final decades of the preceding century. Economic considerations, rather than feelings of personal love and affection, were still predominant in Bavaria, despite the alleged impact of reform legislation and the partial 'modernisation' of both social and sexual attitudes. For the same reason many men continued to seek older and more experienced brides with a larger personal dowry well into the nineteenth century.[58]

But if economic factors continued to determine the choice of brides in rural society, they were even more apparent in the treatment of women within the family unit. Despite the increased discussion of female emancipation in the eighteenth century within enlightened circles,[59] the position of women in rural society remained subject to the mode of production of material life. This was embodied in the attitude of peasants to their womenfolk. Wife-beating in Bavaria was apparently commoner than the ill-treatment of horses and this picture confirms available evidence from other parts of Western Europe.[60] Even well into the twentieth century peasant women were frequently subjected to a strict domestic rule.[61] But the specific role of women was most clearly apparent in the degree of economic exploitation. Like his Swiss counterpart, the Bavarian peasant was relatively slow in applying a rigorous division of labour and the traditional division of work between the sexes persisted well into the late nineteenth and early twentieth centuries.[62] Not only was the overall workload of the wife in excess of that of her husband, but if his was relatively well defined and bound by routine, the wife was expected to modify her labour input in accordance with changing economic needs and circumstances.[63] Her work was seldom limited to household duties, but often encompassed domestic clothing production, the preparation of flax, and agricultural labour at certain times of the year. The role of women was vital in terms of the continued functioning of the family holding. This often precluded any necessary period of rest either during pregnancy or immediately after child-birth.[64] The reform legislation of the early nineteenth century and the significant reduction in Church authority associated with secularisation did not impinge at all on the underlying economic factors which determined the sexual division of labour in rural society and the role performance of women as a whole. Indeed, once again, the form that agrarian development took in Bavaria may well have reinforced existing attitudes. The initial increase in the total demand for labour necessitated by agricultural reform was met by an enforced extension in the workload of peasant women. The rise in infant mortality rates and adult female mortality, together with a further deterioration in the observance of the traditional year of mourning following the premature death of peasant brides,[65] provide tentative evidence of the real cost in human terms of such an economic system. The work role of women in rural Bavaria and the existing sexual division of labour which affected sexual attitudes and relationships within the family remained unaffected by the period of reform. Agrarian reform merely exacerbated the existing state of affairs.

IV

The socialisation of children, both within the first five years of life and during childhood as a whole, was also determined by the primacy of the economic function of the peasant holding. By and large parental attitudes towards children continued to be determined by the economic utility which could be gained from additional family members. Until the child had received some training in a particular, if rudimentary, skill, or had proved its economic usefulness for the domestic household economy, it was seldom accepted either economically or emotionally as a full family member. The amount of attention given by parents to young children and particularly to infants, remained minimal. Young children were rarely regarded as a benefit to the family and once the future of the holding had been secured by the successful rearing of one or two children beyond the critical period of early childhood, the parental attitude to later offspring noticeably deteriorated.[66] In Mittelfels, for example, it was rumoured that a farmer would rather lose a young child than a calf.[67] Peasant indifference to the fate of infants was arguably legitimised by contemporary Catholic ideology. Childhood innocence and early death invariably secured the attainment of lasting salvation. Further evidence of this negative pattern of parent-child relationships can be found in the custom of naming children. The same Christian name occurs with monotonous regularity in parish baptismal records, until it was finally retained within the family through the survival of a particular infant.[68] On this basis, children in Bavaria, at least in the first few years of life, seldom enjoyed a personal existence. The excessively high infant mortality rates in early nineteenth-century Bavaria, the absence of breast-feeding and the fact that children under the age of five years rarely received qualified medical attention prior to their final illness,[69] is further testimony of the prevalence of this general attitude to young infants and children.

However, once a child had survived the perilous rigours of early infancy and had shown both resilience against disease and a potential economic usefulness for the family holding, parental attitudes noticeably changed. But even at this stage, the treatment of children and their socialisation within the family was dictated by economic considerations. Children were employed as soon as possible on menial tasks associated with the management of the holding and incorporated at an early age into the household's economic function. If the family tenement was relatively large, then each child in turn would be employed, perhaps until marriage, in such a capacity. But in the case of small-holdings, which were increasingly predominant in many parts of Bavaria during the early nineteenth century, most surviving children would be employed at a comparatively early age outside the family holding. The Freising census of 1803, for example, reveals the employment of children of only six and eight years of age as domestic servants. The relationship of the child to the parental home and to the family unit as a whole was not only affected by the relative size of the holding and its immediate labour requirements, but also by the presence of other offspring. In peasant legal settlements governing the inheritance of holdings a distinct pattern is observable, both in the late eighteenth and early nineteenth centuries. If only one child was present, in the majority of cases the child retained the right to stay on the holding and to receive food and accommodation in return for labour beyond the age of 16 years. As soon as further children had to be taken into consideration, these rights diminished sharply.[70] In every case, therefore, the position and function of the child was determined by immediate economic considerations.

The reform legislation of the early nineteenth century which contributed, it is claimed, to the partial modernisation of Bavarian society and the transformation of sexual and social attitudes, did not alter the primacy of economic factors in the determining and moulding of inter-family relations. Although the adoption of a more labour-intensive system of production in the primary sector should have re-emphasised the importance of family labour, any radical impact of such a development was minimised by the trend to small-holdings and the collapse of agricultural prices in the late 1820s and 1830s. As a result there was no significant shift in the treatment and socialisation of children in Bavarian rural communities. It is equally important at this juncture to stress the degree to which the peasant household remained unaffected by legislative reform. As Mitterauer and Siedler have shown, the production function of the family unit was traditionally more important than its socialisation role.[71] The nature of work requirement and the relationship between the needs of the holding and family labour provision, invariably led to a noticeable element of compositional change in the peasant household. Role allocation and socialisation in the eighteenth century were essentially determined by this dichotomy. However in Bavaria there is no evidence of any later diminution in the importance of this dichotomy. The critical factors in this respect, such as average age at first marriage and adult mortality rates, did not undergo any radical change in the opening decades of the nineteenth century. There is equally no evidence of a reduction in the production function of the rural family. Agricultural production in Bavaria remained dependent on residential farm labour and not wage labour. The increasing predominance of small-holdings reinforced the production function of the peasant family. Indeed not until the late nineteenth century, with the gradual introduction of mechanisation in the primary sector, was there any change in the traditional production role of the family unit.[72] Under these conditions, therefore, the socio-economic reform legislation of the early nineteenth century could not have produced any radical transition in peasant attitudes and relations.

Given that the mode of family production was the critical factor in determining both the sexual role of women and the socialisation and treatment of children, it is not surprising that educational reform in the early nineteenth century had such a limited impact in rural society. Engelsing has argued that the penetration of new educational theories was a major factor in providing the preconditions for social change in nineteenth-century Germany.[73] In Bavaria, however, a wide gulf continued to exist between the aims of official reform and their impact on peasant consciousness. Despite some improvements in literacy rates, probably between 40 per cent and 50 per cent of peasant society were still illiterate by the late 1840s.[74] Deficiencies in central administration and inadequate funds for educational provision were just two factors which limited reform at the local level. However given the importance of child labour within the rural economy, it was inevitable that the introduction of compulsory primary education would conflict with local labour requirements. The production function of the family remained the prior consideration. School attendance rates were often poor, particularly during the harvest period and until the end of threshing.[75] Many children only attended for part of the year and truancy rates were high. It is clear, therefore, that increasing State control over the teaching profession was not synonymous with greater manipulative powers over peasant society as a whole. Educational reform in the early nineteenth century may have been successful, at a general level, in inculcating loyalty to the ruling house of Bavaria,[76] but in terms of the socialisation of peasant youth and the forming of social attitudes it was largely a failure. The traditional function of the family in the socialisation of children and the reproduction even at an early age of the sexual division of labour, remained unaffected by educational reform imposed from above.[77]

Educational reform was designed to influence the 'mental structure' of future generations and to reduce the socialisation function of the peasant family. Medical reform in early nineteenth-century Bavaria was designed to replace another fundamental function of the family unit. The family holding by definition had functioned as a source of welfare provision for all family dependants. This embraced a wide range of contingencies, apart from the provision of a marriage dowry for all surviving children.[78] In the case of severe physical disablement, for example, children were entitled to remain on the holding and to receive adequate food and accommodation in lieu of a separate marriage settlement.[79] Equally older unmarried children were entitled to return to the holding in the case of sickness and to be cared for at the expense of the household for a specified time. However, the welfare function of the family was not limited to children and adolescent family members. After the devolution of the holding, the heir was legally obliged to maintain the surviving parents. The basic elements of such a parental settlement consisted traditionally of a cash allowance, a specified quantity of food and clothing, an allowance for medical treatment and prescriptions and a provision to cover eventual burial costs. Although the value of the settlement varied according to the relative economic situation of the holding at the time of devolution (Table 3.6), the obligation to make this type of provision was an integral aspect of the local inheritance procedure. To this extent the family, or at least the family holding, functioned as a shelter to its members.[80] The legal obligations to provide welfare were firmly attached to the holding and transcended changes in family composition or the actual ownership of the holding. The sale of the holding, its subdivision, or the re-marriage of a widowed parent did not affect the legal rights of the individual family member. During the three most critical periods of life, therefore, namely youth, marriage and old age, the family holding in Bavaria was traditionally the basic source of welfare provision.

Table 3.5: Social Origin of Marriage Partners in the Villages of Aiterbach, Salmading, Oberkienberg and Allershausen (Upper Bavaria), 1750–99

		Brides (according to size of holding)				
		1	½	¼	$1/8$	$1/16$
	1	19	5	6	5	1
Grooms (according	½	6	4	3	–	2
to size of holding)	¼	7	4	4	2	–
	$1/8$	3	2	1	7	8
	$1/16$	–	–	–	1	18

Table 3.6: Annual Average Value of Parental Settlements: Hofmark Massenhausen, 1770–1829 (fl.kr.)

Decade	Size of Holding			
	1	½	¼	$1/16$
1770-9	142	51	49	–
1780-9	95	61	73	–
1790-9	171	121	–	–
1800-9	166	125	191	–
1810-9	170	153	92	51
1820-9	165	123	150	130

Once again, however, medical reform and the extension of the State's role in welfare provision do not appear to have affected the traditional function of the family. Undoubtedly the increasing intervention of the State in the provision of medical facilities was particularly marked in the early decades of the nineteenth century. There was a radical increase both in the quantity and quality of medical personnel, in midwifery provision and in hospital in-patient facilities.[81] By mid century medical facilities in

Bavaria were probably superior to those of most other German states. But the impact of increasing State intervention would appear to have been very limited. Both infant and adult mortality rates remained disproportionately high and showed little, if any, response to the extension in the infrastructure of official medical provision. This is borne out on the basis of an analysis of both regional mortality rates within Bavaria and the trend in disease-specific death-rates in the first half of the nineteenth century. To some extent the limited impact of medical reform can be traced back to administrative deficiencies and continuing limitations in medical knowledge. However, of even greater significance was the continued existence of traditional peasant attitudes to disease and death. The peasantry still kept their medical problems 'secret' and folk medicines provided by local barbers and midwives, in whom the peasant retained a great deal of 'trust', continued to be preferred to the services offered by the expanding system of official medical practice.[82] Superstitious beliefs and a certain element of class endogamy between the charlatan and the peasant patient were just two factors which undermined the impact of State intervention in the medical sphere. Given the continued availability of traditional medicines, it was unlikely that medical reform would succeed, as this would also have necessitated a fundamental reappraisal of the role of the family. Throughout this period the family holding remained the immediate source of welfare provision in rural society, particularly as far as medical care was concerned. To this extent the continuing preference for traditional medicine and the miracle cures of grave-diggers and urine diviners reflected the localisation of medical provision in general within the family and the immediate village community. In this respect little had changed in relation to the traditional function of the peasant family, and the reform legislation of the early nineteenth century had not impaired this function to any great extent.

V

The structural role of the family extended beyond the confines of the individual peasant household. Central to the traditional historical meaning of kinship structure is the idea that people are related in semi-permanent, biological, legal or economic ways.[83] This was mirrored in Bavaria, as elsewhere in Central Europe, in an extended pattern of cross-connections between and within kinship groups. There are, of course, a number of factors influencing the extent of kinship contacts, including economic ties, residence accessibility, the connectedness of the kinship network and the perceived differences or similarities in social status.[84] However if kin are viewed as a group of individuals who regard themselves as having a special relationship based either on consanguinity (common descent) or affinity (links through marriage),[85] then there is little evidence of any diminution of kinship links in early nineteenth-century Bavaria, or any fundamental realignment of kinship patterns. Economically, kin continued to play an important role in the management of the family household. Not only did kin function as farm and domestic servants, and provide occasional paid labour on the holding, but they often undertook financial support in the form of loans.[86] The new mortgage legislation of the 1820s had no effect on this pattern.[87] Similarly, the geographical interconnectedness of kinship contacts remained intact during the early nineteenth century. The affinitive nature of kinship was reinforced by the fact that marriage partners were still selected within a very narrow geographical radius. In the village of Hetzenhausen, for example, the proportion of brides and grooms originating from settlements within a radius of one mile from the village actually increased from 57.6 per cent of all cases between 1750 and 1799, to 76.6 per cent in the first half of the nineteenth century. Relatives were also still actively involved in negotiating marriage contracts.[88] Residence accessibility was reinforced by the frequency of marriage partners stemming from the same village, which could often be very high indeed.[89] It is not surprising, therefore, that kinship contacts in the period under consideration continued to be very frequent in rural Bavaria.

Participation in traditional rituals and ceremonies, which is commonly taken as being symptomatic of effective kinship relationships,[90] was also very prominent in the early nineteenth century. It was normal for all immediate relatives to be present at court proceedings involving the family holding, and only rarely is it admitted that they could not be traced. Kin continued to play an important role in the life of the family. In Saalgau (Swabia) all close relatives were invited to discuss the individual points of a potential marriage contract.[91] Throughout most regions of Bavaria every relative and close acquaintance within a radius of two to three hours' journey was expected to participate in commemorative services for the deceased.[92] A further indication of the relative strength of family and kinship contacts within the immediate neighbourhood can be found in the practice of naming individual holdings. In certain cases the name of a holding simply reflected its occupational function. However, certain names occur with a surprising frequency both in the late eighteenth and early nineteenth centuries. In the *Landgericht* Freising, for example, the Bartl family first appeared on the 'Thalhausen' holding in Gross Eisenbach in 1745, but the same name can be traced in a further 16 settlements.[93] Clearly the distribution pattern of family names may have been somewhat coincidental, but the available evidence confirms that strong family ties existed within comparatively small geographical regions. Throughout the first half of the nineteenth century and well beyond, the family continued to embrace a network of inter-village contacts, the proximity of which would have reinforced the importance of family and kin relationships. Naturally the precise quality of these relationships is difficult to establish, but in the Bavarian case kinship networks in this period appear to have remained both close-knit and effective.[94]

But if kinship networks continued to play a significant role in supporting the role of the family and the function of the family economy, social change in rural relationships, it is argued, resulted from a fundamental transformation in the role of the village community (*Gemeinde*). Externally-imposed reform, it is claimed, led not only to the 'demise of the village', but the enclosure of common land undermined the associative socialisation function of the traditional community.[95] Economic interdependence, which had been an important force in the maintenance of social conformity, was no longer necessary. As in other parts of Germany the transformation of the village community into a new institutional form (*Landgemeinde*) led to a qualitative change in peasant social relations, which was part and parcel of the general disintegration of European community life during this period.[96] The element of familiarity and both specific and diffuse obligations connected with effective communal bonds, disappeared in the face of increasing State involvement and official central intervention.[97] Certainly in Bavaria the administrative changes of the early nineteenth century did affect the traditional function of the village community. The edict of 1808 established new criteria for the formation of local authorities and destroyed the existing unity between village and *Gemeinde*.[98] Each local authority was now to have a minimum population of between 250 and 1,000 inhabitants and to consist, if necessary, of a group of different villages.[99] This territorial readjustment destroyed the element of cooperation which had existed within the unified village authority.[100] Furthermore, secularisation saw

the transference of court proceedings from individual estates to the
central authority in each administrative region of the country,
weakening once again local autonomy and the supportive structure of
the local or estate community.

However, as in the case of other areas of external reform, the impact
of these changes at the local level was seldom very dramatic. If the
village community had been an important mechanism for the
inculcation of a collective mode of behaviour in the late eighteenth
century, to a large extent it retained this function in later decades. The
closeness of a village community was expressed in face-to-face contact,
the commonalty of purpose and personal familiarity. In the absence of
rapid population growth during the first half of the nineteenth century,
the average size of villages in Bavaria remained small. In the
ecclesiastical diocese of Freising, for example, nearly 70 per cent of all
settlements in 1820 had a population of less than 50 inhabitants
(Table 3.7). This was particularly important in the light of the principle
that the smaller the system, the more frequent the level of internal
communications is likely to be.[101] Personal contact under these
conditions would have remained both frequent and normative during
the period under consideration. Community contacts continued to be
important as a direct support to the functional role of the family. At
one level, the powers of the local communities had been considerably
strengthened. The tighter regulations governing marriage and settlement
of 1825 were to be enforced by the *Gemeinde* and with the abolition
of all seigneurial jurisdiction in 1848 the local authorities were now
empowered to exercise the right of guardianship previously reserved for
patrimonial courts. Such an extension in the powers of the local
authority, however, was not synonymous with greater State control
over rural society. Quite the contrary. The strengthening of community
powers facilitated the retention of indigenous patterns of behaviour. Far
from acting as the State demanded, the *Gemeinde* frequently failed to
fulfil their official role, whether in combating rising illegitimacy,
introducing an improved midwifery service, or in promoting better
educational facilities for the local population.[102] Increased local
autonomy, even allowing for the re-drawing of local authority
boundaries, more than compensated for the limited enclosure of
common land that took place in early nineteenth-century Bavaria.[103]

At a more personal level the local village community still performed
its traditional function. Group contacts had always provided important
support for the individual in rural society, and this continued to be the
case after 1800.[104] Close neighbours (so-called *Not-* or *Kleidernachbarn*)

Table 3.7: Distribution of Settlements in the Ecclesiastical Diocese of Freising by Size of Population: 1820

Inhabitants	No. of settlements	%
1 – 5	13	8.22
6 – 10	27	17.08
11 – 20	35	22.15
21 – 50	35	22.15
51 – 100	23	14.55
101 – 200	18	11.39
201 +	7	4.43

Source: Bischöfliche General-Vicariats-Kanzley (ed.), *Tabellarische Beschreibung des Bisthums Freising nach Ordnung der Decanate* (Munich, 1820) pp. 144-56.

had traditionally been assigned specific functions in the community.[105] These obligations, which constituted important communal bonds between rural families and within individual communities, continued well into the late nineteenth century. At most central family events, such as weddings, during sickness and at burials, immediate neighbours continued to be assigned distinct functions and roles.[106] Equally god-parents were selected with care and were expected to visit the family on every Sunday and public holiday.[107] In many cases, both before and after 1800, god-parents were selected from outside the local parish, but from within the same administrative areas and frequently from neighbouring villages within a radius of 5 to 10 kilometres.[108] The choice also reflected professional and social considerations (Table 3.8), but the application of such criteria in turn undoubtedly reinforced the existing element of local family cohesion. Moreover the village community as such continued to be involved in a general sense in family events. The whole village normally participated in marriage festivities and this also signified communal involvement in the integration of young people within the adult world. Whether in the context of traditional feast days and public holidays, irrespective of the degree to which they were general religious festivals or limited to particular groups within rural society,[109] community involvement in Bavaria continued to be paramount throughout the early nineteenth century.

Particularly in Bavaria, where small settlements predominated, the communal bonds which legitimised and reinforced the traditional role of the peasant family were not radically disrupted by the external changes that took place at the beginning of the nineteenth century.

Table 3.8: Social Distribution of God-parents: Parishes of
Gremertshausen and Allershausen, 1750 –1849

Size of holding of parents	Size of holding of godparents				
	I	½	¼	$1/8$	$1/16$
I	II	30	4	5	–
½	21	3	25	5	4
¼	–	34	9	3	I
$1/8$	14	6	4	10	10
$1/16$	3	–	8	16	47

The local community had always been marked by social and economic
differences, whether expressed in the selection of marriage partners, the
choice of god-parents, or the regular place (*Stammtisch*) in the local
tavern. The organisational structure of community life in the late
eighteenth century had simply stabilised, rather than removed these
differences and had allowed reciprocal expectations and mutual
confidence to develop. Once again, however, the administrative and
economic changes in the early nineteenth century did not seriously
disrupt this function. The redistribution of land within many
communities had in any case tended to reduce even further existing
social inequalities and the strengthening of the decentralised system of
local administration, as it finally took shape in the course of the early
nineteenth century, reinforced the traditional element of local
autonomy and self-reliance. Community organisation continued to
function primarily on a horizontal, rather than a vertical basis,[110] and
informal influences remained of the utmost importance. As a result the
continued independence of local communities, together with their
enhanced administrative responsibilities, effectively worked against any
overall process of radical social change. The village community, whether
in an administrative sense, or in the form of informal rights and
obligations, continued to fulfil its legitimising function and to this
extent contributed to the ability of the peasant family and of rural
society in general to resist increasing State intervention in a variety of
important spheres. It was exactly because of the continuing
autonomous role of the village community that the Bavarian state was
unable to deal with the problem of widespread illegitimacy, to curtail
excessive drinking among the peasantry, or to make any significant
inroads in the elimination of superstitious beliefs in rural society.
Indigenous patterns of behaviour, under these conditions, could

continue to thrive. Social attitudes and family relationships, even if they were at variance with the official norms of the Bavarian state, could also be allowed full expression within the wider framework of the village community as a whole.

VI

It is frequently assumed that the traditional family was characterised by a unity of purpose and inner coherence. This 'pre-industrial' or 'traditional' unity, it is often argued, was broken during the period of 'modernisation' and only recomposed at a significantly later date along totally different criteria. Inner-family coherence was now replaced by personal autonomy and the relative independence of family members.[111] Bavaria is significant as far as this general hypothesis is concerned in that the modernisation process was apparently initiated in the early nineteenth century. This took place not in the context of rapid industrialisation, but in a country still essentially agrarian in nature. The breakdown of the 'traditional' family was a function of the development of agrarian capitalism, the demise of religious values, and perhaps most importantly the intrusion of State control facilitated through educational and welfare reform. The trend towards 'modernisation' in the family sphere was accompanied by a loosening of kinship contacts and community interdependence. In human terms the inevitable concomitant of the development of profit farming and land enclosure was the growth in illegitimacy rates and an increase in the 'caring capacity' of rural youth of both sexes.[112] Such an interpretation, based on the evidence of extensive structural reform in the opening decades of the nineteenth century, has at its core an important assumption. The family is considered as a microcosm of society as a whole, whose dominant values are confirmed in the family through primary socialisation.[113] Not only is the family household 'porous', but kinship systems are also viewed as mutable in response to external pressures.[114] Finally, the village in early nineteenth-century Bavaria was no longer 'a homogenous living space', but increasingly an integral part of the State's administrative machinery.[115]

Such an interpretation suffers from both theoretical misconceptions and a misinterpretation of available data. Above all the analysis provided by the protagonists of modernisation theory of the function of the Bavarian family and household has been generally inadequate. This is particularly true in relation to the treatment of family relationships within a 'traditional' and 'modernising' context and of the role of the family within the framework of kin and community contacts. To view the pre-industrial family as constituting a unity is to ignore the complex variables which acted on the family and determined its function. These included economic pressures, family needs, the demands of the State and other institutional bodies, traditional values governing family work and the value-system of rural society as a whole.[116] Inevitably, both before and after 1800, the specific interaction of these variables determined the function and role of the family and the qualitative nature of family relations. Of critical importance, however, was the production function of the family holding, its changing labour requirements and its ability over time to support and maintain family dependents. For both the State and the Catholic Church, the family throughout this period remained the only recognised unit of social life and any deviation from this norm in both urban and rural areas was criticised and repressed. If the *Hausvater* principle legitimised the relationship of the ruling house with all its dependent subjects, the concept as applied to the peasant family was designed to strengthen its inner coherence within the framework of the existing social order. However even in the eighteenth century the nature of 'traditional' family life rarely conformed to the official norm. In particular economic needs seldom facilitated the acceptance of higher ideals. The treatment of infants and the exploitation of female labour testify to the primacy of economic considerations. Family life was only designed to meet the interests of individual family members provided they were able to contribute to the management of the holding and its economic viability. To this extent the sexual role of women and the socialisation of children in traditional society was dependent on the economic function of the family holding. Individual family rights and interests were subsumed under collective needs. The material condition of peasant life before 1800 determined the quality of family relations and for young children, non-inheriting brothers and sisters, farm servants and the elderly in rural society, the official norm as put forward by the State and the Church was seldom evident in reality.

The economic changes in the primary sector during the first half of the nineteenth century did not affect the underlying production function of the Bavarian peasant family. Indeed the exact nature of agrarian reform in Bavaria, although viewed officially as a contribution to the economic modernisation of the State and to the development of market-oriented capitalist production, merely served to reinforce the existing mode of production. Technological innovation was limited and increased agricultural output was achieved primarily through a more intensive utilisation of existing resources. Land redistribution and the enclosure and subdivision of common land only served to underline the importance of the peasant family economy. The end result was the creation of a peasantry dependent on either medium- or small-scale holdings, which became even less diversified, in terms of economic function, with the later decline of domestic craft production.[117] Agrarian reform in Bavaria, by emphasising the inherent production function of the peasant family, thereby confirmed the traditional sexual division of labour in rural society and the existing attitude towards children and other family dependants. The labour-intensive nature of agrarian reform only served to exacerbate the sexual role of women and the socialisation and treatment of children.

Given that the central economic reforms of the early nineteenth century did not fundamentally alter the production function of the family holding, nor disturb the implicit pattern of social and familial relationships, it was unlikely that other factors, externally induced, would have had any immediate dysfunctional impact in rural society. The significance of secularisation in 1803 has in any case been somewhat exaggerated. The Church in Bavaria had already shown severe structural weaknesses and this situation continued into the early nineteenth century without any marked alteration.[118] What the peasantry took from the clergy, they took on their own terms.[119] After secularisation they continued to show superficial obedience to ecclesiastical rulings, while maintaining their own independent approach to feast days, pilgrimages and other aspects of religious practice.[120]

Equally, increasing State intervention in the educational and welfare spheres did not contribute to a radical change in the functional role of the peasant household or a transformation of existing social attitudes. Even if the extension of State control had not been marred by administrative weaknesses, it is unlikely that the reform measures undertaken in the early nineteenth century would have radically affected existing practice. Both medical care and the socialisation and education of children remained central functions of the family and the family holding. This responsibility reflected a traditional pattern of rights and obligations which were linked with the economic structure of peasant society. In both spheres family interests continued to be predominant. The gap between the aims of State reform legislation and its impact on rural society remained immense throughout the period under consideration. Public education, with its emphasis on industriousness, obedience and order, was not only a means of controlling domestic and farm servants (*Gesinde*), but was viewed in a wider context as a mechanism for securing social modernisation. By the mid nineteenth century, however, official education was still largely ineffective, because the economic needs of family holdings were still paramount. The socialisation of children still took place within the framework of the family holdings and its changing labour needs continued to limit the impact of educational reform. Similarly in the medical sphere, increasing State involvement in the provision of a comprehensive system of medical care did not lead to any significant change in peasant attitudes towards disease and death. Medical care continued to be localised within the family and was still a vital function of the family holding. This traditional function of the peasant family remained unaffected by the development of an official system of medical provision. In the case of both educational and medical reform, therefore, the implicit 'modernising' impact of early nineteenth-century legislation was severely limited by the continuing importance of the production function of the Bavarian peasant family. Other extraneous factors, such as the growth of a standing army based on conscription, were of even less importance in this context.

Family relations in a rural context are inevitably determined by a wide variety of exogenous factors, including the mode of production, inheritance laws and shifts in vital demographic rates. In the case of Bavaria the available evidence would seem to suggest that the factors which determined the nature and quality of family relations in the late eighteenth century had not undergone any noticeable transformation in the first half of the nineteenth century. In particular agrarian reforms had only served to reinforce the existing mode of production in rural areas and had thereby re-emphasised the production function of the family with all the concomitant implications for family and kinship relations. The implications of this analysis in terms of the role of the peasant family in the process of 'modernisation' are considerable. The family and its web of kinship and community contacts was not a pliant object of externally imposed modernisation processes. Nor did it respond positively to increasing State control and manipulation. In two critical areas, in the spheres of educational and medical reform, State initiative in the early nineteenth century failed to transform or to 'modernise' indigenous peasant attitudes.

The precise interplay between the peasant family and externally imposed forces, whether of an economic, cultural or political nature, is difficult to quantify, particularly on a generational basis and over a protracted period of time. Work orientation and the economic needs of production were crucial factors in determining family relationships both in the late eighteenth and early nineteenth centuries. The available work opportunities and work requirements to a large extent structured the interaction between external economic forces and intra-family organisation, and defined at an individual level the perimeters of behaviour.[121] Economic forces impinged on the nature and quality of family relationships, not only through the existing mode of production and the institutional structure of land-holding in the primary sector, but also in the short term as a result of the quality of the annual harvest and the dependent fluctuations in the price of agricultural commodities. To this extent any analysis of the function and role of the peasant family in Western Europe must pay particular attention to the precise nature of the economic forces which helped to define and structure family relationships and to determine their evolution over time. Indeed in relation to the growth in illegitimacy, both in Bavaria and Austria in the early nineteenth century, the significance of underlying economic factors is becoming increasingly evident, as credence in the 'sexual revolution' and the posited radical change in peasant moral attitudes recedes.[122]

However family and communal relationships throughout this period were almost certainly based on subjective feeling, as well as the rationality of economic relations. In the Bavarian case there is every evidence that local custom, superstition and dialect were neither repressed nor transplanted by the institutional reforms imposed by the State in the early nineteenth century.[123] If the production function of the family remained paramount in determining family relationships, this was clearly not the only factor at work. The 'closeness' of village life in many parts of Bavaria, with its realisation of face-to-face contact, familiarity and dependability, was of vital importance in influencing the perceived relations among relationships moulded in the first instance by economic necessity. The continued importance of the horizontal axis in peasant community life also implied that primary group ties and the informal regulation of family and communal affairs persisted well into the nineteenth century. It is of course dangerous to attach too much importance to the concept of peasant traditionalism,[124] but within a social framework largely determined by the production function of the family, the perceived nature of family relationships and the role of the family at a subjective level was still governed by a wide variety of indigenous forces, such as custom, community practice and mutual dependency needs. The constant interplay of these indigenous forces with external changes imposed on the peasant family through agrarian reform and State intervention in the educational and medical spheres, influenced the precise nature of family relationships within rural society. Bavaria is therefore not simply an important test-case for the analysis of the modernisation of the family and family relations in Germany. It serves to highlight the fundamental weakness in the application of modernisation theory to a specific historical case, when the underlying economic factors, including the contemporary mode of production, are misrepresented. There is in any case an implicit difficulty in basing an analysis of the development of the privatised modern nuclear family, with its particular web of personal relationships, on a process of agrarian reform which merely served to reinforce the existing mode of production in the primary sector. But the case of Bavaria also re-emphasises the need to examine in greater depth the nature and strength of traditional values and needs in rural society, both at the family and community level. Without a more rigorous analysis of the complex variables which acted on the family and determined its function, the process of change in attitudes and relationships within the family and within rural society as a whole will not be properly understood.

Notes

The research for this contribution was in part facilitated by the grant of a research fellowship by the Alexander von Humboldt Stiftung, to whom I am greatly indebted.

1. E. Shorter, *The Making of the Modern Family* (New York, 1975), a work relying heavily on Bavarian data.

2. F.M. Phayer, *Religion und das Gewöhnliche Volk in Bayern in der Zeit von 1750-1850* (Miscellanea Bavarica Monacensia, Bd. 21, Munich, 1970), p. 175; G. Schwarz, *'Nahrungsstand' und 'erzwungener Gesellenstand'. Mentalité und Strukturwandel des bayerischen Handwerks im Industrialisierungsprozess um 1860* (Berlin, 1974), p. 29

3. W.K. Blessing, 'Umwelt und Mentalität im ländlichen Bayern. Eine Skizze zum Alltagswandel im 19.Jahrhundert', *Archiv für Sozialgeschichte*, Bd. XIX (1979), pp. 15-21

4. E. Shorter, 'Illegitimacy, Sexual Revolution and Social Change in Modern Europe', *Journal of Interdisciplinary History*, Vol. II, (1972), pp. 237-72.

5. As defined by R.K. Merton, 'Anomie, Anomia and Social Interaction', in M.B. Clinard (ed.), *Anomie and Deviant Behavior* (New York, 1964), p. 226.

6. J.M. Phayer, *Sexual Liberation and Religion in 19th century Europe* (London, 1977), p. 40.

7. F.M. Phayer, *Religion und das Gewöhnliche Volk*, p. 52.

8. W.K. Blessing, *'Umwelt und Mentalität'* p. 16.
9. Ibid., p. 18.
10. K. Böck, *Das Bauernleben in den Werken bayrischer Barockprediger* (Munich, 1953), *passim*.
11. To some extent these more recent works develop an interpretation evident in earlier works, which emphasised the destabilising impact of early nineteenth-century administrative changes on contemporary Bavarian society; see A. Dimpfl, 'Der Einfluss der Bauernbefreiung in Bayern auf den landwirtschaftlichen Betrieb' (Dissertation, Munich, 1916), *passim*.
12. W.R. Lee, 'Bastardy and the Socioeconomic Structure of South Germany', *Journal of Interdisciplinary History*, Vol. 7 (1977), p. 403-25.
13. G. Helling, 'Berechnung eines Index der Agrarproduktion in Deutschland im 19.Jahrhundert', *Jahrbuch für Wirtschaftsgeschichte*, No. IV (1965), p. 118; W.R. Lee, 'Primary Sector Output and Mortality Changes in Early XIXth Century Bavaria', *The Journal of European Economic History (JEEH)*, Vol. 6, No. 1 (1977), pp. 136-8.
14. W.K. Blessing, 'Umwelt und Mentalität', p. 16.
15. J. Mooser, 'Gleichheit und Ungleichheit in der ländlichen Gemeinde. Sozialstruktur und Kommunalverfassung im östlichen Westfalen vom späten 18. bis in die Mitte des 19.Jahrhunderts', *Archiv für Sozialgeschichte*, Bd. XIX (1979), p. 260.
16. B. Goy, *Aufklärung und Volksfrömmigkeit in den Bistümern Würzburg und Bamberg* (Quellen und Forschungen zur Geschichte des Bistums und Hochstifts Würzburg, Bd. XXI, Würzburg, 1969), *passim*.
17. F.M. Phayer, *Religion und das Gewöhnliche Volk*, pp. 111, 255.
18. W.K. Blessing, 'Umwelt und Mentalität', p. 18.
19. W.K. Blessing, 'Staatsintegration als soziale Integration. Zur Entstehung einer bayerischen Gesellschaft im frühen 19. Jahrhundert', *Zeitschrift für Bayerische Landesgeschichte*, Vol. 41 (1978), p. 652.
20. Ibid., p. 681.
21. For further details of state activities in this field; see W.R. Lee, *Population Growth, Economic Development and Social Change in Bavaria, 1750-1850* (New York, 1977), pp. 79-88.
22. W.K. Blessing, 'Allgemeine Volksbildung und politische Indoktrination im Bayerischen Vormärz. Das Leitbild des Volkschullehrers als mentales Herrschaftsinstrument', *Zeitschrift für Bayerische Landesgeschichte* Vol. 37 (1974), p. 490.
23. E. Ebner, *Geschichte des Realschulwesens in Bayern, von 1774 bis 1883* (Munich, 1928), p. 7.
24. W.R. Lee, *Population Growth*, p. 342.
25. This was the case, both during the relatively liberal phase of educational reform under Armansperg, and in the years following 1832, when conservative policies were increasingly prominent; see J. Neukum, 'Die volksschulpolitischen Bestrebungen in Bayern 1818-1848. Ein Beitrag zur bayerischen Schulgeschichte' (Dissertation, Erlangen – Nürnberg, 1964), pp. 147-65.
26. W.K. Blessing, 'Allgemeine Volksbildung', p. 506.
27. W.D. Gruner, *Das Bayerische Heer 1825 bis 1864. Eine kritische Analyse der bewaffneten Macht Bayerns vom Regierungsantritt Ludwigs I. bis zum Vorabend des deutschen Krieges* (Boppard am Rhein, 1972), p. 363.
28. Anon. *Zwey wichtige Briefe von einem baierischen landbewohner an seinen Freund in München über den Krieg* (Munich, 1800), p. 7.
29. F.M. Phayer, *Religion und das Gewöhnliche Volk*, p. 175.
30. G.H. Elder, 'Family History and the Life Course', *Journal of Family*

History, Pt. 2 (1977), p. 279.

31.   T.K. Hareven, 'The History of the Family as an Interdisciplinary Field', *Journal of Interdisciplinary History*, Vol. 1 (1972), p. 411.

32.   G. Eley, 'Some Thoughts on the History of the Family and its Relation to the History of the Working Class' (Unpublished background paper written for the second meeting of the SSRC Research Seminar Group on Modern German Social History, 1979), p. 9.

33.   J. Schlumbohm, ' "Traditional" Collectivity and "Modern" Individuality: Some questions and Suggestions for the Historical Study of Socialization. The Examples of the German Lower and Upper Bourgeoisies around 1800', *Social History*, Vol. 5, Pt. 1 (1980), p. 72; D.C. Tipps, 'Modernisation Theory and the Study of National Societies: a Critical Perspective', *Comparative Studies in Society and History*, Vol. XV (1971), pp. 199-226.

34.   G.H. Elder, 'Family History', pp. 279-304.

35.   W.K. Blessing, 'Umwelt und Mentalität', p. 15.

36.   W.R. Lee, *Population Growth*, p. 12.

37.   P. Fried, 'Die Sozialentwicklung im Bauerntum und Landvolk', in M. Spindler (ed.), *Handbuch der Bayerischen Geschichte. Bd. IV. Das Neue Bayern, 1800-1970* (Munich, 1974), p. 757.

38.   J. Brückl, *Zolling. Aus Vergangenheit und Gegenwart*, Vol. II (Munich, 1968), pp. 358 *et seq.*; G. Hanke, 'Zur Sozialstruktur der ländlichen Siedlungen Altbayerns', *Festgabe K. Bosl zum 60.Geburtstag* (Munich, 1969), pp. 219-69; W.R. Lee, *Population Growth*, pp. 115-18.

39.   H.v. Haag, *Kurze Beschreibung der landwirtschaftlichen Verhältnissen in Bayern* (Munich, 1890), p. 10.

40.   P. Fried, 'Die Sozialentwicklung', p. 758.

41.   G. Wurzbacher and R. Pflaume, *Das Dorf im Spannungsfeld industrieller Entwicklung. Untersuchung an den 45 Dörfern und Weilern einer westdeutschen ländlichen Gemeinde* (Stuttgart, 1954), p. 113. This element of cooperation was also evident in many other areas of agricultural life, for example, in the skinning, cutting and drying of fruit; in the cutting of beans and cabbage, and in spinning and knitting during the autumn and winter evenings. It is also important to note that this degree of economic cooperation was most evident in the case of small-holders; see J. Mooser, 'Gleichheit und Ungleichheit', pp. 248-9.

42.   W.R. Lee, 'Primary Sector Output', pp. 133-62.

43.   J.-L. Flandrin, *Families in Former Times. Kinship, Household and Sexuality* (Cambridge, 1979), pp. 85-6.

44.   I. Weber-Kellermann, 'Die Familie auf dem Lande in der Zeit zwischen Bauernbefreiung und Industrialisierung', *Zeitschrift für Agrargeschichte und Agrarsoziologie*, 26. Jahrgang, Heft I, (1978), p. 69.

45.   D. Sabean, 'German Agrarian Institutions at the Beginning of the 16th century: Upper Swabia as an Example', *The Journal of Peasant Studies*, Vol. 3, Part I (1975), p. 79.

46.   K. Böck, *Das Bauernleben*, p. 32.

47.   P. Laslett and R. Wall (eds), *Household and Family in Past Time – Comparative Studies in the Size and Structure of the Domestic Group in England, France, Serbia, Japan and Colonial North America, with Further Material from Western Europe* (Cambridge, 1972), *passim*.

48.   J. Scheidl, 'Die Bevölkerungsentwicklung des altbayerischen Landgerichts Dachau im Laufe früherer Jahrhunderte. Ein kritischer Versuch', *Zeitschrift für Bayerische Landesgeschichte* (1930), p. 350.

49.   Staatsarchiv für Oberbayern (St.A.ObB.). Regierungs Akten (R.A.), 1104/15679.

50.   J. Hartwig 'Von Anerbenrecht im früheren lübeckischen Landgebiet',

Archiv für Bevölkerungswissenschaft und Bevölkerungspolitik (1941), p. 384.
51.   The general consensus was that the appropriate time for the devolution of a holding to take place was when the father had reached the age of 65 years; see J. Nussbaumer, 'Die Lebensverhältnisse der Bauernfamilien im Homburgertal' (ETH-Dissertation, Basel, 1963), p. 195.
52.   J. Pflaumer-Rosenberger, *Die Anerbensitte in Altbayern* (Munich, 1939), *passim*. According to the law of 1756, preference was to be shown for the eldest male child of a union.
53.   A.Frhr.v. Gügern, *Die Succession in Bauerngüter und landwirtschaftlicher Erbgüter nach den in Bayern geltenden Rechten* (Erlangen, 1891), p. 7. This legislation facilitated the creation of 'Fidei-Kommisse' on the part of the peasantry and was designed to limit any further subdivision of agricultural holdings.
54.   W.R. Lee, 'Primary Sector Output', pp. 133-62.
55.   I. Weber-Kellermann, 'Die Familie auf dem Lande', p. 72.
56.   In this sense there was a clear comparison to be drawn with the position of the capitalist in relation to his immediate employees; see C.C. Harris, *The Family* (London, 1969), p. 81: 'Control over the capital upon which the children depend gives senior [family] members the powers that the capitalist always has over the proletariat.'
57.   G. Lohmeier, *Bayerische Barockprediger* (Munich, 1961), *passim*; A. Hauser, 'Der Familienbetrieb in der schweizerischen Landwirtschaft. Eine historische und sozio-ökonomische Analyse', *Zeitschrift für Agrargeschichte und Agrarsoziologie*, Bd. 26, Heft 2 (1978), pp. 203 *et seq.*
58.   This was specifically the case, for example, in relation to small-holders (1/16) in the Pfarrei Allershausen in the period 1800 to 1849.
59.   K. Epstein, *The Genesis of German Conservatism* (Princeton, 1966), p. 229.
60.   F.F. Lipowski, *Darstellung des sozialen und wirtschaftlichen Volkslebens des königlichen bayerischen Landgerichtsbezirkes Moosburg* (Munich, 1861), p. 24. This picture confirms evidence from other parts of Western Europe. According to Planèse, for example, '. . . rough countrymen have for their womenfolk . . . profound disdain and despotic contempt' (cited in J.-L. Flandrin, *Families in Former Times*, p. 113). On the Thalhausen estate in Bavaria, Theresa Rieger was subjected to corporal punishment in 1791 for having cursed her husband in public on Easter Tuesday (St.A.ObB. Hofmark Thalhausen. No. 5, 20.3.1791).
61.   U. Planck, *Der Familienbetrieb* (Stuttgart, 1964), p. 163.
62.   A. Hauser, 'Der Familienbetrieb', p. 208.
63.   H. Scharnagl, 'Straussdorf, eine sozialökonomische und soziologische Untersuchung einer oberbayerischen Landgemeinde mit starkem Flüchtlingsanteil' (Dissertation, Erlangen, 1952), Anhang, Table 9a. In the areas around Giessen, for example, where the working day corresponded closely with that known to have been common in early nineteenth-century Bavaria, the wife on a peasant holding frequently worked on average 12.8 hours per day, although the upper level could often lie as high as 14.2 hours during the harvest period; see K.v. Dietze, M. Rolfes and G. Weippert, *Lebensverhältnisse in kleinbäuerlichen Dörfern* (Hamburg, 1952), p. 130. In agricultural areas of Switzerland, the woman was expected to work 15 hours per day even in the early twentieth century; see A. Dönz, 'Die Veränderung in der Berglandwirtschaft am Beispiel des Vorderpröttigaus' (ETH-Dissertation, Zurich, 1972), p. 126.
64.   G. Lammert, *Volksmedizin und medizinische Aberglaube in Bayern* (Würzburg, 1869), p. 103; H. Küstner, *Leitfaden der Berufskrankheiten der Frau* (Stuttgart, 1919), p. 90.
65.   In the village of Massenhausen (Upper Bavaria), for example, the

proportion of widows and widowers remarrying before the customary year of mourning had been honoured, rose from 65.2 per cent between 1750 and 1799, to 77.7 per cent between 1800 and 1849. This again reflected the economic importance of a marital partner, rather than the role of personal feelings of affection.

66.   J.v. Hazzi, *Statistische Aufschlüsse über das Herzogtum Baiern*, Bd. II (Munich, 1802), p. 111.

67.   Ibid., Bd. IV (Munich, 1804), p. 412.

68.   W.R. Lee, *Population Growth*, p. 283. However, the original choice of a christian name did frequently reflect the importance of family and kin connections. Certainly in other parts of Germany it was common practice for the eldest son to be baptised with the name of his father's grandfather, and the eldest daughter to receive the name of the father's grandmother; see P. Sartori, *Sitte und Brauch, Teil I: Die Hauptstufen des Menschendaseins* (Leipzig, 1910), pp. 39 *et seq.*

69.   W.R. Lee, *Population Growth*, p. 94. The overall rate of medical attendance in the eight parishes of the Hofmark Massenhausen stood at 8.4 per cent within the period 1800 to 1849. There is no evidence to suggest that this situation changed at all significantly in the course of the later nineteenth century. For the period 1888/9 in the 22 administrative districts of Bavaria, less than 7 per cent of all infants dying from weakness, atrophy or intestinal infection (which constituted 60 per cent of all registered infant deaths) received professional medical treatment prior to death.

70.   In the villages incorporated into the Massenhausen estate (Upper Bavaria) for the period 1750 to 1849, if two children were present at the time of a legal settlement, the right to remain on the family holding until 16 years of age was only accorded in 16.6 per cent of all the listed cases. If three children were present, the proportion accorded this right fell further to 14.2 per cent.

71.   M. Mitterauer and R. Siedler, *Vom Patriarchat zur Partnerschaft. Zum Strukturwandel der Familie* (Munich, 1977), p. 74.

72.   I. Weber-Kellermann, 'Die Familie auf dem Lande', p. 74. Although modern machines, such as the moulding-plough, sowing machines and the 'Exstirpator' had been in use in Bavaria in isolated cases as early as 1811, their general application in the country as a whole was severely retarded; see W.R. Lee, *Population Growth*, pp. 144-5.

73.   R. Engelsing, 'Dienstboten lektüre im 18. und 19. Jahrhundert in Deutschland', *International Review of Social History*, Vol. 13, Part 3 (1968), pp. 385-6.

74.   W.R. Lee, *Population Growth*, pp. 344-6.

75.   Ordinariats-Archiv Munich (O.A.M.). Pfarrei Jarzt, Visitation Protokol of 1813. Pfarrei Massenhausen, Visitation Protokol of 1838.

76.   W.K. Blessing, 'The Cult of the Monarchy in Imperial Germany', *Journal of Contemporary History*, Vol. 13 (1978), p. 361.

77.   One cannot, as in the case of certain areas in late nineteenth-century Russia, speak of the existence of a 'young intellectual stratum' among the peasantry, which was able to initiate and to demand changes in the family and in family life; see P.I. Kushner (ed.), *The Village of Viriatino. An Ethnographic Study of a Russian Village from before the Revolution to the Present* (American edn., New York, 1970), p. 261.

78.   Provisions for a wedding invariably included quantities of bread, beer and brandy, together with suitable wedding clothes which reflected the social status of the family involved.

79.   This was the case, for example, with the sick daughter of the Gaus holding (1/8) in the village of Jarzt (Landgericht Freising). St.A.ObB. Brief

Protokolle. 1238/171.
    80.   M. Mitterauer and R. Siedler, 'The Developmental Process of Domestic Groups: Problems of Reconstruction and Possibilities of Interpretation', *Journal of Family History*, Vol. 4 (1979), p. 267.
    81.   W.R. Lee, 'Medicalisation and Mortality Trends in early 19th century Bavaria' in A.E. Imhof (ed.), *Mensch und Gesundheit in der Geschichte* (Berlin, 1980).
    82.   *Aerztliches Intelligenz-Blatt*, Vol. 4 (Munich, 1857), pp. 450-1.
    83.   E. Litwak and I. Szelenyi, 'Primary Group Structures and their Function: Kin Neighbor and Friends', *American Sociological Review*, No. 4 (1969), p. 467.
    84.   E. Bott, *Family and Social Network* (London, 1968), p. 122. Other factors of importance in this context are the type of genealogical relationship; the presence of 'connecting relatives' and the conscious and unconscious needs and attitudes of the group.
    85.   R. Wheaton, 'Family and Kinship in Western Europe: the Problem of the Joint-Family Household', *Journal of Interdisciplinary History*, Vol. 5 (1975), p. 623.
    86.   M. Mitterauer and R. Siedler, 'The Developmental Process of Domestic Groups', p. 263.
    87.   W.R. Lee, *Population Growth*, p. 197. In the first half of the nineteenth century family loans still accounted for just over one third of all those recorded in the Hypotheken-bücher of the estates of Massenhausen and Thalhausen.
    88.   A. Birlinger and M.R. Buck, *Sagen, Märchen, Volksaberglauben* (Volksthümliches aus Schwaben, Bd. I, Freiburg im Breisgau, 1861), p. 320.
    89.   In the course of the period 1750 to 1850, 13 of the 36 holdings in the village of Massenhausen (Landgericht Freising) were at some time involved in internal marriages. 11.5 per cent of all marriages contracted in the neighbouring village of Hetzenhausen also involved both marriage partners coming from holdings in the villages. Furthermore the fact that marriage partners were by and large selected from the same social stratum in rural society, both before and after 1800, would have reinforced the general quality of kinship contacts; see E. Bott, *Family and Social Network*, p. 122.
    90.   H.M. Bahr, 'The Kinship Role', in F.I. Nye (ed.), *Role Structure and Analysis of the Family* (London, 1976), p. 196.
    91.   A. Birlinger and M.R. Buck, *Sagen, Märchen, Volksaberglauben*, p. 335.
    92.   *Regierungs- Blatt* (Munich, 1821).
    93.   Pfarr-Archiv (Pf.A.) Fürholzen. Familienbuch Gross Eisenbach. Haus No. 4. The name of the Prunner family can also be found in 25 separate settlements and the various branches of the Gratzl family can be traced in a further 26 local villages, including 9 settlements within one fairly small estate: see Pf.A. Fürholzen. Familienbuch Gross Eisenbach, Haus No. 4; Familienbuch Hetzenhausen, Haus No. 6; K. and G. Seitz, *Heimat und Ahnenerbe* (Freising, 1927), p. 38.
    94.   M.B. Sussman and L.G. Burchinal, 'Kin Family Network: Unheralded Structure in Current Conceptualization of Family Functioning', in B. Farber (ed.), *Kinship and Family Organization* (New York, 1966), pp. 125 *et seq*. Evidence of the continuing importance of kin support for lower-class families in the industrial period would seem to indicate that the legislative reforms of the early nineteenth century within the context of an agrarian society would not have exercised a markedly disruptive role.
    95.   J.M. Phayer, *Sexual Liberation and Religion*, pp. 24-5; J. Mooser, 'Gleichheit und Ungleichheit', p. 253.
    96.   K. Blaschke, 'Vom Dorf zur Landgemeinde. Struktur- und Begriffswandel zwischen Agrar- und Industriegesellschaft', in H. Haushofer and

118   *Family and 'Modernisation'*

W.A. Boelcke (eds.), *Wege und Forschungen der Agrargeschichte* (Frankfurt am Main, 1967), p. 238.

97.   C.J. Calhoun, 'Community: Toward a Variable Conceptualization for Comparative Research', *Social History*, Vol. 5/1 (1980), pp. 105-29. This process, in turn, it could be argued reflected the general disintegration of European villages as centres of community life and community control: see J. Blum, 'The European Village as Community: Origins and Function', *Agricultural History* (1971), pp. 162 *et seq.*; W.K. Blessing, 'Staatsintegration', p. 671.

98.   *Regierungs-Blatt* (Munich, 1808), pp. 2, 790: Organisches Edikt über die Bildung der Gemeinden (28.7.1808).

99.   J.C. Fick, *Leitfaden der Statistik des Königreichs Bayern* (Erlangen, 1811), p. 97. Each Gemeinde was to contain not less than 50 families or 250 individuals.

100.   W. Stengel, 'Stand der Archivpflege in der Oberpfalz', *Mitteilungen für die landschaftliche Archivpflege* (1941), p. 6.

101.   J.D. Photiadis and R.A. Ball, 'Patterns of Change in Rural Normative Structures', *Rural Sociology*, Vol. 41/1 (1976), pp. 62-3.

102.   For further coverage of the role of the Gemeinde in these three specific areas; see Ordinariats-Archiv Munich (OAM), Wippenhausen Visitation, 1821, where the local priest in Wippenhausen claimed that one of the main reasons for the decline in contemporary morality was that illegitimacy within the parish boundaries went unpunished by the lay authorities. For the role of the Gemeinde in the spheres of midwifery reform and the promotion of improved educational facilities; see W.R. Lee, *Population Growth*, pp. 89, 347.

103.   Initial encouragement of fallow cultivation through enclosure had been evident in the legislation of 1762 and 1772. However it was not until the Montgelas era that enclosure became fairly common in Bavaria, when within the period 1799 to 1805 a total of 49,963 Tagwerke of fallow land was brought under cultivation. However many communities encountered difficulties in implementing local enclosures and the scale of radical change in this area must not be exaggerated. Even towards the end of the nineteenth century, Bavaria remained behind other areas of Germany in the cultivation of fallow, particularly in contrast to other regions of Germany specialising in grain production. In 1873 the proportion of uncultivated fallow still stood at 13.94 per cent in Upper Bavaria, in contrast to 8.96 per cent in Prussia, 8.9 per cent in Brandenburg, 3.5 per cent in Silesia, 5.7 per cent in Saxony and 2.7 per cent in Hanover; see A. Mucke, 'Umgang des Getreidebaus in Deutschland', *Zeitschrift des kgl. Preussischen Statistischen Bureaus*, Jhg. 22 (1882), pp. 47-8; A. Kalchgruber, *Untersuchungen über landwirtschaftliche speziell bäuerliche Verhältnisse in Altbaiern* (Munich, 1885), p. 37.

104.   K.-S. Kramer, *Grundriss einer rechtlichen Volkskunde* (Göttingen, 1974), p. 82.

105.   J. Mooser, 'Gleichheit und Ungleichheit', p. 247.

106.   P. Sartori, *Sitte und Brauch*, pp. 175-6.

107.   A. Birlinger and M.R. Buch, *Sagen, Märchen, Volksaberglauben*, p. 316.

108.   W.R. Lee, *Population Growth*, p. 280.

109.   In certain communities women celebrated their own feast day; see A. Becker, 'Frauenrecht in Brauch und Sitte', *Hessische Blätter für Volkskunde*, Vol. 10 (1911), pp. 145 *et seq.*

110.   R.L. Warren, 'Toward a Reformulation of Community Theory', *Human Organisation*, Vol. XV, No. 2 (1956); R.M. French, *The Community. A Comparative Perspective* (Illinois, 1969), p. 233.

111.   J. Scott and L.A. Tilly, 'Women's Work and the Family in Nineteenth-

Century Europe', *Comparative Studies in Society and History*, Vol. 17 (1975), pp. 36-64.
112. J.M. Phayer, *Sexual Liberation and Religion*, p. 55.
113. G. Eley, 'Some Thoughts on the History of the Family and its Relation to the History of the Working Class' (Unpubl. Ms., 1979), p. 3.
114. R. Wheaton, 'Family and Kinship in Western Europe: The Problem of the Joint Family Household', *Journal of Interdisciplinary History*, Vol. 4 (1975), pp. 601-28.
115. W.K. Blessing, 'Staatsintegration', p. 649; J. Mooser, 'Gleichheit und Ungleichheit', p. 254.
116. T.K. Hareven and M.A. Vinovskis (eds.), *Family and Population in Nineteenth-Century America* (Princeton, 1978), p. 19.
117. P. Fried, 'Reagrarisierung in Südbayern seit dem 19.Jahrhundert', in H. Kellenbenz (ed.), *Agrarisches Nebengewerbe und Formen der Reagrarisierung im Spätmittelalter und 19/20.Jahrhundert* (Forschungen zur Sozial-und Wirtschaftsgeschichte, Bd. 21, Stuttgart, 1975), pp. 177-94.
118. W.R. Lee, *Population Growth*, pp. 294-7.
119. J. Obelkevich, *Religion and Rural Society: South Lindsey 1825-1875* (Oxford, 1976), p. 279.
120. B. Goy, *Aufklärung und Volksfrömmigkeit in den Bistümern Würzburg und Bamberg* (Quellen und Forschungen zur Geschichte des Bistums und Hochstifts Würzburg, Bd. XXI, Würzburg, 1969), *passim*.
121. V.Y. McLaughlin, 'Patterns of Work and Family Organization: Buffalo's Italians', *Journal of Interdisciplinary History*, Vol. 2, No. 2 (1971), pp. 299-313.
122. M. Mitterauer, 'Familienformen und Illegitimität in ländlichen Gebieten Oesterreichs', *Archiv für Sozialgeschichte*, Bd. XIX (1979), pp. 123-88.
123. This was equally the case in such parts of England as South Lancashire, the West Riding of Yorkshire and the Black Country in the period of early industrialisation; see E.P. Thompson, *The Making of the English Working Class* (London, 1963), p. 446.
124. G. Stedman Jones, 'Class Expression versus Social Control? A Critique of Recent Trends in the Social History of "Leisure" ', *History Workshop*, No. 4 (1977), pp. 167-8.

4 FAMILY AND HOUSEHOLD: SOCIAL STRUCTURES IN A GERMAN VILLAGE BETWEEN THE TWO WORLD WARS

Gerhard Wilke and Kurt Wagner

I

The concept of the family is a relatively new one. Otto Brunner, for example, has argued that in the German context people began to use the term in the eighteenth century. Previously, concepts such as *das ganze Haus* ('the whole house') and 'household' were common usage,[1] indicating that family structures are not fixed entities but are subject to historical change. This applies both to reality and to the definition which we as social scientists use to describe this reality. It follows that we must look at the family historically and get away from assumptions about 'typical' structures for particular countries and forms of society. The form and structure of a family in a society cannot be separated from the way in which its members earn their living, or from their position in the production process. We cannot assume that a certain family type is characteristic for an entire society, as has been done by both functionalist and Marxist sociologists. We must differentiate between the different sections of the population. This means, logically, that several forms of family can coexist within a society at any given stage of development.

Peter Laslett[2] and Michael Mitterauer's[3] studies, using positivist methods, have cast doubt on the 'myth' of the large and extended pre-industrial family. But as their work remains at the level of statistical analysis, they are compelled to accept the classifications of their sources as the 'objective' reflection of reality. This seems to us a doubtful method. It limits their findings to a description of the external and formalistic features of families which provides no insight into the inner dynamics of the family or its significance to individual family members. Mitterauer himself is aware of the inadequacy of the statistical categories of his sources and points out that it is fairly meaningless to accept their definition of maids and farm labourers as 'alien to the family' (*familienfremd*).[4] But his own redefinition remains confined to the statistical categories and fails to describe their social content. By adhering to a strictly positivist approach he prevents himself from speculating on the quality and significance of these

relationships within the household. Yet it is only by getting away from
a narrowly-conceived notion of objectivity and adopting the methods of
social anthropologists and oral historians that students of the social
history of this century at least will be able to gain better insights into
family life. These in turn will allow them to draw inferences about
earlier forms of family organisation. By looking at the family within the
context of social divisions and interrelationships within a German
village our study will try to determine both the external structure of the
'family' (number of generations, children, etc.) and its internal structure
(material basis and social coherence, relationships between people,
between the group and individuals, and between the 'family' and
society as a whole).

Our starting-point is not a set of abstract theoretical assumptions but
the concrete analysis of household structures in a village in northern
Hesse over a given period of time. Our study, which incorporates such
statistical material as exists, is based primarily on 'participant
observation' and 'open interviews'.[5] The findings should not be seen as
generally valid, permanent descriptions of the internal and external
features of household life; they represent working hypotheses, an
impressionist painting, as it were. This is inevitable in a microscopic
study of this nature. The village in question, called Körle, lies in the
valley of the River Fulda in northern Hesse, about 20 kilometres south
of Kassel. It is first mentioned in a document of 1047 in connection
with the transformation of an endowment into a monastery holding
land within the boundaries of the village. Its location and structure are
basically determined by the topographical features – hilly land, and the
River Fulda, which flows past the village. Körle was built on a slope of
land which was safe from flooding, but of little agricultural value. The
agricultural areas connected with the village have always stretched
along the valley floor and across the plateau which rises gently to the
east of the village. Nowadays, large new developments, which clearly
show the growth and transformation of the village, extend to the north,
south and east of the historical centre, which consists of a number of
half-timbered farmhouses clustered around the church. In the four
years from 1971 to 1974, 128 building plots were sold here, mainly to
outsiders attracted by the low price of land and the easy
communications with Kassel.

Built on the main historical trade route of the region – the
Nürnberger Landstrasse – the village enjoyed early links with the
outside world and the regional market centres of Melsungen, Kassel,
Rotenburg and Hersfeld. Communications were greatly improved by

the construction of the railway in 1848 and the opening of a local station in 1892. Politically and administratively the village belonged to the electoral Duchy of Hesse until this was annexed to Prussia in 1866. In 1822 Duke William of Hesse had undertaken a major administrative reform of his duchy, amalgamating rural offices into larger units or *Landkreise*. Until the early 1970s, Körle was an independent parish within the district of Melsungen. In 1971, several surrounding villages were incorporated to form the present amalgamated parish of Körle, with a population in 1973 of 2,336 people.[6]

Nowadays, the village is a place of residence for families whose livelihood depends on industries, craft businesses and administrative posts in and around the village. It is not a rural village in the sense of being primarily a farming community, but neither is it completely urbanised, even though there are only nine full-time farmers left. Today the village is undergoing rapid social and economic transformation. At the centre of this process is the 'local god', the Volkswagen motor-car company. The effects of industrialisation were already noticeable in the 1920s and 1930s, but the pace was slower. In many ways one could describe these years as the second stage in the social transformation of the village. The initial phase, when the majority of the inhabitants became less and less capable of living off the land, was over by the end of the First World War. After that, things could never be the same. Although farming had ceased to be a way of life for most villagers during the Weimar years, it still formed the basis of their self-perception. Despite constant changes in day-to-day living, social status and the villagers' relationship to the outside world, people tried to maintain the village ideals against social division and political difference. Rural identity was married to urban jobs. Over time, however, the marriage ultimately revealed itself to be an uneasy one.

The household is at the centre of any change and a cornerstone of village ideology in a fundamental sense. The protection which it can offer its members is, of course, limited, and must depend on external conditions. Urbanisation got under way much later in Germany than in England, which meant that for many of the villagers the impact of social change was muted. By the time they had to start looking for industrial employment in any numbers, there was already a railway to take them to work. Although the villagers had initially been bewildered by the monstrous 'iron devils' and shocked by the morals of the navvies who built them, the railway did allow them to stay in the place of their ancestors. Unlike many other places, Körle did not significantly suffer from emigration to the city, or across the ocean (*Landflucht*).

Its population, standing at 595 in 1864, had risen to 619 by 1895 and 1,034 by 1939. It rose again very rapidly after the Second World War, when the village was forced to accommodate a relatively large number of refugees from the eastern provinces as well as people evacuated from Germany's bombed-out cities. In 1952 Körle contained 300 refugees and 50 evacuees, mainly from Kassel,[7] people whose integration posed problems.

Throughout the period covered by our research the agrarian economy remained of decisive importance for all villagers, with the exception of one single household. It was basic to this economy that in spite of the progressive industrialisation of society at large, no separation arose between people's residence and their place of work. More and more villagers were drawn into industrial work, but they continued to live as members of the large family household that characterised the village community. The reasons were economic: the industrial wage was held to be inadequate, and self-sufficiency in food produced on one's own land or through odd jobs (*Nebenerwerb*) associated with farming was regarded as vital for survival. This way of life remains important, for even these days there is no division into place of residence and place of production on the surviving farms, whose mode of production continues to depend on the household and not on purely capitalist principles of production.[8] It follows that we must take as our starting-point not the rural family but the 'whole house'[9] as developed by Brunner. We shall try to reconstruct its basic features for the period studied.

Although we assume that some structural elements of household organisation refer to every group of *Bauern* (farmers or peasants), we believe it is necessary to differentiate according to the material and social situation of the individual households. The term *Bauer* is itself too general to be useful, and we have to look more closely into the social stratification of the village and the way this is reflected in the size of households, their division of labour and the relationships between them. While the very process of farming forced every household to use a certain amount of additional labour on a seasonal basis which would have no direct connection with the household, the quantity of land owned by a household does appear to have been *the* decisive factor in determining a villager's status. The owner of 'a lot of' land could remain a full-time professional farmer, employing permanent or seasonal labour. The owner of 'less' land had to supplement their farming income with *Nebenerwerb* (odd jobs). The owner of *ein Fetzen Land*, 'a small patch', had to hire himself out for wage labour and supplement this with some additional provisions produced by farming. These distinctions were reflected in village consciousness and terminology: the inhabitants were divided into horse-farmers (*Pferdebauern*), cow-farmers (*Kuhbauern*) and goat-farmers (*Ziegenbauern*).[10]

The horse-farmers were the full-time professional farmers of whom there were 14 in Körle in 1928. They owned on average between 10 and 30 hectares,[11] producing mainly for the market. Horse-farmers employed maids (*Mägde*) and farmhands (*Knechte*), who were regarded as part of the household. Besides these full-time hands, each of these farms had its so-called *Arbeitsleute*, members of poorer families who would 'help out' at certain times. These *Arbeitsleute*, while vital for every large farm before the introduction of mechanisation, in no way counted as part of the household. They were casual labourers, people from other households. It was common for one household to provide *Arbeitsleute* for a better-off household for several generations. Strong relations of dependence and loyalty developed between these families and their particular horse-farmer. It was common, for instance, for horse-farmers to act as god-parents to members of these families. Although the relations between the horse-farmer and his *Arbeitsleute* was based on unequal distribution of power, the power of the horse-farmer was not entirely arbitrary: attempts to exploit his superior position unduly would meet with censure in the form of malicious gossip or other kinds of ridicule. The horse-farmer was expected to provide his *Arbeitsleute* with some security and certain services; only if both parties kept their side of the bargain could the continuance of the relationship be guaranteed. Villagers accepted as natural the unequal distribution of property and the resulting division of power, and all of them were expected to cooperate to maintain existing social relations and make the best of the situation. In fact the *Arbeitsleute* relationship, based on mutual dependency, allowed the poorer and largest section of the population to stay on in the village rather than have to leave for the city, and on this basis the village community was able to survive. The exception among the larger farms was the mill at the edge of the village, with 47 hectares of land. This was sold to the German State Railway in 1928, who then engaged an estate manager. On this 'estate' capitalist labour relations were dominant. Wage labourers were employed who did not belong to the household and who went home after work at night and came to work from home in the mornings. But these labourers also owned their 'patch of land' and worked as *Arbeitsleute* for one of the other horse-farmers.

In 1928 there were 66 cow-farmer households in the village with an average of between 2 and 10 hectares of land, most of them farming less than 5 hectares.[12] Four of these were full-time farms in 1928, none by 1941. Only one of these households employed a maid; the others depended for their labour force largely on their own relatives. At certain times, such as the harvest, households from this group would cooperate and sometimes even employ members of goat-farmer households, who would be paid in kind. The direct neighbourhood generally formed the basis for such cooperation. The male members of cow-farmer households were generally 'independent' or 'dependent' artisans, i.e. they were basically engaged in occupations that remained part of the agricultural sector. By 1928, however, there were already several who worked as skilled labourers or white-collar workers for industry or the State. A very small number worked full-time in town, cut off during the day from their home base. While we cannot determine precisely how much these households produced for the market, there is no doubt that they regularly supplied the regional markets with foodstuffs including butter, eggs and poultry. At irregular intervals they would sell grain and livestock, especially calves and pigs, to local butchers and dealers.

There were 80 goat-farmer households in 1928, owning an average of less than two hectares, the majority owning less than one hectare.[13] These small-holders would supplement their insufficient holding by additionally renting communal or Church land and by using the herbage growing on river banks, field paths and railway embankments. Although the goat-farmer could generally cultivate his small garden without outside help, he depended on the horse-farmer for the draught animals needed to cultivate his 'patch'. In return the goat-farmer household put the labour of its members at the disposal of the horse-farmer, i.e. it entered an *Arbeitsleute* relationship. Apart from the loan of draught animals, the agricultural work of the goat-farmer household was performed by household members. Already by the 1920s the industrial wage had become the basic income source of these households, but this was supplemented in a variety of ways, with agriculture continuing to provide the household with most of its foodstuffs. In the 1920s only the men took up factory work, while female household members worked on farms in the village or nearby. From the mid-1930s the daughters began to join their fathers and brothers in the factory and the office. But whereas the men endeavoured to obtain a profession, the women worked as unskilled hands, expecting to give up work after marriage.

We can take it that during the time covered by our study all the villagers assumed that farming would continue to form the basis of their livelihood. The central factor in every villager's life was the ownership of land. A villager was what he owned in the shape of material goods (house and land); those who had little were deemed to be of little importance. This is clearly expressed in the three categories of horse-farmer, cow-farmer and goat-farmer and the hierarchical position ascribed to each of these in the village order. Membership of these three categories of farmer not only gave concrete information about the amount of land and livestock owned by a household, but also about its status in the social structure. Property, especially in land, was an integral part of one's consciousness and personality structure. A man without property was accordingly an 'imperfect person' and could hardly expect to be recognised as a person in his own right. The only exceptions were the priest and the teacher, both of whom counted socially with the horse-farmers.

What was on the one hand the natural basis of agricultural production found its natural expression in the social system and became part and parcel of the individual's psychological make-up. It was however not property as such which determined the social structure, but the knowledge that the individual was prepared to use this property in the interest of all the household members dependent on it. No less important than the ownership of land was the labour which a household invested in its cultivation, the harvest that was produced, and the way this would be distributed. It was taken for granted that household members would behave according to accepted village norms, and any household tolerating deviant behaviour among its members lost respect in the village. Both the household and the village as a whole therefore exerted considerable pressure to prevent this happening. The survival of the whole system depended on the effective socialisation of individual household members, as did its ability to provide security for all those who sustained it.

Land was not just part of the physical environment but the very basis of village cosmology. Only when someone owned land and could depend for its cultivation on the support of the members of his household would 'The Lord' prove kind in the hour of need. Security and protection were not automatically associated with State welfare or Christian charity but with cultivating one's holding. Land was seen as an insurance policy. In the days before mechanisation it could only be farmed successfully if you could rely on the cooperation of others. The household or 'whole house' was the ideal vehicle for ensuring this.

Only given this cooperation could the household survive over a number of generations and secure its members a definite place in the village. This was of course the ideal at a time when the village was in some sense for its inhabitants the world. If immobile land was the basis of life then the people living off it had to stay put. Only more recently did people begin to perceive these relationships as binding and possibly oppressive. In the 1920s and 1930s respect for land and for the household and its name was still held to be the very basis for self-determination. Land and household were, then in other words, inseparable and characterised life in a fundamental way between the two world wars and this was reinforced by the industrial insecurity which followed in the wake of both German defeats.

II

Having tried to outline the material basis of village social structure, we shall now attempt an analysis of the various types of household according to their specific groupings. First, it should be stressed that the concept of the 'nuclear family' appears to be inapplicable to village realities between the wars. Even now, in 1980, it fails to describe social relationships in the village, especially where households continue to depend on agricultural production for their main or secondary income. It follows from this, therefore, that since we can assume the unity of place of production (work) and residence (home) for the period under review, it seems useful to base our analysis on the concept of the 'whole house' or 'household' rather than that of the family. While blood relationship is an essential feature of demarcation between households, it is not the only one. Equally important in determining who is to be regarded as a household member is the principle of communal work; by virtue of his work a person can be a household member, with definite rights and duties, without being related to its head. Only in the matter of the inheritance will blood relatives invariably have the absolute advantage. It is therefore important to distinguish between a household's external structure and its internal structure.

By external structure we mean those household features which are visible to the outside world: the number of generations and number of children; which members are related by blood and which are not; the average size of the household. This is the reality reflected in the statistical sources, and, on this level, the family has often been analysed by social researchers. By internal structure we mean the social structure of the whole household: the division of labour and role distribution; the relationship between individuals; the various levels of authority structure; the relationship between the household and other households and the village as a whole. This inner structure forms the main object of our research.

In 1928 the entire village consisted of 161 households, only one of which was not in some way integrated within the agrarian economy.[14] The average household, according to official records, numbered six people, a figure which is extremely misleading in terms of the number of people accepted as forming one 'household' or 'whole house'.[15] The official records give the impression of isolated, closed-off families, leaving out of account the manifold relationships in life and work extending beyond their confines. This definition draws artificial boundaries between the various households and in so doing distorts the inner household structure and its social dynamics, which are made to appear static and in need of no further investigation. The households which we looked at were complex formations, the everyday life of which cannot be seen in isolation from that of other households in the village. They could maintain their economy only by constant cooperation with other households. Everyday situations such as the preparation of meals reflected this reality: it was taken for granted that others beyond the immediate household might share in the meal. At times of marriage or death, household members could be certain that members of other households, neighbours, relatives, work partners and friends would know their part and play it accordingly. This was of great importance in the socialisation process. 'Bonding' relationships were formed not only with one's physical parents and nearest blood relatives, but with a great many people who played a role in the day-to-day life of the household.

These relationships did not of course operate in a moral vacuum. During the 1920s and 1930s, events and actions were still under the influence of taboos which compelled households to cooperate with others. During pregnancy a woman was subject to certain taboos. She was in general not allowed to perform any 'heavy work', lift heavy objects, hang up washing or walk underneath a washing line. Nor might she do any work associated with food preparation. Such jobs had to be carried out by other women of the household or women from other households. These practices clarify and define the nature of social relationships and cosmological principles. Pregnancy is not a normal condition; it puts out of action normal modes of behaviour and work.[16] Such changes in behaviour were endorsed by the threat of retribution and misfortune for those who failed to observe the rules. If a woman worked too hard, this would have repercussions on her health and that of her child. In case of sickness the diagnosis would involve a review of past behaviour. If a pregnant woman walked under a washing line, her unborn child ran the risk of being strangled by the umbilical cord. If a husband hit his pregnant wife, the child would develop a birthmark where the mother had been hit. While pregnancy entitled the woman to special protection, it also made her a potential source of pollution, as is for instance indicated by the rule preventing her from helping in food preparation. These rules served a double function. They tied the person concerned (e.g. the pregnant woman) into the social process and made her dependent on others who would now undertake her normal tasks, and they forced the others to fulfil a social role since they in turn might find themselves in a similar situation and in need of similar support. Thus the village social system was stabilised through mutual obligations.[17]

Child-birth was exclusively the woman's sphere. Preparing for it and helping with the birth itself was the task of the older and more experienced women in the household. A village woman who had shown particular skill in aiding child-birth would also be consulted and called in in cases of emergency. At the end of the 1920s the parish paid for a woman to attend a midwifery course and she became the village midwife. Throughout, child-birth continued to be the woman's business from which men were excluded. Infant care, again, was the woman's sphere, although not exclusively that of the young mother, who after a fortnight's rest in bed would quickly be reintegrated into the household working process. Often it was the grandmother, mother-in-law, some aunt or maid who would look after the infant, which was not allowed to be taken out of doors until it was baptised. Male household members played almost no role during the first years of a child's life. As soon as children were able to walk, their socialisation became an integral part of the everyday life of the household. At first watching and imitating their elders in play, the children soon became actively involved in the household working process. Only now did children begin to form close relationships with the men of the household. Childhood as we know it did not exist. Children went to school on six days a week from 8 till 1. Before they could do their homework certain household tasks were allocated to them which had to be completed before the day was over. If they found time to play as well, all the better, but the concept of play was unimportant. The nature of children's work and their spare time varied depending on the

seasons and the habits of their household, except the sons of some of
the horse-farmers, who attended the grammar school in town and were
given time off to do their homework. These boys were thus less tied
into the household working process than their sisters or the children of
the cow- and goat-farmers.

Children did not regard work as drudgery; it was part of their life.
Through practice and imitation they learned the ways of their elders,
tapping their greater store of knowledge and experience. Their work
was important to the household and no less respected than that of
adults. It was taken for granted that children would help with all the
work, the girls and boys automatically being socialised into different
tasks and skills. The girls' world centred on the house and garden, the
boys' on the fields and stables. On Saturday afternoons the girls would
clean the house, the boys sweep the yard and road. Boys minded the
grazing cattle, girls the chicken and geese. The livestock was classified
into house animals and field animals; cows were primarily draught
animals, geese provided both meat and down for bedding. Where a
household owned a great many geese, these were entrusted to the
village gooseherd – a figure who survived until the early 1950s. Pigs too
were herded professionally until the end of the First World War. Where
a boy or girl showed certain talents these would be encouraged within
the limits of the prescribed sex roles. A girl would be allowed to knit
rather than sew, a boy to chop wood rather than make ropes.

Apart from tasks assigned according to sex there were a great many
which needed everyone's help. Until they took up full-time employment,
all the children had to weed root crops, glean fields, clear the ploughed
fields of stones, plant and harvest potatoes, make hay, fetch grass,
help thresh and act as messengers. During summer and autumn the
children would collect mushrooms and berries which the unmarried
aunts generally took to the market in Kassel. This type of economic
activity was particularly important for the goat-farmers and their
households, though some of the cow-farmers shared in it as well. One
very poor household used to take along its best story-teller to distract
the others while his own family went on picking undisturbed. Also of
importance was the annual collection of herbs for teas and medicinal
purposes which would be supervised by grandmothers or aunts who also
administered the medicines. School-leavers went once a week on foot
to the house of the pastor, six kilometres away, for religious
instruction. Church attendance was compulsory during this two-year
period, and boys and girls had to help in the upkeep of the church and
its rituals. Failure to attend service or disobedience to the pastor usually

resulted in a hiding administered by him.

Thus the object of socialisation within the context of the household was not the development of individualism or of individual needs but an individual's integration into the household, which could only survive if every individual submitted his personality and labour power without reserve. All thought and action was based on the maintenance of the household over and above the needs and inclinations of any of its members. Everything people did had implications for and reflected on the whole household. A child's naughtiness reflected on the adults' inability to raise it properly. The whole household was obliged to repay debts in case of neglect, illness or death. Each household in the village had its own status and moral reputation and people were often concerned primarily with the reputation of 'the house' rather than with the personal behaviour of individual members. Although there was room for individualistic behaviour the household was expected to contain it. Most houses and the people living in them were associated by name and reputation with households who had lived in them generations before the present occupants.

Work was organised on the principle of division of labour according to sex roles. Male and female tasks were further subdivided by age and ability. The male ideology prescribed that men undertook the *heavy* and women the *lighter* work. Men would perform all the tasks associated with the draught animals including ploughing, harrowing, sowing, loading and unloading produce. They also took care of the raising and training of these animals. A horse-farmer would see to everything connected with the horses belonging to this household. Among cow-farmers the work would be divided: while the work with the draught animals and their training was the province of the men, both men and women shared in the care and milking of the cows. Sometimes a woman showed special skill in handling cows for field work, and she would usually earn the title of *Mannsweib* ('man-woman') from her admiring male fellow villagers. More and more women were forced into this role during the war and it became common among war widows after 1945. In the goat-farmer households both sexes saw to the animals; only the rabbits remained a male preserve. Planning the annual field work and deciding which crops were to be raised where was the responsibility of the head of the house, especially among the horse-farmers. Among the cow-and goat-farmers the responsibility for final decisions still rested with the household head, but these were generally arrived at after lengthy discussions among all the members, with the women taking active part. Since in these households the men would generally be working away from home for given periods as labourers or artisans, their women enjoyed greater independence and a greater say than in the horse-farmer households.

Although farming the land was man's work, before mechanisation none of the agricultural work could be carried out without the help of the women and children. In the grain harvest the men would cut the grain while the women took it up, tied it in sheaves and stacked these with the help of the children. In the potato harvest the men dug up the potatoes, while the women put them into baskets which the children emptied into sacks that were loaded on wagons and taken to the farm by another group of men. This work could only be performed if each household could rely on help from other households in the village. Cow-and goat-farmers would help each other. Work on a horse-farm was performed by the household with the help of the *Arbeitsleute* families associated with it, and the horse-farmer in turn would help cultivate the 'patch' belonging to his *Arbeitsleute* by loaning them his draught teams.

The household itself was the centre of the woman's work. This included the house, the garden and the poultry – spheres where the woman enjoyed more or less autonomous authority. The takings from the produce of this sphere such as butter, eggs, poultry, fruit, vegetables, mushrooms, herbs and berries which were sold in the market formed an important part of the household income, and this was mainly at the disposal of the woman. Here again there were important differences between the three types of household. While the horse-farmer had a *Hauskasse* (house money chest) which was controlled by the *Frau* (the wife of the head of the household) and a *Vieh- und Getreidekasse* (livestock and grain chest) controlled by the *Häre* (head of the household), among the cow-farmers the line was drawn more between the income from farming and the income from industrial or craft work, and whereas the former was largely controlled by the woman, the latter appears to have been mostly in the man's hands. Only the goat-farmer households appear to have had no such divisions, since they normally had a cash income only from industrial work and this, according to our informants, was generally paid into the house money chest under the direct control of the woman. None of these divisions is however to be seen as absolute, and the boundaries between the respective household managements are likely to have been fairly variable and fluid.

Typical woman's work included cooking, infant care, gardening, cleaning the house, washing, mending sacks and everything connected with the care of clothing. The laundry was done once a fortnight, ironing was practically unknown. Linen was bleached in the sun, then carefully folded by the girls. Grandmothers were almost constantly knitting, mending and sewing, although during summer only the most urgent repairs would be undertaken. In winter these occupations filled the long evenings and to break their monotony the women of the neighbourhood would gather together in one house and talk while working. These *Spinnstuben* (spinning bees) were of great importance for the survival of the oral culture of the village. The stables formed another important area of work, where again the women had their special tasks. They fed the pigs and sometimes mucked out. They fed and milked the cows and looked after the young animals. When milking machines were first introduced milking for a time became the exclusive province of the men on the assumption that women could not handle machinery. The horse-farmer households employed full-time maids and farmhands who had their own specific tasks allocated to them, mostly in accordance with the division of labour according to sex. The labourers, as is to be expected, were mainly under the control of the head of the household, the maids of the mistress.

Mechanisation brought extensive changes in this division of labour, especially in the horse-farmer households. Women from the 1920s and 1930s were increasingly pushed out of the field work and relegated to the house and to some extent the stables. The number of people working in these households fell, with the maids being the first to go. Apart from this, another additional factor which influenced the organisation and division of labour in the various households during our period was the growing integration of the men – and from the 1920s the daughters – of the cow- and goat-farmer households in the industrial working process. The absence during the daytime of the men forced the women to undertake some of the field work which had previously been mostly a male province. This meant an increase in the women's workload and their sphere of responsibility and an increase in the workload of the children.

The whole system of the household was embodied by the old people who symbolised its rationale. The old people held on to the control of the household as long as they could, and when they eventually became incapable of running it they would dictate the conditions under which the heir took charge. With age they would no longer be able to perform certain tasks, but as long as they could be up and about, the old people remained part of the working process of the household. The older men

(*Opas*) worked mainly in the farmyard and the stables, doing the lighter repairs, chopping wood, preparing the feed, seeing to the fruit trees and the breeding of the animals. With more time on their hands they grew more involved in raising and training the boys. Grandmothers too spent more time caring for the children and in particular instructing girls in certain household tasks. They sewed, knitted, mended and embroidered, looked after the poultry and the garden. With the help of the children the grandmothers in many households would gather and prepare the herbs and herbal teas for the medicine chest. Where the grandmother lived in the house she usually became the household doctor, although this role might be taken by some younger woman or even a neighbour who showed special skill. These women, thanks to their skill in producing and applying medicines, were sometimes credited with the ability to cause sickness in man and animal, and many households banned elderly village women not connected with them from entering their stables. Women who were reputed to be witches might enter neither the house nor stables and this often led to total social isolation.

Every activity within the household and the village had a 'moral' significance. Sickness was not just something that befell one. Concepts like chance or fate were used, but they were invariably amended by the additional query: 'Why did I of all people, or a member of my own household, fall sick? Why not my neighbour, with equal chances of succumbing?' The answer to these questions could be found in an analysis and evaluation of the behaviour of the household concerned – a review that would cover no less than three generations.[18] Illness was an acute threat to the work organisation and livelihood of the entire household and was seen as a punishment. These notions were not confined to interpretations of sickness or accident but were a central part of village cosmology; they formed the background for the division of authority within the household and were a vital part of the socialisation process which tied the individual household members to the acceptable behavioural norms. Failure to observe these norms threatened the household of non-observers with retribution. Not surprisingly these potential sanctions were often actively reinforced. Where a son failed to observe the agreed contract after taking over the farm and household from his parents, the parents could only get their own back by bringing the matter before the village (*ins Dorf bringen*) in the form of malicious gossip – or by placing a curse on their own household. Their house would then 'have a curse on it' (*der Fluch lag auf dem Hause*). Malicious gossip and putting curses on people were tools of social control that could be remarkably effective within a small close-knit community. In 1921 a man predicted that his brother's unborn children would develop a stammer should the brother fail to fulfil his obligations. The brother did, and three out of his four children came to develop a stammer. The sins of the fathers were visited upon the sons.

III

In looking at the household organisation we have to consider the relationships within a given household as well as those between the household and the village as a whole. Both sets of relationship served a multiplicity of functions and were charged with an equally complex set of meanings. A change in the use of space inside a house would usually accompany a redefinition of social relationships. A house was more than just a building: it reflected principles of social organisation and a particular household's way of life. The transition from one social category to another – heir-apparent to owner – involved a 'territorial passage' within the house.[19] The structure of the division of authority and the concomitant allocation of living space within the house in fact became most evident when the farm was handed over to the younger generation. Handing over the house and land was the physical expression of the transfer of authority from the older to the younger generation, involving both the man's and the woman's sphere of work. The male heir now took over not only the formal control of the household but also its representation in the village community and *vis-à-vis* the official authorities. The change was indicated by a redistribution of rooms inside the house. The new head and his wife took over the so-called *Wohnzimmer* (living-room), while the older generation moved to some other room or to the upper floor. This functioned mostly also as a workroom in the daytime and/or bedroom at night. Some of the younger children in these households would generally sleep in the parents' bedroom so that the younger generation had to be allocated the largest room. This living-room had a special status: it was 'properly' decorated and had 'proper' floor covering and visitors would be received in it. Among the horse-farmers the living-room was used purely for receiving guests during summer, in winter it was the place where the women mended the potato and grain sacks. The bedrooms of the maids and farmhands were on the upper floor or right above the stables.

The redistribution of rooms reflected the structure of authority within the household but this did not mean that the older generation — or the female members — had simply to submit to the new household head. The young *Frau*, the wife of the new head of the household, now enjoyed autonomous authority, but since the mother, mother-in-law and other female relatives continued to work in the household she could not exercise this dictatorially. Since decisions concerning the household overlapped with those connected with the general running of the farm, the women appear in general to have been consulted about them. Handing over the farm did not entail a total loss of power for the older generation; the contract of transfer regulated the rights they retained and provided for their material security. None the less the former head of household in particular suffered a grave loss in authority and influence and this often caused serious conflict. Accustomed to making decisions largely on his own, the father had to accept that his son now enjoyed the same authority and often had no intention of consulting him at all.

Problems were likely to arise where the new head had totally different ideas from his father about how to run the farm, especially with regard to investment and mechanisation. Such problems were aggravated where the father had previously controlled the son's behaviour by threatening him with disinheritance. This threat, now no longer a reality, would often still be remembered and held against the father. Since handing over the farm meant a considerable loss of prestige and authority for the former head in both the household and the village, the father would generally try to delay this as long as possible. Often the heir was himself long married, with children growing up, and this led to friction. In these conflicts, the village generally sided with the younger generation. The old man, it was argued, could no longer carry out the necessary work but still wanted to retain his power when his son, by hard work, ability and a 'sensible marriage', had proved his right to run the farm. The village believed that the older generation must hand over to the physically stronger younger one if the household were to function properly. In reality as well as ideologically this was a patriarchal society, with the household head taking the leading role. Women were excluded from public life as late as the 1920s, taking no part in local club life or in Church administration. It was a society where the father was regarded as the ultimate authority in disciplining children: the threat of punishment from him generally led to obedience and submission.

Marriage brought full adult status. During the 1920s and 1930s marriages between horse-farmer households were invariably arranged.

The matchmaker was usually a cattle-dealer or a grain-dealer —
someone who got around in the district and was familiar with the
financial and social situation of the various farms with sons and
daughters of marriagable age. The heads of households would be put
in touch in order to discuss a possible liaison between the households,
a process in which the reputation of the respective households and
young people as well as the size of the dowry and inheritance were
of paramount importance. The household of the future bride would try
to reassure itself by personal inspection that the household their
daughter was marrying into answered their notions of material security,
status and prestige, and that their daughter would be decently treated.
The parents of the heir would assure themselves that the dowry was
adequate and that the future daughter-in-law would be a hard-working,
able-bodied asset to the household and likely to produce a healthy heir.
The marriage arrangements therefore did not correspond to bourgeois
notions but represented in fact a contract between the two households.
Material factors were to the fore, with the participants assuming that
love and affection would automatically arise at some future date.[20]
The marriage broker attached importance to the ultimate success of a
match arranged by him: his name as matchmaker (*Frechesmann*) and
able businessman was at stake. The marriage patterns of the horse-
farmers included what one might call a straight exchange (*Tauschheirat*).
The heir of the one household would marry a girl from another, with
his sister marrying the corresponding heir. Both households gained
since neither had to pay out a dowry.

Marriage across the social boundary between goat- and cow-farmers
was permitted but not between either of these and horse-farmers. Social
conventions reflected these rules. If a horse-farmer's daughter was
asked to dance by a labourer or by a young man from a cow- or
goat-farmer household he had to be ritually refused. Since parents
would accompany their daughters to every dance until they became
engaged this convention was difficult to break. The first marriage across
this boundary took place in 1949 and led to the virtual enslavement of
the labourer's son. These days a horse-farmer's son may call himself
lucky to get anyone's daughter to marry him and undertake the onerous
burdens of a farmer's wife. Love-matches were more common among
cow-farmers, although where the parents objected to a proposed
daughter-in-law the marriage was unlikely to take place. These farmers
too were anxious to find able-bodied girls who would 'bring in
something' as well. While the cow-farmer was anxious not to sink to the
level of a goat-farmer through some careless marriage, for children from

a goat-farmer household marriage with a member of a cow-farmer household offered the only hope of mobility within the village. Marriage was altogether too serious a matter to be left to the decision of the couple concerned. The hard material core of marriage is very much to the fore in village anecdote and ideology. A horse-farmer, asked why during the period under review not a single marriage took place between a horse-farmer and a girl from a cow- or goat-farmer household, offered the following explanation: 'Women from cow-farmer households were too slow to be of use on the larger farms. They were so used to the slow trot of the cattle that they just couldn't keep up with our pace.'[21] The story illustrates the function of marriage in maintaining social differentiation and in tying both the partners not only to each other but to each other's households, something that applied especially to the woman who in all but a few instances moved into her husband's household.

The life of the daughter-in-law was often not an easy one, and she might be treated like a maid until she had proved, by her housekeeping abilities and the production of an heir, that she was not just 'good for nothing'. On the rare occasion where a man married into the woman's household, he too had to prove himself before the household ceased treating him as a labourer. A person who married into a horse-farmer or cow-farmer household was integrated into that household, and any cooperation beyond its confines would be voluntary. On the other hand, marriage into a goat-farmer household meant saddling oneself with a great many obligations extending over several households, because of the *Arbeitsleute* relationship described above, and the daughter-in-law was naturally expected to contribute to this relationship. She would, besides, retain links with her parents' household, which continued to expect certain services from her. The social behaviour of the horse-farmers was determined by the desire to maintain their tradition, ideology and position of power. Almost all the cow- and goat-farmer households suffered from relative or absolute poverty and this created a need for social control to ensure the continuation of the household and a degree of social security for its members. From our own vantage-point of a more secure way of life, this behaviour appears semi-feudal, since individual household members were allowed no opportunity for individual development or freedom of choice. To the people of the time, such thinking would have been alien, preoccupied as they were with everyday needs.

In the horse-farmer households, the choice of life-partners was formally arranged. But where might the marriageable sons and daughters from cow- and goat-farmer households meet their partner? In the 1920s, women attended few public functions. The village clubs held their annual dance, where young people might get together under the watchful eye of the other household members. In November a three-day harvest festival (*Kirmes*) took place, organised by young villagers of both sexes. Relatives and friends from neighbouring villages would be invited and bring along their older children, staying over to attend the dances and celebrations. The young villagers in their turn attended the harvest festival in other villages.[22] There could be problems when a stranger from another village asked a local girl to dance. Ritual quarrels and fights could follow where the stranger would then show his mettle. After leaving school, girls from the goat- and cow-farmer households would generally work on some farm in a nearby village or go into service in town, and they then often married in their place of work. Young villagers similarly often married girls from outside who worked on farms in the village. There were other occasions for young people to meet: the Sunday sports event, followed perhaps by a stroll; Sunday service; the summer evening's saunter up and down the village street. All such meetings took place in public: social control was vital and choosing one's partner for life a public process.

Equally important were the winter *Spinnstuben* (spinning bees) held nightly from November until the end of February, as well as certain agricultural activities involving a large number of helpers. In the spinning bees, women from the various households of a neighbourhood met together to knit or mend socks and sacks, and the older women would retire early, leaving the girls who now admitted the village boys. Although the spinning bees had an intimate air, various ritual censures in the form of pranks (*Streiche*) were played upon the pair that attempted to withdraw unduly from public view.[23] Young people might also meet at the various household feasts held to celebrate important occasions. One of the functions of these was to confirm publicly the cooperation between certain households, which would invite each other and exchange minor gifts. The feasts also confirmed the persistence and relevance to all concerned of traditional values and customs. Hospitality symbolised a household's readiness to give to others what it could spare commensurate with its status. Someone who gained the reputation of being mean and stingy suffered an automatic loss of status, and people would 'speak ill' of the household concerned.

Among the horse-farmers, the 'official' inauguration of a relationship between two young people brought into play a set of rules and regulations which those involved could scarcely escape. There was strong public pressure to complete in the prescribed manner what had been begun, and engagement and marriage would generally soon follow. Among the cow- and goat-farmers, too, the young people were put under pressure to get engaged once they were frequently seen together in public. The young man would visit the girl's house, to show the seriousness of his intentions. Engagement and marriage logically followed. If for some reason marriage did not take place, lifelong enmities between the households were not uncommon. The engagement was celebrated on a Friday evening in the bride's house with only the parents, brothers, sisters and closest friends and relatives invited. The engagement gave the young people the opportunity of getting to know each other and each other's households. It was a time of testing: the would-be bride and bridegroom had to demonstrate their ability to work and their skills as well as moral self-restraint. Where an intended partner failed to carry out certain of the expected tasks the other partner's household was given a chance of preventing the proposed marriage. The requirement of sexual continence could be ambivalent, for while it was morally reprehensible for a girl to become pregnant before marriage, such pregnancy also proved her fertility and ability to carry on the line.

The engagement symbolised the passage from youth to adulthood. Social anthropologists have shown that such celebrations often delineate and clarify social and ideological frontiers.[24] The *Polterabend* ('racket evening', a part of the engagement celebrations) symbolised liberation from the circle of close friends and from village youth as such. Youth was left behind and a new stage – adulthood – entered upon. The celebrations took place in the house of the bride. The village youth met outside the house, equipped with whips and glass objects which would be smashed against the house steps to the accompaniment of the cracking of the whips. Thus a line was drawn between the two social groups – those inside and those outside the house. Only the bride and bridegroom might remove the broken glass; if anyone else from the household or any of their old friends helped them it meant bad luck for the entire household. After smashing the glass outside the house, the village youth would sing a number of woeful songs on the passing of youth and its beauty and the meaning of true friendship lost. The bridegroom would then give the group money to be spent at one of the inns. After drawing this symbolic line, the new adults and their guests withdrew into the house, while their former companions celebrated in the place proper to them – the village inn. This ritual demonstrated the difference between the private sphere of the household and public village life. In the private sphere of the household one could only play an important part as an adult. This was demonstrated symbolically by the bridegroom giving money to his former companions. His first act as an adult was to buy himself out – an act which helped his former companions to drown their sorrow at the loss of a friend in the manner appropriate to village youth. The pastor fixed the wedding date and called the banns. In theory objections might be raised although this seems never to have been done, and the two households drew up their guest lists. The ceremony itself took place at noon on a Sunday at the village church, and the festivities which followed in the bride's house extended over several days. The family, neighbours and members of households with whom one had an *Arbeitsleute* relationship celebrated all day and night, slept it off, and continued celebrating the following day.

These village customs are still in part observed, but they are neither timeless nor unchanging. Passed on as part of the socialisation process, their content is subject to general social change and individual interpretation. The funeral rituals are of interest in this respect. Until the 1920s, villagers were buried in a uniform black shroud, which would be ready long before a person's death. *Totenfrauen*, women from households which specialised in this task, came to the house to wash and dress the body. From the early 1920s a gravedigger replaced these women. It now became customary to bury the men in suits and the women in dresses – generally their wedding clothes. Throughout, funerals remained of great social significance, both for the household and for the village. Neighbours and relatives would help and the members of the household had to observe certain taboos. The number of people taking part in a funeral was a measure of the social status of a person and his household. Funerals moreover offered households an opportunity of 'burying' old hatchets and offering the younger generation a fresh start. By refusing to take part in a funeral one showed one's unwillingness to forget a quarrel – which would then probably carry on for at least another generation.

IV

The founding of a branch of the Nazi Party in the village and the subsequent domination of village politics by representatives of the National Socialist State led to important changes in the village household as regards authority structure and the position of women and children. An examination of these changes casts an unexpected light on the effects of Hitler's 'Third Reich' on German rural society. To begin with, the Nazi takeover fundamentally altered the relationship between father and son. Most of the older horse- and cow-farmers were opposed to Nazism, as were the older goat-farmers. It was the younger generation which became active in the movement, especially in the more authoritarian horse- and cow-farmer households. After the Nazi seizure of power the sons carried their new-found self-confidence into every aspect of village life. Villagers say that this period meant 'war' in every household. Belonging to Nazi organisations strengthened the position of the sons against the head of the household. Loyalty to the various organisations and the State could be set against loyalty to one's household. The household ceased to be the chief focus for the thoughts and actions of its members. The village ideal of working in a community with a tight authority structure was projected on to a 'higher' level, and for many villagers their party organisation took over the function of the household, the nation or State that of the village community. For the deeply committed Nazi villager the *Führer* became the superhuman household head. The values and ideals of village society and the village household were not called into question but in fact became a central feature of Nazi ideology, as is apparent in Nazi concepts such as *Gemeinschaft* (community), *Volk* (people) and *Führer* (leader). This more than anything else perhaps explains the smooth transition to the Third Reich and the successful organisation of large sections of the village within the Nazi state. Basically villagers shared the same concepts of the world, only on another level. If the traditional household heads may have laughed at the political arrogance of the younger generation, they accepted it, for anything else would have meant total conflict within each household, an unacceptable solution. While conflicts were thus very real and brought irrevocable changes, the household structure remained intact.

During the Third Reich the household lost its dominant role in the rearing and training of the children. The school came to serve an even more ideological function. The Hitler Youth conveyed ideals that extended beyond the terms of reference of the village and the household and took up time the children had previously spent working for the household. The younger men were conscripted into labour service or the army where they were exposed to a considerable process of re-education. Again it is worth noting that these obligations were frequently justified in the same terms as those of the traditional household. What mattered in both cases was working for the group, and not the individual's free choice. In both cases the subjection to strict authority structures and the lack of opportunity for individual development were justified by the claim that 'everyone's welfare was at stake'.

The 1930s also saw changes in the role and socialisation of women. The Nazi women's organisations for the first time gave women a chance of entering public life in the village and in the region at large. The National Socialist Organisation of Women (*Frauenschaft*) and the League of German Girls (BdM) allowed women and girls to travel beyond the narrow village confines and brought them into contact with women from other villages and regions and – most important – from other social groups. Women became part of the public life of the National Socialist State and from now on they could form village associations. But as these were part of authoritarian structures with a patriarchal ideology and patriarchal patterns of behaviour they largely failed to bring about the emancipation of women within the household. Before the Third Reich women bore children and worked for the household. Now they bore children, laboured for the household and for the *Führer*. Within the household changes were superficial. Nazi organisations circulated cookery books among other things, and these brought about certain changes in eating habits. Military and labour service helped to relax marriage patterns. While most people still married in the traditional manner, relationships might now be formed with people from other parts of Germany, some of which led to marriage after the war.

The growing demand for workers in industry and the reduced demand for women in agriculture due to increasing mechanisation caused more and more girls during the 1930s to enter industry and offices after leaving school. Before 1934 none of the girls who left school had taken an apprenticeship or learned a profession; after 1935 this occasionally happened. This had a number of positive effects on the household. The girls no longer went to live and work in another household. Because they worked away from home in the daytime while continuing to live at home, they could help in the household after finishing their own job. They now earned an industrial wage, almost all of which was paid into the household fund. This meant a considerable rise in household living standards. The absence of the men during the war greatly enhanced the woman's role and influence. Women now acted as household heads and did work which had been reserved for men, although sometimes the older men remained formal heads of household.

But if this proved a positive experience for the women, it produced no lasting changes. At the end of the war the households resumed their old authority patterns except in instances where the family head failed to return from the war.[25] Only the great expansion of economic opportunity from the 1950s onwards brought fundamental changes in the position of the women. In the horse-farmer households, where the men were not conscripted but allowed to carry on the management of these economically more important farms, the women's position hardly changed.

Different factors determined the development of the horse-farmer household. Here the place of residence and place of work remained the same and the only change was in the composition of the household which employed fewer and fewer labourers from the 1930s and no more maids. The inner structure of these households remained largely untouched and even these days it would be true to say that the surviving horse-farmers have largely resisted capitalist penetration. The organisation and inner structure of these households continues to function according to the principles outlined above. The production process is still based on the household, not on capitalist technology and organisation. It does not, however, follow that the farmers therefore constitute backward and traditionalist groups who by refusing 'to modernise' provide proof for the thesis that 'consciousness' is an independent variable in the process of social change.

Although the villagers' consciousness is of significance, it can only be assessed in connection with the material basis of their life. It is here that social scientists have jumped to premature conclusions. The introduction of the capitalist mode of production does not 'automatically' give rise to capitalist social structures throughout, as is evident from the survival of these rural households. We believe that the farms which have so far resisted structural change will continue to function as households and form the basis of agricultural production in the village. This contradicts Heidi Rosenbaum's thesis,[26] which links the capitalist penetration of agriculture with the gradual disappearance of the rural family farm. While the volume she has edited represents an important advance in family history and family sociology, it is plain that where the 'modern' rural household is concerned she still puts theoretical speculation before research into concrete situations in all their variety.

What we have tried to describe should not be taken as a static portrait of an unchanging rural household. We do not see this form of the household as a relic of the pre-capitalist era, but as the specific reaction of one particular village society, within commuting distance of a town, to industrialisation. Its form of organisation reflects the material basis of life of household members within a developing industrial society; it also shows how integration into the industrial process becomes part of the individual's consciousness.

V

We have tried to show that the concept of the nuclear or small family does not apply to the social reality of the village in the 1920s and 1930s and is an unsatisfactory tool for analysing its structures, which are better seen in terms of the concept of the 'whole house' or 'household'. Any adequate analysis must, we feel, go beyond the external structure, since only the study of the inner structures can provide insights into the possible functions, modes of production and life-styles of these households. It follows that the empirical analysis of the historical process must accompany any definition of social institutions. Works on the family appear often to adopt a different procedure.

Despite the growing integration of villages into the industrial world, the significance of landed property, family and the household did not decline in the period under review. Their importance in fact increased as household members became increasingly aware of the instabilities of the industrial labour market. This applies especially to the 1920s and again to the period of the Second World War. It is worth noting that only some members of a household would be drawn into the industrial process, and that the income they gained would, in their view, never have sufficed to maintain the household. For some of these members there was a separation between residence and place of work, but the result normally posited in sociological writing – the development of something in the nature of the bourgeois family – did not follow. Household members continued to work in their own household after the end of their industrial working day, and, what is more important, they derived their identity as villagers from this sphere. This explains why, in the 1920s, there was no development of a consciousness of independent wage or salary earners, free to dispose of their own wage. The industrial wage remained only one of several incomes contributing to the upkeep of the whole household. Here we must concede these villagers their own 'rationality', regardless of any theoretical concepts, rather than automatically considering their behaviour as irrational. On the whole, therefore, while it is difficult to generalise from a limited case-study, our findings appear to confirm E.P. Thompson's thesis that industrialisation means different things to people in various social groups and occupations, and that their adaptation to industrialisation implies the formation of different ways of life.[27]

Finally we should like to repeat that the villagers in the 1920s and 1930s saw themselves as a village community composed of households which could not have survived in this form without mutual cooperation. This community in no way resembled the nostalgic village idyll: it was a strictly hierarchical social order with tight authority structures and strong social compulsions. These structures derived from the widespread poverty of most of the households, and villagers saw in mutual cooperation within a hierarchically ordered world a precious and necessary safeguard against their poverty. The hierarchical social order was closely associated with control over the land and the household, which often became a source of numerous conflicts within households and between them. These conflicts would always be contained in order to prevent any real threat to the social order as a whole.

Socialisation within village society did not give rise to a uniform character type. The external compulsion of poverty which determined everyday life and the attempts to come to terms with this by securing the greatest possible variety of additional 'incomes' for the household bred highly individual personalities (*Originale*). The very nature of the village community and the household organisation which we have outlined consisted of such contradictions or contrasts; those involved in them did not regard these as contradictory, but as natural.

Notes

This essay is a revised and extended version of a paper delivered to the first meeting of the SSRC Research Seminar Group on Modern German Social History, held at the University of East Anglia in July 1978. It has been translated from the German by Carla Wartenberg.

1.   Otto Brunner, 'Das "Ganze Haus" und die alteuropäische Ökonomik', in Otto Brunner, *Neue Wege der Verfassungs- und Sozialgeschichte* (2nd edn., Göttingen, 1968).

2.   Peter Laslett, 'Size and Structure of the Households in England over Three Centuries: Mean Household Size in England since the Sixteenth Century', *Population Studies*, 23 (1969), pp. 199-223.

3.   M. Mitterauer, R. Sieder, *Vom Patriarchat zur Partnerschaft. Zum Strukturwandel der Familie* (Munich, 1977).

4.   Ibid., pp. 38-65.

5.   For a more detailed discussion of the possibilities offered by oral

history see Paul Thompson, *The Voice of the Past. Oral History* (Oxford, 1978).
6.   *Einwohnerstatistik, Gemeindeverwaltung Körle.*
7.   Ibid.
8.   For a conventional analysis in terms of the 'nuclear family', see Edward Shorter, *The Making of the Modern Family* (London, 1975).
9.   Brunner, 'Das "Ganze Haus" '.
10.   *Kuhbauer:* the locals used their cows for ploughing as well as for milking and breeding. More generally for similar findings, see Albert Ilien, Utz Jeggle, *Leben auf dem Dorfe. Zur Sozialgeschichte des Dorfes und Sozialpsychologie seiner Bewohner* (Opladen, 1978).
11.   *Preussische Viezählungsliste, Gemeindeverwaltung Körle.*
12.   Ibid.
13.   Ibid.
14.   *Vorratsermittlung des Staates Preussen, Gemeindeverwaltung Körle.*
15.   The records in the *Bürgermeisteramt* list the various generations in each household as separate entities. According to our informants they did not constitute self-contained units, and the figures create a false impression.
16.   For an original discussion of the concept of 'taboo', see Edmund Leach, *Culture and Communication: the Logic by which Symbols are Connected. An Introduction to the Use of Structuralist Analysis in Social Anthropology* (Cambridge, 1976).
17.   For a more detailed discussion of the cohesive effect of social obligations, see Marcel Mauss, *The Gift: Forms and Functions of Exchange in Archaic Societies* (London, 1970).
18.   Social anthropologists have studied comparable 'cosmological' systems all over the world. See Max Marwick (ed.), *Witchcraft and Sorcery* (Harmondsworth, 1970).
19.   For a discussion of inheritance and relationships within families and households, see also Sigrid Khera, 'An Austrian Peasant Village under Rural Industrialization', *Behavioural Science*, Vol. VII, pp. 129-36.
20.   For similar examples from France, see Shorter, *Making of the Modern Family.*
21.   Interview with a *Pferdebauer*, 1978.
22.   These *Kirmesen* were held on alternate weekends between the end of July and the last weekend before Advent in the various villages of the area.
23.   The connections between 'joking relationships' and social order are discussed in A.R. Radcliffe-Brown, 'On Joking Relationships', *Africa*, 13 (1940), pp. 195-210.
24.   For a more detailed account, see A.van Gennep, *The Rites of Passage* (London, 1960) and Leach, *Culture and Communication.*
25.   This post-war phenomenon is discussed in Samuel Harvey Franklin, *Rural Societies* (London, 1971).
26.   Introduction to Heidi Rosenbaum, *Seminar: Familie und Gesellschaftsstruktur* (Frankfurt am Main, 1978).
27.   E.P. Thompson, *The Making of the English Working Class* (Harmondsworth, 1968).

5 WOMEN, FAMILY AND DEATH: EXCESS MORTALITY OF WOMEN IN CHILD-BEARING AGE IN FOUR COMMUNITIES IN NINETEENTH-CENTURY GERMANY

Arthur E. Imhof

I

As everyone knows, the sex-specific differences in mortality and susceptibility to illness of the population constitute pressing and consequential problems. Women become ill more often than men and are thus a much greater burden on the medical welfare system of a country; but they (therefore?) live longer. According to the computations of the Federal Office of Statistics in Wiesbaden, girls born in West Germany in 1975-7 could expect to live 75.2 years; boys, on the other hand, only 68.6 years.[1] The life-span of women is one-tenth longer than that of men. Or in other words: for a woman every tenth year — at least in comparison to a man's life-span — is extra, is a gift — whether a welcome one or not is of course another question.

One need consult only some of the relevant statistics for the last decade in the Federal Republic of Germany to get a picture of the higher susceptibility to illness among women. For instance, in 1972/3, 73 of every 100 women (above 14 years of age) consulted a physician in the course of a quarter year; on the other hand, only 59 of 100 men.[2] A poll taken in 1970 showed that 38 per cent of the women polled had already received in-patient treatment at a hospital at least twice, whereas this applied to only 23 per cent of the men. As a rule, the same illnesses lasted several days longer for women than for men.[3] In another poll in 1973, 48 per cent of men characterised their state of health as 'good or very good'; only 40 per cent of women said the same. On the other hand, 20 per cent of the women questioned considered their health to be 'poor or bad', whereas only 15 per cent of their male counterparts were of the same opinion.[4] In 1974 in the Federal Republic, 711 men but 1,011 women per 10,000 inhabitants were considered chronically ill — a state of affairs that cannot be attributed merely to the higher average age of the female population. For both the age brackets 15 to 40 and 40 to 65 the percentages of chronically ill women are greater than those of men of the same age.[5]

None the less, whether we consider the sex-specific mortality rates of infants, children, adolescents, those in their so-called best years, or the aged, the mortality rates for women in all age brackets are lower than those for men. Only a few generations ago this was *not* the case. We need only go back to our grandparents to find the vestiges of an apparently century-old, quite different pattern of mortality for the two sexes. Even as late as the 1920s and 1930s we find a stubborn excess mortality in two age groups: in early adolescence, especially between the ages of 10 and 15 and among women in their more advanced reproductive phase. Within the German borders of 1920, 70 deaths per 10,000 women between the ages of 30 and 35 were registered, as opposed to 63 per 10,000 men (in 1969 the ratio was 9 women to 18 men). For the age group 35 to 40 the relation was similar – 72 to 65 (today, 15 to 25).[6] If we go back another half-century in history to the decade 1871-80, we find not only that the death figures are in general higher, but also that they are higher for women than for men of the same age. Among 10,000 30-year-old women there were 97 deaths per year; among men of the same age only 93. And as for adolescents – here for instance, aged 15 – the figures were 42 to 39 per 10,000, to the disadvantage of the girls.[7]

On the whole, the historical phenomenon of excess female mortality in particular age groups can be verified quite well on the basis of available data – at least in the final phase after the introduction of official statistics. Since a number of researchers have dealt with this question in recent years, it is no longer completely unknown in the literature.[8]

II

It seems appropriate in the context of the present volume to concentrate our attention on one of the two above-mentioned age groups with excess female mortality. We have chosen adult women in their reproductive years. Moreover, both theoretical and methodological considerations suggest that we limit the study to the sex-specific mortality of married persons. Thus the method of family reconstitution, on which historical demographic analyses are based, will allow us at any time to use an equal number of male partners as the basis of comparison for excess female mortality. We have studied 1,869 first marriages contracted in four different German communities between 1780 and 1899. The most important results are summarised in

Tables 5.2 to 5.6 (see below, pp. 159, 162–8); they are presented in histogram form in Figures 5.1-5.4.

Figure 5.1: Excess Female Mortality in Philippsburg 1780-1899

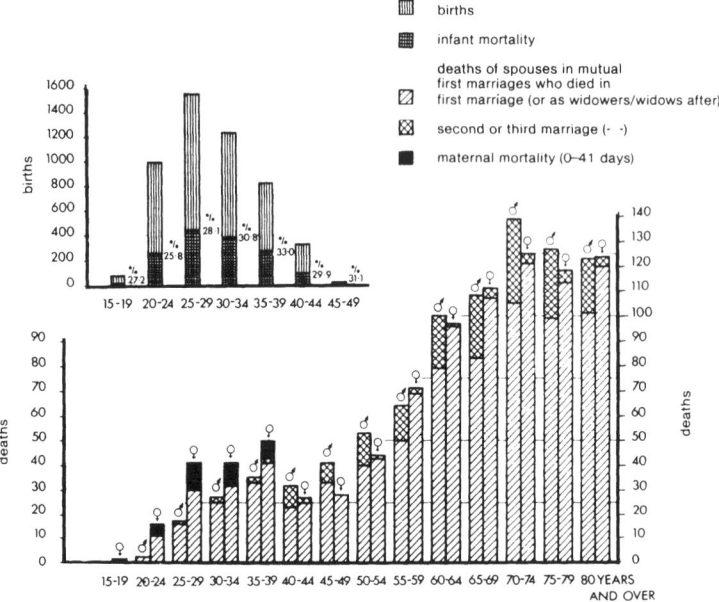

Figure 5.2: Excess Female Mortality in Altdorf 1780-1899

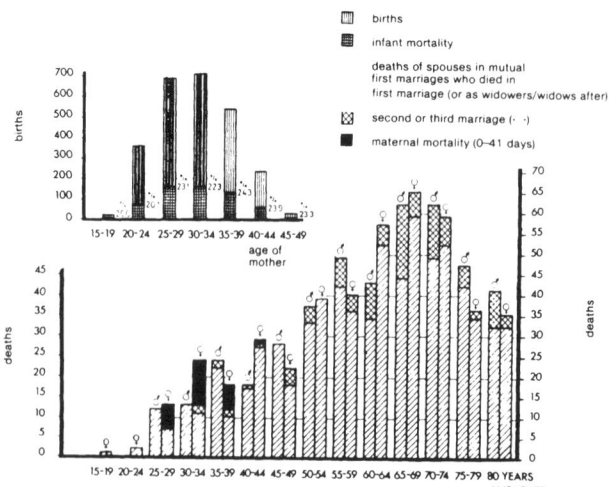

Figure 5.3: Excess Female Mortality in Gabelbach 1780–1899

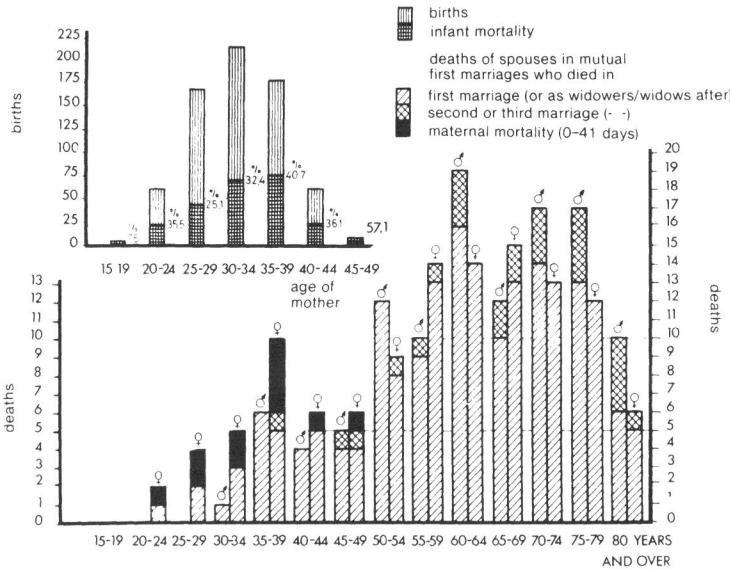

Figure 5.4: Excess Female Mortality in Hesel 1780-1899

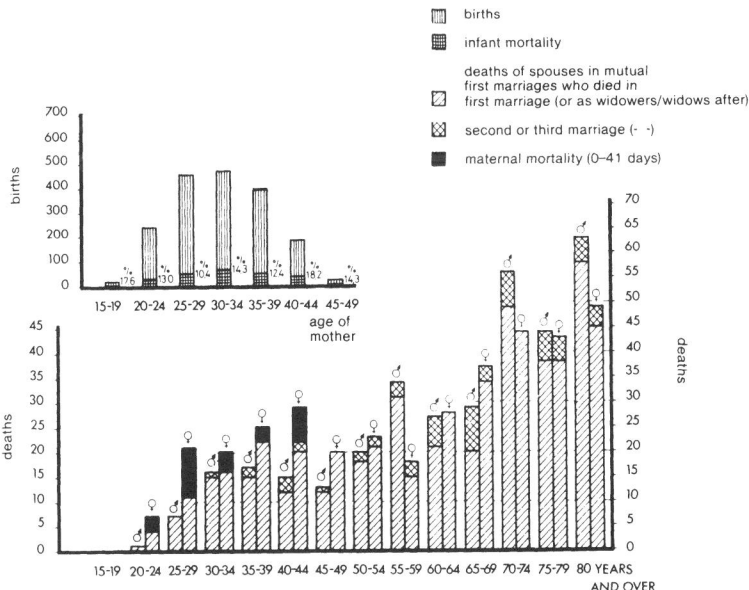

Whenever excess mortality is ascertained for groups of women in their reproductive years (that is, between the ages of 15 and 49), one tends at first to explain the phenomenon with a supposedly extraordinarily high mortality rate of mothers in child-birth. This is however clearly a preconception, which is apparently shared by most of our contemporaries concerning whole generations of mothers in past centuries. For even a casual glance at Figures 5.1 to 5.4 is enough to establish that this argument alone cannot by a long shot explain the indisputable fact of excess mortality among women in child-bearing years. This very common argument deals with only one element of an obviously much more complicated state of affairs. In the mortality charts for women of age 15 to 49, even if we ignore those who died in child-birth – that is, the blocks filled out in black – we can still discern a higher mortality among women in most cases. To allow comparisons with current figures on child-birth mortality, we have adopted the definition of the World Health Organisation, which takes into consideration the deaths of mothers up to 41 days after the birth of the last child. (This corresponds, by the way, quite well to the expression, which appears quite early in our sources: 'died during the six weeks'.) How then do we explain this higher mortality of women in their 'best years', that is, even after subtracting mortality due to child-birth?

A second element of the explanation can also be seen in the upper half of Figures 5.1 to 5.4, namely the great number of births, even at more advanced ages. On average each woman gave birth to more than six children in her first marriage. Although infant mortality (0-1 year) was sometimes frightfully high and in the extreme case of the community of Gabelbach reached 40 per cent for children of mothers between 35 and 39, none the less in most (young) families there were a number of small children to be cared for. Since the so-called 'discovery of childhood' in the eighteenth century, this task has devolved on the wife and mother. The all-present childhood diseases, which often caused the deaths of infants and small children, were at the same time a source of danger for the mother who cared for them. This danger could come from an illness for which the mother in her own childhood had acquired no immunity or only a temporary one, or it could simply consist in the extra burden on the mother as a nurse. Moreover, the self-defined sickness threshold for women was as a rule higher, so that by the time they had acknowledged their sickness, it had reached a more advanced stage than was the case for men. As a consequence of the 'polarisation of "sex characteristics" ' at the time, fathers no longer devoted the same amount of concern to their youngest offspring or to helping out in the household – although of course their own illnesses presented a further burden on their wives.[9] But the 'female condition' in the nineteenth century, as it is reflected in the excess mortality of married women in procreative years, has not yet been adequately described. It is obviously insufficient to cite all these more or less demographic factors as the sole explanation: the repeated pregnancies and births, the care of men and children with infectious diseases, the suppression of one's own illness as long as possible. The era we are discussing here, the end of the eighteenth century and the nineteenth century, was not only a period in which overtaxed wives and mothers – as it might appear in a transfiguring retrospect – in selfless dedication and sacrifice marched in droves to a premature death. It was just as much a period of time in which the working conditions of many married women underwent a fundamental change – for the worse. This observation applies in equal measure to the centres of rapid industrialisation and urbanisation and – of greater importance to us in this discussion – to agrarian regions which became more and more market oriented.[10] Therefore in discussing our results, we shall have to consider very carefully the results of the so-called 'agrarian revolution', or more precisely, the consequences of an increasing workload for women due to the rapid intensification of agricultural production.[11] Even in our own day, current analyses of the present state of health of Central European populations still come to the conclusion, that 'women employed in agriculture . . . due to their multiple burdens probably constitute the most afflicted social group'.[12] The fact that this social group is relatively small today and has no powerful lobby, and that modern medicine is primarily concerned with urban problems, makes it easier to forget this state of affairs.

In my opinion – and I would like to propose it as my hypothesis – the excess mortality of married women of reproductive age during the period investigated here is to be explained by premature physical deterioration due to the multiple simultaneous burdens of women as wife, mother, cook (who was none the less often the most poorly nourished of the whole family), maid, laundress and skilled labourer. Especially with regard to the last two functions, serious changes for the worse occur during this period. Even contemporaries had noticed that more women than men died of cholera, the new pandemic which surged over the entire continent a number of times after the 1830s. The cause of this susceptibility was also just as clear. We can read in a contemporary report on the cholera epidemic of 1866 made by the

Berlin professor of medicine, August Hirsch:

> For the most part, the truly enormous prevalence [of women] is
> probably due to the fact, that the adult part of the female sex, while
> caring for those who have become sick or have died of cholera,
> especially while handling and cleaning the clothes and bedclothes
> soiled by cholera defecations, exposes itself to infection to a much
> higher degree than does the corresponding part of the male sex;
> hundreds of experiences, which have also been made in this year's
> cholera epidemic in Berlin, teach us how remarkably great the
> number of cases of cholera death and disease has been among
> laundresses.[13]

In fact in 1866 in Berlin 1,587 women between 15 and 50 fell victim
to cholera. The number of men of the same age was almost a third less,
namely, 1,131.[14]

More important, however, were the new, additional burdens within
the sex-specifically structured daily working world. Traditionally, the
woman's work area included the care of the smaller domestic animals as
well as the more skilled labour of preparing hemp and flax as well as
milk products.[15] As agricultural production was intensified in the
course of the late eighteenth and the nineteenth centuries, the woman's
duties expanded more and more. It was *her* additional responsibility to
provide the time- and labour-intensive care for the new sorts of
vegetables, the potatoes, sugar beets and fruit trees as well as the larger
number of domestic animals which were now kept all year round in
stalls.

With this in mind, it is hardly to be expected that excess female
mortality should diminish before the end of the nineteenth or the
beginning of the twentieth century, that is, until important alleviations
in house and field work had been introduced – whether through
rationalisation or by replacing manual labour with machines (milking,
butter-making and washing machines, better instruments for work in
the fields, potato-sorting machines, etc.). Should our empirical studies
nevertheless show a decrease in excess female mortality as early as the
nineteenth century, this would indicate that the relief mechanisms in
the areas of burden had at that time already begun to take effect: fewer
pregnancies (which also meant fewer abortions), a lower age at last
birth, improvements in drinking water and sewage systems, a reduction
in infectious (childhood) diseases, quantitatively and qualitatively
improved standards of nourishment, increasing medical, hygienic and

institutional supervision of pregnancy, birth, recovery and child-rearing, of the individual, the family and everyday life.[16] Or should we take the opposite view, that in the light of these aspects of general improvements in the area of health, the wife and mother was loaded down with even more burdens — at least in the early phase — and had little profit from them for her own health?

Whatever the case may be, we have already seen on the basis of highly aggregated statistical data that the real breakthrough in mitigating excess female mortality first occurred in our own century, more precisely, between the two world wars. Only after this time can we discern a lower mortality for women of *all* ages.

III

This study is based on an ongoing historical-demographic research project at the Free University of Berlin. I shall use the results obtained for four communities, which we have already analysed systematically. The selection of these and other localities and the division of the era 1780-1899 into four equal time-periods was not made with the same question in mind as that upon which this report will focus. We chose them according to social-economic and ecological criteria and according to such criteria as inheritance customs, religious confession, and urban or rural location. However the time and labour invested in evaluating the data seemed to justify re-using the data-bank results to analyse a new problem. Moreover, we consider the above mentioned selection criteria in any case to be relevant for our present concern.[17]

The four localities are: the small town of Philippsburg, and three agricultural villages — Altdorf, Gabelbach and Hesel. *Philippsburg* was a French–German border town, situated 25 kilometres south-west of Heidelberg, in a low-lying plain on the upper Rhine. It was predominantly Catholic. A local administrative centre, it also engaged in the cultivation of sugar beets, hops and tobacco, and underwent a modest industrialisation in the course of the nineteenth century, particularly in the development of cigarette and sugar manufacture. Its population in 1779 was 818; by 1900, it had grown to 2,546. *Altdorf,* a village 40 kilometres south of Strasbourg on the right bank of the Rhine, was also Catholic. It relied mainly on grain cultivation, in which it experienced an increasing intensity of production from the middle of the eighteenth century onwards. Cultivation was by an improved three-field system, in which not only corn, but also hemp, tobacco, chicory and clover were grown. The villagers also possessed a number of cattle, kept in stalls. The population in 1813 was 1,140; in 1847 it was 1,358; in 1900 it was 1,125. There was a significant amount of emigration from the village in the second half of the nineteenth century. *Gabelbach*, a village 25 kilometres west of Augsburg, in Swabia, was also Catholic, and also relied mainly on grain production. The extension of cultivated land had been completed at an early period, so that any population increase resulted in severe pressure on resources. In 1810 there were 227 inhabitants; in 1834 there were 234; by 1900 the village's population had grown to 311. Finally, the Protestant (reformed Lutheran) village of *Hesel*, 90 kilometres north-west of Bremen, was situated on infertile soil (heather, sand, moorland) which made cultivation rather difficult. For a time so-called colonists were resettled in the village. The population was somewhat smaller than that of Altdorf, and standards of living were well below those obtaining in the Rhenish community. Like Altdorf, Hesel experienced an increasing amount of emigration during the course of the nineteenth century.

In the systematic evaluation of the family reconstitutions which have been completed for all four communities[18] we took into consideration only families of type I (according to Louis Henry's definition), that is, families for which we knew exactly to the day the data on marriage — beginning and end — birth of the wife, and in this case also the date of death of the surviving partner. The only exception consists of 111 widowers and 55 widows for whom the dates of death are unknown, because they left the parishes after the deaths of their spouses. In order to have an equally large reference group, we also restricted our study to the fates of partners in mutual first marriages (as a rule, four-fifths of all marriages). The time period considered is the years from 1780 to 1899.

Table 5.1: Distribution of the 1,869 Analysed Mutual First Marriages in the Four Communities and over the Four Time-periods

Marriages	Philippsburg	Altdorf	Gabelbach	Hesel	All four communities
1780-1809	91	94	22	69	276
1810-1839	183	114	21	109	427
1840-1869	291	121	31	134	577
1870-1899	344	121	46	78	589
1780-1899	909	450	120	390	1869

It should be indicated that the family reconstitutions on which this report is based are themselves based on so-called *Ortssippenbücher*, genealogical reconstructions of local communities carried out in many areas of Germany since the 1920s, for purposes not unconnected with racial and eugenic 'research'. Whatever the motives behind their compilation, one can still dissipate the misgivings which are often expressed by historians as well as demographers. I should like to quote the summary of a study conducted a few years ago by John Knodel and Edward Shorter, who applied a number of statistical relevance tests to research results based on *Ortssippenbücher*:

> This paper set out to answer the question: is the OSB [Ortssippen-buch] a valid source of data for family-reconstitution analysis? The answer is unquestionably yes. In *comparative* terms the German parish registers on which the OSB's rest are probably superior to the French, on which so much work has been done to date. They permit a higher degree of confidence in making links, and they allow the reconstitution of a higher proportion of families. We have also shown that in *absolute* terms the standards of accuracy of these local genealogists meet the generally established standards of scientific research. Indeed the genealogists appear to have been conscientious in the extreme, and industrious beyond what most professional historical demographers can manage. It goes without saying that the OSBs one selects for analysis must be for communities whose records are substantially intact and whose compiler worked according to the customary practices of local genealogy. But there are many such OSBs.[19]

With regard to the *Ortssippenbücher* that we used, this caution applies especially to the question of whether infant deaths and stillbirths were dependably registered – a question which we scrutinised.

The essentially historical-demographic source base of this study – that is, the *Ortssippenbücher* and the results inferred from them – leads us to focus on *one* central question for which this kind of source is especially fruitful: namely the various aspects of maternal mortality. On this question hardly any historical material has previously been available. However I would like to warn the reader against drawing too extensive consequences from our results. We have studied 1,869 families of type I with a total of 10,063 births. Although these numbers are unusually high for historical-demographic field studies, where each individual event must be laboriously searched out, the number of deaths in child-birth is relatively small. Only 93 women (out of 1,672 fertile marriages) demonstrably died within a period of 0-41 days after the birth of the last child. It should be clear that on this narrow basis we cannot make any precise percentage calculations on the risk of maternal mortality in a particular community *and* in a particular time period *and* in a particular age group *and* for a particular rank-order of birth. Statements of this kind would be statistically irrelevant. Thus in Tables 5.2-5.6, we have given the absolute numbers of these individual categories. However in order to obtain a substantial interpretation, we had to draw them together into larger groups, for instance, the period-specific values for all four localities together or the community-specific figures for all four time periods.

IV

The bottom halves of the Figures 5.1 to 5.4 show the number of deaths among men and among women according to age group for Philippsburg, Altdorf, Gabelbach and Hesel respectively. These are absolute numbers for the entire period of 120 years. The shading in the lower part indicates the deaths which occurred during the first marriage or in subsequent widowhood or widowerhood. The crisscross shading above shows the remarried partners, who died during or after a later marriage. The black sections display the number of women who died in child-birth.

Table 5.2 gives the complementary figures for each of the 30-year periods (i.e. 1780-1809, 1810-39, 1840-69, 1870-99); we have however combined the data for all four communities. The figures here are broken down according to age group and sex, and for women they are given inclusive and exclusive of childbed fatalities. Here we can see a clear and period-specific excess mortality among women between the ages of 15 and 49 years. Even if one excludes child-birth mortality, there are always more cases of death among women than among men of the same age — except in the last period from 1870-99. We must however take into consideration the sex-specific differences in average age at first marriage. As a rule men were about two years older at marriage than women, so that the two partners often belonged to different age groups. Thus there could have been fewer men than women in particular age groups.

Table 5.2: Distribution of Deaths of Partners in Mutual First Marriages
Between Ages 15 and 49 According to Sex during the Four Periods
Investigated 1780-1899 (four communities together)
Women I: inclusive deaths in child-birth (0-41 days after last birth)
Women II: exclusive deaths in child-birth

Marriage cohorts for the years	1780-1809			1810-1839			1840-1869			1870-1899			1780-1899		
Age groups in years	men	women I	II	men	women I	II	men	women I	II	men	women I	II	men	women I	II
15-19	0	0	0	0	1	1	0	0	0	0	1	1	0	2	2
20-24	0	10	7	2	6	4	0	5	2	1	6	5	3	27	18
25-29	8	18	10	8	18	14	8	21	13	12	22	13	36	79	50
30-34	13	15	10	7	22	14	20	31	24	17	22	16	57	90	64
35-39	8	21	18	28	22	18	30	36	30	16	24	17	82	103	83
40-44	12	18	16	9	20	20	27	39	34	21	14	12	69	91	82
45-49	13	16	16	29	22	22	23	20	19	22	18	18	87	76	75
15-49	54	98	77	83	111	93	108	152	122	89	107	82	334	468	374
All ages	276	276		427	427		577	577		589	589		1869	1869	
per 100 men age 15-49 x women of the same age died	100	181	143	100	134	112	100	141	113	100	120	92	100	140	112

In spite of the smallness of the sample, one could perhaps detect a
gradual diminishing of sex-specific differential mortality. In the first
period (1780-1809), for every 100 men between 15 and 49 who died
there were 181 women of the same age who died; in the second period
(1810-39) it was 134; in the third (1840-69), 141 and in the fourth
(1870-99), 120. Any investigations which were to go further than we
have gone here would have to analyse very carefully the causes of death
which had led to the *premature* demise of married men and women,
especially why and how these causes changed. (Note: we have
considered here only those who died before their fiftieth year.) It is, for
instance, quite possible that the gradual improvement in the lot of
women which appears here is deceptive, because in the same period the
'condition of men', which serves as the basis of comparison, had
considerably worsened (industrialisation, urbanisation). Also one
should remember that successes in reducing deaths connected with
pregnancy, child-birth and recovery generally required much greater
expenditure than in other areas due to the necessity of individual care
for the endangered persons. The many infectious diseases could be

combated with extensive and relatively easy-to-manage collective preventive measures such as standardised vaccinations, improvements in drinking water and sewage systems, propagation of personal hygiene, etc.

The top half of each of the Figures 5.1–5.4 shows the number of births in the respective communities ordered according to the age of the mother. The absolute number of children who died in their first year is doubly shaded. The percentages are given to the right of each block. If we subtract this number from the total number of births, the difference gives us the number of small children for whom the mothers had to care.

If we consider the four figures together, we can see a number of features common to all four localities: female excess mortality in reproductive age groups; a relatively low mortality for both sexes around the age of 50; a male excess mortality at more advanced ages. On the other hand, there are particular features characteristic of each community: for instance, the urban–rural difference in the distribution of births according to the ages of the mother. While in Philippsburg fertility is greatest among women between the ages of 25 and 29, in all three rural communities the maximum is reached in the age group 30-34. In the relatively affluent town of Philippsburg many more members of both sexes died at more advanced ages than in the poor rural community of Hesel.

Since this essay concentrates on the excess mortality among women of reproductive age, I should point out here that we are dealing with only one aspect of sex-specific differential mortality. I would especially emphasise that about three-fourths of all married persons in mutual first marriages lived *longer* than 50 years (in Philippsburg 83.1 per cent of men and 77.6 per cent of women; in Altdorf 78.9 per cent and 75.8 per cent; in Gabelbach 86.7 per cent and 72.5 per cent; and in Hesel 82.3 per cent and 68.7 per cent), and at least half or two-thirds of them lived to be 60 years old or older (in Philippsburg 70.2 per cent of men and 64.9 per cent of women; in Altdorf 59.8 per cent and 58.2 per cent; in Gabelbach 68.3 per cent and 53.3 per cent; and in Hesel 68.5 per cent and 58.2 per cent). However, this differential mortality among higher age groups does not really concern us here, since we are primarily concerned with differential mortality in child-bearing age. We also do not want to present the extensive details which are usual in historical-demographic studies (and which have been collected in the larger context mentioned above). Later in the essay I shall introduce such data as figures on the average age of women at the birth of their first and last children, fertility rates, the length of intergenetic intervals, and so on. Here, however, I want to concentrate particularly on the figures for historical maternal mortality, since these have been rather rare in the literature up to now.

Of the 1,869 mutual first marriages in the four communities which we have analysed for the period from 1780 to 1899, 1,672 were fertile (= 89.5 per cent). A total of 10,063 births were recorded (average: 6.02). Ninety-three mothers died in child-birth, 19 of them after the birth of their first child. If one converts these figures to the form which is customary today, the result is 924.2 maternal fatalities per 100,000 births or 1,136.4 per 100,000 first births. We can compare these figures from the eighteenth and nineteenth centuries with modern ones: according to the World Health Organisation definition of death in childbed, 45.9 women per 100,000 births in the Federal Republic of Germany died in childbed in 1973, 38.3 in Japan, 24.0 in France, 22.4 in Austria, 18.3 in Switzerland, 10.3 in the Netherlands and 2.7 in Sweden.[20] The historical course of the decrease in maternal mortality to the low rate of today is especially revealing, since it is quite clear that this is a phenomenon of the *twentieth* century. In the United States maternal mortality per 100,000 births amounted to 916 in 1918; 661 in 1931; 568 in 1936; 317 in 1941; 157 in 1946; 75 in 1951; 41 in 1956; 37 in 1961; and 15.2 in 1973.[21] It is much easier to get a notion of the risks of maternal mortality for women who married at the end of the eighteenth and during the nineteenth century, if one calculates how many of them on the average died in the aftermath of giving birth. Ninety-three cases of death among 1,672 fertile women amounts to a percentage of 5.6. In other words, for every twentieth woman at that time, motherhood was fatal.

Tables 5.3 to 5.6 contain further details on various aspects of childbed mortality. We shall not discuss them here, but the most important results will be brought into the summary discussion. *Table 5.3* shows maternal mortality according to age and rank-order of birth for each community for the entire period studied. *Table 5.4* shows the same thing for each time-period, but with all communities taken together. *Table 5.5* is limited to maternal mortality at the first birth. The top half shows each community for the entire period; the bottom half shows each of the four time-periods for all communities together. *Table 5.6* summarises the period- and community-specific risk of maternal mortality at the birth of the first child for women in mutual first marriages.

Table 5.3: Distribution of Child-birth Fatalities According to Age Group and Rank-order of Birth (parity) in Philippsburg, Altdorf, Gabelbach and Hesel 1780-1899

Risk factor 1: average risk of dying in the aftermath of giving birth, independent of age and rank-order of birth

A: according to age group

Age groups	Philippsburg		Altdorf		Gabelbach		Hesel		All four communities		
	births	deaths	births	deaths	births	deaths	births	deaths	births	deaths	risk factor
15-19	92	0	20	0	4	0	17	0	133	0 }	
20-24	990	5	355	0	61	1	238	3	1644	9 }	0.55
25-29	1550	10	679	6	169	2	456	10	2854	28	1.07
30-34	1236	9	699	10	215	2	468	4	2618	25	1.03
35-39	823	8	527	6	178	4	390	3	1918	21	1.18
40-44	325	0	232	1	61	1	186	7	804	9 }	
45-49*	34	0	30	0	7	1	21	0	92	1 }	1.22
Total	5050	32	2542	23	695	11	1776	27	10063	93	1.00
per 10,000		63		90		158		152		92	

* inclusive 3 births at ages over 50

Table 5.3

B: according to rank-order of birth

Age groups	Philippsburg		Altdorf		Gabelbach		Hesel		All four communities		
	births	deaths	births	deaths	births	deaths	births	deaths	births	deaths	risk factor
1	849	6	380	5	103	2	340	6	1672	19	1.24
2	799	5	358	4	98	2	316	3	1571	14 }	0.95
3	708	4	342	4	90	0	287	5	1427	13 }	
4	610	2	317	3	81	0	229	5	1237	10	
5	520	2	275	1	76	1	199	2	1070	6 }	0.71
6	407	3	245	2	62	1	157	0	871	6 }	
7	327	2	192	1	50	2	110	0	679	5 }	
8	259	3	157	2	40	0	67	4	523	9 }	1.70
9	184	4	113	0	27	1	41	1	365	6 }	
10	140	0	78	1	21	1	24	1	263	3 }	
11	96	1	46	0	17	0	4	0	163	1 }	(0.57)
12	58	0	23	0	13	1	2	0	96	1 }	
13-	93	0	16	0	17	0	0	0	126	0 }	
Total	5050	32	2542	23	695	11	1776	27	10063	93	1.00

Table 5.4: Distribution of Child-birth Fatalities According to Age Group and Rank-order of Birth (parity) During Each of the Four Time-periods Studied (1780–1899)

Risk factor 1: average risk of dying in the aftermath of giving birth, independent of age and rank-order of birth

A: according to age group

Age groups	1780–1809 births	1780–1809 deaths	1810–39 births	1810–39 deaths	1840–69 births	1840–69 deaths	1870–99 births	1870–99 deaths	All four periods 1780–1899 births	All four periods 1780–1899 deaths	All four periods 1780–1899 risk factor
15-19	24	0	37	0	28	0	44	0	133	0 }	0.55
20-24	268	3	374	2	440	3	562	1	1644	9 }	
25-29	402	7	682	4	845	8	925	9	2854	28	1.07
30-34	374	5	617	7	853	7	774	6	2618	25	1.03
35-39	310	3	458	5	616	6	534	7	1918	21	1.18
40-44	139	2	199	0	253	5	213	2	804	9 }	1.22
45-49*	14	0	23	0	33	1	22	0	92	1 }	
Total	1531	20	2390	18	3068	30	3074	25	10063	93	1.00
per 10,000		131		75		98		81		92	

* inclusive 3 births at ages over 50

Table 5.4

B: according to rank-order of birth

Age groups	1780–1809 births	deaths	1810–39 births	deaths	1840–69 births	deaths	1870–99 births	deaths	All four periods 1780–1899 births	deaths	risk factor
1	234	5	384	4	528	5	526	5	1672	19	1.24
2	217	3	364	3	497	5	493	3	1571	14	}
3	199	3	338	2	453	5	437	3	1427	13	} 0.95
4	184	2	300	0	378	3	375	5	1237	10	}
5	166	1	263	2	328	1	313	2	1070	6	}
6	144	0	214	3	260	1	253	2	871	6	} 0.71
7	117	0	166	1	195	2	201	2	679	5	}
8	90	4	123	1	149	3	161	1	523	9	}
9	62	2	84	0	101	2	118	1	365	6	} 1.70
10	49	0	64	1	66	2	84	1	263	3	}
11	29	0	41	0	44	0	49	0	163	1	}
12	15	0	22	0	29	1	30	0	96	1	} (0.57)
13-	25	0	27	0	40	0	34	0	126	0	}
Total	1531	20	2390	18	3068	30	3074	25	10063	93	1.00

Table 5.5: Distribution of Deaths as a Consequence of Giving Birth to the First Child According to Age Group for Four Communities and for Four Time-periods

Ø-age : Average age at first birth (in years)
Risk factor 1 : Average risk of dying in the aftermath of a first birth independent of age
( ) : Source figures too small to be taken into consideration in the discussion

A: In the four communities (for the entire time-period 1780–1899)

Age groups	Philippsburg Ø-age : 24.2 births	deaths	Altdorf Ø-age : 25.3 births	deaths	Gabelbach Ø-age : 27.5 births	deaths	Hesel Ø-age : 26.4 births	deaths	All four communities Ø-age : 25.1 births	deaths	risk factor
15-19	74	0	17	0	3	0	15	0	109	0	( )
20-24	472	3	184	0	31	0	137	2	824	5	(0.54)
25-29	246	3	135	2	39	1	121	3	541	9	1.46
30-34	53	0	35	3	23	0	45	1	156	4	2.25
35-39	3	0	7	0	6	1	19	0	35	1	( )
40-44	1	0	2	0	1	0	3	0	7	0	( )
45-49	0	0	0	0	0	0	0	0	0	0	—
Total	849	6	380	5	103	2	340	6	1672	19	1.00
per 10,000	71		132		194		176		114		

Table 5.5

B: During the four periods studied (in the four communities together)

Age groups	1780–1809 : 24.6		1810–39 : 24.8		1840–69 : 25.7		1870–99 : 24.9		All four periods 1780–1899 : 25.1		
	∅-age births	deaths	∅-age births	deaths	∅-age births	deaths	∅-age births	deaths	∅-age births	deaths	risk factor
15-19	18	0	31	0	23	0	37	0	109	0	( )
20-24	122	2	193	0	236	2	273	1	824	5	(0.54)
25-29	71	2	118	2	194	2	158	3	541	9	1.46
30-34	18	1	35	2	60	0	43	1	156	4	2.25
35-39	5	0	6	0	10	1	14	0	35	1	( )
40-44	0	0	1	0	5	0	1	0	7	0	( )
45-49	0	0	0	0	0	0	0	0	0	0	–
Total	234	5	384	4	528	5	526	5	1672	19	1.00
per 10,000		214		104		95		95		114	

Table 5.6: Risk of Child-birth Fatality for Married Women According to Community and Time-period (only women in mutual first marriages excluding widows and remarried women)

Deaths I: Women who died in mutual first marriages
Deaths II: Women who died in fertile first marriages

Period	Philippsburg deaths I	deaths II	in child-birth	Altdorf deaths I	deaths II	in child-birth	Gabelbach deaths I	deaths II	in child-birth	Hesel deaths I	deaths II	in child-birth
1780-1809	85	81	11	78	73	3	21	18	0	66	62	6
1810-1839	175	170	6	105	99	6	19	18	3	99	97	3
1840-1869	288	283	7	111	105	7	28	25	4	122	115	12
1870-1899	329	315	8	115	103	7	44	42	4	71	66	6
1780-1899	877	849	32	409	380	23	112	103	11	358	340	27
per 10,000	365	377		562	605		982	1068		754	794	

All four communities

Period	deaths I	deaths II	in child-birth
1780-1809	250	234	20
1810-1839	398	384	18
1840-1869	549	528	30
1870-1899	559	526	25
1780-1899	1756	1672	93

deaths in child-birth per 10,000

Period	I	II
1780-1809	800	855
1810-1839	452	469
1840-1869	546	568
1870-1899	447	473
1780-1899	530	556

V

To summarise the content of Figures 5.1 to 5.4 and Tables 5.3 to 5.6, I should like to suggest the following four points as the most important results. In the first place, it is clear that urban (small town) maternal mortality was only about half as high as it was in the country. There were 63 deaths per 10,000 births in Philippsburg but 90, 158 and 152 respectively in Altdorf, Gabelbach and Hesel. On first births alone, Philippsburg had 71 per 10,000 as opposed to 158 for the three rural communities taken together. In Philippsburg, 377 fertile married women per 10,000 died in the aftermath of giving birth; in the three villages: 605, 1,068 and 794. Secondly, it is notable that a slight decline in child-birth mortality occurs between the first and second 30-year periods, that is, at the end of the eighteenth and the beginning of the nineteenth century. No further basic changes can be detected during the course of the nineteenth century. Maternal mortality during the first period reached 131 per 10,000 births, as compared to 75 in the second, 98 in the third, and 81 in the fourth. If one considers only first births, the rates are 214, 104, 95 and again 95 per 10,000 first births; this is the case even though the average age at first birth was lowest (24.6 years) in the first period and highest (25.7 years) in the last. The risk of death in the first period was 855 per 10,000 fertile married women; in the three subsequent periods it was 'only' 469, 568, 473. However, we should remember that these community-unspecific data are strongly influenced by the figures from Philippsburg: 849, or about half, of the 1,672 fertile marriages were in this town. An urban-rural differential development could thus be obscured, and we know that town-country differences were especially accentuated in the course of the nineteenth century. For instance, in the third and fourth periods in Philippsburg, one out of 40 women died as a consequence of motherhood (247 and 254 per 10,000 respectively); whereas in the rural communities the average was one in 10 or 12 (939 and 806 per 10,000).

Paradoxically, the extremely high rate of maternal mortality during the first period might very well be due to the increasing medicalisation of pregnancy in the second half of the eighteenth century, especially to the widespread use of forceps at delivery.[22] Although the use of these instruments helped a growing number of mothers to survive a difficult birth, none the less not a few of them died in childbed shortly thereafter as a result of the operation. In the same manner more children were born alive, of whom however a number died in infancy. For our analysis it is important to note that such cases would be listed in the death registers; this was not necessarily the case if the child was stillborn. If a woman died as the result of a stillbirth, which was listed in neither baptismal nor death registers, our methodological procedure could not identify this state of affairs.[23]

The third conclusion to be drawn from the data presented requires a rather more extended discussion. One can easily discern a differential maternal mortality according to age and rank-order of birth. The risk of death for pregnant women began to increase rapidly at the age of 25. The risk factor was 0.55 for women between 15 and 24, and 1.07, 1.03 and 1.18 for the following age groups — risk factor 1.0 being the average risk independent of age and rank-order of birth. The age-specific risks were even more serious for women giving birth for the first time. For those between 25 and 29 it was already 1.46. In the next group (30-34 years) it rose to 2.25. Today only women over 30 are considered *a priori* to be at risk.[24]

It should thus be clear that the above-mentioned difference in maternal mortality between town and country is connected to a certain extent with the lower age at first birth — and also at last birth — of women in the town. The average ages at first and last birth in Philippsburg during the period we investigated were 24.2 and 37.5 years respectively; in Altdorf the figures were 25.3 and 40.4, in Gabelbach 27.5 (!) and 39.9, and in Hesel 26.4 and 39.0. If we consider the relation between these different ages at first birth and the differing risks of dying as a consequence of giving birth to the first child, we can infer the following values — which in my opinion are directly connected: in Philippsburg the average age at first birth was 24.2 years, the risk of death was 71 deaths per 10,000 births; in Altdorf the age was 25.3, the risk of death 132; in Gabelbach 27.5 years and 194 deaths; and in Hesel 26.4 years and 176 deaths.

Inasmuch as the average number of births for fertile women in mutual first marriages for the entire period from 1780 to 1899 amounted to 6.0 in Philippsburg, 6.7 in Altdorf, 6.8 in Gabelbach, and 5.2 in Hesel, the risk of death for mothers was normally greatest for the birth of the *first* child (risk factor 1.24). It was significantly lower for the rank orders 2-4 (0.95) and 5-7 (0.71). Only with later ranks did a higher risk arise (8-10 had a risk factor of 1.70). With this in mind, it is understandable that the spread of family planning and restriction of the number of births, which proceeded more rapidly among the urban (and Catholic!) population of Philippsburg than it did in the villages, contributed to the lower maternal mortality in the town. This restriction can be seen especially in the lower age at last birth and the

longer intergenetic intervals. Such a reduction in mortality could occur
even without the slightest improvements in hygiene and medical
assistance during pregnancy, birth and childbed. Fertility figures for
Philippsburg were: 1870-1899: 20-24 years: 544 (births per 1,000
married women per year); 25-29: 405; 30-34: 283; 35-39: 186; 40-44:
71; 45-49: 7; average intergenetic interval: 28.9 months. In comparison
the fertility figures for Gabelbach were: 1870-1899: 822, 612, 452,
367, 161, and 42; the intergenetic interval: 22.5 months.[25]

Finally, in spite of the relatively narrow source base, one can discern
a difference between urban and rural maternal mortality. Moreover,
differences can also be found among the various rural communities
with their different economic structures, ecological conditions, and
basic demographic behaviour patterns. We can compare the risk values
for Gabelbach and Hesel. Gabelbach had a 'saturated' Catholic
population, a fact which is expressed in the high average age at
marriage and at first birth (27.5), the high fertility rates with short
intergenetic intervals and an extremely high infant mortality (Figure
5.3). Hesel had a poor Lutheran population; the young people also had
difficulties establishing themselves, as can be seen from the relatively
high age at marriage and at first birth (26.4 years). However the fertility
rates were significantly lower (for instance, in the period 1870-99 for
the age groups from 25-29 to 45-49 the rates were 486, 352, 293, 170,
98, and 10); the average intergenetic intervals were longer (31.2 months)
and infant mortality showed noticeably lower values (see Figure 5.4).
The maternal mortality in these two rural communities can also be
compared with that in Altdorf – a relatively affluent Catholic village
with a rather diversified agrarian economy. The fertility figures here
between 1870 and 1899 were: 540, 481, 410, 317, 157 and 12; the
average time between births was 25.3 months. To recapitulate, we find
the highest figures for infant mortality not in the poor village of Hesel,
still less in well situated Altdorf; rather in Gabelbach. Here there were
158 cáses of maternal death per 10,000 births, in Hesel there were 152;
whereas in Altdorf 'only' 90 (and in Philippsburg even less – 63).
Expressed in terms of 10,000 fertile women: 1,068 died in Gabelbach
in the aftermath of giving birth, 794 in Hesel and 605 in Altdorf (377
in Philippsburg).

VI

We have attempted here to illustrate the effects of marriage, family life, child-bearing and work on women in the nineteenth century with the results of an investigation of the excess mortality of women in child-bearing age. The existing literature on the subject would on the face of it lead one to expect one of two things: either a clear increase in mortality due to the often asserted worsening of the position of women in the course of the nineteenth century;[26] or on the other hand a noticeable decrease in mortality especially among mothers due to increasing medicalisation from the eighteenth century to the beginning of the twentieth,[27] and especially due to the increase in 'institutionalised motherhood' in the course of the nineteenth century.[28] However, apart from striking and easily explicable differences between town and country and also to a certain extent among the different villages, we could not demonstrate any decisive changes in differential mortality in either direction in the course of the nineteenth century; at most there were minor changes. Thus it seems that the negative factors (the worsening of the 'feminine condition' due to intensification of specifically female tasks, an environment which was often ill-disposed towards women, even an anti-feminist ideology),[29] and the positive factors (improvements in nourishment and housing, medicalisation of pregnancy, delivery and recovery, better hygiene in public and private areas) often balanced each other out.[30]

The excess mortality of married women of child-bearing age during the nineteenth century was undoubtedly a reality; and it was largely due to the diversity of simultaneous burdens on women as wife and mother, in the household and in special duties. A woman's condition therefore often stabilised after her fortieth or forty-fifth year when no more pregnancies occurred and when the grown children could help her (note the corresponding reduction in mortality in Figures 5.1-5.4). For the historian, however, it is quite clear that the most interesting aspect of this excess mortality in historical perspective — namely, its disappearance and the emergence of the under-mortality which applies to all female age groups today — is a phenomenon of the twentieth century. Although it no longer belongs to our topic here, the provocative question — why this happened — immediately suggests itself: whether the female organism is better adapted to environmental conditions than the male; and whether the demonstrable excess mortality of women in their prime is not — as the French historian Pierre Chaunu has suggested — merely 'an historical accident of the nineteenth century'.[31]

Notes

The stimulus for this study was an invitation to a conference on 'the condition of women and historical demography' held by the French Demographic History Society in Paris in December 1979. One of the three sessions, chaired by Alain Bideau, was devoted to 'differential mortality'. Earlier versions of this paper were read in November 1979 at the Universities of Geneva and Lyon II in the seminars of Professors Alfred Perrenoud and Maurice Garden. I want to express my thanks to them and to the other participants in the seminars, especially to Annemarie Pinz and Hubert Charbonneau, for their constructive criticism. I would also like to thank the Volkswagen Foundation for its generous material support in carrying out the quantitative analysis; and last but not least my work-group in Berlin, especially Dr Franz Gschwind and Sigrid Stöckel.

1. *Statistisches Jahrbuch für die Bundesrepublik Deutschland: 1979* (Statistisches Bundesamt, Stuttgart/Mainz, 1979).
2. *Daten des Gesundheitswesens 1977* (hg. v. Bundesministerium für Jugend, Familie und Gesundheit, Bonn, 1977), p. 64.
3. Ibid., pp. 65, 112-13.
4. Ibid., p. 62.
5. Ibid., p. 79.
6. *Bevölkerung und Wirtschaft 1872-1972* (hg. v. Statistischen Bundesamt, Stuttgart/Mainz, 1972), pp. 110-11.
7. *Wirtschaft und Statistik* (Wiesbaden, Statistisches Bundesamt, Neue Folge, No. 6 (1954), Tabellenteil, p. 111.
8. L.G. Berry, 'Age and Parity Influences on Maternal Mortality: United States 1919-1969', *Demography*, 14 (1977), pp. 297-310; G. Delille, 'Un problème de démographie historique: Hommes et femmes face à la mort', *Mélanges d'archéologie et d'histoire de l'Ecole française de Rome*, 86 (1974), pp. 419-43; E.I. Hammoud, 'Sex Differentials in Mortality: An Enquiry with Reference to the Arab Countries and Others', *World Health Statistics Report*, 30/3 (1977), pp. 174-206; A.R. Omran, 'Epidemiologic Transition in the United States', *Population Bulletin*, 32/2 (1977); A. Perrenoud, 'L'inégalité sociale devant la mort à Genève au XVIIIe siècle', *Population* (1975), pp. 221-43; A. Perrenoud, *La population de Genève, XVIe - XIXe siècle. Etude démographique* (Geneva/ Paris, 1979).
9. See the essay by Karin Hausen in this volume, pp. 51-83.
10. B. Ankarloo, 'Agriculture and Women's Work: Directions of Change in the West, 1700-1900', *Journal of Family History*, 4 (1979), pp. 112-15.
11. Ivy Pinchbeck, 'Der Einfluss der "agrarian revolution" auf Art und Umfang der produktiven Tätigkeit von Frauen verschiedener Bevölkerungsgruppen in der englischen Landwirtschaft zwischen 1750 und 1850', in Heidi Rosenbaum (ed.), *Seminar: Familie und Gesellschaftsstruktur* (Frankfurt am Main, 1978), pp. 250-1; David Sabean, 'Small Peasant Agriculture in Germany at the Beginning of the Twentieth Century: Changing Work Patterns', *Peasant Studies*, 7 (1978), pp. 218-24. See also the data presented on pp. 95, 131-3 and 226 of the present volume.
12. *Systemanalyse des Gesundheitswesens in Österreich*, Vol. 1 (1978), p. 26.
13. August Hirsch, 'Die Cholera-Epidemie des Jahres 1866 in Berlin. Vom Statistischen Standpunkte geschildert', *Berliner Stadt- und Gemeinde-Kalender und Städtisches Jahrbuch für 1867*, p. 309.
14. Ibid., p. 307.
15. M. Roberts, 'Sickles and Scythes: Women's Work and Men's Work at Harvest Time', *History Workshop*, 7 (1979), pp. 3-28.

16.   L.A. Tilly, J.W. Scott, M. Cohen, 'Women's Work and European Fertility Patterns', *Journal of Interdisciplinary History*, 6 (1976), p. 474; L.-C. Vacher, 'A 19th-century Assessment of Causes of European Mortality Decline', *Population and Development Review*, 5 (1979), pp. 163-70.

17.   A. Imhof, 'Historisch-demographische Grunddaten in Deutschland vom 16. bis zum 20. Jahrhundert' (Typescript, Friedrich-Meinecke-Institut, Free University of Berlin); R. Gehrmann, 'Zum generativen Verhalten in der vorindustriellen Gesellschaft und beim Übergang zur Industriegesellschaft. Ein Forschungsbericht', *Zeitschrift für Bevölkerungswissenschaft* (1979), pp. 455-85.

18.   F. Hauf, *Ortssippenbuch Gabelbach, Landkreis Augsburg in Schwaben* (Frankfurt am Main, 1975); F. Hebbel, W.H. Collum, *Sippenbuch der Stadt Philippsburg, Landkreis Karlsruhe in Baden* (Frankfurt am Main, 1975); L. Janssen, H.R. Manger, *Die Familien der Kirchengemeinde Hesel (1643-1900)* (Aurich, 1974); A. Koebele, H. Scheer, *Ortssippenbuch Altdorf, Stadt Ettenheim, Ortenaukreis in Baden* (Frankfurt am Main, 1976).

19.   J. Knodel, E. Shorter, 'The Reliability of Family Reconstitution Data in German Village Genealogies (*Ortssippenbücher*)', *Annales de Démographie Historique* (1976), pp. 115-54.

20.   *Daten des Gesundheitswesens 1977* (Bundesministerium für Jugend, Familie und Gesundheit, Bonn-Bad Godesberg), pp. 204-5.

21.   Ibid., p. 205; E.R. Shapiro *et al.*, *Infant, Perinatal, Maternal and Childhood Mortality in the United States* (Cambridge, Mass., 1968), p. 329.

22.   J.-N. Biraben, 'Le médicin et l'enfant au XVIIIe siècle. Aperçu sur la pédiatrie au XVIIIe siècle', *Annales de Démographie Historique* (1973), p. 216; J. Dupâquier, *La population française aux XVIIe et XVIIIe siècles* (Paris, 1979), p. 102; J. Gélis *et al.*, *Entrer dans la vie. Naissance et enfance dans la France traditionelle* (Paris, 1978), p. 231.

23.   A. Eccles, 'Obstetrics in the 17th and 18th Centuries and its Implications for Maternal and Infant Mortality', *Bulletin of the Society for the Social History of Medicine*, 20 (1977), pp. 8-11.

24.   J. Manzl *et al.*, 'Einfluss des Alters Erstgebärender auf die perinatale kindliche Morbitität und Mortalität', *Zeitschrift für Geburtshilfe und Perinatalogie*, 181 (1971), pp. 168-73.

25.   Imhof, 'Historisch-demographische Grunddaten'.

26.   'The deterioration in the position of women in Western Europe is in effect considered as one of the major characteristics of the 19th century by all specialists in the condition of women' (D. Tabutin 'La surmortalité féminine en Europe avant 1940', Département de Démographie, Université Catholique de Louvain, Working Paper No. 40, p. 27).

27.   *Annales de Bretagne et des Pays de l'Ouest*, 86 (1979): 'Médicalisation en France du XVIIIe siècle au début du XXe siècle', pp. 177-340.

28.   Gélis *et al.*, *Entrer dans la vie*, p. 233.

29.   Richard J. Evans, *The Feminist Movement in Germany 1894-1933* (London, 1976), pp. 1-33. See also the essay by Karin Hausen in the present volume (pp. 51-83).

30.   W.R. Lee, *Population Growth, Economic Development and Social Change in Bavaria 1750-1850* (New York, 1977), p. 374.

31.   Concluding lecture, conference on 'La condition de la femme et démographie historique' (Paris, December 1979).

6 THE FAMILY LIFE-CYCLE: A STUDY OF FACTORY WORKERS IN NINETEENTH-CENTURY WÜRTTEMBERG

Heilwig Schomerus

I

In the last two decades or so, German social history has devoted a great deal of attention to the emergence and development of the working class. Indeed, it would probably be true to say that no other group or stratum in nineteenth-century German society has attracted so much historical interest as that of the workers. Yet this attention has been overwhelmingly concentrated on the political and organisational history of the proletariat, the emergence of the labour movement, the history of the Social Democratic Party, and the development of strikes, trade unions and other vehicles of workers' protest and self-defence.[1] By contrast, our knowledge of the everyday life of the working class, of the workers' housing conditions, material existence, culture, values and social behaviour, remains surprisingly scanty.[2] Even the recent renewal of interest in the history of the family has not so far encouraged research on workers' families, concentrating instead mainly on family life and family structures among the peasantry. Of course, there were a number of contemporary studies of working-class families in the nineteenth and early twentieth centuries. But essentially as far as modern scholarship is concerned, research on the proletarian family inevitably exists in something of a vacuum. Detailed empirical work must necessarily be carried out on a local level; and since there are up to now very few studies of working-class families of this nature, conclusions must necessarily remain somewhat tentative.

Studies of 'the making of the German working class' tend to be studies of the individual men who took a lead in articulating the social, economic and political demands of the proletariat, the views they held, and the organisations they formed. But these men were not isolated individuals. They were also members of families; they had fathers and mothers, brothers and sisters, wives, and sons and daughters. These family allegiances were not without influence on the organisational and political activities of these men. Above all, in the decisive period of the actual formation of the working class in

Germany, when millions of ordinary people were undergoing the painful process of transition from pre-industrial or traditional forms of making their living to industrial modes of life centred on the factory or the mine, it was of crucial importance for social and political behaviour whether individuals were first-generation proletarians, coming from a non-industrial or country background, or whether they were 'hereditary proletarians', succeeding their parents in the same socioeconomic milieu and class position.[3] For example, as the East German historian Hartmut Zwahr has shown in his detailed study of the formation of the proletariat in Leipzig, there is a noticeable positive correlation between the number of 'born proletarians' and the effectiveness of working-class organisation in the town.[4] It does indeed seem plausible to suggest that the social background and 'traditional' behaviour patterns of the first generation of factory workers inhibited the creation of forms of organisation, conflict and articulation adequate to the capitalist organisation of work and society and the new techniques and structures of production which it involved. But the crucial question of precisely when (and why) these 'traditional' forms of behaviour ceased to be operative has seldom been addressed by historians. In this essay I want to argue that they were not confined to the first generation of factory workers, but continued to play a role for two or three generations (or, more exactly, 40 to 50 years), until they were finally destroyed by economic crisis.

The example on which this study is based is the *Maschinenfabrik Esslingen* (Esslingen machine factory). Esslingen, a town in the former kingdom of Württemberg in South Germany, became an important industrial centre in the course of the nineteenth century. Its economy was dominated by the machine factory, founded in 1846 in the early phase of Germany's Railway Age. The factory's growth during the mid-nineteenth century, based on the production of railway locomotives, made it into the leading industrial employer of the region. In 1840, in the town of Esslingen, some 30 per cent of all employed persons were engaged in the textile industry, and only 15 per cent in the metal and engineering industries. By 1861, however, these percentages had been reversed, and 42 per cent of employed persons were active in metallurgy and engineering, while only 20 per cent were employed in textiles. In 1848 the factory employed 491 workers: by 1858 the number had risen to 1,065, and it remained at about 1,000 until the late 1890s (1,157 in 1868, 1,348 in 1878, 1,202 in 1888, 2,365 in 1898). Correspondingly, the population of the town of Esslingen itself grew steadily from about 11,000 in the 1830s to 13,500 in 1850, 15,000 in 1860, 20,000 in the mid-1870s and 22,000 in 1890. The Esslingen machine factory was from the very beginning a large-scale enterprise, run by a unified administration, with heavy initial capital investment in production machinery that was exceptionally advanced and specialised for its time. Its founder, Emil Kessler, used his experience of English and French engineering works in the creation of the largest, most modern and most highly mechanised industrial enterprise in Württemberg, an enterprise that stood in sharp contrast to the majority of German engineering works, which owed their origins to traditional artisan workshops and frequently consisted of little more than a collection of such workshops with a relatively low level of mechanisation. The Esslingen factory, then, is ideally suited as the basis for a case-study of the recruitment and structure of an industrial labour force.

Moreover, the records relating to this particular factory provide us with sources of unusual richness and precision for the study of the formation of an industrial workforce. In the first place, we have the so-called *Inventuren und Teilungen*, inventories of all household possessions of the factory's employees, comprising savings, cash, books (with titles), clothes and any other items belonging to the household, listed in the year of marriage (*Inventuren*) and in the year of death of either husband or wife (*Teilungen*). Apart from lists of goods and money there is also all the information usually found in parish registers, such as the place and date of birth, the name and profession of the fathers of both husband and wife, the dates of birth of all the children, and, in the *Teilungen*, the profession of the children and their place of work at the time of their parent's death.[5] Secondly, we have the personal registers (*Personalbücher*) of the factory's employees. These give information about the employee's date of birth, the address, date of entry into the factory, qualifications, place of work within the factory, date of any newly acquired qualification, and date of leaving employment within the factory. With the aid of a computer, I have combined these two sources (the latter in a sample of 2,500 out of 12,000 for the years 1846-1914), to form the collective biography of a large proportion of the factory's workers. The important feature of this combination of source material is that it enables us to compare not only four stages in the life-cycle of some 2,500 workers (age 0, 18, 26 and 60) but also three generations (father, son, grandchild) (see Figure 6.1: of course this only gives a very general and superficial idea of the amount and variety of information that can be derived from an analysis of these sources). In the following three sections of this essay, I shall

Figure 6.1: The Quantitative Biography of a Workforce

Information and possible results to be derived from computorized 'Inventuren' and 'Teilungen' and personal registers of the Esslingen machine factory

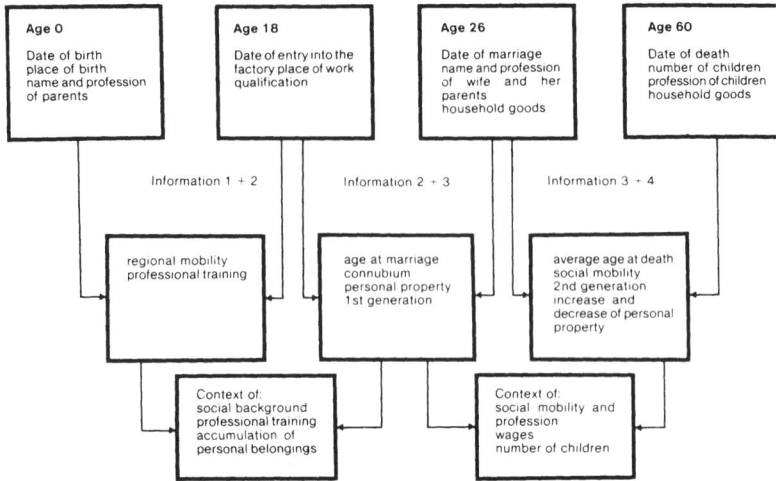

use this material to illustrate the slow, inter-generational process of workers' adaption to the industrial environment by looking at three aspects of the everyday life of employees of the Esslingen machine factory in relation to the social background from which they came. First, I shall examine patterns of regional migration, and the seasonal fluctuation of employment. Then I shall move on to look at patterns of family life – age at marriage, fertility, number of children born or conceived before marriage and financial situation at marriage. Finally, I shall analyse standards of living as shown by the acquisition (or pawning) of material goods according to specific stages of the workers' life-cycle. As we shall see, the crucial linking factor in these various patterns of behaviour is the 'family life-cycle'; that is, the various stages through which a family passes from its formation through marriage, the birth and raising of infants, the acquisition of new earnings as the children begin to work, and finally decay and dissolution as the children leave home and (eventually) one of the original parents dies. Naturally, of course, this pattern was not universal: but factory and State records do show that it formed the experience of the majority of the workforce.

II

Carl Dingler, a second-generation factory worker, was 18 when he wrote the following letter:

> In order to give you an idea of my whereabouts I can say: when I left Esslingen I went to Mainz. At the New Year I got a job there, three hours' walk from Mainz, in Eltville. I stayed there six months and then left for Berlin. On the way I ran short of money and had to earn some, which I did in Burg near Magdeburg for six weeks. I arrived in Berlin in October and there I worked in a factory. In Spring things became difficult because of the war in Schleswig-Holstein and so I started off on the 19th of March together with Paul Döring of Esslingen for Dresden. In Dresden I got a job but as payment was miserable and everything very expensive I left again for Chemnitz, where I found a job with the portefeuille-worker Mr. Ernst and I'm still working at his place.

Carl Dingler Chemnitz 24.8.1864

Before Carl Dingler finally came to Esslingen in 1862, his family had lived at various places in Bavaria, France, Hesse and the Palatinate. We can trace in his biography the typical characteristics of the most highly mobile sector of the early nineteenth-century workforce: pauperised parents, lack of qualifications, and absence of property. For these reasons, such workers were more liable than others to dismissal at short notice. This in turn made it impossible for them to settle down. Their high mobility and frequent changes of residence meant that these workers were not registered anywhere but in the registers of individual firms, so our knowledge of this highly mobile part of the factory workforce is still rather sketchy. However, it is possible to gain at least some information about them from the sources relating to the Esslingen factory.

As shown in the registers of the factory, there were at least three different groups of highly mobile workers in employment at the Esslingen works before the 1880s. First, there were a number of workers who lived in Esslingen but left their jobs without notice in favour of another firm in Esslingen itself. Secondly, there were also many employees who never stayed more than four to six months in one job, at least if their experience in the Esslingen machine factory is anything to go by. After this period, they left the firm and the town but returned in order to start working with the same firm in due turn for a similar period. Finally, there were some workers who were employed for a short time in the Esslingen machine factory, then left and did not come back to Esslingen at all. All these types of worker were highly mobile and only worked in the factory for a short time. Clearly what we are seeing here is an early stage in the creation of an industrial workforce. The kind of mobility involved here bears little relation to patterns of labour mobility observable in a fully mature industrial society. During the later nineteenth century, fluctuations in labour mobility initially did not coincide with economic booms or crises in the machine industry, but as time went on, they became more and more uniform in correspondence to the homogenisation of the social and regional background of the workers as a whole. The well documented fact of growing mass-mobility from the 1880s onwards up to the 1920s was novel in so far as from then on, individual, 'traditional' seasonal mobility vanished and economic boom or slump became 'the' motive for migration. The growing number of 'born proletarians' was thus clearly one of the preconditions of collective behavioural patterns such as collective migration.

The records at our disposal for the study of the workers in the Esslingen factory indicate that the distance of migration was smallest for those workers who worked for some years, then disappeared and came back for at least one, more often two or three more intervals of work in the machine factory. They lived up to 5 kilometres distant from Esslingen, most of them in small villages nearby. From 5 to 25 kilometres was the distance for those who changed form and branch of industry within Esslingen. Predominantly they migrated from villages around Stuttgart. Both these groups were not recruited from urban but rural areas. Of all mobile workers, those who left Esslingen after a short while without coming back migrated the longest distance, most of them departing for a destination between 50 and 75 kilometres away. These differences in regional background were matched by differences in social background. More than half of the workers due to return to the factory at least twice in their life had peasant parents. This also applied to those who did not cling to one factory but changed branch of industry and employer several times a year.

However, although they both had parents who lived in the countryside and retained their roots in rural society, those working seasonally in one firm had parents with small farms or dwarf-holdings. The parents of factory workers with no specific inclination towards one firm but only to the town of Esslingen mostly had rural holdings which concentrated heavily on viticulture. Long-distance migration within these groups of seasonal workers was predominant only with workers whose parents were already employed in factories, that is, in

Württemberg at that time, in textile factories. These factory workers of the second generation not only migrated long distances, they already adopted in the years 1850 to 1860 forms of fluctuation that their 'colleagues' of rural origin did not show before the end of the nineteenth century. Workers of rural origin fluctuated according to the agricultural season whether or not a steady money income was needed by them the whole year round. Of these 'rural' factory workers, 70 per cent stayed in their employment for 4 to 6 months a year, that is only in winter (October-March/April). Those with vineyards did not come each year but they, too, never came in summer. They were not, as the workers of peasant origin obviously were,[6] at any time of their life in desperate need of additional money earnings. A small vineyard was a much more effectively exploitable piece of land than was a less specialised small-holding.

A look at the age-structure of these sons of vine-cultivating families in comparison to those of peasant families gives additional clues to the motives of fluctuation. Children of peasant background started their seasonal work at the age of 16. They then returned every winter up to the age of approximately 40, after which they tried to work for another two to five years without interruption, then left for good. The rhythm of work was quite different with the sons of vineyard-owning peasants. They started their seasonal work in the factories at the age of 30, and they finished when they were about 40. Their rhythm was obviously influenced by the fact that payment for men at the age of 30-35 tended to be best because of the ability of this age group to work hard. But, more important, it was at this age that workers were faced with the most serious drain upon their financial resources because of the expansion of their family, with their children too small to earn money. Here, then, we have two groups of seasonal workers, both working in winter, but for different reasons and at different stages of their life-cycle. Those who needed additional money virtually all the time had to cling to one factory in order to be reasonably sure of getting the job next year as well. These men were 'stem-seasonals', restricted to winter work because of their social background, restricted to one factory because they could not risk losing their reversion to the seasonal factory earnings. In contrast to this the children of vine-cultivators took the job that was best paid, even though, by job-hopping, they ran the risk of getting no job at all the following winter. As they were not as desperately in need of the money as their seasonal colleagues, this risk was worth the chance of better income. The age-structure and seasonal fluctuation of the work of long-distance migrators varied markedly from the two groups mentioned above. When, in summer, the number of workers in the Esslingen machine factory decreased because of these workers leaving their employment for 'agricultural' reasons, the management of the firm tried desperately to keep the number of workers constant.[7] At this time of year they even augmented the minimum daily earnings of their workers in order to discourage their exodus. It was then that other factory workers from the textile industry (mostly 25 to 30-year-old unmarried men) filled in the gaps. Their motive for migration was to find the highest possible earnings at any place within a reasonable distance of home. This meant leaving the textile firms with lower wages near their home towns in which their parents worked, and where they themselves worked during the season when there was no labour shortage in the machine factory.

It is obvious that these individual migrational patterns, adapted to the predominantly non-industrial personal need of seasonal workers of different social backgrounds, could not be maintained in times of economic crisis when the supply of workers was higher than the demand in the specific industry of the region. It was then that fluctuation in employment ceased to be seasonal. Those already in employment tried to keep it, those who were not had to find it elsewhere. The children of seasonal workers of rural background therefore had to leave and adapt the distance and time of their migration to the demand of the industrial labour market, instead of simply working in factories in accordance with the demands of the agricultural cycle. At the beginning of the 1880s, seasonal work lost its agricultural, pre-industrial rhythm. It now became an expression of the fluctuation of a growing number of factory workers of the second generation. Migration more and more became a necessity instead of a choice. And because those who had a job tried to keep it 'regardless' of wages, the age-structure within the factory for some years changed in favour of the 30-45 year-olds, while that of the floating workforce became generally younger (25-30 years old). It might be reasonable, then, to argue that these three developments – the growing number of factory workers of the second generation, the increasing difficulty of getting any employment at all and therefore the compulsion to migrate further afield, and the domination of one age group (25-30) within the mass of the floating workforce in the 1880s and 1890s – almost necessarily intensified the perception of the specific situation of the working class and its specific needs within the working class itself. Differences of background finally melted away, and a more permanent, more unified workforce emerged, more committed to industrial work as a permanent way of life.

III

Regional or seasonal mobility in the first phase of the industrialisation
was to a remarkable extent influenced by personal, individual or
'traditional' behavioural patterns which were none the less closely
related to working and living conditions in the factory, and which lost
their significance when the machine industry entered an economic crisis
in the 1880s. Investigation of fertility, the age of marriage and the
number of children is obviously much more likely to give an idea of
whether or not, and for what time-span, behavioural traditions were
maintained despite changes in working and living conditions. For all
those workers included in this investigation into age at marriage,
patterns of fertility, number of children born or conceived before
marriage, and financial situation at marriage, a number of everyday-life
variables were pretty much the same. They were all working in the
machine factory and living in Esslingen. They were engaged in the
industrial production process and they all got their monthly wages.
Nevertheless, there were remarkable differences in the age at marriage
and number of children. These differences did not coincide with the
workers' qualifications or with their income levels. It is thus necessary
to investigate these differences in connection with the social
background of the workers: to test, in other words, whether workers of
similar social backgrounds maintained similar behavioural patterns
despite the fact that in actual everyday life they had a different status,
different qualifications and different earnings.

Table 6.1: Age at Marriage in Relation to Social Background of Workers
in the Esslingen Machine Factory and their Wives

Profession of fathers of workers	Age at marriage before 1880		Age at marriage after 1880	
	men	women	men	women
Agricultural	32.43	29.11	32.82	29.38
Textile industry	32.75	29.78	32.75	30.07
Metal industry	31.98	27.27	32.20	27.43

It is obvious that before 1880 age at marriage was highest for
workers of a 'textile-background', lowest for those whose parents already
worked in the metal industry. It was fairly similar for workers of rural

origin and those with parents working in the textile industry. This result becomes more comprehensible by realising that 53 per cent of parents working in the textile industry did so in the *domestic* textile industry, living in rural, not in urban areas of Württemberg. The parents of rural profession did not belong to the earlier mentioned group of small farm-owners but were farm labourers. Most probably the higher age at marriage of these two groups of workers (agricultural or textile social background) was due to their financial situation. Marriage in Württemberg at that time was restricted to those with 'sufficient' financial means for a so-called moderate household equipment.

Table 6.2: Amount of Savings and/or Cash at the Age of Marriage in relation to Social Background of Workers in the Esslingen machine factory

Profession of fathers of workers	Amount of savings/cash in Marks					
	0	1-100	101-250	251-500	501-1000	more
Agricultural	47.7	33.2	10.9	5.2	1.6	1.6
Textile industry	58.5	33.8	1.5	3.1	1.5	1.5
Metal industry	46.9	32.7	8.0	2.7	5.3	4.4

The number of workers getting married without any surplus as far as savings or cash was concerned[8] was highest in the group of workers whose fathers worked in the textile industry. As shown in Table 6.2, they were also the group with the highest age at marriage. This direct relation between age at marriage and the height of 'surplus' is typical for all workers included in this table. Age at marriage and financial situation were closely related, due to the fact that, as we have seen, in Württemberg the financial situation and the permission for marriage were bound together by law. But age of marriage never was, and, especially in these years of restricted marriage laws, never could be, identical with age at the actual time of founding a family, or the age at first conception. In order to illustrate this point, and to discover more about behavioural patterns in relation to the individual life-cycles of the workers concerned, we have to look first at the number of children in marriages in general, and then at the number of children born or conceived before marriage.

Table 6.3: Number of Children per Marriage in Relation to Social Background of Workers in the Esslingen Machine Factory

Profession of fathers of workers	Number of children				
	0	1-3	4-6	7-9	more
Agricultural	31.3	33.6	22.8	7.2	4.8
Textile industry	21.4	32.2	25.0	14.2	7.2
Metal industry	17.1	59.9	17.1	2.9	2.9

The number of children per household was highest in those where the father's origins were in the textile industry, that is to say in those that married latest of all groups included in this sample. Workers of this group show the highest percentage of children per marriage. This result becomes less surprising if we look at the percentage of children born or conceived before actual marriage.

Table 6.4: Percentage of Children Born or Conceived before Marriage in Relation to Social Background of Esslingen Machine Factory Workers

Profession of fathers of workers	Born before marriage	Time-span before marriage and birth of child (number of months)				
		1-3	4-6	7-9	10-24	more
Agricultural	25.5	8.5	12.5	8.5	29.8	14.9
Textile industry	35.7	14.3	14.3	7.1	28.6	0
Metal industry	31.6	0	5.3	21.1	26.3	15.8

The singular behaviour of workers with parents working in the textile industry is once more documented in Table 6.4. Approximately 65 per cent of their children were born or conceived before marriage. Their total number of children was higher than in any other group of workers in the factory. Their fertility and their behavioural patterns in this respect differed markedly from those of their colleagues in the machine industry. It did not, as can be shown by results of similar investigations within Esslingen's textile industry, differ from the specific behavioural patterns of workers in the textile industry itself.[9] Social background obviously influenced behavioural patterns in regard to the foundation of families before marriage and the number of children much more effectively than actual profession, the living conditions and the working conditions of the factory worker himself.

The behavioural patterns of workers with parents working in the textile industry bear close resemblance to that Hans Medick has called 'proto-industrial behaviour'.[10] For generations the number of children had been, in domestic textile industry more than in any other branch or profession, a sort of guarantee for increasing income. According to this traditional experience – an experience which did not, however, coincide any more with actual experience – children of textile workers maintained the habit of starting a family (with or without permission to marry) at an early stage of their life and conceiving more children than any of their colleagues. Traditional patterns with regard to fertility obviously did not change immediately with altered conditions of family income, or with new professional skills or requirements.

Only the age at marriage was adjusted to the law. But the 'effectiveness' of these laws, and the meaninglessness of their rigour, could not be demonstrated more impressively than by the fact that they had almost no influence on the actual number of children born. Of course they had, and this is one of the most impressive documented facts of workers' everyday life at the time, a massive influence on the qualitative standard of living of these workers who very often lived for ten and more years with their 'illegitimate' wife and children before they obtained permission to marry. Very often, indeed, they never obtained it despite all the difficulties this imposed on their life and on that of their children.

IV

The biography of the workers, their family life and their life-cycle were of course very much influenced by their actual work, by their qualification and earnings. But we cannot measure this influence or even realise its effect without knowing what sorts of conflicts and difficulties were liable to arise, because there was, as I shall suggest in this last part of the paper, a very specific 'life-cycle' of factory workers and a very different, sometimes vague possibility, for the workers to adapt their behaviour to the stages of this 'factory life-cycle' as they experienced them.

In an important essay on the professional career of workers,[11] Alfred Weber confirmed in 1912 the fact that young workers were liable to obtain well-paid jobs, whereas at the age of about 40 years, their wages deteriorated and they became poor. This general statement can be supported by looking at the wage-earnings according to age of four groups of workers: locksmiths, turners, smiths and unqualified workers. These four groups represented 70 to 80 per cent of the whole workforce of the factory. The course of their earnings and their life-cycle in terms of income originated in the specific forms of 'apprenticeship' and piece-work earnings practised in the factory. Anyone who began work in the factory had to undergo a time when he was not allowed to do piece-work. During this phase of approximately two years he was regarded as an apprentice, whether or not he was actually qualified for a special job. Of course, payment in these years was low. As most workers started their work in the factory at the age of 23-25, this phase of low earnings finished when they were 25-27 years old. They were then allowed to do piece-work which meant an augmentation of earnings of about 20 per cent. Now they had reached the phase of highest earnings. But the worker could not maintain this level of income because at the age of 40-45 he was reduced to his original, 'apprentice' earnings. He was no longer able to work so hard, and for some of the workers the reduction of wages even occurred before the age of 40. Figure 6.2 gives an impression of how these phases of earnings were related to certain age groups, of the increase of income up to the age of 27, the phase of highest earnings, and of the decrease that started earliest in those groups with hardest working conditions, in the groups of smiths and unqualified workers.

Figure 6.2: Phases of Earnings according to Age of Unqualified Workers, Smiths, Locksmiths, and Turners in the Esslingen Machine Factory

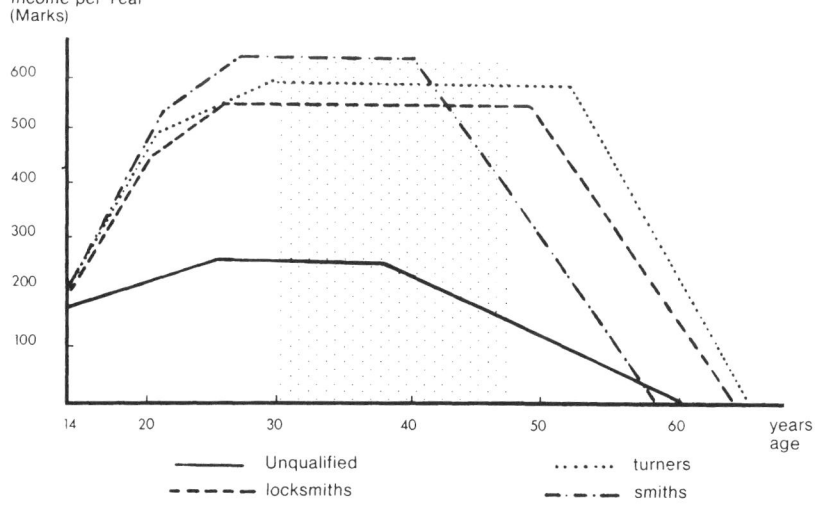

Income per Year
(Marks)

It is important to note that the different stages of income did not coincide with the stages of the family life-cycle: decrease in earnings started when the worker was still in the phase of family expansion and his children were still too small to add to the family budget. There were only two groups of workers whose earnings curve differed markedly from that of their colleagues: the locksmiths and the turners. Under normal economic conditions their phase of highest earnings lasted up to the age of 50. If they had small families and their children were at that time already able to earn money, then there was a very small chance that the poverty of old age could be avoided. For more than 70 per cent of the workers, however, this was impossible.

It is well known that standard of living, income, household and family are not static variables. At least they should not be treated as such because they are components of everyday life which change during everyone's lifetime. Very often these changes are more acute and more dramatic than differences between people of different social classes. As Mark Abrams has suggested,

> . . . in the past and still in many fields today, total consumption patterns have been dominated by class differences . . . it is unlikely that differences of these kinds will retain their significance. Almost certainly they will be replaced in importance by differences related to consumers' position in the life-cycle. Already in some markets the consumption habits of working-class young people have more in common with those of middle-class young people than with those of their parents. Sharp differences in standard of living will in future be related to stages in life-cycle.[12]

This statement does not only apply to the future. It was one of the most important and most typical facts of the worker's life-cycle in the nineteenth century that he had to suffer these sharp differences in standards of living. He may have started reasonably well, but there was no chance whatsoever of ending his life reasonably well. The phase of poverty was apt to become longer the less he was able to restrict his family life-cycle to the stages of earnings forced upon him by factory work.

One possible way to show the effect of these different stages of earnings is to look at acquisitions and at the habit of pawning goods so common to factory workers. In Esslingen, for example, pawnshops came into existence only after the factory and its 500 to 1,000 workers had started production. In 1855 the Industrial Association of Stuttgart published a matter-of-fact statement concerning these phases of different earnings:[13]

> It is generally accepted that a man lays the foundations of his life at the age of 10 to 20, builds it up at the age of 20 to 30, and furnishes it from top to bottom at the age of 30 to 40. But if by this time he has laid no firm foundations, nor built them or furnished the resulting structure, then he becomes once more one of our unhappy beggars.

The restriction on marriage in Württemberg at this time added to the facts which finally forced the workers to try to adapt to these normative stages of the life-cycle. These laws influenced first of all the mode of savings, because for all workers without any dowry it was absolutely necessary to start saving money as early as possible in order to get permission to marry. No more than 24 per cent of all workers succeeded in saving money. More than half (71 per cent) who had savings gathered these before their marriage. The amount of money saved per year was about 8 to 15 per cent of their yearly income. When the sum was sufficient to buy the required 'moderate equipment' of household furniture, the workers stopped saving and started again in one or two years before actual marriage. In the years of no savings the workers bought new clothes, jewellery and books. The surplus they had achieved in the years before their marriage was mainly due to the fact that rent during this time-span of life was lowest compared to any other phase of their life. They did not usually invest more than 7 to 10 per cent of their income in housing, an amount that increased in the years to come sometimes to 25 per cent.

At the age of 25-27 the worker achieved his highest 'standard of living'. Never again during his lifetime would he have so many new clothes, a new silver watch, hats and new shoes, rings and silver buttons. Contemporaries were often annoyed about this 'luxury'. But of course this was not luxury. Only in this stage of his life-cycle did the worker buy new clothes, etc. Whenever in years to come he needed another piece of equipment, either clothes, furniture or whatsoever, he bought second-hand. His 'luxury' was meant to be the last resort in times of acute misery, in times of illness and old age. Any pawning before the phase of decreasing income meant inevitably that poverty started some time earlier. Illness, confinements and premature death, short-term as well as long-term unemployment, all these everyday events added months or years of poverty to the last phase of a worker's life.

Figure 6.3 shows, schematically, to what extent this poverty, this loss of personal belongings was a common event to workers of all professions. The portion of those workers who ended their lives without the smallest possible standard of household equipment was in all four groups of profession higher than at the beginning of their marriage.

Figure 6.3: Household Possessions of Four Types of Workers in the Esslingen Machine Factory

1 = At marriage
2 = At death

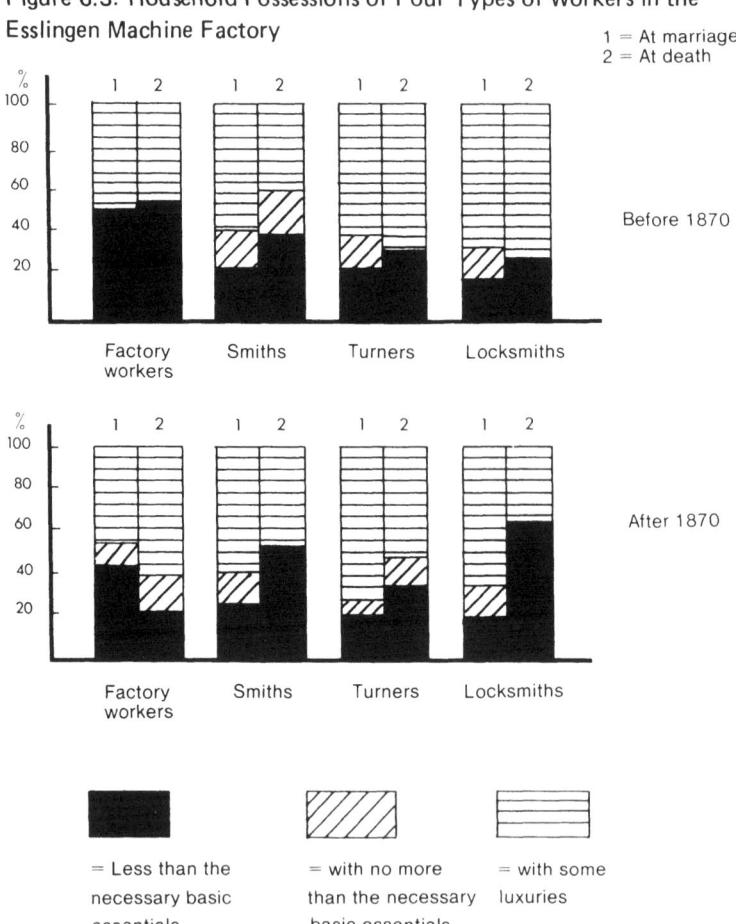

Before 1870

After 1870

■ = Less than the necessary basic essentials

▨ = with no more than the necessary basic essentials

☰ = with some luxuries

Marriage had meant at the beginning another two or three years' additional income and additional household equipment. Workers' wives usually worked in Esslingen's textile industry. They tried to save small sums and to buy some of the furniture necessary to keep up with the requirements of the marriage laws. But the additional earnings of the wife usually stopped when the family had two children. Even though by now rent increased as well as the everyday budget, the worker had no possibility whatsoever of increasing his income. By this age he had reached the highest possible wage and all the family could try to do was to maintain its standard of living as long as possible by some additional, occasional earnings of the wife, mostly sewing. It is in this stage of the life-cycle where social differentiation among the workers becomes most obvious. The varying duration of the phase of highest earnings according to job was combined with the fact that the practice of family planning varied markedly according to the social background of the individual workers. So this stage of the life-cycle was by far the most expensive, especially because industrial wages were not meant to feed a whole family. They were meant for the work done, and it was the worker's own problem whether or not they were sufficient, even though everybody knew that for old age they could never be. The worker had to try to adapt his life-cycle, his age of marriage and the number of his children to the requirements of the different phases of low, high and again low wages. Regardless of his qualification and level of income, he had to realise that when he was 40, his children had to be able to earn their own money: when he finally became 50 or even older they had to be able to support him. Of course these facts were not realised all at one time and by all workers simultaneously, and support in old age was, for all the reasons mentioned above, more often impossible. So old age therefore became the most terrifying prospect of the worker's life. Differences in wages and qualifications, and in general all the aspects of 'social stratification' of workers of one factory, could very seldom touch the extremes that any worker lived through during his lifetime — the relatively well-to-do standards at the age of 25-27, the slow decrease in times of good earnings and expanding family, and the final and inevitable poverty intensified by any 'unusual', that is non-adapted, behaviour or events such as unemployment or illness.

First of all workers tried to adapt their life-cycle to the requirements of their new, specific income situation and to the phases of varying earnings. They did so with varying success according to the behavioural traditions which they 'learned' at home, in their traditional social surroundings. Their standard of living was thus more than just an index of social stratification within the labour force. No more was it simply an indicator of amelioration or deterioration in the economic situation of workers in general. Instead, the biography of any individual worker, as well as 'artificial' collective biographies, shows that sharp differences in the standards of living are related to different stages of the life-cycle. These differences were sharpened by differences in social background much more effectively than by differences in actual income from employment in the factory itself. The inevitable poverty of old age, however, was one of the most influential 'collective' experiences of workers in general. When in the 1880s it became impossible to escape long years of poverty by successful adaptation to the requirements of factory work because of the company's economic difficulties and the general economic crisis in this area, new forms of organisation and protest filled in the gaps. For approximately 40 to 50 years the workers had tried to arrange their inherited or traditional way of life according to the new living conditions of factory work. When at last it became obvious that these efforts were in vain, and that industrial production meant above all that no such thing as traditional behaviour was required anymore, the workers finally began to organise themselves in trade unions and strike movements and to adopt the means of self-articulation which generally characterise the working class in a mature industrial society.

Notes

This essay is based largely on my book *Die Arbeiter der Maschinenfabrik Esslingen: Forschungen zur Lage der Arbeiterschaft im 19. Jahrhundert* (Stuttgart, 1977). It is a revised and extended version of a paper delivered to the first meeting of the SSRC Research Seminar Group on Modern German Social History, held at the University of East Anglia in July 1978.

1.   The bulk of recent work is too great to list here. Two recent major works are: Ulrich Engelhardt, *'Nur vereinigt sind wir stark.' Die Anfänge der deutschen Arbeiterbewegung* (Stuttgart, 1977); Klaus Tenfelde, *Sozialgeschichte der Bergarbeiterschaft an der Ruhr im 19. Jahrhundert* (Bonn-Bad Godesberg, 1977).

2.   Representative selections of this kind of history of workers' everyday lives can be found in Werner Conze *et al.*(eds.), *Arbeiter im Industrialisierungsprozess* (Stuttgart, 1979) and Jürgen Reulecke, Wolf Weber, *Fabrik, Familie, Feierabend: Beiträge zur Sozialgeschichte des Alltags im Industriezeitalter* (Wuppertal, 1978).

3.   For some general speculations on this point, cf. Klaus Tenfelde, 'Zur Diskussion: Arbeiterschaft und Arbeiterbewegung im generationellen Wandel' (paper presented to the Anglo-German Workshop on problems of modern social history, Bad Homburg, October 1979).

4.   Hartmut Zwahr, *Zur Konstituierung des Proletariats als Klasse. Strukturuntersuchung über das Leipziger Proletariat während der industriellen Revolution* (Berlin, 1978).

5.   From the late eighteenth century to the early twentieth century everybody in Württemberg had to register his goods in case of marriage or death, and all these registers (*Inventuren und Teilungen*) were kept at special boards (*Inventurbehörde*), which also carried out the taxation of individual households. Every town had a board of this kind.

6.   For details on the economic and social situation of a number of these workers, see Margarete Ott, 'Das Zubringerdorf Nellingen auf den Fildern' (unpublished 'Zulassungsarbeit' at the Pädagogische Hochschule Esslingen, 1975).

7.   Like a number of Württemberg firms at this time, the Esslingen machine factory paid its workers monthly wages in order to discourage rapid labour turnover and to force the workers to budget their expenditure.

8.   This amount is meant to be additional to the obligatory household equipment taxed by the authorities before giving permission to marry.

9.   Peter Borscheid, *Textilarbeiterschaft in der Industrialisierung* (Stuttgart, 1978).

10.   Hans Medick, 'The Proto-Industrial Family Economy: The Structural Function of Household Production in the Transition from Feudalism to Capitalism', *Social History*, Vol. 3 (1976), pp. 291-315.

11.   Alfred Weber, 'Das Berufsschicksal der Industriearbeiter', *Archiv für Sozialwissenschaft und Sozialpolitik*, 34 (1912), p. 388.

12.   Mark Abrams, 'Consumption in the Year 2000', in Michael Young (ed.), *Forecasting and the Social Sciences* (London, 1968), pp. 39-40.

13.   *Jahresbericht des Stuttgarter Gewerbevereins von 1855* (Stuttgart, 1856).

7 OVERCROWDING AND FAMILY LIFE: WORKING-CLASS FAMILIES AND THE HOUSING CRISIS IN LATE NINETEENTH-CENTURY DUISBURG

James H. Jackson

I

Social critics in the late-nineteenth century were almost universal in their condemnation of cities and the life-styles of their inhabitants.[1] Urban areas were believed to be centres of illness and death, of personal estrangement and rootlessness, of criminality and social revolution. Even though some commentators praised the creative aspects of city life, gloomy portraits of urban conditions were legion. The economist and social commentator Gustav Schmoller likened the city to a primeval forest, where men were gradually but surely stripped of their civilised habits, allowing barbarism and bestiality to reassert themselves.[2] More recently Lewis Mumford reflected a long-standing tradition when he declared that 'between 1820 and 1900 the destruction and disorder within great cities [was] like that of a battlefield . . . Industrialism, the main creative force of the nineteenth century, produced the most degrading urban environment the world had yet seen.'[3] A major component of this urban crisis was the existence of slums where poverty and delapidated, insanitary and overcrowded housing apparently combined to threaten public health and private morality as well as undermine the formation of any sense of social consensus. The misery and desperation that Friedrich Engels observed on the banks of the River Irk in Manchester, Jacob Riis found in the tenements of Cherry Street in New York City, Andrew Mearns and George Sims uncovered in central London, and Gustav Schmoller detected in Berlin.[4]

In the view of many social observers, the most important step that could be taken to halt the social and moral decline of Europe was solving the housing crisis.[5] These critics feared that family life was being progressively undermined because of the lack of adequate shelter and interior furnishings.[6] Presumably, overcrowding created an insanitary living environment and encouraged moral disintegration. Without a comfortable, orderly home to attract him, the man of the house found greater enjoyment in tavern life than in the embrace of his wife and children. Parents and children were forced to sleep together, without regard to health, age or sex, making good child-rearing and proper household decorum impossible. Without proper supervision, young adults were believed to be prone to loose conduct, drunkenness and criminality. These problems were only compounded, according to the critics, by the common practice of taking strangers into the intimacy of the family as lodgers.[7] Poor housing also forced families to change their quarters frequently, in the view of many social commentators. Thus, the home as a symbol of unity with generations past and present was destroyed and, along with it, any chance of developing a sense of stability and belonging.[8]

The central issue of the housing question of the late nineteenth century was, as Gustav Schmoller observed, whether residential conditions affected psychological and moral character.[9] Was social life, more specifically family life, different for slum dwellers who lived in wretched buildings? Both critics and reformers answered in the affirmative. And many social scientists and historians in the late twentieth century continue to believe that overcrowding is directly related to aberrant behaviour.[10] Using animal studies as guides, these researchers have attempted to determine how high density generates social deviance in man, either by directly observing people in dense situations or by correlating densities of physical areas with their rates of social instability.[11] But such crowding studies have been plagued by methodological imprecision and haunted by profoundly contradictory results. While some investigations have apparently established a close association between residential crowding and poor physical health, accidents and dissatisfaction, other inquiries have found many societies in which high-density housing was maintained without the expected pathologies.[12] Thus, no clear-cut relationship seems to exist between density and behaviour, at least in the mid-twentieth century.

Was it possible that such ambiguity could have been present in nineteenth-century cities as well, only to be overlooked by middle-class reformers, city administrators and socialist critics, who all made the housing crisis a captive of their own polemics? If these social observers were correct and the direct links between crowding and behaviour are clearly evident, the way housing conditions helped set the pace of the urban experience must have changed over the past 100 years. How and why this transformation came about is a question that would undoubtedly open up important new areas of research. But if the association of residential density and the organisation of patterns of city life was tenuous, our understanding of the conditions of the nineteenth-century urban experience would have to be revised considerably.

II

How are we to approach this important question of urban social history? The German historiographical tradition offers little guidance. The study of the concrete living conditions of ordinary people in late nineteenth-century Germany has only recently attracted the attention of historians. Those who have ventured into this uncharted territory have returned with complaints about the unsystematic, fragmentary nature of official surveys and statistical reports and about the unrepresentative nature of descriptive evidence. In spite of these frustrations, what they have recounted of this curious land has spurred on the search for more exotic species of data, for detailed information that would facilitate the study of family life and housing conditions. In Duisburg, the industrial town in the Ruhr basin which forms the subject of the present study, such data has been found, consisting of an amalgam of census material (that reveals residency patterns) and housing information (that tells of the physical dimensions of houses). Although this rich data base is not free of some of the same flaws that have plagued earlier studies, it has the great advantage of permitting the analysis of variations in housing conditions and in the behaviour of individual families while controlling for other important variables. One of the central aspects of the nineteenth-century housing question can be addressed directly: did relative crowding make a difference in the way urban families organised their residential patterns?

The census data used in this study was the product of the Prussian Statistical Office and its drive to provide governmental officials with reliable information about national development.[13] By 1890, procedures for a thorough house-by-house numeration had been developed with a formidable reputation for accuracy. The first of December was set as census day. Census cards were distributed to each household head during the preceding two days; then the cards were collected and verified on the afternoon of 1 December. In addition to an address, a person's given and family names, relationship to the household head, sex, exact birth date, marital status, birthplace, religion, occupation, citizenship, place of usual residency (if in transit), and military status, if any, were asked. General statistics were then

generated by local officials and sent on to the Statistical Office in
Berlin.

Although the practice was prohibited after 1890, officials in larger
cities in the lower Rhine area (*Regierungsbezirk* Düsseldorf) saw the
census as an opportunity to correct and supplement their continuous
residency registers. This was also true of Duisburg. Clerks who kept the
residency registers made their own copy of the census cards in the form
of large enumerators' books, which are still to be found in the
Stadtarchiv Duisburg, Bestand 80, GH 74 to GH 78. They contain all
the personal information of the original census cards, except for
relationship to the household head, which was superfluous for the
residency system. Nor were these clerks concerned with maintaining
distinctions between households living at the same address. These two
omissions proved to be formidable obstacles when preparing the
source for computer analysis of family characteristics. They made it
impossible, solely on the basis of the census manuscripts themselves, to
determine who belonged to which household, whether persons with
the same last name were members of the same household with a joint-
family composition or two separate nuclear families or how lodgers
were to be distinguished from single person households.

A satisfactory but time-consuming answer was found by using the
Duisburger Adressbuch (city directory) of 1891 as a guide. City
directories in Duisburg were based on information supplied by the
continuous residency register and the yearly class-tax survey taken each
November. Most probably, directories were assembled and published at
the beginning of the new year. They consisted not only of an
alphabetical listing of tax-paying citizens but also a street-by-street
directory of household heads, i.e., those who maintained an independent
residence. Because the 1890 census was also taken late in the year and
was also organised by street, it was not difficult to locate an address
and identify those who were household heads. Other persons listed
after an identified household head in the census, but before the next
identified head, were assumed to be a household for the purpose of this
analysis. Knowing that the 1890 census instructions specified that
household heads be listed first, with other household members
following in a certain order, the household status of each person could
be inferred. Where possible, Peter Laslett's rules of presumption were
followed.[14] As would be expected, detailed specification of familial
relationships was impossible under these circumstances. Nevertheless,
the broad distinctions of nuclear family members by generation and age,
other relatives, household servants and lodgers were clear. Only in a

handful of cases was the determination of household division and
household status so ambiguous that they had to be eliminated from the
sample. These cases were not, however, clustered in any geographical
area nor did they fall into any one occupational category.

The housing information used in this study was gleaned from
records kept by the city building inspector's office (*Bauordnungsamt*)
on every structure in the city from the late 1850s onward. Where city
planners had failed, these inspectors succeeded in enforcing their
regulations. The basic goal of the researcher using these records was to
determine how houses looked on census day, 1890. But building
dossiers are difficult to use because of their complexity and sometimes
fragmentary nature. Generally, the earliest files contain just a basic
sketch of a building floor plan for new construction. Later on,
however, regulations required much more specific information and
governed such details as distance from the street, amount of courtyard,
waste disposal, height of building, fire safety, construction materials,
and minimum size of occupied rooms. Beginning in 1893, official
concern with residential hygiene was reflected in a series of guidelines
aimed at the living arrangements of poor people, an effort in social
engineering that culminated in the establishment of a formal
inspections office that surveyed multiple-family dwellings from 1901
to 1907. These investigative reports provided important supplemental
information for this study. From this jumble of construction plans,
remodelling permits, sewer and water connection instructions,
apartment inspection forms, appraisals by housing experts of the
structural soundness of a building, descriptions in letters, and old
photographs, the transformation of a particular building could be
traced and the following information assembled: the number of
separate buildings on a lot; the number of floors in the main living area;
whether a building had a cellar, a courtyard, or was part of a large
tract project; multi-purpose use of a building; the total number of
rooms (excluding halls, stairwells, entryways, and sometimes the attic
and cellar); the number of rooms used for business purposes; total
available living area in square metres (including kitchen and bathroom,
if indoors) as well as the attic and cellar, if there was some indication
that they were designed to be used as living areas; the number of
separate kitchens; the number and location of toilet facilities; the total
number of rooms that could be heated, given the placement of
chimneys; the type of construction; and the date when sewer and water
lines were attached. These records do not, however, contain
information on ownership, market values or taxation.

To extract the needed data, three steps were required. First, the proper building dossier had to be found for each sample household. Because *Haus-Akten* ('house files') were listed in archival indices according to current address, problems arose when street names and numbers had changed. In this case, a house had to be physically located on detailed maps of Duisburg between 1867 and 1976. In this way, changes in address identification were clarified. The second step in the process of obtaining the required housing data was to determine the location of the building dossier itself. Documents for those structures presently standing are located in the *Haus-Akten Archiv* (*Mercedes-Haus*). Records of buildings that were either torn down or destroyed are found in the city archive (*Bestand* 610). The third step in reconstructing the housing conditions of Duisburg's families was to determine which architect's plan best described conditions on 1 December 1890. For most houses, no single document could be found specifying these conditions precisely on the desired date. Thus, remodelling plans had to be used to determine how the basic plan had been modified before or after census day. Providing that the continuity of a building dossier was basically sound (e.g. no reference to major reconstruction plans no longer in the file), all documents in the file between 1860 and 1920 were inspected in order to piece together the most complete plan of the building. No assumptions were made about room configuration. If only the ground floor arrangement was shown in the architect's drawings, the plan was considered incomplete and collateral information was sought to determine the character of upper floors.

There are several limitations to the use of housing files that fortunately have had little apparent effect on this study's conclusions. First, the desired information for many buildings could not be obtained, due mainly to the caprice of bureaucratic practice or of wartime destruction. No construction plans existed for houses built before 1860 that did not experience subsequent structural modification, making it difficult to determine which house was standing in 1890. But this restriction was not very significant because nearly two-thirds of Duisburg's housing was built after 1860. Allied bombing raids during the Second World War had a potentially greater effect on the availability of housing records. On the night of 20 December, 1942, the *Stadt-Theatergebäude* (State Theatre Building), where *Haus-Akten* were being stored, was hit and burned. Fortunately, relatively few files were lost. The second limitation in the use of building records concerns the completeness of surviving documents. Certain kinds of structural changes did not have to be formally approved by the building inspector's office, such as changes in non-load-bearing walls and in doors and windows that did not face a street. Thus, a building's room configuration could have changed without becoming evident in official records. But the crucial variable used in this study, space per person, was unaffected by such remodelling. More problematic was the fact that building files did not show conclusively whether attics or cellars were used. But the detailed surveys of housing inspectors who were on the lookout for such problems from 1901 to 1907 showed that few Duisburgers found these kinds of quarters necessary. The final problem in the use of Duisburg's building records was that sample households could not be placed in the precise set of rooms they inhabited in 1890. The exact degree of residential crowding of each family was thereby blurred. Thus, little reliance was placed in this study on fine distinctions between households based on space per person. The use of broader categories would tend to minimise differences between groups living at different densities. And any patterns that do emerge are even more noteworthy.

Housing sanitation inspection questionnaires for older buildings in the inner city of Duisburg presented both unique opportunities and special problems. Even though this information was sometimes incomplete and unsystematic, these forms gave an unusually detailed picture of actual living arrangements of multi-household buildings from 1901 to 1907. Very specific data on the owner's and renter's names, the amount of rent paid, the address and location of the apartment, the number of males and females over and under fourteen years of age, the number and kinds of rooms, size of bedrooms in cubic metres, which household members slept in which rooms, numbers of lodgers, official objections to any living arrangements, the inspection date, and a list of basic sanitation questions was recorded. As rich as this source was, there were a number of limits to its usefulness. First, only buildings with two or more households were inspected. Second, actual record-keeping was not as thorough as the planners of this survey had hoped. Finally, deep social biases about 'proper' living arrangements were apparent. This could especially be seen in the inspectors' judgemental attitudes toward the practice of keeping lodgers and toward the sleeping arrangements of poor people.

Nevertheless, in cases where no earlier building information existed, these questionnaires were considered to be the best estimates of conditions in 1890. The size of living space in square metres was estimated first by totalling the number of cubic metres listed for the bedrooms. In some cases, the volume of all living rooms was given and was used in the calculations instead. Second, this total was divided by the number of bedrooms, giving the average volume of each bedroom. This was in turn divided by a constant of 2.8 metres to give the average number of square metres per room. The 2.8 metre figure was chosen as the average room height of older buildings. The room area average was then multiplied by the actual number of rooms in the building used for living. If only the volume for bedrooms was used, this total was increased by 25 per cent. Bedrooms were, as a rule, smaller than other living rooms. Thus, estimates based on bedrooms alone would have underestimated the true living area. The constant of 25 per cent was determined by figuring total living area based on architectural plans and on housing inspection questionnaires for those buildings where both existed. The former was consistently one-fifth larger than the latter. In the following sections, we shall look at some of the results that may be obtained from a systematic investigation of these sources along the lines indicated.

III

Before the middle of the nineteenth century, there was little evidence that the Ruhr Basin in west-central Germany would become one of Europe's most significant industrial concentrations as well as one of its largest coal-producing areas. The English traveller Thomas C. Banfield found that by 1850, 'castles, ruins, and factories rapidly succeeded each other' on the banks of the Ruhr River itself, but the countryside around Essen remained 'poetically agricultural'. Population statistics reflected the modest tempo of economic life. In 1849, Dortmund with 10,532 residents and Duisburg with 11,725 were the largest Ruhr towns. Essen followed in size with 8,813 inhabitants, and Bochum claimed 4,877 persons living within its boundaries.[15] But the centres of a flourishing textile trade just to the south – Krefeld (36,134), Elberfeld (38,663), and Barmen (35,989) – were far larger. The years after mid-century brought dramatic changes. The area rapidly lost its rural character. The proportion of persons who were employed in mining, metallurgy, machine and chemical manufacture, the building trades and commerce and transportation grew from 6.9 per cent in 1849 to 57.8 per cent in 1895.[16] Drawing migrants from the nearby Sauerland and from more distant areas such as Saxony, Silesia, East Prussia and Poland, the total population of the Ruhr Basin increased from almost 300,000 in 1850 to nearly 2,000,000 by the turn of the twentieth century.[17] The newer towns of the Emscher Valley sprang into existence owing to the expansion of the coal industry. The longer established cities with a wider industrial base also experienced rapid population growth. Dortmund's population increased nearly eleven times, from 13,546 in 1852 to 142,733 in 1900; Essen's from 10,552 to 118,862, or over eleven-fold; and Duisburg's from 13,087 to 92,730, about 700 per cent in five decades.[18]

This kind of growth placed great strains on the resources of these cities, especially on housing. Not unexpectedly, complaints about disintegrating slum conditions became more frequent. Dortmund, Essen and Bochum were the subject of special study when the Social Policy Association dealt with the housing crisis in 1886.[19] And, according to at least one contemporary report, some of the worst living conditions in all of Germany could be found in another major town in the Ruhr, in Duisburg. Literally in the shadow of the city hall, at Schwannenstrasse 13, investigators for the newspaper *Das Volk* found appalling housing conditions and some of their terrible consequences: illness, poverty, child neglect and crime:

> From the entry hall a ladder led upwards. In the cramped space it had to lean against the opposite wall and we could hardly climb up, even after several attempts. A short step from the opening for the ladder we entered a narrow, low ceiling room with two beds and a crib, lighted only by a small roof ventilation hole. A man with a severe lung illness sat on an old crate. He spoke only with great effort, labouring over every word. In his pale face and feverish eyes could be seen the unmistakable march of pain and bitterness of soul out of which sin and desperation burned. Nearby stood another wretched bed in a cramped corner. These four beds and the crib were the resting place for the sickly father, mother, and nine small children. After we had carefully descended the ladder I asked the wife where the other children were, because I only saw a few. She buried her face in her apron and only with great difficulty could we piece the following together because of her sobs: A while back, she had been in the hospital for weeks. Her husband, who was in better health then, was unemployed and finally found work elsewhere. The children were left entirely on their own during this time. One day the oldest boy, who should have been in school, went with his sister down to the coal storage area. They did not even have any fuel to heat the kitchen . . . 'And there they got both of them . . . and now

they have arrested them . . .'[20]

And it appears that such crowded conditions were increasing in
Duisburg. By 1890, the proportion of single-household dwellings
declined markedly (see Table 7.1). At the same time, the percentage of
those residing in buildings with five or more households almost tripled
during the preceding twenty years.

Table 7.1: Proportion of Households in Single and Multiple Dwellings
for Duisburg: 1843, 1867 and 1890.

Type of dwelling	1843	1867	1890
Single-household dwelling	22.8	25.9	13.1
Multiple-household dwelling			
Two households	29.7	24.4	18.1
Three households	20.8	20.0	18.9
Four households	15.6	17.0	17.7
Five households	3.6	7.9	13.7
Six households	3.7	3.6	8.5
Seven households	2.1	0.8	4.1
Eight or more households	1.8	0.5	5.8
Total	100.1	100.1	99.9
(N)	(1089)	(1297)	(1661)

Source: Samples from the 1843, 1867 and 1890 Duisburg census manuscripts

Due to the vicissitudes of bureaucratic neglect and warfare,
documents necessary for a detailed analysis of the human consequences
of the housing crisis of the late nineteenth century do not exist for
Ruhr cities, except for Duisburg.[21] By gleaning information from this
city's collection of official statistics, housing surveys, building permits,
architects' drawings and manuscript census returns, as I have indicated
above, three major questions can be answered. First, how did Duisburg's
housing stock come into being? What was its character? How well were
the city's residents served by this method of creating housing? Second,
was there any association between residential crowding and general
measures of family deviance from the late 1860s, when the first
statistics become available, through the first decade of the twentieth
century? Third, do any systematic differences in the organisation of
family life emerge when the concrete living conditions of individual
households are analysed?

In the early nineteenth century, Duisburg was a relatively

insignificant market town. [22] It still closely resembled the rustic settlement that repelled the Dutch diplomat, Jules Armand Colbert, two centuries before, with its 'low shabby houses' and 'filthy streets'.[23] Although the city had a century-long tradition as a transshipment point for coal and for goods destined for Holland, it was preoccupied primarily with meeting the limited demands of local consumers. Even the expansion of soap manufacturing and the establishment of several sugar processing plants, chemical manufacturing facilities, and a small iron foundry did not change the city's unremarkable economic picture. Before 1850, the geographical expansion of Duisburg was very modest and did not have to contend with the constraints that were later to channel the city's growth. New construction was limited to filling in the low-lying Oederich area within the city walls. The first house outside the dilapidated, vine-covered medieval city walls was not built until 1820, indicative of the slow growth of the town.

As with the Ruhr Basin as a whole, major improvement of the transportation network during the second half of the nineteenth century and several important technical advances allowed iron smelting and metal working to assume leading economic roles in the industrial development of Duisburg. In spite of setbacks in 1858-63 and 1874-85, the city's economy continued to expand and diversify. Building and construction trades benefited from these general trends. It was necessary for these workers to construct both the city's new factories and rows of houses for a burgeoning population. The number of residents in Duisburg was increasing not only because of a relatively high birth-rate but also because of the constant ebb and flow of migrants, more of whom stayed than left. After 1850, the city's settlement expansion became more complex, shaped by the basic framework of an agrarian past, by geographical barriers such as the marshy flood plain of the Ruhr to the north and Dickelsbach to the west, by the coming of the railroad, and by the location of major manufacturing plants.[24] Although the inner city became a business centre and continued to be the site of small-scale manufacture and traditional crafts, it did not experience heavy pressure for land space or have the highest land values because Duisburg had several expansion centres.[25] The thrust beyond the old city walls accelerated toward the east and the new Railway Station. New focal points of settlement were created on the outskirts of town, in Neudorf and Hochfeld, where new industry was located. Local public transportation did not play an important role in shaping the settlement pattern in the second half of the nineteenth century.

Domestic architecture in Duisburg was not characterised by extreme social differentiation.[26] Although better homes were found along Düsseldorferstrasse and Mülheimerstrasse, there was no real 'villa' section. The very well-to-do tended to leave town and settle in more desirable areas, like Düsseldorf. Neither were there large tracts of company housing. Only Krupp and another company, the *Niederrheinische Hütte*, made such facilities available to their employees, and then only in limited quantities. Indeed, the external appearance of housing units did not differ appreciably from city section to section. New housing construction went through two phases after 1850. From mid-century to about 1875, domestic building styles of the inner city were simply extended to the expansion areas.[27] Although street placement was influenced by pre-industrial land-holding patterns, they did not determine housing architecture. Houses were not forced to conform to the haphazard boundaries of agricultural fields. Building lots were simply cut to the desired house size by the builders. Pre-1875 structures were mainly small buildings that did not exceed two-and-one-half floors. Sometimes they were decorated with ornate but unimaginative stucco facades, according to the style of the day. Of brick construction, they usually had a three- to five-window-wide frontage (seven to nine metres). Each floor contained three to four rooms of about eleven square metres each. Except in the more prestigious areas, where free-standing houses were common, buildings were constructed side by side, without open space between them. Single-storey storage sheds, workshops, horse stalls and out-houses occupied most of the area behind the main residence with perhaps some space left over for a garden. After 1875 until the beginning of the twentieth century, housing units grew in size and experienced some basic floor plan changes. Because many building lots were long and narrow, adding an extra floor or two and constructing a rear extension were the only ways land could be used more efficiently. Thus, more three to four storey rental units with rear extensions but with only slightly broader façades (eight to eleven metres) than earlier buildings were popular. Each floor now had four to seven rooms, each averaging 15 to 17 square metres.

In contrast to Berlin and other eastern German cities, Duisburg was not packed with large tenement buildings. This did not happen, however, because city administrators successfully blocked their construction.[28] These officials tried occasionally to control urban development, mainly by attempting to keep living areas and manufacturing sections separate. But because building had already begun, various master plans for the inner city (1841 and 1850), Hochfeld (1864 and 1879), and Neudorf (1878) failed to achieve even this modest goal. Most building went unregulated because the bureaucracy lacked initiative to enforce those regulations already on the books, and did not have the personnel to follow through with oversight, even if they had the will. On the contrary, the development of large tenements was hindered by land-holding patterns. Duisburg's expansion areas were initially splintered into numerous small fields and orchards. This meant there was a large offering of small building lots and no artificial land shortage. In addition, because as many landowners as possible wanted to participate in the city's construction boom, they insisted on building private streets to make their property accessible. Thus the interior land in city blocks was too small to erect large rental units.

One way to understand how well this housing construction pattern served the inhabitants of Duisburg is to analyse residential crowding as measured by the number of persons per room (see Figure 7.1). These statistics became available for the first time in 1866, at the beginning of the second upswing of the local economy in the industrial era. They show that in spite of a construction frenzy between 1866 and 1872, when the city's housing stock expanded nearly 30 per cent, room densities intensified. This was due to an even more powerful increase in total population of about 44 per cent in the same time period. When depression came in 1872, the city's population growth virtually stagnated. At the same time, the housing industry kept on building, still in tune with the tremendous growth of the 'founding period' of the German Empire, the *Gründerzeit*. In fact, construction hit a one-year peak in 1874 when 550 units were added to the city's housing stock, a 17 per cent increase. As a result, residential crowding declined markedly. When a measure of economic vigour was restored in the 1880s and Duisburg's population began to increase again, wary investors held themselves aloof from the real estate market and building lagged behind. Consequently, the number of persons per room again increased, reaching relatively high levels between 1885 and 1890. Thereafter, increases in housing outpaced population growth as the economy entered another phase of relative prosperity, leading to a gradual decline of crowding intensity.

Figure 7.1: Housing Density in Duisburg: 1866-1908

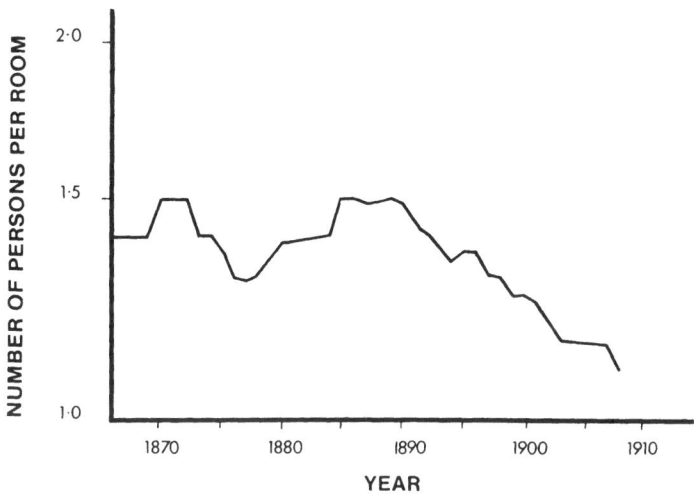

IV

According to the conventional wisdom, variations in residential density like those in Duisburg should have been reflected in various measures of social dislocation, especially those sensitive to family behaviour, perhaps with a slight time-lag. Social ills could have been expected to increase to 1872, when crowding reached its first peak. Between 1873 and 1877, in a period of relative improvement in housing conditions, dislocation in the lives of Duisburgers for this reason should have declined. The long period of increasing crowding from 1877 to 1890, however, should have been accompanied by increasing indication of personal disruption. During the decade of declining density rates, from 1891 to 1901, one would expect to see an easing of social ills. But when changes in residential crowding are compared with those of various measures of dedication to family life, such as the birth-rate, illegitimacy and child neglect, these expectations are not fulfilled.

Residential crowding was believed by many nineteenth-century critics to be one of the most important forces that determined attitudes toward family.[29] When housing density rose, family devotion was thought to wane. Conversely, when density declined, commitment to family presumably intensified. These social observers also held that the birth-rate was a sensitive indicator of devotion to family values.[30] If the willingness to accept the profound social obligation of rearing children changed and if the desire to enjoy the blessings of family life altered, so would the birth-rate. Thus the conventional wisdom would expect housing density and the birth-rate to be reciprocally related to one another. But Duisburg's birth-rates were curiously insensitive to changes in residential crowding (see Figure 7.2). From 1866 to 1872, both the birth-rate and housing density were up. After 1872, crowding went down, but births remained stable for a few years and then began to fall markedly. Between 1877 and 1890, the relationship of housing conditions and family commitment seemed to emerge as expected by nineteenth-century critics. Unfortunately for this view, however, the fall of birth-rates did not begin when residential density rose, but several years before when crowding was becoming less intense. During the last decade of the century, the number of persons per room declined steadily. The birth-rate remained fairly constant, rather than increasing.

Figure 7.2: Crude Birth Rates and Housing Density for Duisburg: 1866-1901

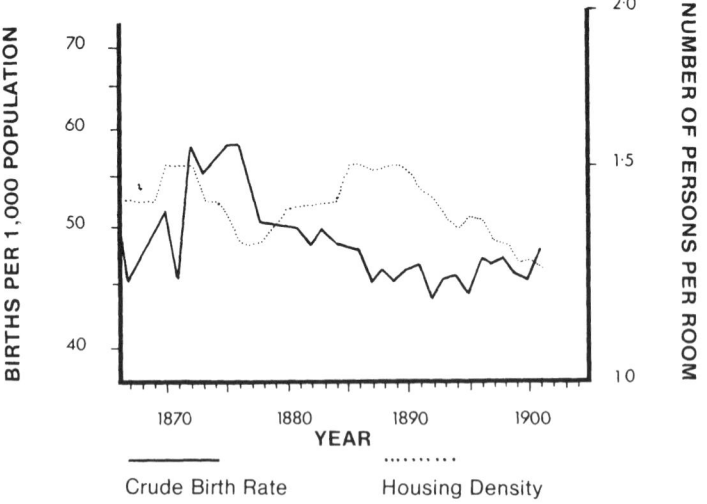

Crude Birth Rate   Housing Density

If birth-rates did not have a clear association with housing conditions, perhaps illegitimacy rates would. Most out-of-wedlock pregnancies would involve impressionable youth, those presumably most sensitive to the corrupting influences of a deteriorating living environment. Many critics felt that crowding encouraged irresponsible sexual behaviour and debauchery that broke through all moral and religious constraints.[31] Thus, residential density and illegitimacy rates would be expected to move in tandem. But unfortunately for this conventional point of view, increases and declines in such births actually anticipated the movement of crowding rates between 1866 and 1872 (see Figure 7.3). From 1872 until 1875, while housing density declined, illegitimacy figures nearly doubled. After another sharp fall and rise that bore little relationship to changes in residential crowding, the number of illegitimacies per 100 births stabilised at just under 3 per cent for the rest of the century. This was the same period during which the number of persons per room began to rise to its peak in 1890 and thereafter to decline. It does not appear, then, that sexual inhibitions were systematically associated with housing conditions.

Figure 7.3: Illegitimacy Rate and Housing Density for Duisburg: 1866-1901

ILLEGITIMACIES PER 100 BIRTHS

NUMBER OF PERSONS PER ROOM

YEAR

Illegitimacy Rate ——— Housing Density . . . .

Some commentators were critical of many late nineteenth-century parents for their apparent lack of concern for their children, letting them become uncouth rowdies.[32] Another measure of this lack of parental concern for family solidarity, according to social observers, was the rate of child neglect. Admittedly an act of desperation, it could be, nevertheless, an indicator of the extremes to which some might go to relieve the tensions brought on by terrible housing conditions, such as those found by the reporters from *Das Volk*. Again, the pattern expected by contemporaries did not emerge. When changes in the number of children supported by public welfare and residential crowding are compared, no consistent relationship can be found (see Figure 7.4). Although housing density intensified between 1873 and 1890, child neglect rates fell fairly consistently throughout the entire period.

Figure 7.4: Number of Orphans and Foster Children Receiving Public Welfare Assistance at the End of the Year and Housing Density for Duisburg: 1873-92

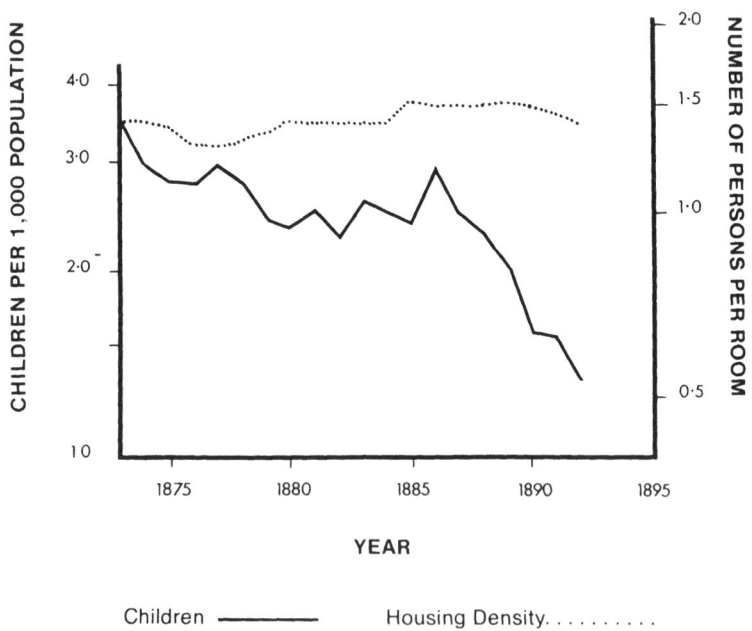

Children ——————   Housing Density. . . . .

V

It is clear then, that these three indicators of unstable family life did not have any consistent relationship to residential crowding in Duisburg during the last third of the nineteenth century. To this extent, the fears of social critics that the quality of family life was disintegrating under the pressures of changing housing conditions were unfounded. But this conclusion must remain tentative because it is based on an analysis of summary measures of behaviour for an entire city. Because associations (or their absence) measured between group variables are not the same as those measured on individuals, the next step ideally would be to collect information on the room size and location of the living quarters of each household and analyse its correlations with such data as physical health, psychological stress, family relations, aggression and social involvement.[33] Of course, this is not possible for residents of nineteenth-century Duisburg. But what can be examined with a more modest data base is of vital importance: did the logic of the conventional wisdom operate at the level of the individual household? More specifically, did a systematic relationship exist between crowding and some general measure of family living arrangements, such as household composition?

At first glance, residential conditions did seem to make a real difference, thereby confirming the expectations of nineteenth-century critics concerning the power of space to shape the texture of family life (see Table 7.2).[34] In Duisburg in 1890, those living in relatively high-density housing tended to organise themselves into simpler nuclear families much more often than those occupying less crowded quarters.[35] Conversely, greater variety in living arrangements was encouraged by average or below average density. Apparently, co-residence was a luxury, permitted only when sufficient privacy between sub-groups of relatives was assured. But looking at all households together obscures the divergent experiences of different socio-economic groups (see Table 7.3). The kind of association between density and family structure found for Duisburg's households as a whole was not present for any group except proprietor and lower white-collar employees. For professional and higher white-collar employees, the relationship was exactly the opposite; for households headed by artisans and unskilled workers, average residential density apparently promoted a greater diversity of living arrangements, while the extremes encouraged households to remain simple families. Clearly, these findings tend to undermine one of the key logical assumptions made by nineteenth-century commentators, that residential crowding affected every household in the same fashion.

Some of these social observers argued, however, that mere space alone was not the basic issue. In their view, residential density was only a proxy measure for a far more significant influence on the living patterns of Duisburg's households: lodging.[36] Taking strangers into the intimacy of the household was thought to be a critical part of the housing crisis of the late nineteenth century, a phenomenon that

Table 7.2: Household Composition by Residential Density for
Duisburg: 1890

Household composition*	Density†		
	High	Average	Low
Simple families	90.7	81.6	79.7
Solitaries	3.9	8.2	12.2
Extended families	2.3	4.5	2.7
No family	1.4	3.5	4.1
Not classified	1.7	2.1	1.4
Total	100.0	99.9	100.1
(N)	(515)	(425)	(74)

*For definitions of household composition categories, see E.A. Hammel and Peter
Laslett, 'Comparing Household Structure over Time and between Cultures',
Comparative Studies in Society and History, 16 (1974), pp. 73-109.

† High density	= 1.0-7.56 square metres per person
Average density	= 7.57-21.58 square metres per person
Low density	= 21.59-111.0 square metres per person

Source: Sample from the 1890 manuscript census and Haus-Akten

involved every social group (see Table 7.4). But critics did not believe
that all status groups responded in the same way to this potentially
divisive force. Higher socio-economic groups apparently managed quite
well. But poorer people were plagued by disequilibrium because they
took in non-family, if the witness of many social observers can be
trusted. Factory inspectors complained that young workers escaped
proper discipline by becoming lodgers.[37] Moralists were attentive to
any rumour of sexual scandal caused by lusty extra-familial household
residents moving into workingmen's homes.[38] To help the less
fortunate escape their plight, reformers sought to instruct them in the
benefits of middle-class domestic values with the aid of meddlesome
bureaucrats.[39] But once again, the evidence from Duisburg confounds
the logic of the conventional wisdom. Except in the case of households
headed by proprietors and lower white-collar employees, the presence
of lodgers was associated with the living arrangements of all status
groups in the same way (see Table 7.5).

Despite accumulating evidence that the logic of the traditional view
of the housing crisis of the late nineteenth century is inadequate, census
data and housing information used alone cannot address the problem of

Table 7.3: Household Composition by Residential Density and
Socio-economic Level for Duisburg: 1890*

Socio-economic level and household composition	Density		
	High	Average	Low
Professional and higher white-collar employees			
Simple families	66.7	75.0	100.0
Solitaries	0	12.5	0
Extended families	33.3	6.3	0
No family	0	6.3	0
Not classified	0	0	0
Total	100.0	100.1	100.0
(N)	(3)	(16)	(11)
Proprietors and lower white-collar employees			
Simple families	89.3	87.5	80.6
Solitaries	3.6	1.3	9.7
Extended families	0	7.5	6.5
No family	3.6	0	3.2
Not classified	3.6	3.8	0
Total	100.1	100.1	100.0
(N)	(28)	(80)	(31)
Skilled crafts			
Simple families	89.9	85.1	90.9
Solitaries	5.9	4.0	9.1
Extended families	3.4	5.9	0
No family	0	4.0	0
Not classified	0.8	1.0	0
Total	100.0	100.0	100.0
(N)	(119)	(101)	(11)
Unskilled workers (position specified)			
Simple families	96.8	93.5	100.0
Solitaries	1.6	3.7	0
Extended families	0	0.9	0
No family	0	0.9	0
Not classified	0	0.9	0
Total	100.0	99.9	100.0
(N)	(188)	(107)	(6)

Table 7.3 (continued)

Socio-economic level and household composition	High	Density Average	Low
Unskilled workers (position unspecified)			
Simple families	94.6	84.9	100.0
Solitaries	0.9	7.5	0
Extended families	2.7	3.8	0
No family	0.9	3.8	0
Not classified	0.9	0	0
Total	100.0	100.0	100.0
(N)	(112)	(53)	(1)

*Definitions for household composition and density are the same as for Table 7.2. A discussion of the socio-economic groupings used here can be found in Jackson, 'Migration and Urbanization', Appendix III.

Source: Sample from the 1890 manuscript census and Haus-Akten

Table 7.4: Presence of Lodgers by Socio-economic Level for Duisburg: 1890

Presence of lodgers	Socio-economic level				
	Professional and higher white-collar employees	Proprietors and lower white-collar employees	Skilled craftsmen	Unskilled workers (position specified)	Unskilled workers (position unspecified)
Not present	71.2	76.8	74.4	86.0	82.4
Present	28.8	23.2	25.6	14.0	17.6
Total	100.0	100.0	100.0	100.0	100.0
(N)	(52)	(224)	(360)	(480)	(301)

Source: Sample from the 1890 manuscript census

deepest concern to social critics: the quality of family life in the slums. Unfortunately, descriptive evidence concerning the question is extremely fragmentary for Duisburg. But that which does exist not only graphically describes the physical, financial and psychic tensions of living in poverty, but also reveals a deep awareness of family ties by dwellers in some of the city's worst housing.[40] This kind of impressionistic data only adds further weight to the critique of the traditional view of housing and social life.

Table 7.5: Household Composition by Presence of Lodgers and
Socio-economic Level for Duisburg: 1890*

Socio-economic level and household composition	Presence of lodgers	
	Lodgers not present	Lodgers present
Professional and higher white-collar employees		
Simple families	93.9	73.3
Extended families	3.0	13.3
No family	3.0	6.7
Not classified	0	6.7
Total	99.9	100.0
(N)	(33)	(15)
Proprietors and lower white-collar employees		
Simple families	84.2	90.4
Extended families	9.1	3.8
No family	3.6	3.8
Not classified	3.0	1.9
Total	99.9	99.9
(N)	(165)	(52)
Skilled craftsmen		
Simple families	94.8	89.1
Extended families	3.2	7.6
No family	0.8	2.2
Not classified	1.2	1.1
Total	100.0	100.0
(N)	(248)	(92)
Unskilled workers (position specified)		
Simple families	96.3	92.5
Extended families	2.5	1.5
No family	0.7	4.5
Not classified	0.5	1.5
Total	100.0	100.0
(N)	(401)	(67)

Table 7.5 (continued)

Socio-economic level and household composition	Presence of lodgers	
	Lodgers not present	Lodgers present
Unskilled workers (position unspecified)		
Simple families	95.8	83.0
Extended families	2.1	11.3
No family	1.7	1.9
Not classified	0.4	3.8
Total	100.0	100.0
(N)	(239)	(53)

*Definitions of household structure and socio-economic level are the same as for Table 7.3

Source: Sample from the 1890 manuscript census

VI

For large numbers of urbanites, living in an industrial city like Duisburg in the late-nineteenth century meant enduring some harrowing conditions.[41] This squalor may still have been better than what was available in the countryside. But it undoubtedly seemed worse to contemporaries because it was so concentrated in unrelenting row upon row of tenement buildings. Social critics constantly lamented the conjunction of slum housing and naive country migrants that resulted in the establishment of an inescapable culture of poverty. Because few suitable homes existed for these new city residents, family life was believed to decay, eventually leading to the destruction of the stability of society as a whole. It is this dismal characterisation that has fundamentally shaped our historical understanding of urban social life.

The evidence presented in this study is at variance with this conventional view, however, and suggests that the presumed debilitating effects of living in crowded slum dwellings did not materialise as expected, at least for the city of Duisburg between 1865 and 1900. There is no doubt that wretched housing conditions were a common part of the city's urban landscape and that they caused great discomfort. But still, no observable association of general measures of family disintegration and residential crowding could be found. In addition, the validity of the logic underpinning the traditional argument is subject to question.

So historians should begin to revise their concepts of urban social development. Onerous housing conditions did not automatically produce alienated, hostile people. On the contrary, evidence is accumulating which points to social stability, not disintegration, among city dwellers. Family life flourished in the city and was one of the basic means by which individuals managed the urban experience.[42] Clearly, much work is still to be done on the relationship of housing and social life in the late nineteenth and early twentieth centuries. Duisburg is but one example and must be placed into a broader context. But at least further exploration of this enormously complex topic should commence without the restraints of old stereotypes.

Notes

1.   Andrew Lees, 'Debates about the Big City in Germany, 1890-1914', *Societas*, 5 (1975), pp. 31-47; Andrew Lees, 'Critics of Urban Society in Germany, 1854-1914', *Journal of the History of Ideas*, 40 (1979), pp. 61-83; Klaus Bergmann, *Agrarromantik und Grossstadtfeindschaft* (Meisenheim am Glan: Verlag Anton Hain, 1970); Elisabeth Pfeil, *Grossstadtforschung. Entwicklung und gegenwärtiger Stand* (Hannover: Gebrüder Jänecke Verlag, 1972); James H. Jackson, Jr., 'Migration and Urbanization in the Ruhr Valley, 1850-1900' (Ph.D. dissertation, University of Minnesota, 1980), chapter 1; Lyle W. Dorsett (ed.), *The Challenge of the City, 1860-1910* (Lexington, Mass.: D.C. Heath and Co., 1968), pp. 1-18.
2.   Gustav Schmoller, 'Ein Mahnruf in der Wohnungsfrage', in *Zur Social- und Gewerbepolitik der Gegenwart* (Leipzig: Verlag Duncker und Humblot, 1890), p. 348.
3.   Lewis Mumford, *The City in History* (Harmondsworth: Penguin Books, 1961), p. 509.
4.   Friedrich Engels, *The Condition of the Working Class in England*, trans. by W.O. Henderson and W.H. Chaloner (Oxford: B.H. Blackwell, 1971), pp. 56-8; Jacob Riis, *How the Other Half Lives: Studies Among the Tenements of New York* (New York: Charles Scribner's Sons, 1890), pp. 17-47; Andrew Mearns, *The Bitter Cry of Outcast London. An Inquiry into the Condition of the Abject Poor* (Boston: Cupples, Upham, 1883), pp. 1-7; George R. Sims, *How the Poor Live and Horrible London* (London: Chatto and Windus, 1889), pp. 11, 44; Schmoller, 'Ein Mahnruf', pp. 345-6. The reasons for the existence of such conditions lies beyond the scope of this essay, but is discussed at length by these authors. A stimulating explanation is also suggested by James E. Vance, Jr., *This Scene of Man. The Role and Structure of the City in the Geography of Western Civilization* (New York: Harper's College Press, 1977), pp. 305-7.
5.   For a review of the most important German literature on the nineteenth-century housing crisis, see Carl Johannes Fuchs, 'Die Wohnungsfrage', in *Die Entwicklung der deutschen Volkswirtschaftslehre im neunzehnten Jahrhundert*, Vol. II (Leipzig: Verlag Duncker und Humblot, 1908).

Representative of analyses of the housing crisis and social life are Paul Lechler, *Nationale Wohnungsreform* (Berlin: Ernst Hofmann and Co., 1895), pp. 9-14; Emil Sax, *Die Wohnungszustände der arbeitenden Classen und ihre Reform* (Vienna: Druck und Verlag von A. Pichler's Witwe und Sohn, 1869), pp. 46-9; Eugen Jäger, *Die Wohnungsfrage*, Vol. 1 (Berlin: Verlage der Germania, 1902), pp. 93-6; Hans Rost, *Das moderne Wohnungsproblem* (Kempten: Verlag der Jos. Kösel'schen Buchhandlung, 1909), pp. 92-101; and Schmoller, 'Ein Mahnruf', pp. 343-51. For a summary of descriptions of the housing crisis in England and France, see Anthony S. Wohl, 'Working-class Housing in Nineteenth-century London', in *The History of Working Class Housing*, edited by S.D. Chapman (London: David & Charles, 1971), pp. 16-31; Gareth Stedman-Jones, *Outcast London. A Study in the Relationship between Classes in Victorian Society* (Harmondsworth: Penguin Books, 1971), pp. 159-235; Louis Chevalier, *Laboring Classes and Dangerous Classes in Paris during the first Half of the Nineteenth Century* (New York: Howard Fertig, 1973), pp. 186-231.

6. For descriptions of the interiors of homes in nineteenth-century Germany for various social groups, see essays by Gottfried Korff, Heilwig Schomerus, and Christa Pieske in Lutz Niethammer (ed.), *Wohnen im Wandel* (Wuppertal: Peter Hammer Verlag, 1979).

7. On the lodger evil, see Schmoller, 'Ein Mahnruf', p. 349; Sax, *Die Wohnungszustände*, p. 52; Jäger, *Die Wohnungsfrage*, p. 95; Lawrence Veiller, 'Room Overcrowding and the Lodger Evil', in *Housing Problems in America. Proceedings of the Second National Conference on Housing* (New York: American Housing Association, 1912); and other references cited by John Modell and Tamara K. Hareven, 'Urbanization and the Malleable Household: An Examination of Boarding and Lodging in American Families', *Journal of Marriage and the Family*, 35 (1973), pp. 467-79.

8. On the question of rootlessness and social disintegration, see Rost, *Das moderne Wohnungsproblem*, pp. 73-4; Lechler, *Nationale Wohnungsreform*, p. 11; Jäger, *Die Wohnungsfrage*, p. 94; Schmoller, 'Ein Mahnruf', p. 349; and the influential work of Wilhelm Brepohl, *Industrievolk im Wandel von der agraren zur industriellen Daseinsform dargestellt am Ruhrgebiet* (Tübingen: J.C.B. Mohr (Paul Siebeck), 1957. See also the essay by Richard J. Evans in the present volume, pp. 257-61.

9. Schmoller, 'Ein Mahnruf', p. 343.

10. David Ward, 'The Victorian Slum: An Enduring Myth? ', *Annals of the Association of American Geographers*, 66 (1976), pp. 323-6.

11. Claude S. Fischer, Mark Baldassare, and Richard J. Ofshe, 'Crowding Studies and Urban Life: A Critical Review', *American Institute of Planners Journal*, 31 (1975), pp. 406-18; Claude S. Fischer, *The Urban Experience* (New York: Harcourt, Brace, Jovanovich, 1976), pp. 154-64.

12. A.L. Schoor, 'Housing and its Effects', in *Environmental Psychology*, edited by M. Proschansky, W. Ittleson, and L. Rivlin (New York: Holt, Rinehart, and Winston, 1970), pp. 319-33; R.E. Mitchell, 'Ethnographic and Historical Perspectives on Relationships between Physical and Socio-spatial Environments', *Sociological Symposium*, 14 (1975), pp. 25-40.

13. See Gustav Seibt, 'Statistik', in *Die Entwicklung der deutschen Volkswirtschaftslehre im neunzehnten Jahrhundert*, Vol. 2, ed. S.P. Altman, *et al.*, (Leipzig: Verlag von Duncker und Humblot, 1908), Section 37; and Richard Boeckh, *Die geschichtliche Entwicklung der amtlichen Statistik des Preussischen Staates* (Berlin: Königliche Geheim Ober-Hofdrucker, 1863); also see '70 Jahre Volkszählung im Deutschen Reich', *Wirtschaft und Statistik* 21 (1941), pp. 409-13.

14. Peter Laslett, (ed.), *Household and Family in Past Time* (Cambridge: Cambridge University Press, 1972), pp. 88-9.

15.   W. Däbritz, 'Entstehung und Aufbau des rheinisch-westfälischen Industriebezirks', *Beiträge zur Geschichte der Technik und Industrie*, 15 (1925), pp. 13-107; Norman J.G. Pound, *The Ruhr: A Study in Historical and Economic Geography* (Bloomington: Indiana University Press, 1952); Hans Spethmann, *Das Ruhrgebiet im Wechselspiel von Land und Leute, Wirtschaft, Technik und Politik*, 2 volumes (Berlin: Reimar Hobbing Verlag, 1933); Heinz Günter Steinberg, 'Grundzüge der Entwicklung des Ruhrgebiets', *Tagungsberichte und wissenschaftliche Abhandlungen. Deutscher Geographentag, 1965* (Wiesbaden: F. Steiner Verlag, 1965); Paul Wiel, *Das Ruhrgebiet im Vergangenheit und Gegenwart* (Essen: Scharioth'sche Buchhandlung, 1963). For the quotation, see Thomas Charles Banfield, *Industry of the Rhine*. Series 1, *Agriculture: Embracing a View of the Social Condition of the Rural Population of that District* (London: C. Knight and Co., 1846), pp. 47-50. Population statistics: Ernst Lutter, *Geographisch-statistische Untersuchungen über die Lage der Städte des Deutschen Reiches mit mehr als 20.000 Einwohnern und ihre Entwicklung im Laufe des 19. Jahrhunderts* (Bonn: S. Foppen, 1909), Anhang.

16.   Jackson, 'Migration and Urbanization', Tables 1-3 and 1-5.

17.   Jackson, ibid., Table 1-4.

18.   Ibid.

19.   See essays by Lange, Arnecke and Wiebe in *Die Wohnungsnoth der ärmeren Klassen in deutschen Grosstädte*. Vol. 30 of *Schriften des Vereins für Sozialpolitik* (Leipzig: Verlag von Duncker und Humblot, 1886).

20.   'Ein Gang durch Jammer und Not', *Beilage zur Zeitung 'Das Volk'*, Number 134 (10 June 1904).

21.   Housing was not the only way in which Duisburg was representative of Ruhr Valley urban centres, especially of the larger, more established cities. Its economic history, its occupational structure at mid-century and in 1895, its population growth patterns, its age structure and balance of the sexes in 1867 and 1890, and its migration rates from 1881-1911 reflect an experience common to all of these cities during the second half of the nineteenth century. See Jackson, 'Migration and Urbanization', Tables 1-3 to 1-7 and Figures 1-1 and 1-2.

22.   The basic literature on the history of Duisburg can be found in Günter von Roden, *Geschichte der Stadt Duisburg*, Vol. 1, *Das Alte Duisburg von den Anfängen bis 1905* (2nd edn., Duisburg: Walter Braun Verlag, 1973); Manfred Schulz, *Die Entwicklung Duisburgs und der mit ihm vereinigten Gemeinden bis zum Jahre 1962. Duisburger Forschungen*, Vol. 24/25 (Duisburg: Walter Braun Verlag, 1977); Kunibert K. Bork, 'Die soziale Wandlungen in der Stadt Duisburg in den ersten Jahrzehnten der Industrialisierung (1850-1880)', *Duisburger Forschungen*, 8 (1965), pp. 54-129; Alfred Fröböse, *Die Industrie im Wirtschaftsraum der Stadt Duisburg. Eine wirtschaftskundliche Untersuchung* (Würzburg-Aumühle: Konrad Triltsch Verlag, 1940); Herbert Lehmann, *Duisburgs Grosshandel und spediton vom Ende des 18. Jahrhunderts bis 1905. Beiheft 1. Duisburger Forschungen* (Duisburg: Verlag für Wirtschaft und Kultur Werner Rencknhoff KG, 1958); Jackson, 'Migration and Urbanization', Ch. 2.

23.   Jules Armand Colbert, Marquis de Blainville, *Reisebeschreibung durch Holland, Oberdeutschland und die Schweiz besonders aber durch Italien*, Vol. I: 1, trans. George Turnbull and Wilhelm Guthrie; ed. Johann Tobias Köhler (Lemgo: Meyerschen Buchhandlung, 1764), p. 63.

24.   Walter Reichardt, *Boden- und Wohnungsverhältnisse in Duisburg von der Mitte des 19. Jahrhunderts bis zum Weltkrieg* (Würzburg-Aumühle: Verlag wissenschaftlicher Werke Konrad Triltsch, 1939).

25.   Reichardt, ibid., p. 134.

26.   Ibid., pp. 7, 85.

27.   Ibid., pp. 81-8.

28. Ibid., pp. 9, 36, 169.
29. Schmoller, 'Ein Mahnruf', p. 347.
30. Adolf Weber, *Die Grossstadt und ihre sozialen Probleme* (Leipzig: Verlag von Quelle und Meyer, 1908), chapter 2.
31. Sax, *Die Wohnungszustände*, p. 52.
32. Schmoller, 'Ein Mahnruf', pp. 347-8.
33. A. Booth, 'Final Report: Urban Crowding Project', Canadian Ministry of State for Urban Affairs (1975).
34. The definition of 'overcrowding' is one of the most formidable problems plaguing the study of the housing crisis of the nineteenth century, preventing good comparative analysis. Not only are these terms dependent on the kind of data available; they are also highly relative terms that take their meaning from cultural norms. See Fischer, *The Urban Experience*, pp. 154-64, for a more detailed discussion of this point. Thus, it seemed advisable to use 'residential density' as measured by square metres per person in a household. Other measures of living area, such as total amount of space per household, persons per room (heated or unheated), or persons per apartment, are clouded because they leave uncontrolled important factors such as household size, apartment size, and room size. No attempt is made in this analysis to specify a level at which a household lived in 'overcrowded' conditions. Instead, Duisburg's households were divided into three general groups according to relative density. The points of separation were selected by adding or subtracting one-half standard deviation from the mean amount of space per person.
35. Although comparison over time is not possible, 1890 turns out to be a good choice to illuminate some aspects of the question at hand. First, local housing problems were presumably most intense at this time. The number of persons per room was at historically high levels. If any impact of residential crowding could be seen, it should be manifest in 1890. Second, some contemporary observers of the housing crisis believed that a generation needed to pass before the debilitating effects of urban overcrowding could be seen. See Schmoller, 'Ein Mahnruf', p. 347. The restraints of religious training and the rural cultural heritage presumably delayed full impact. In 1890, Duisburg was clearly in its second generation of urban-industrial growth and should be a good location to see the effects of high-density living after social constraints have disappeared.
36. See articles cited in note 7.
37. *Jahres-Berichte der mit Beaufsichtigung der Fabriken betrauten Beamten*, I (1876), pp. 270-5; XI (1886), pp. 132-3.
38. See reports to the Social Policy Association and the observations of factory inspectors cited above.
39. These sentiments can be seen in *Jahres-Berichte der Fabriken-Inspektoren für das Jahr 1877*, pp. 269-70 and the introductory remarks in a homemaker's guide written for workingmen's wives by middle-class women, *Das häusliche Glück* (M. Gladbach and Leipzig: Verlag von A. Rissarth, 1882).
40. See further reports in the investigation by *Das Volk*.
41. Hans Kurella, 'Wohnung und Häuslichkeit', *Neue Deutsche Rundschau*, 10 (1899), pp. 814-22; Husi-Huey Liang, 'Lower-class Immigrants in Wilhelmine Berlin', *Central European History*, 3 (1970), pp. 94-111; and articles cited in note 5.
42. See, for example, Michael Anderson, *Family Structure in Nineteenth Century Lancashire* (Cambridge: Cambridge University Press, 1971) and John Modell and Tamara K. Hareven, 'Urbanization and the Malleable Household: An Examination of Boarding and Lodging in American Families', *Journal of Marriage and the Family*, 35 (1973), pp. 467-79.

8 WOMEN'S WORK AND THE FAMILY: WOMEN GARMENT WORKERS IN BERLIN AND HAMBURG BEFORE THE FIRST WORLD WAR

Robyn Dasey

I

Capitalist industrialisation in eighteenth- and nineteenth-century Europe was based upon the specialisation and concentration of work processes in socially organised production, which led to a gradual divorce of workplace and household. The public sphere, populated largely by men from the eighteenth century onwards, became firmly separated from the private sphere of the family, the female domain. This transformation wrought fundamental changes in the economic, social, family and personal lives of women. The diminution of their productive role in the household was not matched by a corresponding expansion of employment opportunities in the new factories and workshops. In nineteenth-century Germany there was a surplus of labour seeking industrial employment; and the developing industrial structure, particularly from mid-century, emphasised employment in construction, railways, mining and engineering, which favoured the employment of male workers. The majority of women were as a consequence confined to more marginal economic activities in or associated with the household, whether as middle-class non-earning wives, or as servants, outworkers, washerwomen or charladies.[1]

This effective exclusion from industry was accompanied by the feminisation of the household. As the nineteenth century progressed, the family as a procreative unit devoted to the psychological, social and cultural welfare of present and future generations became an integral component of bourgeois class consciousness.[2] The fundament of this family was the wife and mother: a woman was defined almost exclusively by these roles. A woman's 'natural profession' was bearer and nurturer; her cause was 'the preservation and cultivation of traditional morality, the defence of the family, and the furtherance of a spirit of self-discipline, moderation and self-sacrifice;[3] and this was ideally to the exclusion of any activity in the public world and particularly paid employment. This middle-class idealisation stood in stark contrast to the material reality of the lives of the vast majority of working-class women, which dictated that most of them had, at some stage in their lives, to contribute income to the household budget. By the late nineteenth century it also contradicted the rising demand for cheap, unskilled casual labour from some sections of employers, notably in the clothing, food processing, office and retail trades. Women were increasingly absorbed into the labour market. This was especially true of married women, the current mothers of the nation. Although only a tiny proportion of married women in Germany were classified as fully occupied, the numbers rose by 300 per cent in the quarter century to 1907.[4] These developments provoked widespread prophesies of the dissolution of the family from politicians and social commentators. The more conservative feared this as a threat not only to the family but to the entire fabric of State and society. This view of the family as a potent factor in the stabilisation of the economic, social and political order, and the threat posed to it by women's employment, underlay German Catholic Centre Party and later conservative and liberal demands for the prohibition or at least limitation of female employment. Bishop Ketteler, an influential figure in the formulation of the Centre Party's social and welfare policies, saw the contemporary family as

> a pillar which alone is able to bear the totality upon which the State and the Church is built . . . The mother has the primary role in this task . . . Were the mother to be torn away into the factory, were she to be alienated from her natural profession, the time-honoured institution of the family would be threatened.[5]

It was the perceived threat to future generations of women's employment in factories, the most advanced form of large-scale production, which provoked the two extensive inquiries of the German Parliament, the Reichstag, into female labour, in 1877 and 1899. Both of these were confined to married women in factories. On similar grounds, the first protective legislation covering German adult workers was a compulsory three weeks' recuperation for women after childbirth (in 1878). It was not the exhausting physical labour done by women as such which concerned the Centre Party or the government – they consistently refused to legislate to protect the even more exploited homeworkers and servants right up until the First World War – but only work done by mothers and future mothers in the non-domestic factory environment. By the turn of the century the bourgeois ideal of motherhood had become so firmly entrenched that successive German

governments concerned about the defence of the fatherland, sought by
the suppression of knowledge of and access to birth control methods,
and by the active encouragement of mother and infant welfare measures,
to reverse the rapid decline in the birth-rate.[6]

Family commitments and, more fundamentally, the generalisation of
this ideal of housewifery and motherhood to all women to the exclusion
of their participation in paid employment and regardless of their actual
family situation, undoubtedly influenced whether, when and where
women worked. The pattern of female participation in the labour force
clearly paralleled the reproductive and family cycles. In 1907 in
Germany almost 70 per cent of single women were fully occupied,
compared with 26 per cent of married women, rising to 40 per cent of
widows.[7] The withdrawal of women from the labour market on marriage
was even more marked in the industrialised urban areas: in Berlin in the
same year only 11 per cent of married women were gainfully occupied
full-time, compared with 70 per cent of single women and 45 per cent
of widows.[8] Whether and when women were in paid employment, and
the types of jobs they did, nevertheless depended heavily upon industrial
structure and conditions of employment and on the relative surplus or
shortage of labour which was regarded as suitable by employers. Thus
the proportion of married women in full-time factory work in the
textile towns of Saxony far exceeded the national average, despite the
fact that working hours were longer than in almost all other factory
industries.[9] In the skilled weaving occupations, married women formed
almost one third of the predominantly female workforce in Germany in
1907.[10] Elsewhere, the structure and conditions of employment set by
the employers were at least partly based on assumptions about whether
and how married women could or should work: outwork industries
grew or were sustained precisely where there was a surplus of married
women seeking earnings; contracts for women workers in domestic
service, shops and offices were usually terminated by the employer on
marriage.

The influence of the family sphere on women's paid employment
during and after the period of industrialisation was thus multi-faceted,
operating at a variety of levels and in both directions. Experience of
employment also affected the family unit and the position of women
within it. At the most general level, the emerging industrial structure
of nineteenth-century Germany, and the surplus of labour seeking
industrial employment, marginalised women's participation in the
industrial proletariat. This was reinforced by a system of social norms
which confined women to procreative and nurturing roles in the

increasingly feminised household. These norms were in turn selectively incorporated into the structure and conditions of employment and used as a convenient rationalisation of inferior working conditions, training and wages. Given these constraints it is scarcely surprising that women with domestic responsibilities sought where possible to avoid adding the burden of a 60 to 70 hour working week in factories to their already heavy household chores.

This interpretative framework of the interrelations of family and work in women's lives is sharply opposed to that of those historians of women belonging to the 'modernisation' school of social history. In their conceptualisation women are more or less explicitly defined by their commitment to marriage and family, which is then forwarded as an explanation for the relegation of women to a peripheral role in the production process. Women 'modernised' along a different, more gradual path than men because this enabled a closer conformity with their goal of marriage and motherhood. At its most extreme this degenerates into a voluntarist theory of history: the majority of working women in nineteenth-century Europe were servants, agricultural labourers, outworkers, etc. because they chose to be so.[11] Despite passing nods in the direction of industrialisation and material circumstances, the economic, political, ideological and social developments which at a specific point in time determined the severely restricted framework within which working-class women (and men) as groups or individuals made these choices, are consistently ignored. In short, the fact that many girls chose domestic service, for example, rather than sewing, waitressing, shopwork or agricultural labour, tells us little about why so few industries and occupations were accessible to women, about why women's wages were uniformly far lower than men's or about why working-class women dramatically reduced the number of children they bore in the precise years they did. At best it simply illustrates the hardheaded practical considerations which informed these women's decisions within the wider economic, political and social systems operative at that time: at worst it reduces to a circular argument.

The present essay analyses the growth of a post-industrialisation outwork industry — garment making — which depended on the reserve of female labour available in many late nineteenth-century cities. This clothing industry exemplifies the way in which capitalist mass production based on a relatively simple and inexpensive piece of capital equipment, the sewing machine, was organised to maximise the use of the cheap female labour force and simultaneously to justify the casualisation of that labour force and its often appallingly low wages by reference to the primarily familial role of the women employed. The focus of the essay's attention is on Berlin and Hamburg. Berlin was the centre of the German clothing industry, and it was there that the putting-out system, which prevailed throughout the many German cities where the industry took root, was most developed.[12] Hamburg, on the other hand, provides an example of a city where the industry paled into relative insignificance compared with the port, shipbuilding and allied industries, but where nevertheless almost one-sixth of the substantial number of women workers were employed as seamstresses. It is not possible to state with certainty that the precise structure was repeated elsewhere due to the paucity of studies of working women in Germany[13] and indeed the wages and conditions were probably superior in these two cities due to the strength of organised labour and a reasonably strong demand for female workers.

The history of working women presents in a most acute form all the problems facing the historian of labour. The marginalisation of women's labour and its concentration in the private domain of the household has as a corollary the absence of the sources customarily used by the historian of male workers, such as the records and comments of employers and government inspectors, or the personal accounts of trade unionists and working-class socialists. This analysis of the German clothing industry derives from a variety of sources, the most important of which for Berlin are assessments of the structure of the industry by academics and Social Democrats and the inquiries of the Berlin Arbitration Commission and the Imperial Office of Labour Statistics which were undertaken as a consequence of the national strike of clothing workers in 1896.[14] The evidence for Hamburg on the other hand derives almost entirely from the Hamburg State Archive. Amongst the diverse sources consulted in this archive, the more general surveys of women's employment come largely from the reports of the factory inspectorate, although until 1910 these regularly include only clothing workers employed in factories. Accounts of the economic position of middlemen and women and clothing workers were gathered from the files of the Hamburg political police, who were responsible for reporting the content of all meetings of trade unionists, Social Democrats and women; from the files of the state authorities responsible for workers' insurance; and from the files of the Poor Law institutions. The first section of the essay provides a brief resumé of the development of female employment in Berlin and Hamburg in the Wilhelmine period. This is followed by a detailed study of the clothing industry in these two cities. The final section points to the relations between family and work highlighted by the study of the clothing industry.

II

The accelerated growth of industry in Germany in the half century up to the First World War, concentrated as it was in particular regions, attracted a mass labour force from rural areas and smaller towns. Within a few decades there was created an urban proletariat whose livelihood was earned in conditions governed by working and social relationships foreign to the large rural property, farm, village or small town. During this process more and more women joined their menfolk in the labour market.

The transition from the agricultural household to urban work was a complex one. The mass exodus of men from the land led to an increased dependence of agriculture on female labour (Table 8.1). Men going off to work on canal, rail, road and building construction from mid-century left their wives and daughters to run their small-holdings.[15] Unskilled men poured into Berlin and Hamburg to do this type of work, living all week in giant dormitories and returning home only on Sundays.[16] Hence their wives and daughters assumed full responsibility for the piece of land, for its few pigs, cows and fowl, for the selling of the surplus and for providing labour for large landowners, especially during the busiest summer and autumn harvest months. The former north German family contract system, under which the husband contracted to provide his own, his wife's and a young person's labour in return for a cottage, some land and payment in kind, as well as a small cash wage, broke down. The single girl, who had either been an agricultural servant or a junior labourer for her own or another tenant family (*Scharwerker*) in return for her keep and perhaps a small cash wage, joined her brothers and father to seek her fortune in the city.[17] The women who remained turned increasingly to day-labouring, with only the more fortunate being able to supplement this with the produce of a small plot.[18] The departure of women as well as men to the industrial cities resulted in a severe shortfall in the number of women agricultural labourers by the turn of the century.[19]

Migration to the city marked a decisive decline in the productive functions of the household, leaving it almost totally as a consumer unit depending on cash earnings. The wife and mother who had formerly contributed to the household economy by keeping the animals, by

Table 8.1: Occupied Women in Germany, 1882 and 1907, by
Economic Sector

| | 1882 | | 1907 | |
Sector	Occupied women '000	Distrib. occupied women	Occupied women '000	Distrib. occupied women
Agriculture*	3,935	47.8	4,599	42.8
Manufacturing & mining	1,127	13.7	2,104	19.6
Trade, commerce & transport	298	3.6	931	8.7
Household service (non-res.) & misc.†	1,466	17.8	1,570	14.6
Civil Service, Army, Professions	115	1.4	288	2.7
Resident domestic servants**	1,282	15.6	1,249	11.6
Total	8,224	100.0	10,742	100.0

* The 1882 figure is adjusted according to Hoffmann's estimates to allow for comparative undercounting of women in agriculture in 1882. The original census figure is 2,535,000.

† This is non-resident service, including miscellaneous day labouring.

** I have included domestic service as a full-time occupation, unlike the census and most statistical series drawn from it. This of course means that the totals and the distribution of women will be different from the usual.

Source: *Berufszählungen*, 1882 & 1907, *Statistik des deutschen Reichs*, Vols. 1 and 203. Hoffmann, *et al., Das Wachstum der deutschen Wirtschaft,* pp. 182-4.

selling the surplus at the local market, by preparing foodstuffs (such as baking bread), and by making the family's clothes, no longer did so to any significant degree. The cramped urban workers' flats and low weekly incomes precluded bulk buying for preserving and storing, and home-made clothing became increasingly uneconomical, undercut by mass-produced goods.[20] In workers' households existing on low and irregular incomes, the cast contribution of the womenfolk became the overwhelming consideration. The family was fundamental in determining incomes, the cash contribution of the womenfolk became the overwhelming consideration. The family was fundamental in determining women's labour in the industrial economy, as it had been in the pre-industrial economy. The assumed primary function of the woman as bearer and nurturer of future and present generations relegated her to dependence on a male bread-winner. Her free labour for the family conditioned her and her male colleagues to expect lower payment for work undertaken in other circumstances. The presumed ability to fall back on family support, usually derived from higher paid male

Thus the Berlin Chamber of Commerce justified starvation wages for women workers in the following terms:[21]

> Those who judge on the basis of the bare facts, that, of four dozen women out-workers two dozen must be content with weekly wages of 3-6 M, would with apparent justification conclude that in home industry most only earn starvation wages. The judgement must, however, be totally different, as soon as . . . it is perceived that the earnings of these twenty-four women are only an addition to the weekly wages of their husbands . . . The low earnings of the women home-workers hence become not a proof of a low standard of living, but indeed . . . can be used to conclude *that the income of the family to which the woman belongs allows her to dispense with higher earnings for herself.* (emphasis in original)

Women's wages rarely reached a level sufficient to keep the woman alone. The fact that up to 47 per cent of working women were the chief breadwinners in late nineteenth-century Berlin, with no husband, father or son to keep them, did not influence the general level of wages, nor the employers' rationalisation of them.[22] Poor women were a reserve of labour which could be utilised when demand was high and left to their family when it was not.

Most women went out to work because the family budget dictated that they must. By the turn of the century, it had become usual for single girls in working-class and many lower middle-class families to earn at least part of their upkeep. Of all the single women aged 16 and over in the Empire in 1907, 72 per cent were so engaged.[23] Many daughters handed over all but the small change to their mother, in return for food, board and clothing.[24] Among married women and widows, family poverty was the overwhelming reason given for factory work.[25] However the shortage of industrial employment, family duties and the expected role of women in the home, and the social stigma attached to factories, led many to seek out other types of employment. Their labour on sewing machines at home was the basis of the mass-produced clothing industry. They also cleaned the houses of the better-off, as well as the stairs and halls of the tenements, offices and shops; they washed and ironed the clothes of others; they sold and delivered milk, bread, vegetables and newspapers.[26] The very nature of this employment tended to make such women workers invisible to their contemporaries, to census-takers, and to the latter-day social historian.

It was in these diffuse service industries, as well as the more public

Table 8.2: Full-time Occupied Women, Hamburg City, 1882 and 1907, by Industry

Industry	1882			1907		
	Occup. women	As % of occup. pers.	Dist. of occup. women	Occup. women	As % of occup. pers.	Dist. of occup. women
A. Agriculture	9	3.2	–	287	8.0	0.3
III Mining	–	–	–	3	1.0	–
IV Brickworks, pottery	10	1.2	–	82	5.2	0.1
V Metal processing	86	1.7	0.2	460	3.0	0.4
VI Engineering, shipb.	48	1.4	0.1	414	2.7	0.4
VII Chemicals	12	2.2	–	444	17.7	0.4
VIII Forestry biprods.	42	9.5	0.1	310	12.6	0.3
IX Textiles	501	43.6	1.3	1,208	53.7	1.2
X Paper } XI Leather }	142	5.7	0.4	576	33.0	0.6
				795	13.2	0.8
XII Wood & wood prods.	257	3.4	0.7	443	3.3	0.4
XIII Food, drink & tobacco	544	7.4	1.4	2,887	14.8	2.8
XIV Clothing } XV Laundries, cleaning }	10,189	54.3	26.9	15,490	59.5	15.0
				4,855	54.3	4.7
XVI Building	39	0.5	0.1	135	0.4	0.1
XVII Printing	87	5.6	0.2	1,236	22.2	1.2
XVIII Art, theatre	10	3.0	–	97	15.4	0.1
Unspecified	–	–	–	50	–	–
B. Manufacturing	11,976	20.7	31.6	29,485	19.2	28.6
XX Trade	2,750	9.5	7.3	16,815	18.0	16.3
XXI Insurance } XXII Transport }	103	1.1	0.3	280	7.9	0.3
				1,445	3.5	1.4
XXIII Hotels, catering	2,376	37.0	6.3	7,919	43.8	7.7
C. Trade, transport, commerce	5,259	11.8	13.9	26,459	16.9	25.7
D. Household service, non-resident	5,211	42.5	13.7	11,041	72.4	10.7
E. Civil Service, army professions, church	1,857	27.6	4.9	7,209	26.6	7.0
G. Domestic service, resident	13,607	97.8	35.9	28,651	99.3	27.8
TOTAL	37,919	28.0	100.0	103,132	26.8	100.0

Source: *Berufszählungen, 1882, 1907, Statistik des deutschen Reichs*, Vols. 3 & 207.

factory and workshop, that most women in Berlin and Hamburg found work. In Berlin one in three of all fully-occupied persons was female.[27] More surprising, given the overwhelming weight of the port and of transport, ship-building and related industries in Hamburg, was the fact that 28 per cent of the full-time labour force were women, as evidenced in Table 8.2. These women were severely restricted in their choice of jobs, with household service, sewing of various types, and cleaning accounting for over three-quarters of those in employment in Hamburg in 1882. Domestic servants residing with their employers alone accounted for about one in three working women throughout the quarter century to 1907. Domestic service together with serving in hotels, restaurants and shops, and sewing and cleaning, accounted for almost all women earning in 1882 in both cities and between three-quarters and four-fifths in 1907. During the 25 years from 1882, however, there was a definite diversification of workplaces for women. By 1907, increasing numbers were to be found working in food processing, the print trades, professional and State employment, leather and paper products and chemical industries, and even engineering and transport. Retailing and wholesaling also became more accessible. The percentage of women and girls living in as servants, or employed as daily women, together with those making, laundering and ironing clothes, declined correspondingly. This concentration of working women in 'female industries', together with the tendency to diversification, was apparent over the entire German economy (Table 8.1), as well as in Hamburg and the largest centre of female labour, Berlin. In the capital in 1907 three-quarters of women were occupied as servants, daily charwomen, seamstresses and laundresses, or in the retail and wholesale branches as detailed in Table 8.3. The major difference between Berlin and Hamburg was the clothing industry, for which Berlin was a world centre, so that seamstresses there outnumbered even the army of servants.

Table 8.3: The Major Female Occupations, Berlin, 1907

Occupation	Number of women
1. Servant, living-in	56,028
2. Retailing & wholesaling	42,956
3. Tailoress	42,430
4. Seamstress	25,186
5. Household service, non-resident	24,375
6. Hotels & restaurants	21,107
7. Washerwomen & ironers	12,303
8. Underwear & linen manufacture	10,052
9. Miscellaneous day labouring	8,534
10. Milliners	5,375
Total	248,346
Total, all full-time occupied women	335,102
% of all full-time occupied women	74%

Source: *Berufszählung 1907, Statistik des deutschen Reichs,* Vol. 207.

'Female industries' supplied goods and services strikingly similar to some of those belonging to the woman's sphere in the pre-industrial household: washing, ironing, cleaning, the preparing, serving and selling of food, and making clothes. This is also true of the female-dominated textile industry in Saxony and the Elberfeld/Barmen region,[28] and of the emergent professional and semi-professional occupations for women in health, child-care and education.[29] The nature of the work and the relationships within which it was undertaken were, however, very different in character from those obtaining in the household economy. The type of product and the conditions of production were dictated by the employer reacting to market pressure, not by household requirements. The hours and the place of work were set quite irrespective of family need, so that, for example, women could not attend to children when required. Specialisation and the need to work hand in hand with others hindered the acquisition of general skills, limited the satisfaction gained from producing an entire item for use, set strict time schedules for the completion of work and frequently necessitated working in the workshop or factory. Above all, most women were employed as individuals, not as part of a family unit, and received payment into their own hands for their labour.

Changes in the organisation of production inherent in the process of industrialisation were, of course, decisive for both men and women. Indeed, they had probably progressed further for many men in large-scale heavy industry.[30] Women, however, unlike their menfolk, bore the major responsibility for the running of the home and the care of the children, a major reason why far fewer of them entered the labour market in the first instance. The transfer of production and its reorganisation outside the sphere of the household, even where the end products and services provided were very similar, divorced the woman's productive activities from her familial ones. The pursuance of the one clashed with the other. In its clearest form, a woman could simply not be in two places – factory and home – at once. While the man could divorce his familial and working lives, largely by minimising the former, the woman, if she was to remain almost exclusively responsible for family care, could not.

It was the attempt to reconcile the work and family spheres which led many women to seek jobs where they could to some extent control the hours they worked in order to avoid absence from the home when the children required care, meals had to be prepared, and so on. They also tried to avoid the sheer toil involved in working in factories and workshops twelve to fourteen hours per day, six days each week, on top of the household labour. Factories employed only a minority of women workers prior to the First World War, though this was rapidly growing. In Hamburg less than one in seven women wage earners worked in factories in 1910, itself an eightfold increase over 30 years

earlier.[31] Single women predominated among female workers in these
workplaces, forming in 1899 more than two-thirds of all factory
women and more than four-fifths of women in the semi-skilled
printing jobs in the city.[32] Married women were concentrated in casual,
part-time employment and outwork. Married women and widows, who
formed about one-quarter of working women in Hamburg, were more
than half the 11,000 paid household helps.[33] Provision of board and
lodging was another major means by which these women supplemented
family budgets, particularly as rents were high. In Hamburg there were
lodgers present in almost one-quarter of all households at the turn of
the century.[34] The division of labour according to sex and, amongst
women, between the single and the married, was characteristic of the
urban economy in Wilhelmine Germany.

III

The mass-production clothing industry provides an excellent example
of the ways in which employers drew upon a female labour force defined
and restricted by familial status and duties. The putting-out system on
which the industry was based was refined to utilise the large reserve
of female labour available in the fast expanding cities. The structure
and success of the industry was intimately linked to the characteristics
of the female labour force, defined by widespread poverty among the
new urban proletariat, the general lack of earning opportunities for
women and their expected and actual role and responsibilities within
the family. A detailed study of this industry, its structure and the
nature of employment, illustrates the relation between women's paid
work and their familial position in industrial Germany at the turn of
the century.[35] The German clothing industry expanded from the 1870s
to become a major international supplier. At the peak of an export
boom in 1883 the 386 women's outerwear clothiers in Berlin, the
centre of this branch, counted sales of 95 million marks.[36] Demand for
ready-to-wear garments continued to grow with urbanisation and the
decline of the manufacture of clothing and linen within the home. The
rising urban middle class, many of whom were unable to support large
establishments, turned increasingly to tailors to have their garments
made up and to patronising the more exclusive stores selling off-the-
peg.[37] In urban working-class households the home-made garment was a
thing of the past, a trend further hastened by the need for women to
devote more time to earning cash.[38] By the turn of the twentieth

century mass-production dominated in women's outerwear — coats, costumes, gowns, jackets — underwear and linen, children's clothes and all cheap lower quality garments. Made-to-measure tailoring retained significance only in better-quality menswear — suits, coats and jackets.

The mass-production garment industry developed on the putting-out system. Its basic features were theoretically simple although the practical operation was often complex. The clothing houses (*Konfektionshäuser*), for whom the goods were ultimately produced, were primarily commercial firms. These put out the materials to middlemen (*Zwischenmeister*) who were responsible for having them made up either in their own workshops or by further putting out the cut cloth to homeworkers or by a combination of both. The putting-out system had numerous advantages for the clothiers, so long as the low cost of labour on the universal sewing machine more than offset the higher productivity of more capital-intensive factories. The clothiers minimised capital costs, disclaimed all responsibility for the workforce, evaded protective legislation and insurance laws, and could expand and contract output at will. In short, the costs of production were transferred to the middlemen and homeworkers, a particularly strong advantage in the fashion-dominated and highly seasonal clothing industry.[39] The clothiers undertook virtually no investment in the actual production of the garments and employed very little direct labour besides the sales staff. A contemporary described these establishments in Berlin:

... An office, in which some sales employees work, and a relatively primitive storeroom filled with completed garments and rolls of cloth. An outfitter, some buyers and perhaps some service personnel who are employed in packing the cloth, this is the entire staff. Depending on the size of the firm we find one or several more storerooms. Through the office we enter a room in which there is a cutting machine driven by . . . motive power. Besides this we might find a few more tailors who select the accessories and attach them to the cut cloth . . .[40]

In season a large clothier might have 120 to 140 middlemen under contract. The Berlin Arbitration Office estimated there were 400 to 500 such businesses in Berlin in 1896 employing 3,000 to 4,000 middlemen and 80,000 to 90,000 indirect workers.[41]

The middlemen and women almost always specialised in one type of garment and maintained a workshop, normally consisting of one or two rooms in their own dwelling, in which might be employed up to 20 women in season. Workshop equipment, accumulated over a period of time, consisted in the mid-nineties of two to six sewing machines at 160-180M each, irons and ironing boards, scissors, needles and thread, with only the bigger shops owning the new button-holing machine costing 420-450M.[42] The workshop owner agreed with the clothier on the price per piece and after allowing one to two-thirds for his own costs and profit, set the piece rates for the workshop and homeworkers.[43]

This domestic industry system was capable not only of mass output but also of rapid expansion and contraction. Sales in Berlin of manufactured women's garments increased tenfold between 1865 and 1884.[44] The seasonality in the fashion-dominated women's branch was extreme. Production peaked in February-March for the spring/summer and July-August for the autumn/winter wardrobes. Whilst some work was available in January, April, June and September, there was almost a total standstill in May and from October to mid December.[45] The clothiers minimised overhead costs and the central core of permanently employed labour, together with potential losses from unfashionable stocks, by passing them and the associated risk onto the middlemen. As they had no idle unproductive hands or capital equipment, the clothiers concentrated production into a shorter and shorter period after the fashion trend for the season had been established. The middlemen in their turn passed the risks onto the seamstresses, especially those producing at home, who had to suffer regular cycles of overemployment and unemployment, in addition to providing the sewing machines, light and heating. The linen and underwear and low-quality workmen's clothing branches were less subject to fashion changes and hence less seasonal in production. The overwhelming consideration in these staple lines was cheapness. By the end of the nineteenth century production in factories had become more attractive to linen and underwear firms because of the more advanced and expensive equipment such as specialised sewing and button-holing machines, whose productivity was far greater than that of the universal sewing machine, let alone hand sewing. This coupled with the tighter discipline and control in factories and increasing demand for full-time female labour in cities such as Hamburg, led to the growth of larger workshops and factories where staple goods were produced more or less all year round. Even these factories, however, employed some outworkers in peak periods.

The structure of the industry and the casual nature of employment for a large proportion of its workforce led to large variations in the numbers employed between years, seasons and even weeks. The very definition of who comprised the workforce was imprecise. A small tailor might cater predominantly for individual customers but also contract occasionally for garment firms. While clearly occupied in the clothing industry his involvement in the mass-production sector was rarely specified. Factories and workshops varied their in-house and domestic workforces greatly according to the season. Many seamstresses were primarily engaged in household duties but sewed for neighbours and middlemen when the work was offered. Even factory seamstresses in relatively permanent employment suffered short time and unemployment in some periods. For official and private investigators these problems of timing and definition were compounded by common perceptions of social respectability. The wives of better-off workers and white-collar employees were particularly prone to denying that they had to supplement their husband's incomes, or to describing themselves as more prestigious self-employed tailoresses. For similar reasons small tailors might neglect to mention working for middlemen or clothiers. The desire to conceal taxable earnings also inhibited disclosure of employment.[46] Thus estimates of the number of people employed must be treated with caution. It is, nevertheless, quite clear that the number of more or less fully occupied women clothing workers overall was very large. In Berlin it rose from roughly 34,500 in 1871 to 97,500 in 1907, when women formed approximately 70 per cent of all workers in the clothing industry.[47] Most of these women were engaged in sewing women's outerwear, children's clothing, underwear and linen, and 35-45 per cent of them worked from home.[48] Production of men's and women's outerwear, underwear, linen and millinery were also firmly established in Hamburg. In 1907 about 25,000 men and women were occupied in the industry there. The industry had experienced a four- to five-fold expansion in employment over the previous two decades, when the number of women engaged grew at a faster pace than men, rising from 2,500-3,000 in 1896 to about 15,000 in 1907-13.[49] By 1907 clothing engaged one-quarter of all fully occupied women in Berlin and one in seven in Hamburg (Tables 8.1 and 8.2).

Men and women did not perform the same jobs nor often work in the same type of workplace in the clothing trade. The sexual division of labour paralleled the structure of the industry. Men were concentrated into two groups: skilled tailors and middlemen. Skilled tailors were mostly found in the made-to-measure men's outfitters where they owned or worked in small workshops to customers' individual orders, or worked as cutters and tailors with clothiers and in factories. The background of middlemen working in mass production was far more diverse. Some were trained tailors. Many more were from unrelated trades, including butchers, cigar-rollers and building workers, who frequently entered the industry as a consequence of marrying seamstresses. These often acquired the minimum tailoring skills from their wives, who were in practice often the real managers of the shop with the husband only their business representative and cutter.[50] Women, on the other hand, were concentrated in the mass-production and outwork sectors producing women's garments, underwear, millinery and standard workmen's clothes. In 1913 the Hamburg factory inspector concluded that there were about 8,000 women employed in supervised shops and factories with a further 5,500 homeworkers. By this count women formed four-fifths of workers in Hamburg's clothing factories and workshops and three-fifths of homeworkers and self-employed tailors.[51] Women outworkers were far more numerous than men and totally dominated the cheap staple underwear branch: of the 1,616 outworkers traced by the factory inspector in Hamburg in 1913 in this branch, only 26 were male.[52] A similarly disproportionate concentration of women in the outwork sector was clear in Berlin. There in the mid-nineties around 35-45 per cent of female clothing workers worked at home compared to around 25 per cent of men, including an unspecified number of self-employed tailors.[53]

By the turn of the century substantial factories, dealing in the less seasonal lines, were employing large numbers of women. In Hamburg in 1907 almost 2,000 women worked in clothing establishments employing 100 persons or more. The Axien underwear factory, for example, employed 300 women and girls.[54] Many of these operated on a similar basis to greatly enlarged workshops. The Hamburg firm of Oppenheim & Rappolt employed 150-200 factory workers in the mid-nineties producing a wide variety of better-quality sporting clothes, night gowns, cloaks, evening wear and rubber clothing on contracts from large stores dispersed throughout Germany.[55] The hundreds of different garments, together with the women who sewed them, were known only by number, a common practice in both workshops and factories designed to prevent women comparing items and piece rates. As in workshops, unsatisfactory goods had to be resewn in the seamstress's own time.[56] Workshops varied from establishments virtually indistinguishable from factories to one or two women operating a machine in a kitchen. Larger workshops included those in the new department stores and the alterations rooms of large clothiers who sold direct to the public. C & A Brenninkmeyer employed 47 seamstresses supervised by 5 tailoresses in addition to 51 sales staff and 7 support workers in their Hamburg clothing store in May 1913.[57] The majority of workshops, however, employed between five and ten people, rising to ten to twenty in seasonal peaks.[58] Most of Hamburg's mass-production workshops produced women's and children's clothing. In 1907, 963 of the workshops supervised by the factory inspectorate manufactured these items with a further 195 in the millinery, 62 in the underwear and 47 in the menswear branches.[59] The workshop was frequently a room in the middleman's or woman's dwelling and the smallest were run by women who were themselves subtenants in a larger flat. In the coldest months the kitchen often doubled as a workroom to save fuel.[60] Overcrowding was common in the season.[61] The tailoress Augusta Koch had employed eight women in the two rooms of her flat for twelve years prior to 1905 when the sanitary policy ordered that this be cut to a maximum of four for reasons of hygiene.[62] Nor was overcrowding confined to the smallest businesses. The millinery and clothing firm Münzer until 1907 occupied twenty-seven women in a basement barely adequate for ten.[63]

Hours, conditions and regularity of work, and wages were in general better in large factories than in workshops or outwork. Nevertheless, the hours worked in the clothing factories were longer than in almost all other factory organised trades, with the exception of textiles. The normal day was 12-13 hours between 7a.m. and 8.30p.m. including 2-2½ hours for the midday meal and coffee breaks. On Saturdays most workers did not finish until the legal deadline of 5.30p.m. after working the full 9-10 hours allowed.[64] As Saturday afternoon and evening was the busiest shopping period, employers bitterly resisted 5.30p.m. finishing for seamstresses who were completing last minute orders or doing alterations. Employers often evaded or simply broke the law. The most common methods of evasion were to gain classification as a 'workshop' outside the industrial code; nominally to divide establishments into 'independent' firms after the code was extended to workshops of more than ten employees in 1910; to classify seamstresses as saleswomen whose hours were far less restricted; or to put the work out to their own seamstresses to do after hours or to uncontrolled homeworkers.[65] The Hamburg women's clothing manufacturer Albert Levy pursued the first course when he succeeded in his claim that his factory workforce of 82 women did not comprise a factory under the industrial code. The overtime at his factory was in addition to an 8.30a.m. to 8p.m. working day and the then legal maximum of eight hours' work on Saturdays.[66] The factory inspector reacted sharply to the second practice when it was brought to his notice but condoned the classification of seamstresses as salesgirls in some cases.[67] Despite limited jurisdiction and associated difficulties of prosecution, half of the 34 employers of women prosecuted in 1902 by the Hamburg factory inspector were engaged in clothing manufacture. Almost all the cases involved illegal Saturday and Sunday working. One particularly crass employer was convicted of illegally working his 19 seamstresses aged under 18 years on Saturday evenings for a full three months.[68] The custom of giving women work to take home with them at the end of the day was widespread in Berlin in peak season despite its illegality.[69]

IV

Factories and workshops employed large numbers of young girls, often supposedly in training, and the majority of their women workers were under 21 years. In the 1,310 establishments supervised by the Hamburg inspectorate in 1908, the labour force was made up of 456 girls under 16 years, 2,675 aged 16 to 21 and 2,249 adult women, plus 277 males.[70] The quality of training varied enormously depending on the family's ability to pay the master's fee and to do without the daughter's wages, in addition to social connections and a large element of chance in the selection of workplace. A skilled tailor charged 10-20M for a six to twelve month training period during which the girl received no wage and then started her on 5-7M weekly. In Berlin training was often as brief as two to six weeks, cost 10-12M, and was followed by up to six months on 3-4M weekly. The least reputable workshop owners doing low-grade work collected the fee, used this free labour as long as possible in peak season and then simply sacked the girl. The trainee would at best learn the sewing of plain garments; at worst she would be occupied running errands, collecting and delivering to the putter-out or even looking after the master's children.[71] Factories usually paid the girl 2-3M on commencement and relied on her to pick up the limited tasks from an experienced woman. Generally it was true that

> In the employment of young girls . . . there is no sign of any regulated training period either in the factories or in the clothing workshops. Especially in the clothing workshops the girl trainee wanders from one job to another and there are cases of individual women having 3 or 4 different training masters or mistresses entered in their workbooks.[72]

Workshop seamstresses suffered regular periods of unemployment and overemployment. This was particularly marked in the highly seasonal women's fashion lines. In the mid-nineties the Imperial Statistical Office found 48 seamstresses in Berlin worked an average of 41 weeks but in only 8 of these were they fully occupied. In general, workshop women worked 3-4 weeks longer and were fully occupied 1½ weeks longer than homeworkers.[73] Workers in women's clothing in Hamburg were totally unemployed for an average 8-10 weeks per year and worked reduced hours for most of the remaining months, while full employment and considerable overtime prevailed during the peak season.[74] In June 1913, the Brenninkmeyer store followed standard practice when it laid off 26 women, half their seamstresses, after the peak season.[75] The need to accumulate extra earnings to tide themselves over the almost certain periods of unemployment compelled women to work very long hours during the short period when plenty of work was available. This cycle was characteristic of factories, workshops and outwork in both the made-to-measure and mass-production sectors. Most workshops concentrated their legal overtime of 60 days per year into the season when hours were already exceptionally long. The women's clothing workshop of Schmersahl in Hamburg, for example, obtained permission to work late every night of the week in the season of 1904. Their seamstresses who worked beyond 10p.m. were limited only to a maximum shift from 12 noon to 12 midnight with ten hours between shifts should these be done consecutively.[76] Employment among outworkers was so discontinuous that many obtained work only at the height of the season, when they might however force themselves to work up to 16 hours daily in order to compensate for the 6-7 months when 'earnings . . . are only worth mentioning where the woman owns a machine and takes on aprons, underwear, etc'.[77]

The middlemen and women who ran the workshops ranged from the well-to-do to poor widows scraping a living little better than that of their seamstresses. Setting up a business required little training or capital outlay. Thus skilled tailors desirous of becoming their own masters were joined by men from many unrelated trades. Seamstresses sometimes set up in their own home, took on a neighbour's girl or young relative as helper, acquired a sewing machine on time payment and thus gradually expanded to perhaps six women in the season and one or two in the slack period. This was a simple extension of the homeworkers' custom of utilising relatives' or children's labour to maximise the work that could be done when it was available. Typical of such a small workshop was that of the tailoress Martha Bormann in a workroom above her Hamburg flat. She employed in 1905 five women in an overcrowded room suitable only for two. She had been a middleman for 18 years during which her carpenter husband had been only irregularly in work due to lung disease.[78] The tailor Holzapfel, by contrast, ran a women's garment workshop and store which had required considerable investment in sewing machines, cutting equipment, flat irons, stove and shop rental. Illness during the eight years he had had the business had resulted in large debts so that his household and business effects were all mortgaged and his family had to sublet two rooms of their flat above the shop. His five seamstresses worked in an overcrowded unhygienic basement amidst the steam and heat generated by the ironing equipment.[79] Many middlemen and women did, however, earn a handsome living. In 1890 the middleman Platzke in Hamburg employed 18 seamstresses making coats in workrooms of his house. From the 5-6M he received for each coat he paid 2-2.50M to the women; his own income was estimated at 70-80M weekly.[80] A large Berlin middleman employing 50 women, mostly as homeworkers, delivered 1,800 pairs of men's trousers weekly for a net income of 200M.[81]

The putting-out system encouraged many seamstresses to set up independently in the hope of being able to handle more work when it was plentiful. They, like many homeworkers and workshop seamstresses, relied on private custom when the clothiers and middlemen did not want their services. Independent tailoring shops, workshops and homework shaded into each other and the one seamstress could be engaged in all three simultaneously or in rapid succession. The Hamburg tailoress Helene Siek, for example, had worked with the firm of Glass & Co., first in her own home, then in their workshop for 4½ years, before reverting to outwork in 1907, apparently because the firm was short of space. At this point she bought an additional sewing machine and took on another woman who had sewed in Glass's workroom and made clothes for other parties when the work from Glass was insufficient. She paid this woman a daily wage and netted an income of 18-20M weekly for herself. Siek was subsequently judged by the authorities to be a self-employed independent tailoress with one employee, while the firm of Glass bore no responsibility for either woman despite the fact that most of the work was done for them.[82] This case clearly illustrates the advantages of the putting-out system for the clothier and the large middleman: overhead costs of machinery, workspace, lighting and fuel were born by the outworkers; neither clothier nor middleman was required to pay insurance contributions, nor observe legal regulations with respect to conditions of work; they could utilise the women's labour at will and leave them to earn a living elsewhere when orders were short.

Wages were usually based on piece rates for the garment or part of the garment made. The two most striking features of the wages system, both intrinsic to the putting-out method of production, were the profusion of piece rates and fluctuations in earnings. Any estimates of average earnings thus conceal as much or more about the wages system and actual earnings for particular groups as they reveal, particularly given the very limited and patchy data available. Rather it is more fruitful to indicate the range of earnings in Berlin and Hamburg according to whether workers were employed in factories, workshops or outwork, were male or female, in full or part-time employment, and the variation over a period of time. Piece rates on which earnings were calculated varied between models, quality, time of year, employers and even individual workers. Very few workers did identical work at the same piece rate even within the same factory or workshop. The Tailors' and Tailoresses' Union in Hamburg, in an attempt to negotiate uniform established rates, presented a claim for 94 rates for basic items in the men's outerwear branch alone in 1896.[83] For each item there were up to 30 quality grades, the rates for which were to be determined with individual employers.[84] Union-negotiated piece rates in this branch in Hamburg yielded minimum earnings of 27M weekly in 1896 rising to 33M in 1911 for fully-trained tailors.[85] Union rates for expert tailoresses in these made-to-measure workshops in the same years were 15M and 18M respectively, or 55 per cent of male rates.[86] These women were exceptional in being highly skilled and working alongside strongly unionised tailors in comparatively permanent jobs in shops catering for the top end of the market. Even so the trade union was aware that these minima for women were frequently not met.[87] The top rates for tailoresses in women's tailoring shops were 23-25M for a 57½ hour week around 1910. Regular trained seamstresses in these establishments received 12-15M weekly.[88] Women overseers and experienced machinists in Hamburg factories earned a maximum of 12-15M in the 1880s and 1890s while their poorest colleagues took home 5-6M.[89] The wages of the majority of workshops lay between the two at about 7-12M weekly.[90]

Wages in Berlin displayed similar differences between male and female clothing workers. In clothing factories in the late 1890s tailors averaged 27-28M weekly with some earning 40M and more; female supervisors 20-25M; seamstresses and ironing women 12M and women workers under 16 years 6-7M.[91] One Berlin underwear factory employing 145 workers more or less steadily throughout the year paid its workers the following for a 57½ hour week (excluding meal breaks) in 1891:[92]

5 tailors	24-30M	1 woman ironing supervisor	45M
4 tailoress supervisors	19-31M	50 ironing women	5.50-17M
60 seamstresses	5.45-28M	1 laundryman overseer	30M
		5 laundrywomen	13M
	7 diverse women workers	12M	
	12 girls under sixteen	5M	

Experienced tailoresses in high-quality workshops and factory workers were generally the best paid in the clothing trade. Factories relied heavily on young single women, particularly the urban-born daughters of workers attracted by the opportunity of earning higher wages relatively quickly more or less all the year round, and by the more regulated hours. These women were also less influenced by the social stigma attached to women's factory work.[93] However, they rarely earned enough to support themselves from sewing or ironing alone. In Berlin in the 1880s, renting a bed in a working-class household and a very basic diet of bread, potatoes and coffee cost about 8.40M per week. In Hamburg a single self-supporting woman needed 7-8M to subsist in this way.[94] Women earning less than 10M every week of the year had an extremely deficient diet. The comparative luxury of sharing a rented room and having a wardrobe similar to that of a working-class daughter living at home required a regular wage of 18-20M weekly in Berlin and 15-17M in Hamburg at the turn of the century.[95] Most seamstresses could only hope to attain these wages in the few weeks when business was at its peak. Self-supporting women – and in Hamburg in 1905 there were more than 12,000 females living as boarders and dependent on their own earnings,[96] – survived by doing as much overtime as possible in season and living in the slack period from whatever savings they had, on credit from landladies and shopkeepers, by sewing for private customers, by doing odd jobs and, at worst, from casual prostitution. The many female clothing workers on near-subsistence incomes suffered dire poverty when average wage levels were forced down in the 1890s. From the peak of the late 1880s, average money earnings across the Berlin clothing industry had by 1897 fallen by as much as 60 per cent,[97] leading the Berlin Arbitration Office to conclude in 1896 that 'wages paid in many cases have sunk so low that even with the most strenuous and diligent effort, no existence worthy of a human being is possible for the worker'.[98] Workshop and factory seamstresses in Berlin in this period averaged perhaps 9M weekly when in full work and despite a gradual, if erratic, increase in the subsequent 15 years, real wages throughout the period never rose above the levels achieved in the latter half of the 1880s.[99]

It was, however, outworkers and the more marginal workshop seamstresses whose wages were lowest and most subject to fluctuation. As with workshop seamstresses, piece rates for outwork varied with the quality of the sewing required, the time of year and the employer. Earnings, however, were usually lower because the pieces or garments put out to homeworkers were frequently of inferior quality, spells of employment were shorter, working hours were more restricted by household duties and overhead costs had to be met. The range of earnings in the outwork sector was extreme. In Hamburg in 1912 the factory inspector found that the hourly rates varied between 7Pf and 90Pf with the lowest paid engaged on oilcloth coats and underwear. Average wages were 20-35Pf per hour.[100] The cost of the sewing machine, needles, thread, lighting and heating reduced this by 5 to 15 per cent.[101] Theoretically, a woman working at the machine for 50 hours per week without interruption and exclusive of the several hours spent in the collection of cloth and delivery of garments, would net 10-12M. Outworkers, however, could on average obtain no work for three months each year and only limited work for a further six to eight months, while their ability to earn the maximum in peak season was restricted by housework and the limits of physical endurance. Thus of the 16 regular outwork seamstresses working for Müller & Hager, Hamburg, over the two years 1891-3, four averaged wages of less than 5M weekly, seven averaged 5-7.50M, four averaged 7.50-10M, while one averaged an exceptional 22M.[102]

Marriage or the arrival of the first child was a decisive turning-point in the working life of women garment workers. The vast majority gave up paid employment only often to turn later in their lives to outwork, where they were joined by thousands of other married women who had held other jobs prior to marriage, mainly as servants.[103] While workshop and factory seamstresses were almost entirely single women, married women dominated the outwork sector. A survey of 1,350 homeworkers in a number of German cities in 1912 revealed that 73 per cent of them were married, widowed or divorced.[104] In 1913 the Hamburg factory inspector reported that of 1,187 outworkers, 53 per cent were married and a further 22 per cent widowed or separated. At least three-quarters of these homeworkers gave household responsibilities as the reason for doing outwork. This despite the fact that 30 per cent of these women had no children or other pressing grounds for preferring outwork and

20 per cent were married to lower state employees in secure jobs.[105] Among a group of Berlin homeworkers in 1912, 56 per cent had formerly been servants while 37 per cent had continued as seamstresses, although before marriage many had been engaged in workshops. Some 68 per cent of these gave 'care of household' as their reason for doing outwork.[106] The desire of better-paid skilled workers and State employees to appear to be maintaining their wives undoubtedly encouraged the women to work at home rather than in workshops if extra money was needed. This was clear in a 1907 inquiry of Berlin metal and engineering workers. The wives of skilled men were far less likely to be earning than those of unskilled workers, even when the family depended on the same low income. The wives of the more status-conscious skilled and semi-skilled men were, moreover, far more likely to be outwork seamstresses when they did earn.[107]

Households whose circumstances were such that they could partially meet the living costs of the female members but which still needed some supplement to their income were hence a major source of female garment workers. The clothing industry appeared to offer them light, clean, respectable work in workshops less rigorously controlled than factories, nearer to home, which could be, according to family duties or choice, followed by work in the home after marriage should the need arise. It was able to exploit the family orientation and position of these women by utilising their labour only when demand was high and cutting earnings to below independent subsistence level. The earning of other family members had to supply the difference.

Dire family need nevertheless drove many to seek work as domestic seamstresses, especially when there were dependants in the home. Illness, unemployment or general low and irregular earnings of the husband left the family dependent on whatever earnings the wife or daughter could scrape together from various sources. Typical of this was a seamstress who testified before the Berlin Arbitration Office in 1896 that she tried to support her husband, who had been ill for 22 weeks, and their two children, from net earnings of 4.95M weekly. Another worked 15-16 hours daily for 5M a week to keep herself and her unemployed husband.[108] Frau Richter in Hamburg worked as a seamstress in winter when her husband was out of work simply to keep her family alive. Despite the low wage of 1.40M daily for up to 18 hours work, she stated she was satisfied if she got any work at all.[109] The husband's death — and women lived on average five years longer than men — left the widow with the alternatives of Poor Law assistance, the workhouse or a return to the labour market. Half the widows of

workers in Hamburg in 1907 chose to work full or part time, mostly as
casual seamstresses, cleaning women, washerwomen and bread and
newspaper sellers.[110] However neither earnings nor Poor Law assistance
were sufficient by themselves to keep even a single woman. The widows
who worked at Schenkolewsky, Hamburg, earned an average of 10-23M
monthly.[111] Many had to seek earnings wherever else they could,
commonly by taking in lodgers. The 61-year-old widow Sophie Cordes
earned an average 9.75M monthly with Schenkolewsky and in many
weeks could not net 1.50M. She and her dependent 81-year-old mother
took in lodgers and washed clothes in order to survive.[112] Poor Law
assistance did not obviate the need to earn elsewhere: in 1905 the vast
majority of widows and unsupported wives received less than 18M per
month outdoor relief.[113] Clothing workers comprised almost 30 per
cent of female recipients judged fit for work and inadequate earnings
was the primary ground for granting relief to these women.[114]

V

The case of the garment workers in two of the largest cities of Wilhelmine
Germany highlights aspects of the relations between work and family;
between the public economy and the household economy; between the
spheres of production and reproduction. The extent and nature of
female participation in the workforce was determined by economic,
political and social factors, including those encapsulated in and mediated
through the family. In late nineteenth-century Berlin and Hamburg tens
of thousands of women were seamstresses because of the need to earn
cash and the few alternative opportunities open to them. Women's paid
labour was confined to a limited number of jobs which bore distinct
similarities to those they had performed in the rural and proto-industrial
household. Where these skills and aptitudes were in demand such as in
textiles, food processing and garment industries and domestic service,
they found employment.

   The concentration of female labour within this limited range of
occupations and the lack of practical alternatives was largely determined
by the industrial structure and employment policies of employers. The
large reserve of labour of both sexes encouraged the casualisation of a
very high proportion of labour in, for example, construction, the docks,
catering and the food processing and clothing industries, the profitability
of which was at least as much determined by the utilisation of large
quantities of cheap labour as by the investment in high-cost capital

equipment. This casualisation was particularly true of women workers because employers chose to define them as primarily committed to the family. This was backed up by and in turn reinforced the growing social and political emphasis on women as mothers in the later decades of the nineteenth century.

The implications in practice of the social definition of women as wives and mothers to the exclusion of their other roles in society were complex. It did not lead employers to confine their demand for women's labour to lighter, non-injurious occupations. Rather, they sought to exploit the economic, social and psychological dependence of women on the household and family and their reputed subsequent pliability, obedience and acceptance of poorer wages and conditions. Women and particularly married women were to be found amongst the lowest paid in the least hygienic and often most exhausting jobs such as brickyards, rag-and-bone sorting, laundries and hotel service.[115] Industries employing very large numbers of women – textiles, clothing and food processing – were characterised by the lowest wages and longest hours, with married women commonly even more disadvantaged than their single counterparts.

The clothing industry exemplified the marked sexual division of labour which had become firmly established in capitalist industry in Germany by the end of the nineteenth century. The organisation of clothing production on the putting-out system was only possible because of the availability of this cheap marginalised labour force. Within the industry itself, men and women filled different occupations, in different workplaces and in largely different branches. Amongst the women there was a sharp division between the younger single women working in factories and workshops and the married women and widows who dominated the outwork sector.

Clothing workers' wages were subject to continual downward pressure from employers who quite consciously calculated an adequate female wage as that which supplemented income earned by a male breadwinner. The supply of a large number of working-class and lower middle-class daughters and wives who had at least a minimum of the necessary skills and whose upkeep was partly met by a male bread-winner enabled employers to hold wages at a level below that necessary to lead an independent existence. These below-subsistence wages of women who did not have to provide entirely for themselves were reinforced by the competition of the thousands who did. The poorest homeworkers who had to support dependants were forced to undertake all the work they could get, regardless of how low the rates of pay were. Here the ability of the clothiers and middlemen to exploit the double burden of women workers was most extreme. Numerous contemporary reports document the appalling poverty and degradation of these women garment workers, the extreme overwork, chronic ill-health, sickness and substandard diets and accommodation which characterised their lives. Paradoxically, wage work within the home, which apparently allowed women to combine earnings and household duties, was probably equally or more detrimental to the woman's and family's long-term welfare than extra-household employment.

Working women were defined by their actual or potential position as wives and mothers regardless of their real circumstances and hence treated as temporary, casual and peripheral workers, even or particularly in industries such as clothing where they formed the bulk of the workforce. Employers explicitly used women's position in the family to justify their employment practices and low wages. They denied that any seamstresses were solely dependent on their own wages. They claimed that both married and single women sewed only for pocket money and were satisfied with their earnings. These were also justified by recourse to general insinuations about their personal lives: 'the work is done by women whose husbands either earn too little or drink their wages away . . .'[116] The logical extension of this view was that seamstresses were not really workers at all, despite the industry's heavy dependence on their labour, as they had family responsibilities. One Hamburg clothier successfully used this argument to avoid payment of insurance contributions for his female outworkers:

> The seamstresses employed by us pursue their household activities and only work as they please in their free hours . . . at any moment the woman can refuse to take on further work, or the employer refuse to offer her further work . . . she has sufficient work space in the corner where her sewing machine stands; why should the seamstress fit herself up with a larger workplace, if any old space satisfies her? . . . that some of the . . . seamstresses achieve only extremely low earnings clearly shows that they are more or less taken up with household and other activities and accordingly should not be seen as occupied wage workers . . . that these . . . persons had not worked for other firms or private customers . . . is because . . . they either could gain no work elsewhere or . . . have too little spare time to sew for other firms; in any case such people, who . . . through casual work earn in part only 2M to 2.50M weekly should not be seen as dependent wage workers.[117]

The case of the clothing industry emphasises a more general facet of industrialisation: the relationships between the spheres of production and reproduction which are easily neglected when these are too sharply divorced. The exclusively familial obligations and orientation ascribed to women as the bearers of the next generation were fundamental to the sexual division of labour not only between public paid employment and non-paid domestic work but also between men and women within the labour force. The very structure of the garment industry in Wilhelmine Germany depended crucially on the availability of women who, even in their capacity as workers and despite the fact that in that group the majority were single, were defined by employers as wives and mothers, not as workers. Working women were in this view not wage workers dependent on the employer for their living, but family members dependent on the husband or father. Wages below subsistence level were thus possible and justified because the responsibility for a woman's upkeep lay with the male bread-winner. Where their employment was feasible, employers substituted cheaper female labour for male so reducing average wage rates over time.

Within the female working-class population the family situation influenced whether and when they were in paid employment. Participation in the workforce was largely determined by material need and household obligations. In the working class the vast majority of women were workers in their own right at some time in their lives. Unlike their male counterparts, however, their working lives paralleled the reproductive and family cycle. By and large these women were in paid work when single, left the labour force on marriage, only frequently to return to it later as the husband's declining earnings or death dictated. Women's work in the clothing industry illustrates that the type and conditions of work at this later stage in women's lives were not the same as when they were single. Older women were far more likely to work in the home than in the factory or workshop and to call on the assistance of children or relatives for at least a few hours per week. Married women as a group were the most marginalised of a largely casual workforce in the putting-out system the very structure and continuation of which was dependent on their labour.

The gradual divorce of the sphere of production from the household under the conditions of nineteenth-century industrialisation in Germany severely limited the range of productive earning activities open to the rapidly increasing number of poor women in the cities. Industries which did offer them employment in large numbers were able to exploit the characteristics of the female labour force which arose out of the socially-defined family role of women. Commitment to marriage and family on the part of women did not determine where they worked and under what conditions: the sexual division within the labour market arising out of the longer-term incorporation of women's family roles into the employment structure certainly did.

Notes

This essay is a revised and extended version of a paper first delivered to the first meeting of the SSRC Research Seminar Group on Modern German Social History at the University of East Anglia in July 1978. The following abbreviations are used in the notes: StA Hbg – Staatsarchiv Hamburg; AA – Allgemeine Armenanstalt; PP – Politische Polizei; DHSG – Deputation für Handel, Schiffahrt und Gewerbe; BVZ – *Berliner Volkszeitung; FS – Fachzeitung für Schneider* (Berlin); HE – *Hamburger Echo;* VW – *Vorwärts* (Berlin); SDR – Statistik des deutschen Reiches; SHS – Statistik des Hamburgischen Staates; SMH – Statistische Mitteilungen über den Hamburgischen Staat; SVSP – Schriften des Vereins für Sozialpolitik.

1. To date, there has been little systematic investigation of the marginalisation of women's work in the nineteenth-century industrial economy. For the general argument, see Eric Richards, 'Women in the British Economy since about 1700', *History,* Vol. cxcvii (1974) pp. 337-57. The development of a casual labour market in late nineteenth-century London is analysed in Gareth Stedman–Jones, *Outcast London* (Oxford, 1971), esp. Part I. On the concentration of women in casual work, see Sally Alexander, 'Women's Work in 19th-century London: A Study of the Years 1820-1850', in Juliet Mitchell, Ann Oakley (eds.), *The Rights and Wrongs of Women* (London 1976), pp. 59-111; and for the USA, Susan J. Kleinberg, 'The Systematic Study of Urban Women', in Milton Cantor, Bruce Laurie (eds.), *Class, Sex and the Woman Worker* (Westport, Conn., 1977), pp. 20-42. The author of the present essay is currently writing a doctoral thesis on the social and economic position of women workers in Hamburg 1880-1914, to include detailed material on the female casual labour market.

2. Rolf Engelsing, 'Das häusliche Personal in der Epoche der Industrialisierung', in R. Engelsing, *Zur Sozialgeschichte deutscher Mittel- und Unterschichten* (Göttingen, 1973), pp. 225-61, and Margarete Freudenthal, *Gestaltwandel der städtischen bürgerlichen und proletarischen Hauswirtschaft unter besonderer Berücksichtigung des Typenwandels von Frau und Familie 1760-1910* (Würzburg, 1934).

3. Wilhelm Heinrich Riehl, *Die Familie* (Stuttgart, 1889), p. 80.

4. *Statistik des deutschen Reiches* (SDR) Neue Folge (NF) Vol. 211, 43. This prints the results of the Imperial census of the economically active population, carried out in 1907. Like the earlier occupational censuses of 1882 and 1895, this included all economically active persons, referred to here as 'gainfully occupied' or 'occupied' and further distinguished four major groups: the self-employed, business owners and managers; salaried staff; workers; and servants. The term 'workers' or 'employees' used throughout this essay includes servants but not salaried staff unless specifically stated. In all cases the figures include only those occupied or working full-time. Although more than two-thirds of these occupied women were still in agriculture in 1907, the number of married women occupied

full-time in manufacturing also rose by 200 per cent in the period between the census of 1882 and that of 1907.

5. Quoted in Rose Otto, *Über Fabrikarbeit verheirateter Frauen* Münchener Volkswirtschaftliche Studien, No. 104, Stuttgart and Berlin, 1910) p. 143. See also the essay by Richard J. Evans in the present volume, pp. 256-88.

6. Ulrich Linse, 'Arbeiterschaft und Geburtenentwicklung im Deutschen Kaiserreich von 1871', *Archiv für Sozialgeschichte*, Vol. XII (1972), pp. 205-72; Anna Davin, 'Imperialism and Motherhood', *History Workshop – A Journal of Socialist Historians*, 5 (1978), pp. 9-65.

7. 4,787,000 single women, including those working in family businesses, of a total of 6,625,000 single women (SDR, Vol. 211, pp. 12-13).

8. SDR, Vol. 207, Table 2.

9. Kleinberg, 'Systematic Study', adopts a similar approach. On textiles, see Wilhelm Feld, *Die Kinder der in Fabriken arbeitenden Frauen und ihre Verpflegung mit besonderer Berücksichtigung der Crimmitschauer Arbeiterinnen*, Vol. III (Dresden, Abhandlungen der Centrale für private Fürsorge in Frankfurt am Main, 1906). A study of a large textile mill in Mönchengladbach illustrates this in detail: Marie Bernays, *Auslese und Anpassung der Arbeiterschaft in der geschlossenen Grossindustrie* (Schriften des Vereins für Sozialpolitik (SVSP) Vol. 133/1, Leipzig, 1910). Studies of the textile industry in other countries seek to analyse the relations between family and married women's work. See e.g., R. Burr-Litchfield, 'The Family and the Mill: Cotton Mill Work, Family Work Patterns and Fertility in Mid-Victorian Stockport', in Anthony Wohl (ed.), *The Victorian Family* (London, 1978), pp. 180-96; David Walkowitz, 'Working-class Women in the Gilded Cage: Factory, Community and Family Life among Cohoes, New York, Cotton Workers', in Peter Stearns, David Walkowitz (eds.), *Workers in the Industrial Revolution* (New Brunswick, 1974), pp. 255-77.

10. SDR, Vol. 203, Table 3.

11. A very readable critique of the 'modernisation' school of social history is Tony Judt, 'A Clown in Regal Purple: Social History and the Historians', *History Workshop*, 7 (1979), pp. 66-94. Particularly extreme examples in the field of women's history are Patricia Branca, *Women in Europe Since 1750* (London, 1978) and Theresa McBride, *The Domestic Revolution* (London, 1976).

12. The clothing industry was a major employer of women in many German cities, including Breslau, Stettin, Dresden, Erfurt, Halle, Posen, Bielefeld, Stuttgart, Aschaffenburg and Aue.

13. One of the few recent social-historical works on the garment industry is Karin Hausen, 'Technischer Fortschritt und Frauenarbeit im 19. Jahrhundert. Zur Sozialgeschichte der Nähmaschine', *Geschichte und Gesellschaft*, 4 (1978), pp. 148-69. For a general appraisal of recent work on the social history of the working class in Germany see Richard J. Evans, 'The Sociological Interpretation of German Labour History' in Richard J. Evans (ed.), *The German Working Class 1888-1933: The Politics of Everyday Life* (London, 1981). A collection of essays expanding on the social and historiographical theories pursued by modern German social historians is Jürgen Kocka (ed.), *Geschichte und Gesellschaft*, Vol. I (1975).

14. This strike occurred in February and March 1896 and involved upwards of 50,000 workers, including a very large number of women, in Berlin, Breslau, Stettin, Erfurt, Dresden, Halle and Hamburg. The strike and its outcome merit separate consideration and are not dealt with here.

15. Theodor von der Goltz, *Die ländliche Arbeiterfrage und ihre Lösung* (Danzig, 1872), p. 82.

16. Johannes Schult, *Geschichte der Hamburger Arbeiter 1890-1919* (Hannover, 1967), p. 27.

17. Goltz, *Ländliche Arbeiterfrage*, pp. 78-82.

18. In 1882 there were 748,000 men and 118,000 women day labourers having their own land; by 1907 this had fallen to 214,000 men and 46,000 women, although this does not tell us who actually worked these plots as opposed to who owned them. The number of day-labourers with the use of land owned by others, or with no land at all, rose from 786,000 men and 588,000 women to 865,000 men and 714,000 women by 1907. At the latter date, the completely landless stood at 646,000 men and 697,000 women. See A.V. Desai, *Real Wages in Germany 1871-1913* (Oxford, 1968), p. 145. For the condition of agricultural labouring women, see Goltz, *Ländliche Arbeiterfrage*, ch. I-II and Elly zu Putlitz, *Arbeits- und Lebensverhältnisse der Frauen in der Landwirtschaft in Brandenburg,* Schriften des ständigen Ausschusses zur Förderung der Arbeiterinnen-Interessen, Vol. 5 (Jena, 1914). See also the essay by Arthur E. Imhof in the present volume, pp. 148-74.

19. A. Geyer, *Die Frauenerwerbsarbeit in Deutschland* (Jena, 1924), p. 23.

20. Freudenthal, *Gestaltwandel*, ch. 3, 5.

21. *Die Heimarbeit in Berlin. Bericht der Handelskammer zu Berlin* (Berlin, October 1906), p. 11.

22. Otto, *Über Fabrikarbeit,* p. 113.

23. 4,787,000 single women, including those working in family businesses, of a total of 6,625,000. SDR, Vol. 211, 12-13.

24. Marie Baum, *Drei Klassen von Lohnarbeiterinnen in Industrie und Handel der Stadt Karlsruhe* (Karlsruhe, 1906), pp. 61-5; Käthe Mendé, *Münchener jugendliche Ladnerinnen zu Hause und im Beruf* (Stuttgart, Berlin, 1912), pp. 203-5.

25. *Die Beschäftigung verheirateter Frauen in Fabriken* (Reichsamt des Innern, 1901), pp. 33-45.

26. These jobs were done by large numbers of women and children in both Berlin and Hamburg either as a part-time employment or as part of a full working day in which a variety of such jobs were combined. There is to date nothing published on this form of work for women in Germany. Sally Alexander, 'Women's Work', gives examples from London in the mid-nineteenth century.

27. SDR, Vol. 207, Table 1.

28. Elisabeth Altmann-Gottheimer, *Studien über die Wuppertaler Textilindustrie und ihre Arbeiter*, Staats- und sozialwissenschaftliche Forschungen, Vol. 22, No. 2 (Leipzig, 1903); Marie Bernays, *Auslese*, is a detailed study of the workforce at one large textile mill in Mönchengladbach; Jürgen Kuczynski, *Die Geschichte der Lage der Arbeiter unter dem Kapitalismus*, Vol. 18, *Zur Geschichte der Lage der Arbeiterin in Deutschland von 1700 bis zur Gegenwart* (East Berlin, 1963) contains a great deal of scattered information on women textile workers in Saxony from the mid-nineteenth century.

29. See for example Mary Kathleen Benet, *Secretary. An Inquiry into the Female Ghetto* (London, 1972).

30. For a detailed study of this process in German industry of the period, see Clemens Heiss, *Auslese und Anpassung der Arbeiter in der Berliner Feinmechanik* (SVSP, Vol. 134, Part II, Leipzig, 1910).

31. StA Hbg. Senat, Cl. I, Lit. T, No. 8, Vol. 30, Fasc. 2, 25: *Jahresberichte der Gewerbeinspektion 1879, 1910.*

32. StA Hbg. Senat, Cl. I, Lit. T, No. 8, Vol. 30, Fasc. 10: *Jahresbericht der Fabrikinspektion 1899,* 2-9.

33. SDR, Vol. 207.

34. *Statistik des Hamburgischen Staates* (SHS), Vol. XXV, Part 3 (Hamburg, 1910), p. 75; R. May, *Kosten der Lebenshaltung und Entwicklung der Einkommensverhältnisse in Hamburg seit 1890* (SVSP), Vol. 145, Part IV, p. 292.

35. The only attempt recently to evaluate the importance of the sewing

machine and the clothing industry for paid employment and its relation to the
family in women's lives is Hausen, 'Technischer Fortschritt', to which more
general background this article is in many respects complementary.

36. J. Krengel, 'Das Wachstum der Berliner Bekleidungsindustrie vor dem
ersten Weltkrieg', p. 6 (MS. kindly given me by the author), Table 1. 57 per cent
of these sales were on the international market.

37. Engelsing, 'Häusliche Personal', p. 234.

38. Freudenthal, *Gestaltwandel,* ch. 3, 5.

39. On the organisation of the outwork clothing industry, see H. Grandke,
'Berliner Kleiderkonfektion' in *Die Hausindustrie der Frauen in Berlin* (SVSP),
Vol. 85, (1899), pp. 129-389; W. Stieda, *Die deutsche Hausindustrie* (SVSP),
Vols. 39-42, (1889); J. Timm, *Das Sweating-System in der deutschen
Konfektionsindustrie* (Flensburg, 1895); A. Dodd, *Die Wirkung der
Schutzbestimmungen für die jugendlichen und weiblichen Fabrikarbeiter und die
Verhältnisse im Konfektionsbetriebe* (Jena, 1898), pp. 146ff.

40. Timm, *Das Sweating-System,* p. 9.

41. Grandke, 'Berliner Kleiderkonfektion', p. 343. This estimate seems too
high; see pp. 230, 235 of the present essay.

42. Dodd, *Die Wirkung,* pp. 173, 157.

43. Ibid., p. 161; Timm, *Das Sweating-System,* p. 15, gives an example of a
large middleman's income and expenditure.

44. Krengel, 'Das Wachstum', Table 1.

45. Dodd, *Die Wirkung,* p. 170; K. Stülpnagel, *Uber Hausindustrie in Berlin
und den nächstgelegenen Kreisen* (SVSP), Vol. 42, (1890), p. 14.

46. Krengel, 'Das Wachstum', p. 7; Dodd, *Die Wirkung,* pp. 147-8; A. Weber,
Die Entwicklungsgrundlagen der Grossstädtischen Frauenhausindustrie (SVSP),
Vol. 85, (1899), p. lvii, suggests that many women understood 'independent' &
'self-employed' as meaning 'not a bound servant'.

47. Krengel, 'Das Wachstum', Tables 3, 14.

48. Weber, *Die Entwicklungsgrundlagen,* p. xix; J. Krengel, 'Die
Arbeiterschaft der Berliner Bekleidungsindustrie' (MS. by courtesy of the author),
comparing Tables 2 and 1 (pp. 9, 6).

49. In 1897, the Chamber of Commerce stated that there were 211 people
employed in menswear, 282 in women's clothing and 390 in clothing war factories.
This left 1,727 of their total figure for those in the clothing industry unaccounted
for (StA Hbg, DHSG, II, Spezialakten 371-8 II, XXX, A1.2, Bd. 1, *Bericht der
Industriekommission der Handelskammer . . . 1897,* pp. 5-6). In the peak season
of 1896, the police found 1,200 women engaged in the four largest factories alone,
and agreed with the Tailors' Union estimate of 2,500 women employed in the
industry (StA Hbg, PP, S5310-58, Bd. 1, Police report, 7 January 1896). In 1900
the factory inspectorate estimated a total of 10,000 workers in 3,000 workshops,
with an unknown number of domestic workers (StA Hbg, Senat, Cl. I, Lit. T, No.
8, Vol. 30, Fasc. 11: *Jahresbericht . . . 1900,* p. 5). By 1906 the inspector
supervised 1,154 workshops with 6,386 women and 235 men workers, but
claimed many still evaded control, and this in any case did not include domestic
workers (ibid., Fasc. 20: *Jahresbericht . . . 1906,* p. 22). The 1907 industrial
census counted 10,926 'businesses' in clothing manufacture, of which 8,622
employed no non-family labour – i.e. were outworkers. On this count there were
22,918 persons in the clothing industry, 13,769 of them women (SMH No. 4,
Table 1). The occupational census conducted concurrently, however, found
26,020 persons in the clothing industry, 15,490 of them women (Table 8.1). The
occupational classification of this census and of the factory inspectorate reports
do not allow a breakdown according to branch. By 1913, the inspectorate
supervised 1,600 workshops and factories employing 8,000 women and 1,620

men and estimated that there were an extra 5,500 women and 1,500 to 2,000 men outworkers (StA Hbg, Senat, Cl. I, Lit. T, No. 8, Vol. 30, Fasc. 30, Conv. 1: *Jahresbericht . . . 1913*, pp. 2-4).

50. Grandke, 'Berliner Kleiderkonfektion', pp. 168-9; Stülpnagel, *Über Hausindustrie*, pp. 13-14; Dodd, *Die Wirkung*, p. 155.

51. StA Hbg, Senat, Cl. I, Lit. T, No. 8, Vol. 30, Fasc. 30, Conv. 1: *Jahresbericht . . . 1912*, pp. 5, 32, and *1913*, pp. 4-5.

52. Ibid.

53. Krengel, 'Die Arbeiterschaft', pp. 6, 8, calculated from Tables 1, 2.

54. SMH No. 4, Table 1; StA Hbg, Senat, Cl. I, Lit. T, No. 8, Vol. 30, Fasc. 7: *Jahresbericht . . . 1907*, p. 20; and Fasc. 30, Conv. 1: *Jahresbericht . . . 1912*, p. 4; Sta Hbg, Senat, Cl. XI, Gen. No. 2, Gewerbewesen, Vol. 121, Fasc. 2.

55. Sta Hbg, PP, S5310-58, Bd. 1: Police report 2 March 1896, 8 April 1896; Bd. 2, FS 21 March 1896.

56. Ibid., Bd. 1, police report 30 March 1896; Bd. 2, FS 21 March 1896.

57. Sta Hbg, Senat, Cl. XI, Gen. No. 2, Vol. 53a, Fasc. 13, Inv. 2: *Bericht des Versicherungsamts 15 June 1913*.

58. SMH No. 4, Table 1; StA Hbg, Senat, Cl. I, Lit. T, No. 8, Vol. 30, Fasc. 19: *Jahresbericht . . . 1905*, p. 7.

59. Ibid., Fasc. 21: *Jahresbericht . . . 1907*, pp. 6, 7.

60. Ibid.

61. Ibid., Fasc. 10: *Jahresbericht . . . 1899*, p. 20; Fasc. 11: *Jahresbericht . . . 1900*, p. 5.

62. StA Hbg, Senat, Cl. XI, Gen. No. 2, Vol. 115b, case 2.

63. Ibid., case 9.

64. StA Hbg, Senat, Cl. I, Lit. T, No. 8, Vol. 30, Fasc. 10: *Jahresbericht . . . 1899*, p. 20; Fasc. 21: *Jahresbericht . . . 1907*, p. 7. StA Hbg, Senat, Cl. XI, Gen. No. 2: *Gewerbewesen*, Vol. 99b, Fasc. 39; Vol. 121, Fasc. 43, 46, 50; Vol. 125, Fasc. 12.

65. StA Hbg, Senat, Cl. I, Lit. T, No. 8, Vol. 30, Fasc. 5: *Jahresbericht . . . 1894*, p. 5; Fasc. 7: *Jahresbericht . . . 1896*, p. 3; Fasc. 10: *Jahresbericht . . . 1899*, p. 20; Fasc. 11: *Jahresbericht . . . 1900*, p. 5; Fasc. 18: *Jahresbericht . . . 1904*, p. 3; Fasc. 25: *Jahresbericht . . . 1910*, p. 7; Fasc. 30, Conv. 1: *Jahresbericht . . . 1911*, pp. 8-9.

66. StA Hbg, Senat, Cl. XI, Gen. No. 2, Vol. 121, Fasc. 43, 1. Anlage. Another example is of a factory employing 140 workers, removed from inspectorate supervision in 1894 (StA Hbg, Senat, Cl. I, Lit. T, No. 8, Vol. 30, Fasc. 5: *Jahresbericht . . . 1894*, p. 5).

67. Ibid., Fasc. 25: *Jahresbericht . . . 1910*, p. 7; Fasc. 30, Conv. 1: *Jahresbericht . . . 1911*, pp. 8-9.

68. Ibid., Fasc. 14: *Sonderbericht. betrifft Bestrafungen . . . 1902*, case 75.

69. StA Hbg, PP, V327-86, HC 15 Nov. 1900; Senat, Cl. I, Lit. T, No. 8, Vol. 30, Fasc. 30, Conv. 1: *Jahresbericht . . . 1912*, p. 10; Fasc. 22: *Jahresbericht . . . 1908*, p. 7.

70. Ibid., p. 24.

71. Ibid., p. 6. For training in Berlin, see Grandke, 'Berliner Kleiderkonfektion', pp. 263-6; Dodd, *Die Wirkung*, p. 182.

72. StA Hbg, Senat, Cl. I, Lit. T, No. 8, Vol. 30, Fasc. 20: *Jahresbericht . . . 1906*, p. 6.

73. Dodd, *Die Wirkung*, p. 171.

74. StA Hbg, PP, V709, HE 9 Dec. 1912; Senat, Cl. I, Lit. T, No. 8, Vol. 30, Fasc. 22: *Jahresbericht . . . 1908*, p. 6.

75. StA Hbg, Senat, Cl. XI, Gen. No. 2, Vol. 53a, Fasc. 13, Inv. 2: *Bericht des Versicherungsamts*, 15 June 1913.

76. Ibid., Vol. 99b, Fasc. 39.
77. *Ergebnisse der Ermittelungen über die Lohnverhältnisse in der Wäschefabrikation und der Konfektionsbranche* (Drucksachen des deutschen Reichstags, 1887), p. 9. Grandke, 'Berliner Kleiderkonfektion', p. 256, gives an average of 15 hours 45 minutes in peak season in Berlin. Also, K. Gaebel, *Die Lage der Heimarbeiterinnen* (Gewerkverein der Heimarbeiterinnen, Berlin, 1912), p. 9.
78. StA Hbg, Senat, Cl. XI, Gen. No. 2, Vol. 115b, Bl. 4.
79 Ibid., Bl. 8.
80. StA Hbg, PP, V157, Bd. 2, police report 16 Feb. 1890.
81. Report of the 1896 Berlin Arbitration Office Inquiry in HE 22 April 1896 (StA Hbg, PP, S5310-58, Bd. 4).
82. StA Hbg, Senat, Cl. XI, Gen. No. 2, Vol. 71b, Fasc. 16, Inv. 18, case 3/08.
83. StA Hbg, PP, S5310-58, Bd. 1, Lohntarif, Firma Oppenheim & Rappolt.
84. Ibid., police report 8 April 1896.
85. StA Hbg, PP, V327-86, Bd. 2, Lohntarif, and S18030-88, HE 3 Feb. 1911.
86. Ibid., also S5310-58, Bd. 1, Lohntarif, Firma Oppenheim & Rappolt.
87. StA Hbg, PP, V709, FS 27 March 1909.
88. StA Hbg, Senat, Cl. I, Lit. T, No. 8, Vol. 30, Fasc. 20: *Jahresbericht . . . 1906*, p. 6; StA Hbg, PP, S18720-31, HE 9 March 1913.
89. StA Hbg, PP, V327-86, Bd. 2, FS 11 Jan. 1896; S1053 Burgerzeitung, 26 June 18
90. StA Hbg, PP, S5310-58, Bd. 3, HE 13 Feb. 1896, BVZ 17 Feb. 1896.
91. *Ermittelungen über die Lohnverhältnisse in Berlin* (Statistisches Amt Berlin, Berlin, 1888), pp. 6-8.
92. Ibid., (Berlin, 1892), p. 120.
93. Dodd, *Die Wirkung*, pp. 191-4; Grandke, 'Berliner Kleiderkonfektion', pp. 260, 373.
94. *Ergebnisse . . .* (note 77, above), p. 8.
95. Dodd, *Die Wirkung*, pp. 210, 218.
96. SHS Heft XXV (Hamburg, 1910), p. 124.
97. Krengel, 'Die Arbeiterschaft', p. 13.
98. Quoted in full in Grandke, 'Berliner Kleiderkonfektion', pp. 351-9.
99. Krengel, 'Die Arbeiterschaft', 12, Tables 4, 5.
100. StA Hbg, Senat, Cl. I, Lit. T, No. 8, Vol. 30, Fasc. 30, Conv. 1: *Jahresbericht . . . 1912*, p. 6.
101. Grandke, 'Berliner Kleiderkonfektion', pp. 237-40.
102. StA Hbg, Senat, Cl. XI, Gen. No. 2, Vol. 71b, Fasc. 16, Inv. 3, case 2/93.
103. In her 1912 survey of outwork seamstresses, Gaebel *Die Lage*, found that 56 per cent had been servants before marriage. Grandke, 'Berliner Kleiderkonfektion', p. 261, found that 20 out of 52 domestic workers had been servants.
104. Gaebel, *Die Lage*, p. 7.
105. StA Hbg, Senat, Cl. I, Lit. T, No. 8, Vol. 30, Fasc. 30, Conv. 1: *Jahresbericht . . . 1913*, p. 5.
106. Gaebel, *Die Lage*, pp. 97, 107.
107. Of the metal and engineering workers with the lowest earnings of less than 900 Marks per annum, 23.5 per cent of the skilled men's wives also earned, compared with 37.5 per cent of the semi-skilled and 43 per cent of the unskilled men's wives. See D. Lande, 'Arbeits- und Lohnverhältnisse in der Berliner Maschinenindustrie zu Beginn des 20. Jahrhunderts', SVSP, Vol. 134 (1910), Part 7, pp. 442ff.
108. StA Hbg, PP, S5310, Bd. 4, HE 29 Feb. 1896.
109. StA Hbg, PP, V43, police report 16 June 1896.
110. Among the 17,331 widows of workers, 8,719 had full or part-time

employment; 3,924 relied on Poor Law benefits; 2,599 were living in institutions
and 2,089 relied entirely on relatives. See SMH No. 2, 261.

111. StA Hbg, Senat, Cl. XI, Gen. No. 2, Vol. 71b, Fasc. 16, Inv. 4, case 4/94.

112. Ibid., letter from widow Sophie Cordes in case file.

113. Ibid., in 1900, widows and separated wives accounted for 6,451 of the
8,819 recipients of outdoor relief. Seamstresses, milliners etc. were 1,421 of the
total 4,972 of these women judged to be fit for work. See *Die Ergebnisse der am
1.Dez. 1900 erfolgten statistischen Erhebung über die in Hamburg in offener
Armenpflege unterstützten Personen unter besonderer Berücksichtigung der
Wohnungsverhältnisse* (Armenkollegium Hamburg, 1902), pp. 6, 32-3.

114. StA Hbg, AA II, 123: 'Übersicht über den Bestand der Armenparteien
am 1 Januar 1905'.

115. *Die Beschäftigung . . .* (note 25, above), pp. 87-113.

116. StA Hbg, PP, S5310-58, Bd. 4, VW, 20 Feb. 1896.

117. StA Hbg, Senat, Cl. XI, Gen. No. 2, Vol. 71b, Fasc. 16, Inv. 4, case
9/94, appeal of Schenkolewsky, pp. 3-5.

9 POLITICS AND THE FAMILY: SOCIAL DEMOCRACY AND THE WORKING-CLASS FAMILY IN THEORY AND PRACTICE BEFORE 1914

Richard J. Evans

I

In the nineteenth century most people agreed on the central importance of the family for the social and political order.[1] The family was still, though to a diminishing degree, a public institution; its formation was a matter for communal concern, its transactions were carried out under the public eye, and its activities played an important role in public life. As it has become removed from the public sphere, however, and transformed (at least in theory) into a place of refuge from the world outside,[2] so the family has also been removed from the historian's concept of past politics. Its incorporation into a 'private sphere' removed from society has been followed by its removal from history in a wider sense and its incorporation into a depoliticised history of private life.[3] In this essay I want to take up the neglected question of the connections between family and politics in the late nineteenth and early twentieth centuries,[4] and to look at how people thought the two were related, and how far these ideas had any base in reality. The starting-point of the essay is the belief, widely accepted then and now, that industrialisation and the spread of the capitalist mode of production, by drawing women and young people into the labour market as wage earners, removed them from the orbit of the family and politicised them by exploiting them directly, as individuals, instead of indirectly, through the male head of the family or household.[5] The importance of the family within society itself was reduced as it lost its productive role with the coming of factory production and its socialising and educative functions (which of course included the imparting of political beliefs and attitudes) with the spread of primary education and the growth of organised youth and women's movements. Increased exploitation and the break-up of the family led to political mobilisation. Women entered the factory, worked alongside men, shared their experiences of exploitation and resistance, and made common cause with them in political organisations. Women and children, it is argued, moved into politics as independent actors, no longer content to leave the

256

representation of their interests to the male head of household.

This argument applies principally, of course, to the women and children of the industrial proletariat. It received a dramatic illustration in Germany with the rise of the Social Democratic movement (SPD), which by 1914 was the largest and most highly-organised socialist movement in Europe, with over a million members, many of them women. With its demands for the complete democratisation of all political and social institutions, its radical socialist programme drawn up under the guidance of Marx's collaborator Engels, its Marxist rhetoric, and its resolute refusal to contemplate working within the existing political system, the SPD aroused massive anxieties within the ruling classes. Not least because it extended its critique of the bourgeois order to include social and economic aspects of capitalism as well as political ones, it was regarded by the ruling classes as a threat to the very principles and institutions on which their lives were based. It was natural enough, therefore, that its emergence and rapid numerical growth should have been regarded as a threat to the integrity of what conservatives saw as the most fundamental of all social institutions, the family.

Right-wing politicians and journalists in Germany saw a contented family life as a major bulwark against the radicalisation of the newly emerging industrial proletariat. In 1899, for example, the newspaper *Die Post,* which represented the views of heavy industry, voiced its concern at the attempts of the SPD to politicise working-class women:

> As in all fields, so in the question of women's rights, the influence of Social Democracy will prove openly destructive of civilisation. It desires only too eagerly the complete destruction of the family, whose beneficent influence has shown still to be a strong, if not at every place an impregnable barrier against social agitation. It is for this reason that the doctrine of free love and the promotion of the most radical emancipatory aspirations belong to the most important points in the programme of the international revolutionaries.[6]

In alleging that the Social Democrats aimed at the destruction of the family, *Die Post* was giving vent to a feeling that was almost universally held on the right of the political spectrum. 'There is now a species of men', a State primary school teacher was reported to have told his (largely working-class) pupils, 'who call themselves Social Democrats; they want to destroy marriage and family life . . .'[7] The effect of Social Democratic agitation on women was especially alarming to right-wing observers, for women were seen as the cornerstone of the family unit. The political mobilisation of women, indeed, appeared as the practical expression of the Social Democrats' attack on the integrity of the family. As right-wing 'National Liberal circles' quoted in a major daily newspaper, the *National-Zeitung,* in 1913, asserted:

> Instead of thinking clearly about the real reasons for their poverty and need – I mention only the modern desire for pleasure and amusement, the tendency of husbands to take to drink, and the often quite exaggerated involvement in societies and clubs – she (the working-class woman) gives her bitterness free rein and simply ascribes the blame for all her misery to the disorganised and unjust circumstances of our present social order . . . She does not incline to logically correct thought, but is quickly won over by strongly expressed sentiments and outward impressions, which lead above all the woman of the people to follow more easily whatever is crudely obvious, harsh, hard and coarse. But has there ever been a movement with a stronger self-confidence, a more obviously coarse sureness of its aims than Social Democracy? These qualities . . . alone can explain why women fail to see through the boundlessness and impracticality of Socialist aims.[8]

What really disturbed middle-class and conservative commentators was the fact that from the turn of the century onwards increasing numbers of women began to join the SPD. By 1914, indeed, their numbers had reached the considerable total of 175,000. Right-wing politicians and administrators in Wilhelmine Germany ascribed this alarming development above all to the employment of women outside the home, which, they believed, was breaking up the working-class family and creating an alienated male and female proletariat ripe for socialist agitation. It was clear to the senior official of the Prussian administration in the Ruhr district in 1902 for example that the SPD had failed to recruit women in the industrial towns under his supervision because 'there is no female factory proletariat in the Ruhr area'.[9] The most extreme remedy offered by conservatives was to send women back to the home in order to build up a contented family life as a bulwark against revolution,[10] a view that was eventually shared by Hitler and the Nazis, who indeed went some way towards putting it into effect.[11]

The recruitment of women by the SPD thus appeared as a by-product of the destruction of family life by the Industrial Revolution; and the employment of women outside the home was the source not only of their own mobilisation against the existing order, but also of their husbands'.

Thank God, the family life of our working class is still a healthy one. [remarked a Catholic Centre Reichstag deputy from the Ruhr area] A happy family life is the best reward for a worker; the feeling that he is working to support his wife and offspring gives him encouragement in his work; and in his family he finds peace and contentment. But such is only the case when the wife can devote herself to the family. If she is out of the house the whole day, then the house becomes dirty and untidy; the husband cannot get a proper meal, just cold food the whole day through: coffee, potatoes, sausages, cheese; and this is *not* conducive to the creation of a feeling of contentment within the family.[12]

If the working class were not to be driven to revolution by a diet of cold potatoes, sausages and cheese, however, the first necessity was clearly for married women at least to remain at home; and the whole tenor of the opposition to female emancipation was to emphasise this necessity. Yet with masses of married women providing cheap labour for the very classes that provided some of the most vocal opponents of the employment of women, it would clearly be economically disadvantageous to translate these social principles into social reality. It was the consciousness of this contradiction between social reality and social ideology which prompted the German Government to introduce over a number of years a series of measures designed to minimise the allegedly harmful effects of employment on the family and home life of the working classes. The factory legislation of 1878 and subsequent years limited women's hours of work and type of employment. It was mainly designed to protect married women workers and their families. As the Government's spokesman in the Reichstag declared, in justifying an extension of these measures in 1890, the aim of the new regulations was to ensure 'that the ennobling spirit of family life and the blessings of hearth and home, which seem at present to be seriously under threat, remain assured to the worker and his own'.[13] The aim, therefore, was to minimise the allegedly harmful effects of female and child labour outside the home on proletarian family life.[14] Thus where the family, with its supposedly calming influence on the worker, and its allegedly deterrent effect against the blandishments of Social Democracy, was not considered to be in danger, the Government took no action. The regulations of 1878, 1890 and later periods did not extend to domestic labour, where conditions were often far worse than in large factories; nor did they cover shops employing less than ten workers, although such places often saw the worst evils of sweated labour. The only exception was the stipulation that women workers who had worked the maximum permitted hours in a given day were forbidden to take any other employment that day. This too was a measure to protect the family. Domestic service and agricultural labour were also exempt from these regulations; here the paternalistic influence of the employer was seen, as it was not in the more impersonal circumstances of factory employment, as providing a reinforcement of family morale.[15] Thus the right-wing daily *Die Post* accused the Social Democrats in 1899 of fighting against all attempts 'to persuade the daughters of the lower classes to become domestic servants rather than factory workers. The Social Democrats . . .', declared the newspaper, 'want to remove the girls from the beneficent influence of an orderly family life in order to drive them into the ranks of the discontented.'[16] Even within the factories that were covered by protective laws, little seems to have been done by the Government to improve working conditions; what it was really concerned about was that married women workers should be able to get away from the factory enough to keep their family going, their husband contented and their children alive, and that children and adolescents should remain as far as possible confined within the family sphere.

A classic statement of this ideology was William Heinrich Riehl's immensely popular *Die Familie*, a book which went through ten editions between its publication in 1858 and the year 1889.[17] Riehl's book was a romantic hymn of praise for the patriarchal peasant family, though perhaps as he portrayed it it was to a great extent the product of his imagination.[18] Riehl saw the institution of the patriarchal family and household as a model for the whole of society:

> Modern times unfortunately, only know of the family; they no longer recognise the household, they no longer accept the joyful and hospitable idea of the 'whole house', which includes not only the natural members of the family, but also all those voluntary comrades and helpers of the family who are traditionally described as living-in-servants. In the household, the beneficent influence of the family is also extended to people who otherwise have no family; these people are drawn in, as it were by adoption, to the moral system of authority and piety. This is of the profoundest importance for the social stability of the entire nation.[19]

Society as a whole, in this view, was — or should be — a gigantic patriarchal family, in which, to use the vocabulary employed by Riehl, the mass of the people became 'voluntary comrades and helpers', and behaved with 'piety' towards their superiors, above all the monarch, who, as supreme patriarch, exercised 'authority' over his people. Riehl believed that women were naturally inferior to men, just as children were to adults, and that inequality and authority were basic elements in human society. His views were but a literary expression of patriarchal assumptions which permeated the attitudes, behaviour and legislative practice of the classes and groups who wielded effective political and administrative power in Imperial Germany. The family was seen as a microcosm of the State, and it was entitled to the same kind of legal protection; so much so, in fact, that the 'Revolution Bill' (*Umsturzvorlage*) of 1896 proposed to commit to prison anyone who criticised the family as an institution.[20]

The attitude of the dominant culture to the family was thus an overwhelmingly positive one. A stable family life was held to be a guarantee of social peace; the family was regarded as the very basis of the social and political order. Conversely, the undermining of family solidarity appeared to conservatives as one of the most worrying aspects of industrialisation; while the conviction that the socialists were busy destroying the integrity of the family in word and deed, through propaganda on the one hand and the political mobilisation of women and children on the other, was one of the deepest sources of bourgeois anxiety about the political future of the Imperial system. At the same time, there existed a dramatic contradiction between the platitudes and shibboleths mouthed by bourgeois commentators about the sanctity of family life, and the realities of the social praxis of the bourgeoisie. To begin with, the very employers whose spokesmen in papers such as *Die Post* so eloquently delineated the consequences of female employment on proletarian family life, were at the same time engaged in the wholesale employment of women and children, often at starvation wages, or, alternatively, in creating an urban environment which offered neither sufficient wages to men to enable them to set up a family, nor sufficient employment opportunities to women to make up the family wage. Evasions of Government regulations on female and child labour by industrial employers were commonplace. In their own lives, too, the members of the bourgeoisie were possibly even more contradictory, as indeed Social Democratic spokesmen were not slow to point out. Late or loveless bourgeois marriages, the consequence of making marriage dependent on property, created a massive bourgeois demand for the sexual services of prostitutes, thus further undermining the integrity of the proletarian family circles from which those who supplied these services – often better-paid than the more legitimate forms of employment which the bourgeoisie had to offer women – were drawn. Wilhelm II's own court circle, despite the official idealisation of family life, was to a large degree homosexual in tone. Sexual scandals in the ruling class were frequent: the cases of the industrialist Krupp, who was discovered keeping a love-nest of Italian boys on a Mediterranean island, or of the millionaire Sternberg, convicted of a particularly unpleasant rape in 1900, were only the tip of an iceberg of sexual hypocrisy.[21] Nevertheless, if the ruling classes themselves were not always prepared to follow their own precepts, they certainly intended the proletariat to; and the belief that the Social Democrats were actively undermining the stability of family life was one of the most important aspects of middle-class insecurity in the industrialising society of the Wilhelmine age.

II

Bourgeois observers certainly had some justification for believing that the SPD was hostile to the family as an institution. The classical texts of Marxism, so often cited by Social Democratic theorists, presented the dissolution of the family under the impact of the spread of capitalist industry as a generally positive development. 'The emancipation of women', wrote Engels in *The Origin of the Family, Private Property and the State* (1884), 'has as its first precondition the return of the whole female sex to public industry, and . . . this again demands the removal of the individual family in its character as an economic unit of society', and Engels predicted that the upbringing of children would be a public not a family matter in the future socialist society.[22] Marx himself, in a much-cited passage of *Das Kapital*, remarked that 'the dissolution of the old family structure within the capitalist system' through the employment of women and children outside the home provided 'the economic basis for a higher form of the family', and he added that the 'Christian-Germanic form of the family', was as socially determined as any other, and just as likely to be superseded.[23] August Bebel, the SPD leader, in his book *Woman and Socialism,* the most widely-read of all Social Democratic tracts, repeated these views at greater length and in more detail;[24] and like Bebel and Marx, Lily Braun, the author of the only other large-scale work on women's emancipation to emerge from the Social Democratic movement, also argued that the family would give way in the future socialist society to communal forms of social organisation.[25] Likewise, in 1891, the editor of the SPD's women's magazine, Clara Zetkin, who subsequently became the leading theorist on women's questions within the party, looked forward to the rapid dissolution of the family in the last phases of capitalism.[26]

It was a corollary of these beliefs that the SPD, like its conservative enemies, believed that the spread of female wage labour outside the home would lead increasing numbers of women into its own ranks. Capitalism, it held, was drawing increasing numbers of women into factory work and full-time employment. In doing so, it politicised them by exposing them to direct forms of exploitation in which the reasons for their oppression, both as women and as workers, became clear. By breaking down the sexual division of labour, capitalism forced women and men to undergo similar forms of exploitation, thus making clear to both their common interest in overthrowing the existing social order. As the employment of women in industry increased, so growing numbers of proletarian women joined their male working-class comrades in the fight for emancipation and social justice. Thus – in the eyes of the Social Democrats – the political mobilisation of working-class women was part of the same inexorable process of economically determined political and social change that would eventually bring them to power.[27]

The place accorded to the family in the formal ideology of the SPD seems clear enough, then: but in view of the gulf between theory and practice noted by many historians of the party,[28] it should come as no surprise to discover that in day-to-day party life, attitudes to the family were very different. The easiest way to approach the practical reality of the party's view of the family is through investigating the extent to which the SPD's recruitment of women and young people actually reflected the break-up of the working-class family, whether through conscious agitation or through social and economic circumstances. If the SPD women's movement, in particular, consisted above all of women factory workers, then we could consider the party's theories on the subject vindicated. If this were not the case, then we might perhaps have to think again about them. Unfortunately there is no easy way to answer this question. National statistics do not give any indication of the social or marital status of women SPD members.[29] However, some scattered local figures are available.[30] The earliest we have date from the period of the Anti-socialist Law, when socialist women's groups already existed, but in heavily disguised form, as trade unions or educational associations. There is no doubt, however, that they were in effect the female arm of the socialists. On 16 June 1886, for instance, a straw poll revealed that all 50 women at a meeting of such a women's society in Hamburg, at that time the main centre of the nascent socialist women's movement in Germany, were married.[34] After this, the Hamburg society carried out a more detailed survey. Completed in October the same year, it revealed that only 16 of the society's members were factory workers. Thirty-three did some form of paid domestic work, while no fewer than 74 did not work at all.[32] At a much later date, a survey of eight of the SPD's 'Women's Reading Evenings', designed for the political education of Social Democratic women, showed that the overwhelming majority of participants were married and did no paid work.[33] To a large extent, then, it seems that the Social Democrats were recruiting housewives rather than factory workers.

We can see this much more clearly, in fact, when we turn from the rather scattered and unsatisfactory statistical evidence to an examination of the actual techniques which the SPD used in trying to attract women to its organisation. The initial appeal of the SPD to the uncommitted was made through mass public meetings,[34] which were carefully designed to provide entertainment – rousing songs, fiery speeches, colourful banners and so on – as well as to arouse political enthusiasm. During the meetings, volunteers stood ready in the wings with membership forms, waiting to swoop on the audience the moment the speeches finished.[35] The subjects announced as the topics for the women's meetings were very revealing of the direction in which the party was launching its appeal. The major issue after the turn of the century was the inflation of food prices, which the SPD ascribed to high corn import tariffs and low meat quotas imposed in their view to protect large farmers against foreign competition.[36] In 1905-6, for example, the SPD in Hamburg, at that time the only big city in which it was legal for women to join the party, held the following meetings for women: six on 'The Trade Treaties and Women', three on 'Our Daily Bread', three on 'Podbielski, the Hamburg Beef Cattle Exhibition and the Meat Shortage', two with the title 'Hunger and Whips', two on 'How the German *Michel* (the equivalent of John Bull)'s bread basket is being hung ever higher', and two on 'Can women still keep house properly in view of the high food prices?'. Apart from these, all of which referred in one way or another to the high cost of food, there were two meetings on primary education and three on a current scandal about brutality in the army, all of which could be seen as appealing to women as the mothers of schoolchildren or conscripts; and finally there was one meeting attacking the Christian religion's attitude towards the female sex.[37] Similar examples could also be taken from subsequent years, and from the experience of other towns and cities.[38] In Dortmund, for example, an industrial town dominated by iron and steel, mining and building, and with relatively few employment opportunities for women, the police reported in 1907-8 that the SPD had launched an intensive recruiting drive to bring women into the party, and that its success was due to the high price of food.[39]

Another important means of recruitment and mobilisation was through the SPD women's magazine, *Die Gleichheit* ('Equality') which from the turn of the century onwards was increasingly directed towards a popular audience, more and more of whom were not members of the SPD.[40] In 1905, while remaining officially a 'Magazine for the Interests of Women Workers', it began to include regular supplements for mothers and children. From about the same time, as its editor Clara Zetkin had hoped, its circulation began to increase sharply and it moved from a situation in which it made regular deficits to one in which its profits were reasonably healthy.[41] Here too, then, the mass recruitment of women began when campaigns and propaganda were explicitly directed towards their interests as housewives and mothers, rather than towards their interests as workers. It seems, therefore, that the political mobilisation of working-class women in Wilhelmine Germany did not take place as a direct and immediate result of politicisation through the experience of exploitation in the factory labour force. Actual mobilisation did not generally occur until women were married and out of full-time industrial employment.[42] This becomes even more paradoxical if we take into consideration the fact that the unmarried woman worker was likely, despite long hours, to have more leisure time available for political activities than the married woman in her thirties or forties with small children and a household to look after. Yet many married women entered the SPD from 1905-6 onwards, paid regular membership dues, attended weekly meetings, went to mass demonstrations, helped the party organisation at election time and involved themselves actively in party affairs, while few younger unmarried women did.

The most important clue to understanding this phenomenon lies in the fact that the SPD women were overwhelmingly the wives of men already active in the party. Local evidence is unambiguous on this point. Thus the Hamburg political police noticed in 1886 that the husbands of the members of the socialist women's organisation were 'all known to be zealous Social Democrats'.[43] The 1911 survey of women's reading evenings in Berlin showed that the great majority of the participants had husbands in the SPD; many of the husbands were in the trade unions also.[44] On the eve of the First World War, a survey of the 11,684 female members of the SPD in Hamburg revealed that only 1,601 were engaged in paid employment: as the historian of the Hamburg party in this period concludes, 'the majority of female members were the non-working wives of the organized comrades'.[45] And at an earlier date, a social investigator of working-class life noted that young women workers were largely unpolitical, and added: 'those who really possessed a knowledge of the teachings of Social Democracy were the married women, who were brought into the ferment of agitation by their husbands and finally in this way they took part in it themselves'.[46] Similarly, a recent study of the SPD in the South German state of Baden has concluded of the period before the First World War that 'the Social Democratic women's movement was formed to a decisive degree of married women . . . A strong part was taken by the wives of the local party leaders'.[47] On a more general level, too, there was increasing recognition by party workers that the women in the SPD were mostly the wives of men already active in the labour movement. Since this contradicted the ideology of the SPD by disproving the theory of direct mobilisation through factory work, it was the source of a certain amount of embarrassment and disquiet. One of the leading SPD men in Leipzig, for example, asked with evident irritation in 1913: 'Whom do we have, then, in the organisation? The wives and daughters of party comrades, but not women factory workers.'[48] The women themselves were equally concerned. In the same year, 1913, the SPD women's organisation in Berlin held a conference in which a special session was devoted to the topic 'How do we recruit unmarried women workers?' The speaker began by saying:

> For the most part it is only the wives of our comrades who belong to the party organization. The great mass of female industrial workers is still lacking. I think we've been somewhat remiss in directing our women's recruitment efforts too much at women in their role as housewives and mothers. Our propaganda addresses itself too much to the housewife and mother. We don't have material for agitation among unmarried women workers.[49]

The leading recruiter of women for the SPD, Luise Zietz, also admitted in the same year that she had only really succeeded in winning over women with husbands already active in the party.[50] How this situation was to be remedied, however, nobody could convincingly say; and the SPD women's organisation continued to be a movement of party wives right up to the First World War.

Now of course there are a number of problems with the evidence which I have presented for this statement. It is, inevitably, drawn from scattered sources. In the final analysis it is perhaps suggestive rather than convincing. Certainly this is a subject on which a great deal more research is called for. But it is significant that all the concrete evidence which we possess does actually point in the direction I have indicated. No one contradicted those leading SPD activists who complained that women workers were not being recruited. There are no figures available which indicate that the SPD's women members in any part of the Empire were predominantly engaged in full-time wage labour. There is no evidence to suggest that any more than a handful of them joined the party independently of their husbands, let alone in opposition to them. This is not to say, of course, that SPD women were never confronted with the exploitative power of capitalism as workers as well as in their role as housewives at some stage of their lives. Most of them must have undergone full-time employment before marriage and this may well have been a source of later commitment. Moreover, it is clear that at some stage during their married life most of them would have taken part-time casual jobs to help out in times of economic difficulty for the family. It may well be the case that the evidence which I have cited underestimates the numbers of working women in the SPD because at least some wives of Social Democratic men may have concealed their involvement in the labour market for fear of compromising their husbands' respectability. And in addition to this, of course, it may well be that for some of them at least, political considerations, even if only of the vaguest sort, may have played a role in the choice of marriage partner. In many ways, women had a lot to gain by joining the SPD, and would have realised this when considering commitment. None the less, when all these various reservations and provisos have been made, the point remains that there was no simple one-way process of the politicisation of women through their emancipation from the family unit and incorporation into the productive process outside the home. On the contrary, such evidence as we have suggests that the decisive act of political mobilisation – joining the party – took place within the framework of the family. It reflected the realities of women's role within the working-class family as much as, or even more than, their earlier experience as full-time wage labourers, or their continuing engagement in part-time, casual employment. Not only did the party address itself to women in their roles as mothers, consumers and wives, to a greater extent than it concerned itself with them in their role as wage earners, but as often as not, this was the kind of appeal which proved most effective in arousing their interest.[51]

III

Of course, this angling of the SPD's appeal to women reflected the extent to which the men who dominated it accepted the conventional bourgeois concept of the sexual division of labour and the nature of sex-role divisions – women in the home, men out at work. Yet the men of the SPD had good reasons of their own for desiring the recruitment of women into the party. Had they been as hostile to women's involvement in politics as were their counterparts in the French labour movement, for example, then it is hardly likely that women, however strong their own reasons for committing themselves to socialism, would have entered the party in such massive numbers. But there is no doubt that the women who joined the SPD were actively encouraged to do so by their husbands save in a very small minority of cases. Again, a few local examples may serve as illustrations. Thus the 1911 analysis of members of the eight Berlin women's reading evenings already referred to showed that only 3 per cent of them were attending against their husbands' wishes. The analysis was carried out by women for women, so it probably reflected the true situation.[52] The attitude of many male activists in the party was well conveyed by Karl Böttger, a speaker at a meeting of the SPD women's group in Lindenhof, an industrial suburb of Mannheim, in 1912, when he remarked that 'you're a bad comrade if you stand at the top and can't even manage to bring your wife into the association'.[53] In earlier years, up to 1906, the SPD women constantly complained about the indifference shown by their male comrades towards the recruitment of women.[54] But this constant insistence that it was wrong for men to take this attitude was bound to have an effect. Indeed, there is evidence that in the case of Dortmund the local party was spurred into launching a drive to recruit women precisely by this kind of complaint, which implied that it was backward, old-fashioned and inactive.[55] As time went on, then, it seems that the prejudice against the recruitment of women was gradually eroded.

One reason for this was a growing impatience with the hostility which working-class women often displayed towards the involvement of their menfolk in socialist politics. Joining the SPD in Imperial Germany could have severe consequences — it could lead to arrest and imprisonment, for even after the lapsing of the Anti-Socialist Law in 1890, police harassment of socialists, using a whole battery of legal pretexts, was very widespread; or it could lead to dismissal and, if the worker rented company housing, eviction by the employer, for many industrialists refused to tolerate active Social Democrats in their workforce. The economic consequences of all this for the working-class family were clear above all to the housewife, whose role it was to keep the family fed and clothed. A local newspaper commented with some feeling after the defeat of a miners' strike in Zwickau in 1900:[56]

Women do not want to know about politics and organization, they do not 'understand' it at all; they appreciate a Mayday festival, with singing and speeches and dancing, that makes sense to them, but they do not appreciate political and trade union meetings, working-class women seem to lack the capacity to think in abstract terms. The female members of a workers' family become directly hostile, however, when a strike threatens or breaks out. They see only the missing weekly pay-packet of their husband, brother or father, not the circumstances which lead him to strike, and what the strike hopes to achieve . . . They think he has been 'stirred up' by others and 'forced to strike', compelled to be idle, and because they cannot get any money from him during the strike, they drive him from his comrades' side into the ranks of the strike-breakers, blacklegs and Judas Iscariots!

Further evidence of this can be found in workers' autobiographies.[57] A recent analysis of 33 autobiographies of pre-1914 Social Democrats has found that not one of the writers had experienced any sympathy from his mother for his decision to join the party. One writer commented that his mother had made life hell for him after he joined the SPD. Another reported that his mother had said to him on hearing the news, 'Out, you godless boy! You're not going to eat with us in the kitchen any more . . . I'm not going to let the children be corrupted by someone who'll end up in gaol or on the gallows.' Several writers mentioned that their political convictions were opposed by their wives as well as by their mothers. Two of them actually ended up by divorcing for this reason.[58]

These experiences indicated another way in which women were believed to damage the interests of the labour movement: by bringing up children in opposition or indifference to the tenets of socialism. According to the sexual role division common in the German working-class home in the late nineteenth century, the care of children was left almost exclusively to women; the men spent most of their leisure time in all-male pubs, singing clubs, sports associations or, of course, political meetings. While father was out helping to run the SPD, mother or grandmother was at home making sure the children did not follow in his footsteps. To a movement as concerned as the SPD was with the future, this was a serious problem. It was present above all in Catholic areas, where working-class women continued to support the Church long after a large part of the male population had gone over to the SPD. Even in the Weimar Republic, when women had the vote, the Catholic Centre Party was supported by proportionately more women than men at the polls in these areas, while the reverse was true of the SPD.[59] In an area such as Düsseldorf, indeed, the loyalty of women to the Catholic Church in the 1890s was so strong that the men in the SPD regarded it as a complete waste of time even to try to recruit them to the party.[60] The same pattern could be observed, though to a much lesser extent, in Protestant areas.[61]

The turning-point in the SPD's attitude towards the recruitment of women is hard to pin down precisely, and varied from area to area, but as the national statistics suggest, it can most plausibly be dated to the years 1905-6. An important role here was played by the great miners' strike of 1905, when the active participation of women in support of the strikers made a great impression on observers, who contrasted it with the women's hostility to the last great strike, that of 1889, as well as with their attitude in many smaller strikes such as the one in Zwickau in 1900, mentioned above. This support, of course, had its ideological limitations: one commentator described 'how they streamed in their thousands to the women's meetings and often a dozen of them marched onto the platform one after another and gave their opinion: "Fight to the end, God and the Kaiser will take care of us" . . .'. These assemblies made what the same writer called an 'eternally unforgettable impression' on the labour movement in the area.[62] They seem to have convinced the men that there were positive advantages to be gained by the recruitment of women. The will to support the labour movement was clearly present in large numbers of women; all it needed was to be given a more permanent and more politically educated form. It was after the strike of 1905 that the first successful women's recruiting drives were launched in places such as Bochum and Dortmund, in the Ruhr;[63] and significantly they were virtually the first to be aimed specifically at housewives and mothers.

Not only the men, but also the women of the SPD were quite explicit that the major purpose of the political mobilisation of working-class women was to strengthen the ideological solidarity of the Social Democratic family. Thus at a meeting of a local branch of the SPD's women's association in Mannheim, for example, the participants resolved in 1905 to take note of the fact that 'we women are at last waking up and not leaving it to the men alone to fight for the general well-being of the family'.[64] The SPD women were constantly insisting that their intention was to fight 'shoulder to shoulder' alongside the men in the party to achieve a general improvement in the life of the working class, and they were always careful to reassure the party that they had nothing whatever to do with the 'bourgeois women's rights enthusiasts' of the liberal feminist movement, whose fight was directed not against capitalism, but against men.[65] The major theorist of the women's section of the SPD, Clara Zetkin, editor of the women's magazine *Die Gleichheit*, expressed her ideal of the socialist woman in the following terms:

> Rooted and active in the world and in the family, she is able to make the husband completely at home in the house again. From her own rich, wide circle of influence there grows in her an untroubled understanding of his aspirations, his struggles and his work. She stands by his side no longer as a faithful and solicitous handmaid, but rather as a convinced, warm guardian of his ideals, as a companion in his struggles, as a comrade in his efforts and his exertions, giving and receiving intellectual and moral support.[66]

The efforts, struggles and so on were the man's; the woman's role was to support them. Beyond this, too, as a member of the Mannheim-Lindenhof SPD women's society remarked in 1911 – 'women can contribute a great deal towards making their children familiar with our efforts from an early age'.[67] Once more Clara Zetkin put this view in its most explicit form:

> The more she can be the educator and the moulder of her children, the more she can enlighten them and ensure that they carry out in rank and file the struggle for the emancipation of the proletariat with the same enthusiasm and spirit of self-sacrifice as we do. When

the proletarian then says 'my wife', he adds to this in his mind: 'the comrade of my ideals, the companion of my exertions, the educator of my children for the future struggle'.[68]

A major purpose of the political mobilisation of women, as of young people, therefore, was to provide backing for the Social Democratic man in his struggle against Government, police, capital and reaction, by sealing off his family as far as possible from outside influences. His wife was to be removed from the reactionary influence of the Church, and she in her turn was to immunise their children against the nationalistic and conservative ideology purveyed in the schools.[69]

IV

When we turn from high socialist theory to the everyday practice of the Social Democratic movement, therefore, we find, not hostility towards the family, but an overriding concern for its integrity and solidarity. Indeed, it is not difficult to find SPD members — both male and female — deploring the effects of industrialisation on the family as sharply as any romantic conservative. Early tracts and manifestoes of the socialist women's movement are full of outrage that every woman who was neither an heiress nor married into a propertied family was compelled to work,[70] that woman's work spelled ruin for the family,[71] and that men often had to look after the home; and the aim of the movement was declared to be the creation of 'circumstances in which a woman can fulfil her duties as wife and mother'.[72] A local SPD women's branch in Hamburg looked forward in 1894 to a time 'when our men will earn more, so that we don't need to work any more and can devote ourselves more to bringing up our children'.[73] A male speaker in the Mannheim-Lindenhof women's branch in 1910 met with no contradiction when he envisaged a time when men would earn enough for their wives not to have to work.[74] It was a common complaint that capitalism had driven women out of the home; and many ordinary party members evidently thought that the socialist revolution would put them back there.

Some support for this view could even be found in the classic Marxist texts. For although Marx, Engels, Bebel and Zetkin all insisted that the decline of the existing form of the family under capitalism heralded the emergence of a new form of the family under socialism, this insistence only took up a small part of the space which they devoted to the subject. What they devoted most attention to were the harmful effects which capitalism had on the existing family structure; and it was all too easy for ordinary Social Democrats to forget the dialectic of decay and renewal and concentrate their attention exclusively on the former, especially because Marxist accounts of the decay of the existing family were rich in moral indignation, heavily laden with shocking examples, concrete and passionate at the same time, while accounts of the future family structure, by contrast, were necessarily pitched at a rather vague and abstract level. Both Marx and Engels, in the *Communist Manifesto* and Bebel, in *Woman and Socialism*, depicted in lurid detail the moral collapse of bourgeois and proletarian family ties under the influence of capitalism; and their detailed analysis of the evils of female factory labour could all too easily be interpreted as the obverse of a tacit plea for returning women to the home. Ordinary Social Democrats, then, tended to select from the range of ideas available to them those which emphasised the damage done by capitalism to proletarian family life, and drew the conclusion that everything possible should be done to maintain or restore the family's integrity. Significantly, the more the leading theorist on women's questions within the SPD, Clara Zetkin, came into contact with the views of ordinary party members on this subject, the more she was forced to modify her original beliefs. In 1896 she confessed that her earlier statements on the family had claimed with 'one-sided sharpness' that the family had no future because it was being undermined by the development of capitalism.[75] Instead, as we have seen, from 1896 onwards she fully accepted the validity of the family as an institution.

The accommodation of the Social Democrats to the institution of the family and their conversion to the view that family solidarity should be strengthened, can be viewed as a response to the common accusation that their main aim in this area was to subvert the family rather than maintain it. It can also, to a limited extent and subject to reservations which I shall discuss later on in this essay, be regarded as part of a complex socio-political process, commented on by many historians, through which the Social Democratic movement, denied influence on the political system, ostracised by respectable middle-class society and cut off from full participation in national life, turned in on itself and built up a social subculture, a 'society within a society', in which all social activities could be carried out within the orbit of Social Democracy, thus keeping the movement's members uncorrupted by contact with bourgeois society until the coming of the revolution. By the early twentieth century, it has been argued, it was possible for a male Social Democrat to live almost his entire life within this subculture; he could eat food bought in a Social Democratic cooperative, read nothing but Social Democratic newspapers and magazines, spend his leisure time in a Social Democratic bicycling or gymnastics club or a Social Democratic male voice choir, drink in a Social Democratic pub and be buried with the aid of a Social Democratic burial society. It was only a small step from this to make him a happy home life in a Social Democratic family, with a Social Democratic wife and Social Democratic children.[76] However, the precise political meaning and significance of this elaborate subculture are complex and difficult to unravel. Some historians – indeed so many that their views can now be described almost as an orthodoxy – have argued that the Social Democratic subculture closely resembled the dominant culture of Imperial Germany despite the superficial differences and apparently irreconcilable hostility between them, and instead of sealing off the party from bourgeois influences, the SPD subculture acted as an unconscious transmitter of the dominant values of Wilhelmine Germany to the new working class. The party's emphasis on the importance of the family as an institution would seem to be a classic instance of this contribution to the *embourgeoisement* of the proletariat. The party was inculcating reverence for the bourgeois family ideal in the working classes; it was even trying to insist on the need for the family to be as cohesive and unified as possible in its outlook on life.[77]

It could also be argued that the SPD was trying to import the bourgeois reverence for the family into its own organisation as a whole, rather as the dominant culture of Wilhelmine Germany argued that the state was but a larger version of the family, and should be bound by the same values and modes of behaviour. The Austrian socialist leader Viktor Adler commented in 1915 for example that the SPD provided for its members 'the family home and the stuff of life'.[78] In this larger family of the SPD as a whole, the women's and youth sections occupied the same subordinate and supportive positions as women and children were supposed to occupy within the individual household.[79] The recruitment of women and young people, however much effort was devoted to it, always appeared as a secondary objective in the eyes of male party activists: 'One should try to organise the men', a woman delegate to the Party Congress in 1906 reported the men of her local party organisation as saying; 'then after that one could approach the women'.[80] Clearly it would not do to recruit women and children unless the adult male membership of the local party organisation was already numerous and firmly established. Once in the party, women were expected to maintain a low profile; as Clara Zetkin's statements, quoted above, suggest, their role was intended to be a supportive one. Women who tried to take an active role in running general party affairs ran into a lot of opposition from the men. There were few more hated people in the party than Rosa Luxemburg; and at a lower level, the experience of Klara Haase, a more humble party activist, when she was elected to the committee of the First Berlin Reichstag Constituency party organisation, was probably far from untypical.[81] She wrote later:

> I came to the first session and the men tried to show their courage by using the vilest expressions and the foulest words in order to annoy me. However, I sat down and made a list of all these words with the corresponding names besides them. At the end, I said: 'If you men think you can frighten me off, you'd better take note: I'm going to take this list in person to the Party Executive tomorrow so that it can see what sort of people it's dealing with!' . . . After that, they were very decent to me.

In addition, of course, many SPD men must have been worried that it would arouse sexual gossip and suspicion if they spent long hours closeted behind committee-room doors with women to whom they were in no way related. The result of all this, however, was that the women did not take a significant part in general party affairs. Instead, they had their own areas of competence within the party. They were made responsible for so-called 'women's questions', children's welfare, family affairs, legal protection for women workers, consumer interests, health and so on. As a consequence they lacked a voice in party affairs as a whole. Here too, therefore, they could be seen as extending their prescribed role within the family, itself defined by bourgeois values and norms, to their activities in the party in general.[82] In these ways, therefore, Social Democratic attitudes to the family would seem to bear out many of the claims advanced by historians of the party in recent years: the divorce of theory and practice, the creation of a sealed-off subculture, the failure of ordinary party members to grasp Marxist ideology, and the function of the party as a contributor to the *embourgeoisement* of the proletariat.

In fact, however, this is only part of the picture; and the conclusions which have been drawn from the existence of a Social Democratic subculture are open to question. In the first place, it is incorrect to emphasise exclusively the subordinate nature of women's role in the party. Women joined the Social Democrats for their own reasons. They were not mere cyphers, enrolled in a cause in which their role was purely passive and supportive. Membership in the party, whatever its limitations, did represent a significant gain in status for working-class women. And although the SPD women were largely confined to 'women's questions', they asserted themselves in this area with a vigour, a determination and an independence which clearly antagonised male party leaders. Despite formal incorporation into the party on the passage of the Imperial Law of Association in 1908,[83] the women continued in effect to run an autonomous women's organisation within the party. The SPD men did everything they could to stop this. In 1912 they closed the women's bureau, the only central institution of the SPD women in Germany as a whole.[84] After 1908, the male party leadership was so hostile to the holding of separate national SPD Women's Conferences, previously held every other year, that only one more was ever held before the First World War, in 1911. The local women's conferences which replaced them were supposed to have the advantage that they were put on by local party organisations, and so more easily controlled by the men, but even here the fact that they were led by women brought calls for their abolition. As one local party leader put it: 'The Women's Conferences are a dubious institution. We now have a unified organization, into which the women have been incorporated. But the women still believe in many cases that they form a special organization on their own.'[85]

In the same way, most party leaders viewed the existence of a separate socialist youth movement with profound distrust. 'If we had such a movement', remarked Hermann Molkenbuhr in 1904, 'we would have to fight against it, since all the efforts of the Party are directed towards centralization and greater unity.' The trade unions were particularly hostile to the SPD's youth movement. When in 1908, worried by the anti-militaristic tone of the movement, the Government banned all people under the age of 18 from taking part in political activities, the party and the unions moved to bring the youth organisations under tighter control by placing its branches under the aegis of the local party organisations. None the less, youth groups within the SPD continued to show signs of radicalism and rebellion, and clashes with the parent organisation were frequent, rising to a new pitch of intensity during the First World War, when the youth organisations in towns such as Hamburg were centres of opposition to the moderate policy of the party majority.[86] Similarly (though to a much greater extent), the complaints of party leaders about the women's separatism after 1908 indicate that the women were not entirely unsuccessful in defending their autonomy within the SPD.

The position in particular of women in German Social Democracy should be seen in terms of a process of conflict and bargaining with the men in the party, in which both sexes made their own demands, yielded some and saw the realisation of others. If the political mobilisation of women involved their acceptance of the male-dominated family, then it was a negotiated acceptance, in which the end result was a significant shift in the balance of power between the sexes within the labour movement as a whole.[87] The redefinition of women's roles which occurred, in other words, was a result not of the simple coopting of a passive mass of women who supinely acquiesced in the perpetuation of their own subordination, but rather the outcome of a constant process of conflict, of resistance and accommodation, in which the terms of women's subordination were constantly being renegotiated.[88]

Similarly, in the broader context of the labour movement as a whole, the recruitment of women on a mass basis in the last decade before the First World War, as part of a drive to secure the ideological cohesion of the Social Democratic family, should be seen not as a result of the straightforward downward transmission of cultural values – the acceptance of the bourgeois family ideal by the German working class – but as part of a more complex process of cultural bargaining and social change.[89] The SPD did not simply accept the bourgeois family as it stood; it turned it to its own purposes, using it against the effects of clerical and educational conservatism on women and children, and it brought about, in however limited a way, a redefinition of the division of roles and power between the sexes in the family. So the party did not simply accept *the* family; rather, it could be argued that it accepted a negotiated version of the 'higher form' of the family which Marx believed would emerge from the ruins of capitalist society. Clara Zetkin in particular entered a powerful plea for the conversion of the family from an 'economic unit' into a 'moral unit', bound together by love and resting on a basis of far greater equality between its members than was the case with the patriarchal family of the dominant culture;[90] and, as we have seen, there were many influences at work to ensure that Zetkin's views were indeed likely to have been a reflection of the family life at least of a large number of the women who joined the SPD before the outbreak of the First World War.

By the eve of the First World War, therefore, SPD leaders and activists seem to have been convinced that the political mobilisation of working-class women would aid male trade unionists and SPD men in labour disputes, benefit the numerical expansion of the party, and socialise their children into socialist attitudes and beliefs. It is important to look for longer-term changes which were bringing more SPD men to recognise these facts and to attach increasing importance to them. Underlying this process of recognition, it may be suggested, was the growing social differentiation of the German working class. Although some 175,000 women had joined the SPD by 1914, these by no means constituted a majority of SPD wives, and in the context of the working class as a whole they represented an even smaller minority. Contemporary social surveys suggested that as men's wages rose, their wives tended to work less outside the home. Wives provided 3.5 per cent of the income of skilled workers' families in the 1890s but 7.7 per cent of the income of unskilled workers' families. Even unskilled workers, however, if they earned over 1,000 marks a year, tended to have wives who did no paid work.[91] A survey carried out in 1899 among married women factory workers found that over half of them worked because their husbands earned too little to support the family, and many more because he was chronically ill or unemployed.[92] Married women who worked also generally had to carry out all the household chores after hours,[93] a fact which provides additional support for the argument that most women members of the SPD were not engaged in full-time employment, for given the fact that husbands were unlikely to carry out more than a limited amount of housework and child-minding, it was only in this way that they could have sufficient leisure time to take part in Social Democratic activities.

It seems likely, therefore, that the husbands of SPD women came from the better-off sectors of the working class. Many of these men, as the insistence of SPD propaganda and comment on the paramount importance of the wives of leading officials and activists joining the party suggests, were undoubtedly paid officials in the party or the unions. Others were benefiting from the long period of rapid increases in real wages which set in at the end of the 'Great Depression' in 1896.[94] Among the groups represented by the SPD, patterns of leisure were beginning to change. The all-male clubs and activities which dominated social life both among old-established artisan communities, reflecting the tightly-knit organisation of craft work, and in the newer industrial districts, where the population was predominantly young, male and unmarried, were declining in importance as artisan culture disintegrated and the balance of ages and sex in the new industrial areas became more even as the new communities gained a measure of permanence and stability. These men began to spend an increasing amount of their leisure time within the home, so that the political opinions and attitudes of wife and family, which they might not previously have had the inclination to notice, now began to acquire a new importance.[95] Seen in a wider social perspective, then, the emergence of a mass socialist women's movement in Germany could appear as part of the growth of a 'respectable' upper stratum of the working class.[96]

As Jane Humphries has recently remarked, 'all too frequently in the modern literature, the family is seen as engendering false consciousness, promoting capitalist ideology, undermining class cohesion and threatening the class struggle. In short, it stands charged with being a bourgeois institution acting in collaboration with capital against the real interests of the working class.'[97] This is not how it appeared to the leading socialist movement in Europe before the First World War. The mere fact that the official idealisation of the family in Imperial Germany was turned against the ruling classes by the Social Democrats indicated that the proletarian family was no simple vehicle for the downward transmission of bourgeois values. Yet, although Humphries has rendered a service by pointing out the inadequacies of the traditional Marxist view of the family, it is equally erroneous to claim, as she does, that the family was on the contrary an essential element in the economic defence and solidarity of the proletariat. Such a view ignores the explicitly educational and socialising functions of the family as envisaged by the German Social Democrats; but much more importantly, it glosses over internal divisions within the working class — vital for the understanding of political behaviour — and presents the family in far too unproblematic a way. A more fruitful way of approaching the working-class family is to see it as the object of a struggle between rival political creeds for its allegiance, the permanent scene of a conflict between rival political ideologies. To some extent, this conflict was fought out between forces imported into the family from outside: socialism and unionism, brought in by the father, religion brought in by the mother, nationalism and monarchism brought in from school by the children. But real conflicts of interest within the family (ignored in Humphries's model) were also involved: conflicts of authority between man and wife, parents and children, and economic conflicts between the primary breadwinner and the house-keeper, most evident in strikes and lockouts. Here again conservative and socialist ideologies represented different concepts of how the family should be structured, ranging from patriarchalism at the one extreme to egalitarianism at the other; so that conflict within the family was political not merely in the sense of being about power, but also in the sense that it related directly to theories about the distribution of power advanced by the major political movements of the day.

Social Democrats in Germany were ambivalent towards the family as an institution. While doubts about the virtues of patriarchalism do not seem to have troubled the ruling groups of Wilhelmine society to an undue degree, the Social Democrats, once the decision to mobilise women and youth for the party cause had been taken, found themselves faced with a prolonged intra-party struggle, with the women members and the youth movement attempting to assert their independence and the men trying to stop them. Role conflicts between men and women within the family, in other words, had been extended upwards into the party; and parallel conflicts emerged as a result of the growth of the Social Democratic youth movement at roughly the same time. Social Democratic attitudes towards the family were not just developed in isolation by Marxist theorists and imposed on the labour movement from above; they were worked out by ordinary Social Democrats themselves in the course of trying to explain, and ultimately to change, the conditions of their own existence; they were fought out in a series of conflicts of interest within the labour movement, and between the labour movement and the dominant culture. The resulting attitudes were an amalgam of personal and political experience, theoretical understanding, and parts of the cultural apparatus of the society in which the Social Democrats lived, so it is difficult to talk of a simple contradiction between theory and practice, or to argue that a creeping reformism was the main characteristic of the evolution of Social Democratic ideas about the working-class family. Rather, here as in other spheres, we should pay more attention to the changing conditions under which Social Democratic attitudes developed, and the ways in which they related to the changing exigencies of everyday life in the working class under a booming, rapidly expanding form of industrial capitalism.

Table 9.1: Circulation and Profit/Loss Figures for *Die Gleichheit* 1901-14

Year	Profit/Loss (Marks)	Circulation
1901-2	-4,430	4,000
1902-3	-3,010	9,500
1903-4	- 381	11,000
1904-5	74	28,700
1905-6	3,996	44,000
1906-7	12,584	67,000
1907-8	15,701	75,000
1908-9	15,389	77,000
1909	7,564	82,000
1910	13,239	85,000
1911		94,000
1912		107,000
1913		112,000
1914		125,000

Sources: Hilde Lion, *Zur Soziologie der Frauenbewegung* (Berlin, 1926); Dieter Fricke, *Die Deutsche Arbeiterbewegung, 1869-1914. Ein Handbuch über ihre Organisation und Tätigkeit im Klassenkampf* (Berlin, 1976), p. 433.

Table 9.2: Age Structure of Social Democratic Membership (Male and Female) in Two Cologne Reichstag Constituencies (Köln-Stadt and Köln-Land) 1914

Age group	Male	Female	% of male members	% of female members
18-20	174	23	2.34	2.36
21-25	735	95	9.90	9.76
26-30	1,441	173	19.40	17.78
31-35	1,604	191	21.60	19.63
36-40	1,392	187	18.74	19.22
41-45	886	126	11.93	12.95
46-50	527	79	7.10	8.12
51-55	354	55	4.77	5.65
56-60	180	30	2.42	3.08
61-65	90	13	1.21	1.34
66-70	33	1	0.44	0.10
over 70	11	—	0.15	—
Total	7,427	973	86.90	13.10

Source: Dieter Fricke, *Zur Organisation und Tätigkeit der deutschen Arbeiterbewegung 1890-1914* (Leipzig, 1962), p. 79.

Table 9.3: Age Structure of Social Democratic Membership (Male and Female) in the 13th Saxon Electoral District (Sachsen 13-Leipzig-Land) 1909

Age	Male	Female	% of male members	% of female members
18-21	643	252	3.28	7.19
21-25	1,976	410	10.09	11.70
25-30	3,868	624	19.75	17.80
30-40	6,807	1,149	34.75	32.78
40-50	4,882	818	24.92	23.34
50-60	1,148	223	5.86	6.36
60-70	243	28	1.24	0.80
70 +	22	1	0.11	0.03

Source: Dieter Fricke, *Die deutsche Arbeiterbewegung 1869-1914. Ein Handbuch über ihre Organisation und Tätigkeit im Klassenkampf* (Berlin, 1976), p. 273

Table 9.4: Age Structure of Women in Employment, 1907

	Total	% under 30	% 30-50	% over 50
Agriculture	4,254,488	49.5	32.0	18.5
Industry	1,562,698	69.8	22.6	7.6
Trade and transport	605,043	63.0	28.2	8.8
Total	6,422,229	55.8	29.3	14.9

Source: Fricke, *Die deutsche Arbeiterbewegung,* p. 316.

Table 9.5: Membership of the SPD Women's Movement 1905-14

Year	Women party members	Female 'voluntary subscribers'	Women's educational societies (SPD)
1905	4,000	1,000	3,000
1906	6,460	4,933	8,890
1907	10,943	8,751	10,500
1908	29,458	Female party membership	
1909	62,259	legalised	
1910	82,642		
1911	107,693		
1912	130,371		
1913	141,115		
1914	174,754		

Note: Registering as members of 'unpolitical' women's education clubs or
subscribing 'voluntarily' to party funds were means of joining the party where
to do this formally was illegal.

Source: Lion, *Zur Soziologie;* Fricke, *Die deutsche Arbeiterbewegung;* W.
Thönnessen, *The Emancipation of Women: The Rise and Decline of the
Women's Movement in German Social Democracy 1863-1933* (London, 1973).

Notes

Parts of this essay were read as a paper to a conference on 'Women in the Labour
Movement in Central and Eastern Europe' held at the School of Slavonic and East
European Studies in the University of London in April 1978. I am grateful to the
participants for their comments, and also to Robert Lee for his constructive
criticism of an earlier draft. The essay also draws on material and arguments
presented in my book *Sozialdemokratie und Frauenemanzipation im Deutschen
Kaiserreich* (Verlag J.H.W. Dietz Nachfolger, Berlin-Bonn, 1979).

1. See for example the essays by Karin Hausen and Robyn Dasey in the
present volume (pp. 51-83; 221-55).
2. See Jean-Louis Flandrin, *Families in Former Times: Kinship, Household
and Sexuality* (Cambridge, 1979), pp. 1-2, 118-45, and Jürgen Habermas,
*Strukturwandel der Öffentlichkeit. Untersuchungen zu einer Kategorie der
bürgerlichen Gesellschaft* (Neuwied-Berlin, 1969), pp. 55-63, 171-9.
3. Lawrence Stone, *The Family, Sex and Marriage in England 1500-1800*
(London, 1978); Edward Shorter, *The Making of the Modern Family* (London,
1973); Peter Laslett, *The World We Have Lost* (London, 1971).
4. For a sustained critique of recent literature in the field, see Geoff Eley,
'Some Thoughts on the History of the Family and its Relation to the History of
the Working Class' (unpublished paper presented to the second meeting of the
SSRC Research Seminar Group on Modern German Social History, University of
East Anglia, January 1979).

5. See T.W. Adorno *et al.*, *The Authoritarian Personality* (New York, 1968) and Erich Fromm *et al.*, *Autorität und Familie* (Paris, 1936). See also the discussion of anti-feminism in my book *The Feminist Movement in Germany 1894-1933* (London, 1976) chap. 6; and, much more generally, the stimulating and extraoₒdinary work of Klaus Theweleit, *Männerphantasien* (2 vols., Frankfurt am Main, 1978). For Nazi anti-feminism, see Tim Mason, 'Women in Nazi Germany, *History Workshop: A Journal of Socialist Historians*, 1-2 (1976) pp. 74-113, 5-32.

6. Staatsarchiv (StA) Hamburg (Hbg), Politische Polizei (PP) S8897: *Die Post*, 18 November 1899.

7. W.T. Bromme, *Lebensgeschichte eines modernen Fabrikarbeiters* (Jena, 1905), quoted in Günther Roth, *The Social Democrats in Imperial Germany. A Study in National Integration and Working-Class Isolation* (Totowa, N.J., 1963), p. 60.

8. StA Hbg, PP, S8897/*IV: National-Zeitung.* 28 August 1913.

9. Stadtarchiv Bochum/480: Regierungspräsident Arnsberg to Prussian Ministry of State, 24 Nov. 1902. I am grateful to Stephen Hickey for this reference.

10. See for example the debate in *Stenographische Berichte über die Verhandlungen des Deutschen Reichstags,* 8. Leg. Per., I. Sess., 20 May 1890; or the views outlined in Werner Heinemann, *Die radikale Frauenbewegung als nationale Gefahr!* (Hamburg, 1913) and in StA Hbg, PP, S18848: Deutscher Bund zur Bekämpfung der Frauenemanzipation.

11. Tim Mason, 'Women in Germany'.

12. *Stenographische Berichte über die Verhandlungen des deutschen Reichstags,* 9. Leg. Per., V. Sess., Bd. I, pp. 564-5 (MdR Hitze).

13. Jürgen Kuczynski, *Die Geschichte der Lage der Arbeiter unter dem Kapitalismus. Bd. 18. Studien zur Geschichte der Lage der Arbeiterin in Deutschland von 1700 bis zur Gegenwart* (Berlin, 1963) pp. 142, 153 ff.; *Stenographische Berichte über die Verhandlungen des Deutschen Reichstags,* 8. Leg. Per., 1. Sess., 20 May 1890.

14. For child and youth employment, see Alex Hall, 'Youth in Rebellion: the Beginnings of the Socialist Youth Movement 1904-1914', in Richard J. Evans (ed.), *Society and Politics in Wilhelmine Germany* (London, 1978), pp. 241-66.

15. Kuczynski, *Die Geschichte,* pp. 154-5, 181ff.

16. StA Hbg S8897/1: *Die Post,* 16 Nov. 1899.

17. Ingeborg Weber-Kellermann, *Die Deutsche Familie, Versuch einer Sozialgeschichte* (Frankfurt am Main, 1977), pp. 87ff; George L. Mosse, *The Crisis of German Ideology. Intellectual Origins of the Third Reich* (London, 1966), pp. 19-24

18. Peter Laslett (ed.), *Family and Household in Past Time* (Cambridge, 1974). Introduction.

19. Quoted in Weber-Kellermann, *Die Deutsche Familie,* p. 88.

20. For the *Umsturzvorlage,* see E.R. Huber, *Deutsche Verfassungsgeschichte seit 1789, Bd. IV: Struktur und Krisen des Kaiserreichs* (Stuttgart, 1968); Klaus Saul, 'Der Staat und die "Mächte des Umsturzes": Ein Beitrag zu den Methoden antisozialistischer Repression und Agitation vom Scheitern des Sozialistengesetzes bis zur Jahrhundertwende', *Archiv für Sozialgeschichte,* XII (1972), pp. 293-350.

21. See, in general, Alex Hall, *Scandal, Sensation and Social Democracy. The SPD Press and Wilhelmine Germany 1890-1914* (Cambridge, 1977). For evasions of Government regulations, see Robyn Dasey's contribution to the present volume, and Hall, 'Youth in Rebellion'.

22. Marx-Engels, *Ausgewählte Schriften,* Vol. 2, p. 216.

23. *Das Kapital* (Berlin, 1955), Vol. I, p. 515.

24. August Bebeal, *Die Frau und der Sozialismus* (50th edn., Berlin, 1970).

25. Lily Braun, *Die Frauenfrage: ihre geschichtliche Entwicklung und wirtschaftliche Seite* (Leipzig, 1901).

26. Clara Zetkin, *Die Arbeiterinnen – und Frauenfrage der Gegenwart* (Berlin, 1891).

27. The best general discussion of SPD ideology is still Hans-Josef Steinberg, *Sozialismus und deutsche Sozialdemokratie. Zur Ideologie der Partei vor dem 1. Weltkrieg* (2nd edn., Bonn, 1972).

28. E.g. Steinberg, ibid.; or Roth, *Social Democrats in Imperial Germany;* see also Carl Schorske, *German Social Democracy 1905-1917: The Development of the Great Schism* (Cambridge, Mass., 1955).

29. See the tables in Dieter Fricke, *Die deutsche Arbeiterbewegung 1869-1914. Ein Handbuch über ihre Organisation und Tätigkeit im Klassenkampf* (Berlin, 1976).

30. For a more sustained statistical analysis, see my *Sozialdemokratie und Frauenemanzipation.*

31. StA Hbg, PP, V43: Versammlungsbericht, 16 June 1886.

32. StA Hbg, PP, V43: Versammlungsbericht, 13 October 1886; StA Hbg, PP, S1053: *Bürgerzeitung,* 26 June 1886 and 17 October 1886. According to the latter, the figures were: 33 domestic workers, 16 artisans, 49 'women workers' (Arbeiterinnen) and 74 without employment.

33. *Die Gleichheit,* Vol. XXI (14 Aug. 1911).

34. Cf. Jochen Loreck, *Wie man früher Sozialdemokrat wurde* (Bonn, 1977).

35. See the elaborate instructions for the holding of such meetings in Luise Zietz, *Gewinnung und Schulung der Frau für die politische Betätigung* (Berlin, 1914).

36. Cf. the advertisements and reports in StA Hbg, PP, S8897.

37. StA Hbg, PP, S8897: Versammlungsberichte, 1905-6.

38. In 1912, there was a campaign of mass women's meetings in Berlin against rising food prices (Staatsarchiv Hamburg, PP, S8897: *Vorwärts,* 25 Sept. 1912).

39. Ralf Lützenkirchen, *Der sozialdemokratische Verein für der Reichstagswahlkreis Dortmund-Hörde* (Monographien zur Geschichte Dortmunds und der Grafschaft Mark, Vol. II, Dortmund, 1970), pp. 114-32.

40. This was because an increasing proportion of each edition of the magazine was taken up by bulk orders from the unions.

41. See Table 9.1, p. 281 above.

42. See Tables 9.2 and 9.3, pp. 281-2 above.

43. StA Hbg, PP, S1053: Hamburg police to Berlin police, 3 November 1886.

44. *Die Gleichheit,* Vol. XXI (14 August and 28 August 1911).

45. Volker Ullrich, *Die Hamburger Arbeiterbewegung vom Vorabend des Ersten Weltkrieges bis zur Revolution 1918/19* (Hamburg, 1976), p. 77.

46. M. Wettstein-Adelt, *Dreieinhalb Monate Fabrikarbeiterin* (Berlin, 1893), p. 71.

47. Jörg Schadt (ed.), *Im Dienst an der Republik: die Tätigkeit des Landesvorstands der Sozialdemokratischen Partei Badens 1914-1932* (Veröffentlichungen des Stadtarchivs Mannheim, 4, Stuttgart, 1977), p. 42 and note 86.

48. Badisches Generallandesarchiv Karlsruhe, Nachlass Adolf Geck, 1907: Stizungen der Kontrolkommission: Partei-Ausschuss, 7 Nov. 1913. The speaker was Richard Lipinski.

49. StA Hbg, PP, S8897: *Vorwärts,* 17 Nov. 1913.

50. *Die Neue Zeit,* Vol. XXXI (12 Sept. 1913), p. 881.

51. These points are made in response to criticisms advanced in Willy Albrecht *et al.,* 'Frauenfrage und deutsche Sozialdemokratie vom Ende des 19. Jahrhunderts bis zum Beginn der zwanziger Jahre', *Archiv für Sozialgeschichte,* Vol. XIX

(1979) pp. 459-510, esp. pp. 472-3. For overall figures on the SPD's recruitment of women, see Table 9.5.

52. See the interesting discussion of these reading evenings on pp. 193-200 of Jean H. Quataert, *Reluctant Feminists in German Social Democracy 1885-1917* (Princeton, 1979). The original figures are in *Die Gleichheit*, Vol. XXI (14 August 1911, 28 August 1911).

53. Stadtarchiv Mannheim, Kleine Erwerbung No. 43: Protokollbuch des Sozialdemokratischen Frauenvereins Mannheim, Zahlstelle Lindenhof, 13 Dec. 1912.

54. Molly Nolan, 'Proletarischer Anti-Feminismus. Dargestellt am Beispiel der SPD – Ortsgruppe Düsseldorf 1890 bis 1914', in *Frauen und Wissenschaft. Beiträge zur Berliner Sommeruniversität für Frauen Juli 1976* (herausgegeben von der Gruppe Berliner Dozentennen, Berlin, 1977), p. 386; StA Hbg, PP, V43: Versammlungsbericht, 15 Dec. 1886; *Parteitagsprotokolle*, 1894, p. 179; 1896, p. 170; 1906, pp. 407-9.

55. Lützenkirchen, *Der sozialdemokratische Verein*; Table 9.5 above.

56. StA Hbg, PP, S8897/III: *Sächsisches Volksblatt*, cited in *Fachzeitung für Schneider*, 21 April 1900.

57. For an introduction to this rich literature, see Wolfgang Emmerich, *Proletarische Lebensläufe* (Reinbeck bei Hamburg, 1974).

58. Loreck, *Wie man früher Sozialdemokrat wurde*, pp. 238-9.

59. Gabrielle Bremme, *Die politische Rolle der Frau in Deutschland* (Göttingen, 1956); Brian Peterson, 'The Politics of Working-class Women in the Weimar Republic', *Central European History*, Vol. X, No. 2, (June 1977), pp. 87-111.

60. Nolan, 'Proletarischer Anti-Feminismus', p. 366.

61. Bremme, *Die politische Rolle der Frau in Deutschland.*

62. Erhard Lucas, *Arbeiterradikalismus. Zwei Formen von Radikalismus in der deutschen Arbeiterbewegung* (Frankfurt am Main, 1976), p. 66, citing Anton Erkelenz, *Kraftprobe im Ruhrgebiet* (Düsseldorf, 1905), p. 49.

63. Lützenkirchen, *Der sozialdemokratische Verein* (for Dortmund); reports in Münster/Bochum Staatsarchiv Münster RA/I/96 and Stadtarchiv Bochum 480 (for Bochum: I owe these last references to the kindness of Stephen Hickey).

64. Stadtarchiv Mannheim, Kleine Erwerbung No. 43: Protokollbuch des Sozialdemokratischen Frauenvereins Mannheim, Zahlstelle Lindenhof, Minute for June 1905 meeting.

65. The classic statement of this view can be found in Clara Zetkin's speech to the 1896 Party Congress, printed in Clara Zetkin, *Ausgewählte Reden und Schriften*, I (Berlin, 1957).

66. *Die Gleichheit*, Vol. VIII, No. 2 (19 Jan. 1898), pp. 9-10.

67. Stadtarchiv Mannheim, Kleine Erwerbung No. 43: Protokoll des Sozialdemokratischen Frauenvereins Mannheim, Zahlstelle Lindenhof, minute of meeting on 6 April 1911.

68. *Die Gleichheit*, Vol. VIII, No. 2 (19 Jan. 1898), pp. 9-10.

69. Brief (if simplistic) delineations of the influence of Church and *Volksschule* in: Hans-Ulrich Wehler, *Das deutsche Kaiserreich 1870-1918* (Göttingen, 1973).

70. StA Hbg, PP, V43: *Bürgerzeitung*, 27 Feb. 1886.

71. StA Hbg, PP, V43: Versammlungsbericht, 23 Feb. 1887.

72. StA Hbg, PP, V46: *Hamburger Echo*, 19 Nov. 1889.

73. StA Hbg, V581: Versammlungsbericht, 18 Oct. 1894.

74. Stadtarchiv Mannheim, Kleine Erwerbung Nr. 43: Protokoll des Sozialdemokratischen Frauenvereins Mannheim, Zahlstelle Lindenhof, minute of meeting of 7 December 1910.

75. *Die Gleichheit*, Vol. VI, No. 25 (9 Dec. 1896) and No. 26 (23 Dec. 1896), pp. 197-200 and 203-7.

76. For the idea of a Social Democratic 'subculture', see Günter Roth, *The Social Democrats in Imperial Germany. A Study in National Integration and Working-class Isolation* (Totowa, N.J., 1963).

77. Ibid.; and particularly in Peter Lösche, 'Arbeiterbewegung und Wilhelminismus: Sozialdemokratie zwischen Anpassung und Spaltung', *Geschichte in Wissenschaft und Unterricht*, 20 (1969), pp. 519-33; also in Dieter Groh, *Negative Integration und revolutionärer Attentismus. Die deutsche Sozialdemokratie am Vorabend des Ersten Weltkrieges* (Frankfurt am Main, 1973) (using the phrase 'Verbürgerlichung des Proletariats'); more generally, in the various essays in Hans Mommsen (ed.), *Sozialdemokratie zwischen Klassenbewegung und Volkspartei* (Frankfurt am Main, 1974). For a more sustained discussion of the concepts of 'subculture' and *embourgeoisement* in contemporary German labour history, see my essay on 'The Sociological Interpretation of German Labour History' in Richard J. Evans (ed.), *The German Working Class 1888-1933: The Politics of Everyday Life* (London, 1981).

78. Quoted in Alex Hall, *Scandal, Sensation and Social Democracy. The SPD Press and Wilhelmine Germany 1890-1914* (Cambridge, 1977).

79. Cf. Alex Hall, 'Youth in Rebellion: the Beginnings of the Socialist Youth Movement 1904-14', in Richard J. Evans (ed.), *Society and Politics in Wilhelmine Germany* (London, 1978), pp. 241-66.

80. *Protokoll des Sozialdemokratischen Parteitags zu Mannheim* (1906), pp. 407-9.

81. Friedrich-Ebert-Stiftung, Bonn-Bad Godesberg; Archiv der Sozialen Demokratie, Nachlass Gerda Weyl; Lebenserinnerungen von Klara Weyl.

82. See also the conclusions of Nolan, 'Proletarischer Anti-Feminismus'.

83. Fricke, *Die deutsche Arbeiterbewegung* gives the relevant documents. The Law of Association (1908) made it possible for women to join political parties in all parts of Germany.

84. Fricke, ibid., p. 329.

85. Badisches Generallandesarchiv Karlsruhe, Nachlass Adolf Geck, No. 1907: Sitzungen der Kontrollkommission: Partei-Ausschuss, 7 November 1913.

86. Hall, 'Youth in Rebellion'; Fricke, *Die deutsche Arbeiterbewegung;* Johannes Schult, *Geschichte der Hamburger Arbeiter* (Hanover, 1967).

87. For the idea of the negotiated acceptance of bourgeois values and institutions by the working class, see Frank Parkin, *Class Inequality and Political Order* (London, 1972), pp. 79-102.

88. For the application of this approach in the context of women's history, see for example Linda Gordon, *Woman's Body, Woman's Right. A Social History of Birth Control in America* (Harmondsworth, 1977), esp. pp. xiii-xiv.

89. For 'culture bargaining', see R.J. Morris, 'Bargaining with Hegemony', *Bulletin of the Society for the Study of Labour History*, Vol. XXXV (1977), pp. 59-63.

90. *Die Gleichheit*, Vol. VI, No. 25 (9 Dec. 1896) and No. 26 (23 Dec. 1896), pp. 197-200 and 203-7.

91. Peter N. Stearns, *Lives of Labour. Work in a Maturing Industrial Society* (London, 1975); see also the same author's 'Adaptation to Industrialization: German Workers as a Test Case', *Central European History*, Vol. III (1970), pp. 303-31.

92. Rose Otto, *Über Fabrikarbeit verheirateter Frauen* (Stuttgart/Berlin, 1910), pp. 114-15.

93. See for example Johannes Schult, *Geschichte der Hamburger Arbeiter 1890-1918* (Hanover, 1967), and descriptions of the life of working-class women in *Die Gleichheit* Vol. IV, No. 16, Vol. V, No. 19, and subsequent issues.

94. Ashok V. Desai, *Real Wages in Germany 1871-1913* (Oxford, 1968),

Thomas J. Orsaghy, 'Löhne in Deutschland 1871-1913: Neuere Literatur und weitere Ergebnisse', *Zeitschrift für die gesamte Staatswissenschaft* 125 (1969), pp. 467-83. Otto, *Über Fabrikarbeit,* shows that the husbands of women factory workers were overwhelmingly employed in poorly-paid or casual jobs (they are described as 'factory workers', 'day-labourers', 'other workers' etc., rather than being assigned to specific trades requiring training).

95. See Wolfgang Nahrstedt, *Die Entstehung der Freiheit. Dargestellt am Beispiel Hamburgs* (Göttingen, 1972), esp. pp. 217-26 and 183-91; also Robert Q. Gray, 'Styles of Life, the "Labour Aristocracy" and Class Relations in Later Nineteenth Century Edinburgh', *International Review of Social History,* Vol. XVIII (1973), pp. 428-52; and Gareth Stedman Jones, 'Working-class Culture and Working-class Politics in London 1870-1900: Notes on the Remaking of a Working Class', *Journal of Social History,* Vol. VII (1974), pp. 460-508. I owe this point to work in progress by David Crew.

96. E.J. Hobsbawm, 'The Labour Aristocracy in Nineteenth-Century Britain', in E.J. Hobsbawm, *Labouring Men* (London, 1964), pp. 272-315.

97. Jane Humphries, 'Class Struggle and the Persistence of the Working-class Family', *Cambridge Journal of Economics,* Vol. 1, No. 3 (1977), pp. 241-55.

NOTES ON CONTRIBUTORS

Robyn Dasey was born in Australia in 1946 and graduated in economics from the University of New South Wales in 1967. In 1972 she took a Master of Science in Economics at the University of Bradford, and she is at present completing a doctoral dissertation for the University of London on the social and economic conditions of working women in Hamburg between 1890 and 1914. She has taught at Highbury Technical College and Portsmouth Polytechnic, and since 1978 has been Research Assistant to the trade union APEX.

Richard J. Evans was born in Woodford, Essex in 1947 and studied history at Jesus and St Antony's Colleges, Oxford, graduating in 1969 and gaining his doctorate in 1972. From 1972 to 1976 he taught at the University of Stirling, and since 1976 he has been Lecturer in European History at the University of East Anglia. Among his publications are *The Feminist Movement in Germany 1894-1933* (London, 1976), and articles on the social history of prostitution in Imperial Germany, the suffrage riots of 1906 in Hamburg, and the German labour movement before the First World War. He is the editor of *Society and Politics in Wilhelmine Germany* (London, 1978). In 1980 he was Visiting Associate Professor at Columbia University, New York, and in 1981 he worked at the Free University of Berlin as a Research Fellow of the Alexander von Humbolt Stiftung, on aspects of poverty, crime and punishment and disease in nineteenth-century German towns.

Karin Hausen was born in Hamburg in 1938 and studied history and sociology in West Berlin, Tübingen and Paris. In 1969 she completed her doctorate at the University of Münster. From 1968 to 1978 she taught at the Free University of Berlin, and in 1978 she became Professor of Economic and Social History at the Technical University of Berlin. She is the author of *Deutsche Kolonialherrschaft in Afrika: Wirtschaftsinteressen und Kolonialverwaltung in Kamerun vor 1914* (Freiburg, 1970) and of a number of articles on the social history of technology, on social protest, on women's history and on the history of the family. She is at present engaged in a study of middle-class families in nineteenth-century Germany.

Arthur E. Imhof was born in the Valais canton of Switzerland in 1939 and studied history at the Universities of Zürich, Brussels, Paris and Rome. He has taught at universities in Switzerland, Sweden and Germany, and since 1975 has been Professor of Social History at the Free University of Berlin. Among his publications are a two-volume study of Scandinavian population history in the eighteenth century (*Aspekte der Bevölkerungsentwicklung in den nordischen Ländern 1720-1750*, Bern 1976), and a general introduction to demographic history (*Einführung in die Historische Demographie*, Munich 1977). In 1980-81 he was Visiting Associate Professor at the Ecole des Hautes Etudes en Sciences Sociales in Paris. He is at present engaged on a number of research projects in demographic history and the quantitative social history of medicine, death, and disease.

James H. Jackson was born in Oakland, California in 1946 and studied history at Pasadena College and at the University of Minnesota, where he took his MA in 1969 and his PhD in 1980. He has taught at Northwest Nazarene College, Idaho, at Boise State University, Idaho, and at the University of Minnesota. Since 1978 he has been Assistant Professor of History at Point Loma College, San Diego, California. He is the author of 'Wanderungen in Duisburg während der Industrialisierung' in Wilhelm H. Schröder (ed.), *Moderne Stadtgeschichte* (Stuttgart, 1979), a study of migration in the Ruhr, and he is at present engaged on research on families, migrants and urban growth in the Ruhr Valley during the later nineteenth century.

Robert Lee was born in Birkenhead in 1946 and studied history at Corpus Christi College, Oxford, where he obtained his doctorate in 1972. Since 1972 he has taught at the University of Liverpool, where he is now Senior Lecturer in Economic History. He is the author of *Population Growth, Economic Development and Social Change in Bavaria 1750-1850* (New York, 1977), and of articles on the history of illegitimacy, mortality and taxation structure in nineteenth-century Germany. He is the editor of *European Demography and Economic Growth* (London, 1978, Vol. I; Vol. II in preparation). After spending part of 1980 as Research Fellow of the Alexander von Humboldt Stiftung at the University of Münster, he is now engaged on further research on aspects of the economic, demographic and social history of nineteenth-century Germany.

Heilwig Schomerus was born in Wittenberg (Saxony) in 1944 and studied at the Universities of Marburg and Heidelberg. From 1970 to 1972 she was a student of St Antony's College, Oxford, where she carried out research on aspects of poverty and disease in early nineteenth-century Edinburgh. The author of *Die Arbeiter der Maschinenfabrik Esslingen* (Stuttgart, 1977) and a number of articles on the social history of the sixteenth and nineteenth centuries, she taught in the Institute for Social and Economic History at the University of Heidelberg from 1977-80 and is now on the staff of the Institute for European History in Mainz, where she is researching German social history.

Kurt Wagner was born in Körle, Hesse, in 1952, left school in 1967 and served an apprenticeship in agriculture. From 1969 to 1972 he studied agrology and from 1973 to 1975 he worked as a volunteer in the Agricultural Extension Scheme in Afghanistan. Since 1976 he has been studying sociology at Frankfurt University.

Gerhard Wilke was born in Körle, Hesse, in 1948, left school in 1962 and served an apprenticeship as a butcher. He went to Ruskin College, Oxford, in 1969 and studied sociology and social anthropology at King's College, Cambridge from 1971 to 1974. He is at present Lecturer in Sociology at a College of Further Education in London. Together with Ernest Parkin he published a study of the major plays of Samuel Beckett 'Schluss mit Warten', in *Das Werk von Samuel Beckett* (Suhrkamp, Frankfurt 1975), and he has given a radio talk for the Open University on 'The Impact of War on a German Village'. With Kurt Wagner he is continuing his research on the oral history and historical anthropology of the village in which he grew up.

INDEX